MACHINES OF THE MIND

MACHINES OF THE MIND

Personification in Medieval Literature

KATHARINE BREEN

THE UNIVERSITY OF CHICAGO PRESS
CHICAGO AND LONDON

The University of Chicago Press, Chicago 60637
The University of Chicago Press, Ltd., London

Published 2021
Printed in the United States of America

30 29 28 27 26 25 24 23 22 21   1 2 3 4 5

ISBN-13: 978-0-226-77645-3 (cloth)
ISBN-13: 978-0-226-77659-0 (paper)
ISBN-13: 978-0-226-77662-0 (e-book)
DOI: https://doi.org/10.7208/chicago/9780226776620.001.0001

The University of Chicago Press gratefully acknowledges the generous support of the Alice Kaplan Institute for the Humanities and Northwestern University toward the publication of this book.

Library of Congress Cataloging-in-Publication Data

Names: Breen, Katharine, 1973– author.
Title: Machines of the mind : personification in medieval literature / Katharine Breen.
Other titles: Personification in medieval literature
Description: Chicago ; London : The University of Chicago Press, 2021. | Includes bibliographical references and index.
Identifiers: LCCN 2020051233 | ISBN 9780226776453 (cloth) | ISBN 9780226776590 (paperback) | ISBN 9780226776620 (ebook)
Subjects: LCSH: Literature, Medieval—History and criticism. | Personification in literature. | Literature—Philosophy.
Classification: LCC PN682.P475 B74 2021 | DDC 809/.02—dc23
LC record available at https://lccn.loc.gov/2020051233

♾ This paper meets the requirements of ANSI/NISO Z39.48-1992 (Permanence of Paper).

CONTENTS

ACKNOWLEDGMENTS

It is a great pleasure to thank those who have given generously of their time and treasure to help make this book a reality. I am especially grateful to my colleagues at Northwestern University. Barbara Newman, Laurie Shannon, and Susan Manning have been wonderful mentors, guiding me along the sometimes ill-mapped path of associate professorship. Susie Phillips has been the best "big sister" a medievalist could hope for, while Nick Davis, John Alba Cutler, Kelly Wisecup, Harris Feinsod, Rebecca Johnson, Helen Thompson, and Viv Soni have been indispensable comrades in arms. Richard Kieckhefer has been cheerful and generous in consulting on tricky passages of medieval Latin. I would not have been able to finish this book without their collective support. I also owe a debt to the many Northwestern students who have challenged me to clarify key ideas, especially in my graduate seminars and in two undergraduate iterations of "Allegory from Rome to *Star Trek*." My advisee Sarah Wilson was a model of intellectual companionship as we worked on our projects together.

Like much of my academic work, this project began and ended with *Piers Plowman*, and I'm grateful to the many Langlandians who have taught me to think deeply about how the poem works, beginning in Anne Middleton's spring 1997 graduate seminar at the University of California, Berkeley. Since then, Masha Raskolnikov, Liz Schirmer, Katie Vulić, Katherine Zieman, and I have traveled a long way with the poem, and with each other. More recently, I have learned a great deal from Alastair Bennett and Eric Weiskott, my coeditors at the *Yearbook of Langland Studies*, as well as from the journal's contributors, peer reviewers, and past editors, especially Andrew Galloway, Fiona Somerset, Emily Steiner, Rebecca Davis, and Frank Grady. I've enjoyed intense conversations at the intersection of *Piers* and personification with Fiona, Nicolette Zeeman, Bruce Holsinger, and Tekla Bude, and about person making more broadly with Kellie Robertson, Cathy Sanok, Claire Waters, and Julie Orlemanski, often extending from one conference venue to the next over the course of years. Julie helped make many of these conversations possible by organizing an unbeatable sequence of panels and events, and she, Claire, and Alastair kindly commented on sections of this book in progress. So, too, did members of the Midwest Middle English Reading Group, including Mike Johnston, Lee Manion, Shannon Gayk, Lisa Cooper, Robyn Malo, and Jessica Rosenfeld, who intervened at a key juncture to keep the project from turning into something much less interesting (at least to me!). Nicholas Watson offered support at an early stage, and Rebecca Krug has been a consistent voice of sanity, which I appreciate enormously.

I am likewise appreciative of institutional support, beginning with a Charles A. Ryskamp Research Fellowship from the American Council of Learned Societies that gave me the time and space to conceive of such a wide-ranging project, and continuing with Northwestern's Alice Kaplan Institute for the Humanities, which offered a year of fellowship to keep me going and stepped up with last-minute publication funding in the midst of the pandemic. Portions of chapters 6 and 7 have been published previously as, respectively, "The Need for Allegory: *Wynnere and Wastoure* as an *Ars Poetica*," *Yearbook of Langland Studies* 26 (2012): 187–229, and "Langland's Literary Syntax, or Anima as an Alternative to Latin Grammar," in *Answerable Style: The Idea of the Literary in Medieval England*, edited by Frank Grady and Andrew Galloway (Columbus: Ohio State University Press, 2013), 95–120, and I am grateful for permission to republish them here in revised form. The manuscript draft I sent to the University of Chicago Press has been greatly improved by the incisive and detailed commentary of two anonymous press readers. I am especially grateful to the reader who invented the character of Milly the Medievalist as an imagined interlocutor and to my editor, Randy Petilos, for shepherding the project so carefully along its way.

I owe the most profound thanks to my family. Elizabeth and Samantha O'Hara have patiently supplied me with bike rides and homemade bread. Douglas O'Hara has been my most generous and my most hostile reader. To answer his most frequently asked question of the last ten years: yes, I am done with the book! I dedicate it to him, and to our daughters, with love.

Introduction

WELCOME TO THE MACHINE

In the early twenty-first century, the tech world rediscovered personification. A popular product-design textbook credits software engineer Alan Cooper with creating *"personas"* by "put[ting] a face on the user." That is to say, it credits him with inventing the rhetorical trope of personification, or prosopopoeia, a Greek compound derived from *prosopon* (face, mask, person) + *poiein* (to make). Tamara Adlin and John Pruitt's *The Essential Persona Lifecycle: Your Guide to Building and Using Personas* promises that "personas play an essential role in the development of successful products. Without creating profiles of target customers and studying them throughout your product development lifecycle, it's impossible to truly understand user need, context, and pain points."[1] Cooper himself argues that "personas are the single most powerful design tool that we use."[2] Following their advice, corporations in recent years turned to personas to design software, websites, and control panels; to renovate showrooms; and even to build cars. In other words, after years of using a self-consciously scientific vocabulary to describe their work, they began to recognize the commercial and even ethical value of a popular premodern literary device.

According to Adlin and Pruitt, personas allow engineers to design products that people actually want to use. Although product-design teams were accustomed to conducting polls and interviews to gather data about potential customers, they had difficulty translating that information into an intuitive user interface. When engineers at Ford Motor Company began turning their statistical profiles into personifications, however, they were enthusiastic about the results. As Moray Callum, then executive director of Ford Americas design, explained to the *New York Times* in 2009, "Invented characters get everyone on the same page. . . . Sometimes the target demographics are difficult to relate to by, say, a 35-year-old male designer. . . . We found in the past that if they didn't understand the buyer, designers would just go off and design something for themselves."[3] While a complex numerical sequence is quickly forgotten, an equally complex personification can remain available for productive imaginative work. For Ford, these functions proved so valuable that the company began to design each of its new models for a specific persona: Antonella, the fun-seeking twenty-eight-year-old driver of the Ford Fiesta; Natasha, the tech-savvy "social achiever" owner of a Lincoln luxury vehicle; Ashley, the "cool mom" driver of a post-SUV family hauler; and so on. At Microsoft, one researcher counted more than two hundred product-design personas.[4]

But how, and why, has personification become so useful? While simile and metaphor compare objects at the same level of abstraction, allegory asserts likeness between unlike things at different levels of abstraction. Personification allegory is thus ideally suited for representing a body of data as a human body. Although the techniques for gathering data have changed over the centuries, both Ford's Antonella and the title characters of the fourteenth-century alliterative poem *Winner and Waster* are derived from empirical observations of particular individuals, which are then aggregated into a single, representative form. Antonella reflects market research data about hedonistic urban twentysomethings, while Winner reflects a series of behaviors typical of increasingly urbanized late-medieval lawyers and friars, vintners and wool merchants. Critics of persona-based design often confuse personification with more novelistic forms of representation, with one scholarly article complaining that only 0.000048 percent of the American population, or approximately 134 people, possess all of the attributes of Microsoft's Patrick, a personification of a small business owner.[5] Such criticisms, however, miss the point. Where novels often create an illusion of individuation through an accumulation of nonsignifying details, personifications are instead composed of exemplary or characteristic details.[6] Antonella lives in Rome because it is imagined as a hotbed of dance clubs and other fashionable nightlife and because its narrow streets, heavy traffic, and tight parking spots define, in an extreme form, the most salient challenges of urban driving. As a result, Rome can represent other major metropolitan markets for the Ford Fiesta insofar as they, too, are characterized by young, fashion-conscious consumers and terrible traffic. Adlin and Pruitt suggest that engineers avoid confusion by giving their personas hybrid names like "Toby the Typical Teenager" and "Connie the Conscientious Consumer" that would be right at home in a poem like *Piers Plowman*.[7] Personas lend themselves to "real world" applications precisely because they yoke empirical detail to more abstract categories, mediating between them in a way that makes the concepts accessible, memorable, and easy to manipulate.

According to their proponents, personas also foster the development of social-emotional skills. In lending voice and body to abstract ideas, personification brings them under the jurisdiction of the moral codes, disciplinary regimens, social formations, and economic structures that organize human societies. Personification endows inanimate entities with sex and gender and often with other socially significant characteristics such as race, age, ability or disability, and level of attractiveness. The discourse of a young and beautiful female personification will inevitably be understood differently than that of an old, bald, lame, and impotent male personification—with the latter, perhaps counterintuitively, the persona of choice for medieval writers including Langland, John Gower, and the author of the *Parliament of the Three Ages*. An important body of recent criticism argues that the gender of personifications is neither arbitrary nor an inevitable inheritance from the grammatical gender of Latin and Romance abstract nouns.[8] As seen through the lenses of critical race theory and disability studies, other bodily attributes reveal themselves to be equally meaningful, carrying ethical, social, and political significance. Beyond these individual characteristics, personifications' figural bodies are often situated within human communities. Unlike the abstractions from which they are derived, personifications are defined by human relationships such as friendship, kinship, and marriage. Both within and outside of these social and legal structures, they also exhibit and elicit human emotions.[9] Langland's dreamer desires Meed, fears Holy Church and Scripture, and loves Haukyn the Active Man and Piers Plowman—emotions inflected by the supposed "accidents" of age and gender. Cooper emphasizes that personifications help software engineers to empathize with the generally older and less technologically savvy purchasers of their products, enabling them to develop more usable computer programs.

Together, these attributes make personifications especially useful for complex, large-scale imaginative work. Because personifications are dynamic rather than static—that is, because they can be imaginatively manipulated—they are particularly helpful for understanding movement. How will Antonella operate her car's dashboard control panel? How does she customarily navigate her urban environment? More broadly, personifications facilitate the imaginative exercise of walking a mile in someone else's shoes. For Pruitt and Adlin, they promise an end to product-design disasters such as the VCR clock perennially flashing 12:00, the result of an interface created for the convenience of programmers rather than users. By offering a concrete and memorable locus of common attention, personas also help groups to think collectively about problems that are too large or intractable to tackle individually. Adlin and Pruitt thus offer step-by-step instructions for "building" personas specific to each project, promising that this sizable investment of time at the beginning of the product lifecycle will pay for itself many times over.

Many of these advantages derive from two basic characteristics of personification that the guidebooks, confident as they are in other aspects of their treatment of personas, are not entirely sure how to handle. The first we might simply call literary pleasure. Apparently the halls of Microsoft's "campus" in Redmond, Washington, are full of posters of personifications,[10] and Ford found Antonella so appealing that it made her the centerpiece of the advertising campaign for the redesigned 2011 Fiesta.[11] Since statistical profiles do not receive similar treatment, these displays suggest that personifications have an inherent dynamism, even a life of their own, that motivates people to engage with them, to think with them and on their behalves, in ways that straddle the line between work and recreation. Even as Adlin and Pruitt encourage designers to incorporate "storytelling elements" into their personas, they caution them to "know when to stop," warning against investing too much time and energy in personas, building villainous personas, and other forms of overengagement. They also warn their readers that personifications tend to expose hidden assumptions and so may uncover "bad decisions that were made in the past and other 'dirty corporate secrets' some of your colleagues might not want illuminated." Since personifications, by their nature, lend presence to that which is absent and give voice to that which is voiceless, they can disrupt existing power structures, prompting Adlin and Pruitt to advise readers to "proceed with extreme caution" unless they have "buy-in from high-level stakeholders."[12] Once a personification has been set in motion, they suggest, there is something inexorable, and potentially even threatening, about the way it follows its own internal logic. Although Cooper characterizes personification as a "design tool," in this respect it may be more accurate to think about it as a design engine, or even a form of artificial intelligence.

If I have begun this project by looking at corporate uses of personification, it is not because I believe the trope can or should be reduced to commercial ends. As we have seen, even carefully constructed, business-friendly personifications tend to escape from their assigned purposes. Instead, it is because our contemporary business world, with its relentless prioritization of return on investment, perceives the utility of personification allegory so clearly. Technology companies' embrace of personification to solve twenty-first-century problems demonstrates that it is not exclusively a premodern literary device, much less one of merely antiquarian interest. Indeed, these companies' understanding of personifications as complex design tools, as machines for building other machines, harmonizes surprisingly well with medieval writers' own understanding of the form, suggesting that examining medieval practices may help to illuminate modern problems. The remainder of this book, then, will consider the ways in which personifications were used as machines of the mind from the patristic period through the end of the fourteenth century. It will look at the main varieties of personification that survive from this period, examining how they work and the different kinds of tasks they are designed to accomplish. By investigating the operations of personification during this period of exceptional variety and vitality, it aims to generate a clearer understanding of the trope as such, while also revising its literary history.

Writing at the turn of the seventh century, Gregory the Great anticipated contemporary technological discourse by characterizing allegory as a *machina*—a term that encompasses devices of all kinds but most often refers to building equipment such as hoists, cranes, and scaffolding. As he puts it in the preface to his *Commentary on the Song of Songs*:

> Allegory makes, as it were, a kind of machine, whereby a soul placed far from God may be raised up to God. If enigmas are placed between God and the soul, when the soul recognizes something of her own in the language of the enigmas, through the meaning of this language she understands something that is not her own and by means of earthly language is separated from earthly things.
>
> Allegoria enim animae longe a deo positae quasi quandam machinam facit, ut per illam leuetur ad deum. Interpositis quippe enigmatibus, dum quiddam in uerbis cognoscit, quod suum est, in sensu uerborum intellegit, quod non est suum, et per terrena uerba separatur a terra. (2.14–18)[13]

In the context of the *Commentary*, the chief allegorical machines to which Gregory refers are the Bridegroom and Bride of the Song of Songs, whom he understands as personifications of God and the church. When interpreted properly, these personifications lift the soul toward God *in excelsis*. Just as a crane amplifies force through mechanical advantage, allowing its user to lift loads that far exceed human strength, so, too, the figures of the Bride and Bridegroom allow human beings to exceed human nature and ascend toward divinity. The soul, here depicted as possessing earthly weight, is simultaneously she who lifts and that which is lifted. Although the goal is spiritual transcendence, the means of elevation are strikingly concrete and mechanical.

When Gregory calls these allegorical devices enigmas, he does not seem to refer to a subtype of allegory distinct from personification, as in some modern taxonomies of allegory, but rather to the complexity of their machinery.[14] He also alludes, inevitably, to Augustine's famous discussion of enigma in *On the Trinity*, which connects the rhetorical trope to 1 Corinthians 13:12: "We see now through a glass in a dark manner; but then face to face" (videmus nunc per speculum in enigmate tunc autem facie ad faciem).[15] For Augustine, the difficulty of enigma simultaneously measures the soul's present distance from God and offers a means for select readers to approach the unapproachable. For Gregory, the overtly sensual language of the Bride and Bridegroom—"in this book, kisses are mentioned, breasts are mentioned, cheeks are mentioned, thighs are mentioned" (nominantur enim in hoc libro oscula, nominantur ubera, nominantur genae, nominantur femora)—similarly acknowledges fallen human nature even as it offers a mechanism for rising above it (3.27–29). Instead of lingering over the external, sensory dimension of these descriptions, Gregory admonishes, "When we discuss the body, let us become as if separated from the body" (loquentes de corpore, quasi extra corpus fieri) by reading the Bride and Bridegroom as personifications—that is, as user interfaces—rather than as embodied human beings (4.42–43). Readers of the Song of Songs must use its allegorical machinery to push their souls away from their bodies because otherwise "the very machine employed to lift us will instead burden us and not lift us" (machina, quae ponitur ut leuet, ipsa magis opprimat ne leuemur) (4.40–41). In other words, readers must themselves strive to become personifications by distancing themselves from their physical bodies. Just as the soul is both that which lifts and that which is lifted, so personification is simultaneously the mechanism of lifting and a representation of the intermediate ontological state, the state of quasi-embodiment, that the reader seeks to attain.

In the *Craft of Thought*, Mary Carruthers cites Gregory's preface to the *Commentary on the Song of Songs* as evidence for a broader early medieval concern with thinking machines that includes—but is not limited to—personification. She argues that monks understood their meditative practice as a craft analogous to that of a mason or a carpenter, drawing on an earlier passage in 1 Corinthians:

> According to the grace of God that is given to me, as a wise architect, I have laid the foundation; and another buildeth thereon. But let every man take heed how he buildeth thereupon. For other foundation no man can lay, but that which is laid; which is Christ Jesus. Now if any man build upon this foundation, with gold, silver, precious stones, wood, hay, stubble – every man's work shall be manifest, for the day of the Lord shall declare it, because it shall be revealed in fire; and the fire shall try every man's work, of what sort it is.
>
> Secundum gratiam Dei quae data est mihi / ut sapiens architectus fundamentum posui / alius autem superaedificat / unusquisque autem videat quomodo superaedificet / fundamentum enim aliud nemo potest ponere praeter id quod positum est qui est Christus Iesus / si quis autem superaedificat supra fundamentum hoc / aurum argentum lapides pretiosos / ligna faenum stipulam / uniuscuiusque opus manifestum erit / dies enim declarabit / quia in igne revelabitur / et uniuscuiusque opus quale sit ignis probabit. (3:10–13)

According to Saint Paul, the "work of each builder" is to follow Christ by remaking the self in his image, with the self, again, being both that which builds and that which is built. Zealous Christians build with gold, silver, and precious stones, while those whom Paul rebukes build with wood, hay, and straw. Patristic writers build on Paul's foundation by elaborating the tools with which the "wise master builder" plies his craft. Augustine describes the *machina* of knowledge as building up the edifice of charity, while Gregory classifies not only allegory but also contemplation and love as *machinae mentis*, machines of the mind.[16] In Isidore of Seville's *Etymologies*, Paul presides over a detailed description of empirical building equipment. The apprentice monks in Carruthers's study accordingly learn not to have ideas but to make them, using a combination of inherited rhetorical, mnemonic, and interpretive tools and more specialized machines, including the personified Virtues and Vices of Prudentius's *Psychomachia*. Hugh of Saint Victor's *Didascalicon* extends this metaphor of thinking as building into a full-fledged allegory, imagining the entire liberal arts curriculum as a construction project while lending the crafts themselves, via their connection to this work, a dignity they had not enjoyed since Plato.[17]

Both as rediscovered by engineers in the early 2000s and as conceived over the course of the Middle Ages, then, personifications are powerful machines of the mind. That is to say, they belong to the group of mental devices Daniel Dennett describes as "prosthetic imagination-extenders and focus-holders," which "permit us to think reliably and even gracefully about really hard questions." For Dennett, these "hand tools of the mind" are continuous with "the precise, systematic machines of mathematics and science," including Pascal's probability theory and Newton's and Leibnitz's invention of calculus. In part because they fall within the modern disciplinary category of the humanities, however, we tend to use them without recognizing them as such. One strength of Dennett's conceit is that it presents the humanities and sciences as engaged in the common project of knowledge production. At the same time, it acknowledges the importance of disciplinary expertise, understood as the ability to choose the right tool for the job, use it adeptly, and create new ones as needed. Another strength of Dennett's approach is that it reestablishes continuity between the present and the past. Dennett himself makes somewhat eclectic use of the past, pairing Ockham's razor, which warns against multiplying entities unnecessarily, with "Occam's Broom," which "describe[s] the process in which inconvenient facts are whisked under the rug."[18] By reconnecting the quantitative and qualitative disciplines, however, his thinking machines have the effect of more systematically reconnecting the Enlightenment to the so-called Dark Ages. In this model, rather than being defined by their failure to invent calculus, the Middle Ages can be valued for the thinking machines they did invent, adapt, and upgrade. We can give the period credit for making machines that still work as well as for its instructive failures. In doing so, we should be able to avoid the mind-boggling inefficiency of reinventing a device as venerable, ubiquitous, and useful as prosopopoeia—a device that by all accounts we are still struggling to relearn how to use and, at times, even how to recognize.

The purpose of this book, then, is to dust off personification, as if it were a machine stored overlong in someone's attic, in order to understand how it works as an engine of thought, as well as the uses to which is has been, and potentially can be, put.[19] This is not to say that medievalists, or even literary critics in general, ever lost sight of personification to the same degree that the worlds of business and technology did. Relatively little literary critical work on the topic, however, treats personifications as useful, much less as specialized machines of the mind. On the contrary, for much of the nineteenth and twentieth centuries, personification was characterized, often via its connection with the Middle Ages, as an inherently archaic or archaizing form, as that which any serious modern writer or thinker must avoid. Presented as the binary opposite first of transcendent symbolism and then of mimetic realism, it was the literary device that everyone could weigh in the scales and find wanting. While to an important extent this valuation changed in the last quarter of the twentieth century, when Paul de Man famously championed prosopopoeia as the "master trope of poetic discourse," his declaration had the effect of turning personification into a battleground in the theory wars.[20] Critics tended to characterize personification as either strongly nominalist or strongly realist and then praise or censure it in keeping with their own philosophical, religious, or political commitments.[21]

In contrast to these earlier accounts, which generally seek to discover what personifications do or do not mean, I am most interested in investigating how they work. That is to say, I take as my starting point the assumption that personification is as personification does. How are personifications constructed? What kinds of force do they amplify? What do they accomplish? Considering personifications as fictions, in Hans Vaihinger's sense of "hypotheses which are known to be false, but which are employed because of their utility," I seek to evaluate them according to their use value rather than their truth value, subjecting them to "justification" rather than "verification."[22] This understanding of personifications as fictions is consonant with the way medieval authors, regardless of their philosophical commitments, understood personification as a rhetorical device.[23] From Augustine onward, medieval sign theorists recognized a discontinuity between sign and signified that was, if not inherent to language itself, then at least endemic to human language after the Tower of Babel.[24] Classical treatments of personification as a rhetorical device were read, copied, cited, and reworked throughout the Middle Ages. For all of these writers, a given personification might point the way toward the abstraction it designates, but it can never coincide with it. In this context, the most important measure of a personification is almost axiomatically its utility—that is, its effect upon a work's intended audience. For Gregory the Great, the purpose of the Bride and Bridegroom in the Song of Songs is not so much to communicate doctrinal content as to lift readers toward God in the manner of a builder's hoist. He concerns himself not only with what these personifications mean but also, and perhaps more importantly, with what they do.

In order to evaluate personifications according to their use value, we must also recognize that not all personifications work in the same way. For Kathleen Hewett-Smith, Langland's Hunger fails as a personification because it does not uplift readers in the way that "such successfully transcendent figures as Wit or even Envy" do.[25] But what if Hunger is not a poorly designed machine for transcendence? What if Hunger is a different kind of machine altogether, one that helps readers to grasp the practical and moral dimensions of food policy in a subsistence economy? Rather than seeing figures like Hunger as failures or eccentric anomalies, I will consider the multiple ways personifications might operate. I argue not only that personification is one machine of the mind among many but also that we can usefully identify different types of personification that work in different ways toward different ends. Within the category of hand tools, wrenches are distinct from hammers and screwdrivers, but open-end wrenches are also different from box-end wrenches, hex-key wrenches, socket wrenches, and torque wrenches. And all of these multipurpose wrenches are distinct from a purpose-built tool such as the basin wrench, which specifically facilitates the work of connecting and disconnecting the water supply under a standard sink.

In seeking to define types of personification, I engage with the work of Kellie Robertson, Barbara Newman, and Suzanne Conklin Akbari, each of whom connects changes in personification to the philosophical paradigm shift that followed the rediscovery and translation of Aristotle's metaphysics and natural philosophy.[26] In contrast to the dominant discourses of the twentieth century, these recent studies acknowledge that personification does not inherently embody any one metaphysics, and they even find that a single work can contain both realist and nominalist personifications. The present study draws on their work while also seeking to define a more comprehensive and detailed set of categories that better describes the versatility of medieval personifications as machines of the mind. What are we to make, for instance, of the flagrantly nontranscendent personifications in Prudentius's fifth-century *Psychomachia*, where Faith grinds her opponent's eyeballs into the dust and Chastity runs her sword through the throat of Sodomitic Lust? Are these figures, like Langland's Hunger, simply failures, as C. S. Lewis and Jon Whitman have argued?[27] Why do the personifications in Bernardus Silvestris's twelfth-century *Cosmographia* look and act so differently from those in Guillaume de Deguileville's fourteenth-century *Pèlerinage de la vie humaine* (*Pilgrimage of Human Life*), despite both texts' strong doctrinal emphasis on transcendence? Does the nominalist or conceptualist Aristotelianism of someone like Ockham produce different personifications than the moderately realist or immanent Aristotelianism associated with Aquinas and Albert the Great? How do personifications relate to the classical deities with whom they often rub shoulders in medieval literary texts? How do all of these different types of personification work? In order to answer these questions, I will set medieval personifications in conversation with the major metaphysical systems that were either directly or indirectly available to medieval writers, both highlighting the variety of medieval allegorical practice and accounting for some of the patterns within it. Neither ignoring the relationships between personifications and the universals or concepts to which they refer nor assuming a single or straightforward mode of reference, I will instead outline a number of different models of personification allegory in order to examine how they work.

It may be here that my project most strongly courts misunderstanding. For in attempting even a basic classification of medieval personification allegory, it runs counter to what Sarah Kay has called "the current liberal orthodoxy," which "privilege[s] playfulness, irony, multiplicity, and indeterminacy" over even provisional attempts at classification.[28] I thus wish to clarify that these categories, like the personifications from which they are derived, are intended not as static manifestations of eternal truth but rather as dynamic engines of thought. I recognize in advance that they cannot provide an adequate account of every aspect of every individual case, any more than Linnaeus's biological taxonomy can account for all of the characteristics of flora and fauna. Instead, returning to Vaihinger, they *"deliberately substitute a fraction of reality for the complete range of causes and facts"* in order to produce a set of tools that are useful to think with.[29] Aiming for justification rather than verification, they are intended to be used exactly insofar as they are useful—and modified insofar as they are not. At the same time, I want to make a case for the value of classification and more broadly for the value of universality. A commitment to particularity at the expense of universality is incoherent, in the sense that a particular without a universal is not a particular at all but merely one phenomenon amid a welter of phenomena. To distinguish or isolate for consideration one particular phenomenon from others is already to posit, at the very least, a universal particularity in which it might participate. Universality, then, seems to be an inescapable fact of human consciousness, or at least of human language. Like Kay and Fredric Jameson, I find allegory to be a fruitful site of investigation precisely because it confronts this inevitability. Sometimes its goal is critique, as when, in Jill Mann's account, Langland's Liar "shows us *lying being made respectable*" as he infiltrates one powerful social institution after another.[30] Often it involves the formation of an impersonal, and thus at least potentially collective, identity, whether that of John Bunyan's unworldly Christian or John Ball's politically active "Jon Treweman and alle his felawes," elaborated as instruments of rebel solidarity in the 1381 Peasants' Revolt.[31] My point is not that a concern with the universal is inherently radical but rather that it is not inherently reactionary. The same is true of a concern with particularity. As David Lawton puts it, "Allegory deals in power, knowledge, authority; equally, it can challenge or negate them."[32] As machines of the mind, personifications amplify force by connecting individuals to collectivities, as well as to the ideas in whose name they act.

From here, it follows that the force, or even the violence, exerted by personification is not inherently destructive or immoral. Gordon Teskey's influential account of personification allegory claims that the process by which personifier is attached to personified is akin to the capture or *raptus* of an individual, empirical being—generally represented as feminine because of its association with matter rather than form—by the totalizing, masculine *logos*. In Dante's *Inferno*, for instance, the adulterous Francesca is violently stripped of her human complexity in order to be reduced to a univocal sign of lust. While this reading offers a plausible account of the Dantean pilgrim's response to Francesca, it cannot reasonably stand in for all possible relationships between personifier and personified, much less all relationships between particular and universal. When the thirteenth-century German mystic Mechthild of Magdeburg sought union with Christ via a personified Love, she certainly did not understand herself to be reduced in any way by her experience. Quite the contrary. To the extent that she experienced violence, it was the violence of her ardent, explicitly erotic desire for her beloved, shaped by the high medieval discourse of *fin'amour* as well as by the allegorical "machine" of the Song of Songs. More recently, the Occupy Wall Street protesters who personified themselves as Penny Less and Owen Lots represented themselves as violently captured by their student loan debt—symbolized by the signs they carried and the chains draped around their necks—which prevented them from living fully autonomous adult lives.[33] Far from compounding their oppression, their acts of self-personification helped them to emancipate themselves by reframing student debt as a social and political problem rather than an individual moral failing. Like the "people's microphone" also employed by the Occupy protesters, personification allowed Penny Less and Owen Lots to amplify their individual voices in order to speak on behalf of student debtors as a disenfranchised class.[34] It is of course possible to interpret both of these examples as instances of false consciousness, what Teskey calls "the practice of ritual interpretation by which [ideological] structures are reproduced in bodies and reexpressed through the voice."[35]

Doing so, however, requires overwriting the participants' compelling accounts of their own experiences. In both cases, the personifiers affiliate themselves with their personifieds voluntarily, in ways that run counter to the dominant gender and class narratives of their respective historical moments. In Vaihinger's terms, their use of personification does violence not to their human autonomy but "to thought itself" by demanding that its audiences think in challenging new ways.[36] Instead of being exerted by the personified on the personifier, this violence amplifies the power of those who are otherwise comparatively powerless. The moral and political value of personification thus depends upon its use.[37]

REALISM AND ITS DISCONTENTS

Much of the controversy surrounding personification is derived from the fact that it often mediates between individuals or particulars on the one hand and universals or concepts on the other. Particulars and universals have been, if not indissociable, then at least empirically inseparable since the time of Aristotle, who famously defined them relative to each other in *On Interpretation*. In this context, subject and predicate are philosophical rather than grammatical categories, referring to logical propositions rather than to Greek, Latin, or English sentences (the Latin translation is that of Boethius, standard throughout the Middle Ages):

> Some things are universal, others individual. By the term "universal" I mean that which is of such a nature as to be predicated of many subjects, by "individual" that which is not thus predicated. Thus "man" is a universal, "Callias" an individual.
>
> Sunt haec quidem rerum universalia, illa vero singillatim (dico autem universale quod in pluribus natum est praedicari, singulare vero quod non, ut 'homo' quidem universale, 'Plato' vero eorum quae sunt singularia). (*On Interpretation* 7, 17a37)[38]

In this account, *man* is a universal because it can serve as the predicate to many different subjects ("Callias is a man"; "Socrates is a man"; "Plato is a man"), whereas *Callias* is an individual because it can serve as a predicate to only one subject ("Callias is Callias"). But what does it mean, in metaphysical terms, to say, "Callias is a man"? The first of these terms seemingly refers to an empirical and potentially identifiable individual. If we are not sure whether Aristotle refers to the Callias who was a wealthy

Athenian soldier, diplomat, and statesman of the fifth century BCE or to a different person of the same name, that is a historical rather than a metaphysical problem.[39] (It is also a problem that Boethius sidesteps by substituting the more easily identifiable Plato for Callias in his translation.) It is not possible, however, to identify *man* in the same way as Callias or Plato. To begin with, is the predicate *man* an independent substance? A divine idea? A human idea? A regulative idea? A mere word? Just as important, in what way "is" Callias any of those things? It depends not only on what your definition of *is* is but also on what your definition of *man* is. Is *man* a stable category, or can it change? Does it describe or prescribe? What kinds of demands can be made in its name? If an adult male human is not an instantiation of *man*, as I define that universal, then what is he? A woman? A child? An animal? An entirely alien Other? How should I relate to this not-*man*? How should the polis treat him? How should he understand himself? It is not difficult to see how these metaphysical questions quickly become epistemological, ethical, and political. Far from being specifically medieval, the debate over universals is alive and well in contemporary discussions of race and class, gender and sexuality, as well as in the development of emerging categories such as the Anthropocene. Universals are a characteristically medieval problem only to the extent that, in Paul Vincent Spade's terms, medieval philosophers discussed the topic "with a level of insight and rigor it has never enjoyed since."[40]

These rhetorical, political, and ethical questions should also begin to indicate some of the ways in which debates over the status of universals have influenced critical accounts of personification allegory. Late-medieval morality plays such as *Mankind*, *Everyman*, and the *Castle of Perseverance* seem to take Aristotle's definition of predicative universals as their point of departure—except that they imagine the universal *man* as having the physical traits of an individual such as Callias. That is to say, these plays represent *man* as having a voice, a body, and other attributes of material existence that characterize individuals while maintaining its philosophical universality. In contrast to studies that extend their purview only to "genuinely abstract personified[s]" such as emotions, faculties, and ethical qualities, this understanding of personification accommodates the full range of medieval practice, in which figures such as Everyman and Mankind interact with abstractions such as Lust-Liking and Mercy as ontological equals.[41] It can also include social categories such as Kindred and Cousin, figures with compound names such as Pernele Proud-Heart, beast-personifications such as Reynard the Fox, and even figures with individual names who represent universal qualities.[42] On such a reading, Pernele is a personification because, appearing alongside Envy, Wrath, Covetousness, and the like, she confesses on behalf of all who are prideful. In doing so, she highlights one of the tensions inherent in Aristotle's definition of universal and particular. Aristotle's Callias and Boethius's Plato are men both generically and specifically: they are not only instances of universal human being but also particular adult Athenian males of high social status. In contrast, the awkwardness of a proposition such as "Pernele is a man" demonstrates that an individual woman's relationship to the universal *man* is necessarily more fraught.

By their nature, then, individual personification allegories almost inevitably make claims about the relationship between particulars and universals, allying themselves, either implicitly or explicitly, with one or another school of metaphysics. These allegiances, in turn, help to account for critics' intense, often polarizing, reactions to specific works of personification allegory. They do not, however, explain the more puzzling critical tendency to associate *all* personifications with a specific position in the debate over universals. Twentieth- and twenty-first-century accounts usually represent personification either as inherently realist or as inherently nominalist, praising or blaming it in keeping with the critic's own philosophical commitments. Mann speaks of personification as such when, in a 2014 essay, she claims that "personification allegory . . . quasi-inevitably embodies a 'Platonizing' tendency." Although Mann sees this Platonizing function as positive, arguing that in its absence allegory would be reduced to "just a game," most critics who perceive a similar connection between personification and philosophical realism find it insidious.[43] In the 1940s, Erich Auerbach defined the Middle Ages as a period in which mimetic representation "was in danger of being choked to death by the vines of allegory," while at the height of the Cold War, Angus Fletcher associated allegory not only with medieval backwardness but also with "communist Russia and China."[44] Teskey, in the 1990s, dubbed it "the logocentric genre par excellence," which "actively sustains" a Neoplatonic "ideological order."[45] All three regard personification as inherently dangerous, threatening to engulf both empirical individuals and mimetic characters in totalizing doctrine.[46] Indeed, one might say they allegorize the problem. They first stage a contest between personification and mimetic characterization and then interpret that contest as a battle between philosophical realism and nominalism, medievalism and modernity, totalitarianism and individualism—in short, between bad and good. In this schema, medieval personification allegory is itself an object of ideological capture. The Middle Ages and its characteristic literary form serve, both jointly and severally, as the Other whose complexity must be reduced to a univocal ideological position. Having described medieval allegory in the most rigid, narrow, and reductive terms, these critics proceed to condemn it as rigid, narrow, and reductive.

In contrast to this understanding of allegory as inherently realist, twentieth-century post-structuralists, above all de Man, understood personification as inherently nominalist, indeed as a figure for the discontinuity between language and reality. Comparing the disagreements in his own day between theoreticians of rhetoric and traditional literary critics to "the disputations between nominalists and realists in the fourteenth century," de Man emphasized "the sheer strength of figuration . . . [its] power to confer, to usurp, and to take away significance from grammatical universals."[47] Personification thus serves as "the very figure of the reader and of reading" because it gives face to the faceless and voice to the voiceless, at the same time bringing into being a self-conscious fiction and acknowledging that fiction's lack of a real referent. Understood in these terms, prosopopoeia is not only innocent of upholding Teskey's "ideological order" but becomes the single most "powerful and indispensable tool in the unmasking of ideological aberrations." Because it is always simultaneously making and unmaking itself, personification reveals ideological discourse to be constructed rather than natural or eternal. Where Teskey categorically condemns personification, de Man's language instead verges on deific, albeit via a theology of negation. "Hallucinatory" and "uncanny," prosopopoeia becomes a central, all-powerful mystery, "the visual shape of something that has no sensory existence."[48] Thus described, it not only loses much of its particularity as a rhetorical trope but also becomes just as univocally virtuous as it is, for Teskey, univocally vicious.[49]

This tendency to characterize personification as either inherently realist or inherently nominalist extends to medieval studies. Analyses of medieval personifications must contend, either implicitly or explicitly, with the long shadow cast by Johan Huizinga's ultrarealist *Waning of the Middle Ages*, published in Dutch in 1919 and first translated into English in 1924. Even de Man cites Huizinga, briefly but apparently uncritically, using Huizinga's realist account of medieval personification as a foil for his own nominalist understanding of personification in the Romantic era and beyond.[50] Huizinga, however, attributes to the Middle Ages a realism so extreme that no medieval author ever endorsed it. He first characterizes his subject as realism "in the scholastic sense" in order to distinguish it from the literary realism of the nineteenth-century novel, concerned with the mimetic representation of the material world. Just a few lines later, however, this scholastic realism gives way to a more pervasive but largely unarticulated religious realism, defined in terms of a general habit of mind rather than specific philosophical propositions. Indeed, Huizinga insists that in order to understand this deeper realism, we must deliberately set aside our knowledge of medieval metaphysics:

> We should be careful not to think too much of the quarrel about the universals . . . [for] it is in the domain of faith that realism obtains, and here it is to be considered rather as the mental attitude of a whole age than as a philosophic opinion. In this larger sense it may be considered inherent in the civilization of the Middle Ages and as dominating all expressions of thought and of the imagination.

Huizinga's problem with scholastic realism, evidently, is that it is not realist enough. Where medieval philosophical realists overwhelmingly followed Boethius in understanding universals as real but not substantial, Huizinga describes "a sort of magic idealism" in which abstract ideals actually become concrete beings. Just as important, where scholastic realism acknowledges, by its very argumentative structure, the existence of other metaphysical systems, Huizinga claims for his realism a powerful unanimity that renders other paradigms literally unthinkable. His "men of the Middle Ages" understood abstract ideas to be substantial, in the sense of existing as independent substances, in almost exactly the same way as an empirical man or horse—an extreme form of realism that Huizinga, in the anti-Catholic vein typical of many early-twentieth-century northern European medievalists, links with religious practices such as the veneration of saints, the worship of the real presence in the communion host, and recourse to the treasury of merit.[51] The doctrine of the real presence, Huizinga suggests, depends upon a metaphysical system in which all abstract entities are naïvely and vulgarly understood to exist not just substantially but concretely.

Huizinga, however, soon finds even this religious definition of realism to be too weak, setting it aside in favor of an underlying folk belief that verges on animism. He argues that even though "the Church . . . always explicitly taught that sin is not a thing or an entity," the mass of medieval Christians nonetheless understood vice in corporeal terms, often as a hideously deformed supernatural being. As proof of this "popular" belief system, he primarily cites works of literary personification allegory, attributing the animation of the deadly sins to Prudentius's *Psychomachia*, adopted into the medieval literary tradition "as a waif of decadent

Antiquity" and honored after its adoption with a reverent literalism. Tracing the medieval afterlife of the *Psychomachia*, he sees this literalism as extending not only to audiences of popular sermons on the virtues and vices but also to elite readers of the *Roman de la Rose* (*Romance of the Rose*), of whom he asks, in all seriousness, whether "Bel-Accueil or Faux Semblant did not appear as real as Saint Barbara and Saint Christopher." For Huizinga this folk realism seems to serve as a condition of possibility for most medieval literary writing, and certainly for all medieval personification allegory. If not for these structuring assumptions, "the *Roman de la Rose* would have been unreadable." Operating within them, the *Rose* simply manifests, in a particularly elaborate form, an inherent cultural tendency toward personification. For Huizinga, "Having attributed a real existence to an idea, the [medieval] mind wants to see this idea alive, and can only effect this by personifying it." The result is an impulse toward personification "so spontaneous that nearly every thought, of itself, took a figurative shape." Huizinga goes on to link this folk realism to a generalized primitivism, declaring that "every primitive mind is realist, in the medieval sense." Via its association with a "very remote cultural past," Huizinga's allegory is timeless in the sense of literally preceding historical time, even as it gathers together a geographically and chronologically disparate subset of cultural groups in the name of a shared primitivism.[52]

Strikingly, however, Huizinga argues that classical antiquity and early modernity should be exempted from this list of primitive societies despite the prevalence of allegorical personification in both periods. In his account, the turning point between the Dark Ages and "the dawn of the Renaissance" is the work of the late-fourteenth-century French poet and chronicler Jean Froissart:

> In the poetry of Froissart, Doux Semblant, Refus, Dangier and Escondit are seen contending, as it were, with mythological figures like Atropos, Clotho, Lachesis. At first the latter are less vivid and coloured than the allegories; they are dull and shadowy and there is nothing classic about them. Gradually Renaissance sentiment brings about a complete change. The Olympians and the nymphs get the better of the allegorical personages, who fade away, in proportion as the poetic glory of Antiquity is more intensely felt.

At first this explanation simply seems incoherent. While Huizinga condemns the Middle Ages for populating its literary works with divinized abstractions akin to the classical Pallor and Panic (Pavor), he praises the

Renaissance for populating its literary works with actual classical divinities and even imagines a *Psychomachia*-like contest in which the latter defeat the former in a battle for ontological supremacy.[53] The crucial difference seems to be that Huizinga interprets the Renaissance Olympians as literary characters while understanding the medieval personifications as actual divinities. That is to say, the ontological status he attributes to textual persons depends almost entirely on his historically specific judgments of literary value. Recognizably literary works produce literary characters, while nonliterary works produce at best naïve representations of faith and at worst idols and abominations.

If I have dwelt at length on a work more than one hundred years old, it is because Huizinga's extreme realism casts an exceptionally long shadow, setting the terms for discussion well into the twenty-first century. Like Huizinga, Owen Barfield posits a medieval realism stronger than any claimed by actual medieval realists, conflating metaphysical realism, which grants a category such as *man* an objective existence, either separate from or within empirical men, with so-called Cratylic realism, which asserts a real or natural relationship between words and the things they designate. Barfield's "man of the Middle Ages" was accordingly incapable of distinguishing between literal and figurative uses of language in any way we now recognize.[54] Other critics accept Huizinga's account of allegorical realism but see Ockham's early-fourteenth-century nominalism, rather than Renaissance humanism, as sounding the death knell for allegory as a characteristically medieval mode of thought. Within this group, Newman and Mann describe personification as primarily if not exclusively realist but value it positively rather than negatively, characterizing nominalist allegory as mere rhetoric. Most critics, however, accept both Huizinga's characterization and his valuation, even as they oppose realist personification to Enlightenment rationality, the development of capitalism, and the nation-state. Critics ranging from Jorge Luis Borges to Sheila Delany to Akbari understand personification as a device that short-circuits thinking, leading it in circles that offer the illusion of forward movement without going anywhere.[55] As such, it becomes a machine for unthinking, at once the Middle Ages' most characteristic literary form and not truly literary in our modern sense of the term.

It is perhaps an even greater mark of Huizinga's influence that his work likewise sets the terms of debate for critics who strongly disagree with him. Although James Paxson's influential *Poetics of Personification* does not cite Huizinga by name, Paxson accepts Huizinga's negative characterization of realist personification as the all-but-automatic expression of a naïve religiosity. Paxson departs from Huizinga, however, by attaching these qualities to philosophical realism rather than to personification per se. He accordingly sees any self-conscious or self-referential use of personification as evidence that a text is neither religious nor realist. Analyzing medieval works of narrative personification allegory in terms that invert those of Huizinga, he argues that they demonstrate a nominalist self-awareness constructed in opposition to realist naïveté:

> One might say that narrative personification works as a parody of or *satire* on the kind of philosophical Realism described by Barfield. Nominalist or Terminist logic always comes down to lively self-criticism. Terms are terms. There were, for Ockham and his followers, no "universals." Only propositional logic—a logic self-aware of its own rhetorical and nominational underpinnings—formed the meaningful basis of ontology or epistemology. *Piers Plowman* reflects this philosophical sentiment again and again.[56]

Although Paxson attributes this nominalism to Ockham and his followers, it is actually considerably broader. To begin with, many of the medieval works of narrative personification allegory Paxson discusses were composed before the fourteenth century and thus can only have been Ockhamite avant la lettre. In some respects, the nominalism Paxson describes is difficult to distinguish from literariness, understood as an author's self-conscious awareness of craft. In other respects, however, it is less indebted to Ockham than to de Man's theorization of prosopopoeia as the "master trope" of poetic discourse. For Paxson, Langland anticipates twentieth-century post-structuralism by understanding that "terms are terms," with no referent outside the human mind—a position that Ockham himself in fact rejects, as we will see in chapter 5. In order to counter Huizinga's extreme realism, Paxson attributes to the Middle Ages what he himself would later call "the ruthless nominalism of postmodernism."[57] Both Huizinga's and Paxson's approaches to personification, then, are shaped by the assumption that one believes either naïvely or not at all.

FROM UNIVERSALS TO PERSONIFICATIONS

In tracing this long afterlife of Huizinga's account of medieval personification, I intend neither to represent his influence as all-encompassing nor to reduce the studies I cite to their engagement with his ultrarealist paradigm. I do, however, seek to trouble the binary of extreme realism versus extreme nominalism that continues, either implicitly or explicitly, to inform many analyses of medieval personification.[58] As my description of Huizinga's legacy shows, we need an account of personification that sees nonrealist medieval personifications neither as failures or exceptions nor as anachronistic instances of postmodern nominalism. I thus seek to offer a more nuanced account of the metaphysical and epistemological frameworks that would have been available to medieval authors and readers of allegorical works. That is to say, I wish to explore the theories of personification allegory implied by—and on occasion explicitly derived from—the intertwined Platonic, Aristotelian, and religious traditions as these were available to and developed within the Latin Middle Ages. Although a comprehensive treatment of these traditions is beyond the scope of this project, even my restricted survey suggests the range of ways in which medieval authors and audiences might have understood personification. To begin with, what kinds of concepts did these authors and audiences understand as susceptible to personification, and to what effect? What was the ontological status of those personifications, and how did it relate to the ontological statuses of persons and divinities? What kinds of relationships were possible between personifications and persons, or between personifications and gods? To what extent were personifications understood as real, to what extent were they understood as literary representations of reality, and to what extent were they understood as mere fictions? The answers to these questions obviously differ according to time, place, and social milieu, both within the Middle Ages and beyond. Nonetheless, it is possible to identify distinct sets of plausible answers corresponding to the relationships between universals and particulars in classical religion and rhetoric, in medieval Platonism, and in the moderately realist and nominalist or conceptualist branches of the medieval Aristotelian tradition.

At one end of the spectrum of medieval metaphysics, the naïve realism described by Huizinga is largely an empty category—albeit one so frequently cited that, as we have seen, it has become constitutive of the field.[59] While it is certainly possible that some people who lived during the Middle Ages subscribed to a naïvely realist metaphysics, they would have been considered naïve in their own time much as they are today. Instead, medieval thinkers overwhelmingly accepted Aristotle's critique of Plato's forms, as transmitted by Boethius. They understood universals not as the substantial beings described by Plato but as ideas in the mind of God. These ideas, they all but unanimously agreed, served as the templates for the creation of the world recounted in Genesis. Even when medieval philosophers disagreed about the immediate sources of human knowledge, then, they agreed that it ultimately refered to the divine mind. This, however, was where the consensus ended. Although there were almost as many medieval understandings of metaphysics as there were medieval metaphysicians, the paradigms can be divided into three main groups. During the Middle Ages, Platonic realists, moderate realists, and nominalists understood the relationship between particulars and universals in fundamentally different ways.

The Platonic realists held that the ideas or universals in the divine mind not only directed the original act of creation but also play an ongoing role in human cognition. They followed Augustine and other late-classical Neoplatonists in professing that the corruption of the postlapsarian world and the unreliability of sense perceptions prevent human beings from gaining knowledge independently. Instead, the human mind can attain genuine knowledge only insofar as it participates in divine ideas, often via the metaphor of divine illumination. For the Platonic realists, every human act of cognition thus requires divine intervention; in theological terms, it is mediated by Christ the Divine Wisdom and Divine Word. Although most medieval Aristotelians likewise understood universals to exist in the divine mind, they differed from the Platonic realists in the role they attributed to them in human cognition. One important medieval tradition of interpreting Aristotle, usually denominated moderate realism, holds that human beings can attain knowledge by abstracting it from universals located within empirical objects. They argue that empirical horses contain within themselves the form of *horse* and that humans can understand the form of *horse* by observing, reflecting on, and reasoning about empirical horses. Although moderate realists such as Aquinas continued to posit important roles for divine illumination, including as the first principle of cognition and as the basis for prophecy and other inspired forms of knowledge, they no longer considered it essential for ordinary cognitive acts. The group of philosophers known as *nominales* or *nominalistae* during the Middle Ages, and now conventionally referred to as nominalists, likewise depended heavily on Aristotle. They departed from the moderate realists, however, in positing a material realm consisting entirely of individuals. Empirical horses do not contain within themselves the form of *horse*: they are simply this horse, and that horse, and that other horse. The mature Ockham did continue to posit the universal *horse* in the human mind, but instead of understanding it as a mental entity, in the manner of the moderate realists, he understood it as a cognitive act. It does not follow, however, that for Ockham *horse* was just a human concept. Whereas the word *horse*, like the word *equus*, the word *cheval*, and the word *caballo*, signifies contingently and conventionally as the product of a particular time and place, Ockham argues that the concept to which they all refer has a natural and essential connection to that slice of reality we might call the equine. Although I will continue to refer to Ockham and his followers as nominalists in deference to the term's medieval origin as well as the general practice among medievalists, his philosophy should not be conflated with that of de Man.[60] Like other medieval thinkers, Ockham neither equates concepts with things nor disassociates the two completely. Instead, the medieval metaphysical tradition defines a series of nuanced relationships between particulars and universals.

This book argues that the range of positions in the medieval debate over universals—Platonic realism, moderate realism, and nominalism—roughly corresponds to the range of ontological statuses attributed to medieval personifications. Since virtually all medieval metaphysical paradigms treat universals as ideas rather than substantial beings, it follows that encounters with personified universals should generally be understood as taking place inside the mind. Almost by definition, these encounters represent the author's process of coming to know a personified universal and thus—albeit in a way that is necessarily imperfect and incomplete—of aligning himself or herself with the divine mind. The specifics of this process, however, differ significantly within as well as among philosophical schools. For realists in the Augustinian tradition, universals are transmitted to the human mind by divine illumination, as transcendent images perceptible to the mind's eye. Not unexpectedly, they correspond to a subset of personifications that are likewise resplendent and often explicitly the product of visionary experience. Other Neoplatonic personifications do not correspond to the forms at all but to daemons, semidivine beings ontologically intermediate between humans and the Neoplatonic One. These daemons bequeath to the corresponding subset of medieval personifications their specifically tutelary function as well as their tendency to rub shoulders with Olympian gods and other pagan divinities. Formal Neoplatonic personifications speak with great authority, as befits their status as embodiments of the Platonic forms. Daemonic personifications, in contrast, are much less authoritative and can even be faintly ridiculous. Together, these models suggest a much greater range within the category of Neoplatonic personification than critics have generally recognized.

Among medieval Aristotelians, the moderate realists understood universals to exist both within empirical things and within the human mind as so-called beings of reason abstracted from sense perceptions of empirical things. Whereas Augustinian personifications are timeless and nearly always virtuous, moderately realist personifications can be positive, neutral, or negative, depending on the sensory data they seek to organize. Because they are derived from sense perceptions, moreover, they can be strikingly historically specific and tend to be characterized by a wealth of empirical detail. By their very existence, moderately realist personifications thus complicate attempts to distinguish protonovelistic characters from personifications on the basis of verisimilar detail. Instead, they are associated with what we might call representative detail, while novelistic characters are associated with idiosyncratic detail. Although medieval *nominalistae* depart from the moderate realists in holding that only individuals exist in the material world, they continue to posit universals in the human mind, albeit as acts of cognition rather than as mental beings. It follows that nominalist personifications do not represent universals as much as they prompt readers to conceptualize them. They tend to be puzzles or enigmas, engaging readers through their incongruity rather than through visionary imagery or verisimilar detail. Although both kinds of Aristotelian personification are often dismissed as failed attempts at Platonism, together they arguably constitute the dominant form of personification in the later Middle Ages. Neither mere rhetoric nor "just a game," they refer either to universals that are part of material objects or to universals as cognitive acts.

I also investigate a third variety of personification, which I call "Prudentian personification" in honor of its most prominent literary practitioner. In doing so, I address the misunderstanding that structures Huizinga's and Paxson's shared assumption about the naïveté of belief. Despite their different philosophical orientations, both critics hold that personifications must be understood either as real or as self-conscious human creations: they can never be both at once. But do we, as moderns, become less committed to the ideals of liberty, equality, and fraternity when we analyze Eugène Delacroix's *Liberty Leading the People* as a work of art produced at a particular historical moment? Does it lose its guiding power, or its moral seriousness, when we understand it as the historically contingent construction of a more or less self-aware individual? I hope not. The same was true, I argue, of medieval allegorical works. Having asked how medieval writers and readers could believe in personifications when their contingent creation was manifest, we should not have to choose between answering with Huizinga that they were innocent and primitive and did not understand what they were doing or answering with Paxson that they were canny and literary and didn't believe in their personifications at all. Instead, this book poses an easier, more plausible, and generally more sympathetic question. How did people in the Middle Ages self-consciously create and then subject themselves to personifications in an attempt to achieve moral, political, or spiritual ends? Once again, I am less interested in *what* people in the Middle Ages believed than in *how* they believed. More precisely, I am interested in the ways medieval authors used personification as a critical tool for self-formation, at once a representation of a higher state of being and a machine that helps writers and audiences to attain that higher state.

I argue that Prudentian personification is derived from classical religion and rhetoric and is transmitted to the Middle Ages to an important extent via the *Psychomachia* and its tradition. It is "formative" in much the same sense that experience is formative, with persons and personifications mutually forming or informing each other in either a virtuous or a vicious cycle. In these cycles, the person forms or creates the personification, either individually via the rhetorical trope of prosopopoeia or collectively via the kind of deliberate, self-conscious deification practiced in Roman state religion. The personification, in turn, helps to form or reform the person, rendering him virtuous or vicious and ultimately—if the process is taken to its logical conclusion—turning him into a personification of Virtue or Vice. To borrow a turn of phrase associated with Marshall McLuhan, "We shape our tools and thereafter they shape us."[61] Prudentian personifications resemble their Platonic counterparts in being both religious and realist. Their worshippers understand abstractions such as Honor and Courage to be either divinities or aspects of divinity, with the power to respond to prayers and punish transgressions. They resemble Aristotelian personifications, however, in being self-consciously human creations. Instead of descending from above, Prudentian personifications are built up from below via religious practice. They thus come into being through a process of tropic deification, as contrasted with Platonic emanation or illumination on the one hand and Aristotelian abstraction on the other. Although many critics treat this combination of divine power and self-consciously human origins as a contradiction in terms, it goes a long way toward explaining personifications such as Prudentius's Faith, whose gruesome victory over Worship of the Old Gods demonstrates both her great power and her total lack of transcendence. In later texts, it also illuminates the phenomenon of persons turning themselves into personifications. In the opening lines of *Piers Plowman*, those who "putten hem to pride" idolatrously serve and conform themselves to the vice as if it were a deity. Prudentian personification troubles the chronology of recent accounts of the *longue durée* of medieval personification, which often assume that before the twelfth-century rediscovery of Aristotle all personification was necessarily and exclusively Platonic.

The types of personification that I elaborate in the rest of this book are suggestive rather than exact or exhaustive. There is necessarily much that I leave out. The same holds true, inevitably, for my analyses of particular allegorical texts. They are intended as case studies, as illustrations of the utility of my approach to personifications as machines of the mind. There is, however, a principle of selection. In keeping with my understanding of personifications as tools for thought, I privilege authors who create new kinds of mental engines or rework old ones for new purposes. The initiatory role of Prudentius's *Psychomachia*, as the first work of narrative personification allegory in the Western tradition, is widely acknowledged. So, too, is the influence of Boethius's *Consolation of Philosophy*, whose title character served as a paradigmatic example of Neoplatonic personification for more than a thousand years. Both of these late-antique texts also play a crucial role in linking classical theories of personification to medieval allegorical practice. Few medieval readers of the *Consolation*, for example, read it alongside Apuleius's theorization of Neoplatonic daemons in *On the God of Socrates*—and those who did overwhelmingly followed Augustine in condemning Apuleius's paganism. Yet medieval readers were attentive to the qualities Boethius's Philosophy inherited from Apuleius's daemons, including her tutelary function and intermediate ontological status. When we understand Philosophy as a daemonic personification, then, it gives us new insight not only into the *Consolation* itself but also into its medieval successors. In these texts, Philosophy and her heirs are, for lack of a better term, more novelistic than we usually acknowledge. Instead of speaking with transcendent authority, they embody a specific, limited point of view, subordinate to that of the author. The medieval texts I examine, which range from scholastic commentaries on the *Consolation* to the alliterative allegorical poem *Winner and Waster*, simultaneously initiate new modes of personification and position themselves as inheriting and adapting the classical allegorical tradition.

Because personification assigns bodies to ideas, I pay special attention to the relationship between personification and gender in all of these works. In languages like English that do not have grammatical gender, gender often functions as a minimum marker of embodiment: to refer to an inanimate object with a masculine or feminine pronoun is to personify it. Texts written in languages with grammatical gender likewise emphasize the gender of personifications in order to situate them relative to persons, whether other characters or the text's imagined readers. In a very early decision allegory, recounted by the sophist Prodicus of Ceos in the fifth century BCE and paraphrased in Xenophon's *Memorabilia*, the hero Hercules must choose between feminine personifications of Virtue (Arete) and Vice (Kakia). Both are defined in sexual terms: Virtue is "fair to see and of noble stock; her body adorned with purity, her eyes with modesty" while Vice "had grown plump and soft with high feeding. Her skin was made up to heighten its natural white and pink, her figure to exaggerate her height. She had wide-open eyes and clothing that showcased her young beauty" (*Memorabilia* 2.1.22). The gendered structure of this allegory represents moral choice as both normatively masculine and deeply intimate: a decision about how to orient desire. Where the named character Hercules represents the masculine self, the abstractions Virtue and Vice are defined by their femininity as potentially desirable Others. In later allegories, a personification's gender is often bound up with its ontological status. The most familiar varieties of Neoplatonic personification are overwhelmingly feminine, with their gender marking both their desirability and their ontological distance from their normatively masculine interlocutors. Moderately realist Aristotelian personifications, in contrast, are disproportionately masculine. Their gender reflects their relative proximity to male authors and readers, as well their origin in empirical observations of a male-dominated social world. In other cases, the gender dynamics are more complex: Prudentius starts to describe his feminine personifications of Virtue in masculine terms as soon as they begin to slacken in their battle against Vice. I argue that the *Psychomachia* encourages its male readers to transform themselves into Virtues by divesting themselves of their assigned gender. Their newfound femininity then represents their difference from their old selves, their hard-won status as "higher" and "Other." In all of these cases, gender becomes an important means of representing the relationship between particular and universal, between a reader or character who strives to become virtuous and virtue itself.

Machines of the Mind is divided into three main parts corresponding to Prudentian, Neoplatonic, and Aristotelian personification. Within each section, a first chapter examines a particular metaphysics and its implications for personification, while a second offers a detailed literary case study. Part I traces the origins of medieval personification to the late-classical period, in which embodied abstractions were worshipped as gods. Instead of seeing religious and rhetorical personification as incompatible, the products of distinct historical eras, I argue that classical texts such as Cicero's *On the Nature of the Gods* (*De natura deorum*) and *On the Laws* (*De legibus*) simultaneously support the worship of abstractions such as

Honor and Courage and recognize that these divinities are self-conscious and historically contingent human creations. Like Cicero, Quintilian regards the processes of religious and rhetorical personification as continuous, producing a model of personification as tropic deification in which ancestors and abstractions are consecrated as deities so that they can form their worshippers to virtue.

The second chapter in this section turns from theory to practice, examining the personifications in Prudentius's *Psychomachia*. I argue that the poem enacts a battle over the nature of personification allegory itself. Prudentius's Vices are none other than the deified abstractions of the ancient world, interpreted as Saint Paul's "spirits of wickedness," and his Virtues destroy them not once but twice: first as moral categories, then as a pagan form of personification that will give way to its Christian counterpart. Prudentius's model of formative personification adapts rather than dismantles that of Cicero and Quintilian, however. His feminine Virtues are simultaneously supernatural beings battling against wicked spirits as ontological equals and human creations. Indeed, as soon as they slacken in their fight against vice, their bodies revert to those of male persons, indicating that for Prudentius virtue is not a state but a process of self-personification, even self-deification, through religious practice. He invites his readers to reform or re-create the poem's personifications as they read, so that they will in turn be reformed by them, remade first as virtuous readers and ultimately as personifications of virtue. In the final lines of his poem, Prudentius suggests that the endpoint of this process is Neoplatonic personification, represented by the transcendentally beautiful Wisdom seated on her jeweled throne. However, the passage's otherworldly imagery, borrowed from Revelation, makes it clear that a figure like Wisdom can only exist outside of time. In this world, formative personification remains Prudentius's most powerful weapon in the fight against wickedness.

Part II considers medieval Neoplatonism and the allegorical forms associated with it. Rather than reestablish the existence or general characteristics of Neoplatonic personification, it examines the different varieties of Neoplatonism available in the Middle Ages and their correspondingly different implications for personification allegory. Strikingly, the category of Neoplatonic personification includes not only the tradition's most thoroughly awe-inspiring and numinous personifications but also some that are notably irreverent and unreliable. The most transcendent Neoplatonic personifications, associated with an Augustinian understanding of the Platonic forms, tend to be allegorical goddesses, often introducing themselves as the brides or daughters of God magisterially described by Newman. Daemonic personifications, in contrast, are much less authoritative, and can even be mildly ridiculous, as befits daemons' tutelary role in texts ranging from Plato's *Symposium* to Apuleius's *On the God of Socrates* to Calcidius's commentary on the *Timaeus*.

The second chapter in part II tests both formal and daemonic personification against a work often regarded as the paradigmatic example of Neoplatonic personification allegory: Boethius's *Consolation of Philosophy*. Examining the *Consolation* both within its original late-classical context and through the lens of the medieval tradition of commentary and translation, I argue that Boethius's Philosophy inherits her basic mode of being from classical daemons—and is thus neither transcendent nor fully authoritative. For Boethius himself, as for medieval commentators including William of Conches and Nicholas Trevet, this intermediate status is encoded in Philosophy's femininity, which allows her to nurse the young and care for the sick but limits her authority over full-fledged philosophers. Neither in the *Consolation* itself nor in its medieval tradition does Philosophy lead the way to transcendence, as we would expect of an allegorical goddess. Instead, she accompanies the prisoner for a portion of his upward trajectory before turning back with him to consider moral and political philosophy. In the *Consolation*, the prisoner finally seeks God through humble prayer rather than Neoplatonic ascent, redefining philosophy as a fundamentally worldly discipline concerned with moral probity and political justice. Medieval commentaries on and translations of the *Consolation* likewise cordon off the highest reaches of philosophy as ill-suited for personification, leaving Philosophy as the mistress of a diminished and downward-looking discipline, suitable for beginners and those who deliberately look away from the heights to devote themselves to the public good. Understood in these terms, Philosophy embodies a specific, limited point of view, explicitly subordinate to that of Boethius as author.

Part III examines the relatively unexplored category of Aristotelian personification allegory. Seeking an account of the relationship between universals and their earthly instantiations, Aristotle dismissed the Platonic doctrine of formal participation as nothing more than "empty words and poetical metaphors," instead positing that humans derive universals such as *man* and *horse* from their observations of empirical men and horses. For moderately realist medieval Aristotelians, these universals are abstracted from sense perceptions and exist in the mind as beings of reason. The personifications corresponding to these universals are ontologically dependent on the individuals from which they are abstracted, sometimes even emerging from and reverting to them before our eyes in the manner of Langland's Liar. Nominalist personifications, in turn, tend to be puzzles or enigmas. Like Guillaume de Deguileville's Penance, who carries a broom in her mouth to signify the tongue's cleansing power in the confession of sin, they tend to be described in terms that are worldly but not verisimilar. Deguileville's Penance does not look like penance but is instead a machine for generating the concept of penance in the minds of readers and would-be penitents. Strictly speaking, a nominalist personification does not represent a given universal but prompts its audience to conceptualize it, often via an "aha moment" as they come to appreciate the puzzle.

Part III's second chapter focuses on two satirical allegories that, while certainly less well known than the *Psychomachia* or the *Consolation of Philosophy*, play a similarly initiatory role. Raoul de Houdenc's early-thirteenth-century *Songe d'Enfer* (Dream of Hell) rewrites Prudentius's *Psychomachia* as the earliest first-person, fictional dream vision, while the alliterative debate poem *Winner and Waster* offers the first account of a dream in post-Conquest English. In both cases, the dream structure lends itself to Aristotelian personification, since it makes no claims about the existence of universals, or the personifications who represent them, outside of the human mind. Instead, their personifications present themselves as a means of coming to grips with the poets' self-consciously modern world. Raoul's Vices grow in strength and stature as more and more people abandon idealized feudal values in favor of the values of the marketplace, suggesting that they represent Aristotelian universals abstracted from the qualities of empirical human beings. The titular personifications of *Winner and Waster*, for their part, make a dizzying multiplicity of economic actors available to ethical and political analysis. These poems' shift from feminine to masculine personification contrasts with both the *Psychomachia* and the *Consolation*, suggesting that their authors understood themselves to be producing a new variety of personification, one defined by its ability to represent the male-dominated social and political world rather than by its distance from it.

In these first three parts, the book seeks to isolate the different varieties of Prudentian, Neoplatonic, and Aristotelian personification for the sake of analytical clarity. Its final chapter recognizes that during the later Middle Ages hybrid metaphysical systems were in fact the rule rather than the exception. Built in part on the shared Neoplatonic and Aristotelian understanding of cognition as inner vision, hybrid models of metaphysics tend to describe the intellection of "higher" cognitive objects in terms of divine illumination and that of "lower" objects in terms of Aristotelian abstraction. These models give rise to allegorical works in which numinous and mundane personifications appear together, either side by side or sequentially. The chapter examines *Piers Plowman* as an instance of this mixed allegory, arguing that it includes instances of Prudentian, Neoplatonic, and Aristotelian personification. Indeed, the often remarked shift in the gender of Langland's personifications over the course of the poem reflects a larger shift from characteristically feminine Neoplatonic personifications to characteristically masculine Aristotelian ones. More broadly, Langland's willingness to experiment with different varieties of personification offers a fitting riposte to critics who insist that personification is either inherently realist or inherently nominalist, as he builds, rebuilds, and tinkers with his personifications as machines of the mind designed to answer specific questions or solve specific problems. Like the tech-world personifications Connie the Conscientious Consumer and Abe the Active Administrator, Langland's personifications are valued for their representational power.

PART I

Prudentian Personification

CHAPTER ONE

Consecratus Manu: Men Forming Gods Forming Men

The personification called Pheme in Greek, Fama in Latin, and Fame or Rumor in English comes into being at the same moment both as a goddess and as a rhetorical personification. She takes shape before our eyes in the final lines of the "Works" section of Hesiod's *Works and Days* (c. 700 BCE) as the authorial persona warns his brother of the danger of rumors:

> Do these things, and avoid the wretched talk [*pheme*] of mortals, for talk [*pheme*] is evil, lightweight, and very easy to lift, but painful to carry and hard to put aside. No talk [*pheme*] that many people talk [*phemizo*] perishes completely. She herself is a kind of god [*theos*].[1]

Repeated three times as a common noun and then as the root of a verb, Pheme becomes a personification only gradually, as she begins to pass a series of "grammatical tests" for identifying personifications. Discussed as early as Priscian's *Institutes of Grammar* (*Institutiones grammaticae*) but elaborated most fully by Morton Bloomfield, these tests include the use of a common noun as a proper name, the use of grammatical forms that imply animateness, and the use of verbs that normally apply only to living beings.[2] In this case, Fame is first accorded a moral bearing ("*pheme* is evil"), then gains a physical body ("very easy to lift, but painful to carry"), then becomes the subject of a verb normally applied to living things ("perishes"), and finally is characterized as fully animate ("a kind of god"). Strikingly, she does not become a person but a divinity—albeit a divinity of a peculiar sort. Although the "Works" begins with a traditional invocation of Zeus and the Muses, it ends with a goddess who is created, and to an important extent mediated by human beings. Hesiod cautions his prodigal brother to avoid loose talk specifically in order to limit Fame's power over him. In doing so, he suggests that if all mortals hold their tongues, Fame will lose her divine power, and perhaps even perish. At the same time, Hesiod presents Fame as his own poetic invention, with the circumlocution in the last line suggesting, as the classicist Emma Stafford puts it, "a poetic way of emphasizing rumour's power rather than a reference to a deity already recognized by Hesiod's audience."[3] Even as Hesiod recognizes that Fame is dangerous, then, she also represents the ambition of his poem, which likewise seeks to rise from low origins, as something akin to "the wretched talk of mortals," to achieve immortality. Hesiod may encourage his brother to avoid loose talk, but he also urges him to talk up his poem. From the very beginning, Fame's verbal power parallels that of the poet, while she herself is both larger and smaller than he is.

My reading of Fame highlights her status as both a goddess and a rhetorical personification because these two categories are usually treated as incompatible. As we have seen, the early-twentieth-century critic Johan Huizinga understood personification to be both inherently religious and inherently naïve. In his account, medieval personification allegories are not crafted by individual authors as much as they are generated, almost automatically, by the period's ultrarealist conception of universals. Later critics, including James Paxson, accept Huizinga's category of naïve religious personification but oppose it to a category of self-aware literary personification. Jon Whitman most clearly articulates this bifurcation:

> It is necessary to distinguish two meanings of the term "personification." One refers to the practice of giving an *actual* personality to an abstraction. This practice has its origins in animism and ancient religion, and is called "personification" by modern theorists of religion and anthropology. . . . The other meaning of "personification," the one used throughout this study, is the historical sense of *prosopopoeia*. This refers to the practice of giving a consciously *fictional* personality to an abstraction, "impersonating" it. This rhetorical practice requires a separation between the literary pretense of a personality, and the actual state of affairs.[4]

As described here, the differences between these two types of personification are both disciplinary and chronological. While the first falls within the domains of religion and anthropology, the second belongs to literary studies and the history of rhetoric. The second also develops later than, and as a refinement of, the first. Although the creators of both kinds of personification engage in the identical activity of "giving . . . personality to an abstraction," only the later and implicitly more refined creators of literary personifications understand what they are doing.

This chapter argues that, on the contrary, many personifications categorized as religious are also rhetorical, in the sense of being self-conscious human constructions, while many personifications categorized as rhetorical are also religious, in the sense of giving voice to divine or semidivine beings. Personifications such as Fame—first as elaborated by Hesiod, then as reimagined by Virgil, Ovid, and Chaucer—occupy an ambiguous middle ground. In a given rhetorical context, it is not necessarily clear whether Fame should be understood as a divinity, a semidivinity, a potential divinity, or as something similar or analogous to a divinity. Likewise, it is not necessarily clear to what extent each subsequent author who writes about Fame creates her anew and to what extent he describes an existing superhuman being. I will focus on the classical period, in which the worship of abstract ideas was commonplace, in order to demonstrate that the critical binary of naïve religious personification versus self-conscious rhetorical personification is not always tenable. But I will also argue that classical theories of personification illuminate the medieval practice of personification to a greater extent than is usually recognized. To be sure, classical treatments of personification that we now think of as rhetorical enjoyed both a wider medieval readership and a more favorable medieval reception than classical treatments of personification that we now think of as religious. Both sets of texts, however, exerted an important indirect influence on medieval writers. When medieval writers looked to the classical world for literary models, they encountered personifications who emerged from the same discursive, and sometimes authorial, matrix as the theoretical texts discussed in this chapter. Although the theoretical texts helpfully make explicit what is only implicit in the personifications themselves, the same metaphysics is embedded in the personifications for attentive and perceptive medieval readers to intuit or even unfold.

I will begin by examining Cicero's theorization of religious personification in *On the Nature of the Gods* and *On the Laws*. In these texts, the deified virtues are both fully numinous and, without contradiction, the product of human intellectual craftsmanship. Indeed, Cicero recognizes that the process of deification is contingent, in the sense that the number of potentially deifiable virtues far exceeds those actually deified. In these circumstances, the Roman people rightly deify the virtues they most value and those of which they have the greatest need. The remainder of the chapter examines the parallel theorization of personification in rhetorical treatises, arguing that just as religious personifications can be rhetorical, so rhetorical personifications can be religious. In guides to rhetoric ranging from Demetrius's *On Style* to the *Rhetorica ad Herennium*, Cicero's *Orator*, and Quintilian's *Institutes of Oratory* (*Institutio Oratoria*), the paradigmatic examples of personification are not abstractions at all but the spirits of ancestors and localities. In this context, prosopopoeia becomes a form of religious invocation as well as a site for rhetorical invention. I thus argue for classical religious and rhetorical personification as continuous, sometimes overlapping, categories rather than binary opposites. Together they define what I am—admittedly anachronistically, at least for the purposes of this chapter—calling Prudentian personification. Like Platonic personifications, Prudentian personifications are religious, and thus realist. Like Aristotelian personifications, however, they are also self-consciously created, the product of human craftsmanship. They come into being through a process of consecration or deification, as contrasted with both the characteristically Platonic process of divine illumination and the characteristically Aristotelian process of abstraction from sense perceptions. Prudentian personification is accordingly formative in the same sense that experiences are formative. As such, it disrupts the categories as well as the chronologies of recent accounts of the *longue durée* of personification allegory.

THE RHETORIC OF RELIGIOUS PERSONIFICATION

In his influential essay "Did the Middle Ages Believe in Their Miracles?," Steven Justice objects to the axiomatic equation of medieval religious belief with credulity, an equation which he describes as constitutive of the field of medieval studies, indeed a primary means of defining the Middle Ages as modernity's incomprehensible Other.[5] In alluding to Paul Veyne's book *Did the Greeks Believe in Their Myths?*, Justice's title implicitly compares medievalists to classicists, who in recent years have treated the same subject matter quite differently.[6] Where medievalists see a stark opposition between religious naïveté and literary self-consciousness, classicists emphasize the "ontological ambiguity" of Greek and Roman personifications, including their slippage from literary to religious and back again.[7] H. L. Axtell identifies over forty literary personifications who were also the beneficiaries of attested cults, while Amy Smith defines personification "as the representation of a thing, place, or abstraction as a person, where person may be human, mythical, and/or divine."[8] In a characteristically subtle reading, Stafford points out that since Quiet (Hesychia) is only personified in Pindar's odes, "it is quite reasonable to suppose that the implied attribution of deity is a product of poetic license"—but then goes on to caution that Pindar's hymnic invocation of Quiet represents her as "a being *capable* of receiving worship, whether or not her cult is actually observed anywhere."[9] Dunstan Lowe argues that when the goddesses of vengeance were "translated" from the Greek to the Roman pantheon, their ontological status shifted along with their name. Although the Greek proper name Erinys classifies them as personal deities, the Latin common noun Furia (Furies) situates them in a liminal space between divinity and personification—a space where Lowe likewise locates Virgil's and Ovid's Fame and Sleep (Somnus) and Ovid's Hunger (Fames) and Envy (Invidia).[10] Classicists thus tend to represent abstraction and deification, both separately and together, as processes rather than absolutes. They understand abstract ideas as susceptible to deification even when not empirically deified, while recognizing that deities were likewise susceptible to abstraction, whether through translations such as the one undergone by the Erinys; epithets such as Aphrodite Peitho (Aphrodite-Persuasion) and Athena Nike (Athena-Victory); ritual linkages such as altars to Health (Hygieia) in shrines of the personal deity Asclepius; or well-worn metonymies such the substitution of Dionysius/Liber for wine and Demeter/Ceres for bread—the latter so common that it gave rise to the modern English word *cereal*.[11] In doing so, classicists treat belief not as a refusal to engage with facts but as a commitment to ideals such as Divine Order (Themis), Peace (Irene), and Democracy (Democratia).

In short, classicists now give little credence to the once popular claim that deified abstractions represent a primitive form of religious expression, gradually superseded by personalized deities.[12] As early as the eighth century BCE, deities with abstract names mingled with the Olympian gods in the works of Homer and Hesiod, with the relationships among them both intimate and intricate. In Hesiod's *Theogony*, Zeus takes as his first wife the titaness Metis, whose name means skill or wisdom, but, fearing that she will bear a son who will surpass him, incorporates her into himself by swallowing her whole. Thus internalized, she bears not a son but a daughter, the Olympian Athena, who emerges from her father's head fully armed to become the goddess of skill and wisdom. In the Homeric poems, Metis becomes a quality or aspect of Zeus, who gains the epithet *metieta*, wise counselor. In other cases, gods with abstract names were understood as the children of gods with personal names, with Love (Eros) the son of Aphrodite, Youth (Hebe) the daughter of Zeus and Hera, and Hygieia the daughter of the deified mortal Asclepius. As these relationships indicate, many deified abstractions were venerated alongside, and sometimes in competition with, personalized deities. In Greece, there was an altar to Fame in Athens, a shrine to Divine Order and Retribution (Nemesis) at Rhamnous, and altars to Hygieia and Peitho in temples of Asclepius and Aphrodite. In Rome, sanctuaries were dedicated to Victory (Victoria), Fortune (Fortuna), Concord (Concordia), War (Bellona), Faith (Fides), Youth (Juventus), and a host of others. The temple of Victory was built at virtually the same time as a temple of Jupiter Victor—that is to say, of Jupiter in his aspect as Victor—and presumably competed with it for offerings, much as the cults of Good Reputation (Euclea) and Artemis Euclea coexisted in Athens. Where records are available—as for the fourth-century cults of Peace, Democracy, and Good Fortune (Agathe Tyche) in Athens—they suggest that the festivals of personified abstractions were conducted on the same scale as celebrations of Athena, Dionysius, and Zeus Soter.[13] These juxtapositions undermine not just the older position that divine personifications gave way to personalized deities but also the more recent claim that later cults of divine abstractions were "more propaganda than religion," with "the profusion of robed female statues of an allegorical character arous[ing] no more than dusty, aesthetic antiquarian interest."[14] Instead, personified abstractions seem to have been understood in largely the same terms as the personalized, anthropomorphic deities who were their fathers and mothers, sons and daughters, with the qualification that, as Stafford suggests, personifications often governed narrower, more clearly defined fields of responsibility.

None of these accounts associate religious personification with credulity. On the contrary, the divinity of personifications was subject to philosophical deliberation within the classical period itself. Cicero's *On the Nature of the Gods*, which was known and copied somewhat sporadically during the Middle Ages, offers the best surviving evidence for the arguments of the major philosophical schools.[15] It stages a debate among Velleius the Epicurean, Balbus the Stoic, and Cotta the Skeptic, with Cicero speaking in propria persona only in brief opening and closing statements. Although Velleius's arguments are demolished so thoroughly that he is reduced to the position of spectator, the debate between Balbus and Cotta ends without a clear victor. The situation is complicated yet further by the fact that Cotta does not necessarily endorse the views he articulates. As an Academic Skeptic, he adopts a variety of hypothetical positions with the goal of identifying flaws in his opponents' logic rather than advancing arguments of his own. Even as Cotta challenges the Stoic account of the divinity of abstractions, then, he accepts the worship of deified abstractions as part of the larger structure of Roman civic religion, as defined by its high pontiffs. This lack of a definitive conclusion may reflect the state of public discourse at the time it was written and seems to indicate that, at least for Cicero, the question remained open to debate. Even more fundamentally, it reflects the extent to which Roman religion was governed by orthopraxis, or correct ritual performance, rather than revelation or doctrine. Cotta's last statement expresses both a desire and an expectation that Balbus will ultimately defeat him. Even if he does not, Cotta sees no conflict between his attempts to demolish Balbus's philosophical arguments and his obligation to "uphold the beliefs about the immortal gods which have come down to us from our ancestors, and the rites and ceremonies and duties of religion" (opiniones quas a maioribus accepimus de dis inmortalibus, sacra caerimonias religionesque defenderem) (3.2.5). John Scheid argues that since "relations with the gods were conducted under the sign of reason," they were neither threatened nor undermined by reasoned critique.[16] In this context, with both Balbus's and Cotta's positions articulated and defended with full awareness of the other—indeed, articulated most strongly in response to the other—it is virtually impossible to characterize either argument as naïve.

As the title of Cicero's work indicates, his debaters are primarily concerned with the nature of the gods—that is to say, with the kinds of beings properly venerated as divinities. As a Stoic, Balbus argues in favor of divine personifications, assigning what Whitman calls an "actual" rather than a "fictional" personality to abstractions. He characterizes them, however, in terms diametrically opposite Whitman's. Rather than being primitive or naïve, the cults of divine personifications demonstrate rationality and cultural advancement. Contrasting the worship of abstractions in his own day with earlier devotions to monsters such as the Hippocentaur and the Chimaera, he asks, "Where can you find an old wife senseless enough to be afraid of the monsters of the lower world that were once believed in?" (Quaeve anus tam excors inveniri potest quae illa quae quondam credebantur apud inferos portenta extimescat?) (2.2.5). He claims that where monsters once presided over feminine ignorance and irrationality, the current Roman deities "have with good reason been recognized and named both by the wisest men of Greece and by our own ancestors from the great benefits they bestow" (ex magnis beneficiis eorum non sine causa et a Graeciae sapientissimis et a maioribus nostris constitutae nominataeque sunt) (2.23.60). Balbus bases his argument in favor of divinized abstractions in part on the social position of those who support these cults, naming the prominent citizens who have recently paid to renovate or construct shrines to Faith, Mind (Mens), Courage (Virtus), and Honor (Honos) as evidence of the bona fides of these divinities. Pointing to a renovated temple that was evidently visible from the portico of Cotta's mansion, where the dialogue is set, he suggests that the social and architectural fabric of Rome itself authorizes the worship of divine personifications. Associating Faith, Mind, Courage, and Honor with masculinity, rationality, and high social status, he defines them as civic gods, both contributing to and—as they receive offerings at newly built altars—benefiting from Rome's cultural, political, and economic progress.

Even more strikingly, Balbus argues in favor of the divinization of abstractions as a recent, indeed ongoing, religious practice. In keeping with his understanding of divine abstractions as "modern" gods, contrasted with primitive monsters such as the Chimaera, he describes them as brought into being through enlightened acts of interpretation. In such cases,

> some exceptionally potent force is itself designated by a title of divinity, for example Faith and Mind; we see the shrines on the Capitol lately dedicated to them both by Marcus Aemilius Scaurus, and Faith had previously been deified [*consecrata*] by Aulus Atilius Calatinus.

> res ipsa in qua vis inest maior aliqua sic appellatur ut ea ipsa nominetur deus, ut Fides, ut Mens, quas in Capitolio dedicatas videmus proxime a M. Aemilio Scauro, ante autem ab A. Atilio Calatino erat Fides consecrata. (2.23.61)

For Balbus, deification is thus an explicitly human act, performed through individual and collective ritual practices, including the construction and maintenance of shrines, the provision of priests, the dedication of offerings, and the observance of festivals. Indeed, the verb *consecro*, which he uses to describe Calatinus's deification of Faith, means inextricably "to dedicate, devote something as sacred to a deity" and "to elevate to the rank of deity, to place among the gods, to deify."[17] It is also an act performed by named individuals within historical memory: Calatinus was a prominent statesman of the third century BCE, while Scaurus was one of Cicero's own clients. Implicitly, those who participate in the cults of Faith and Mind corroborate and continue this work of deification. Rather than being artificial or arbitrary, these rituals are necessitated by the *vis*—strength, force, vigor, power—of Faith and Mind, Virtue and Honor. As Balbus explains, "because the power of all these things was so great that it could not be governed except by divinity, they were designated as gods" (quarum omnium rerum quia vis erat tanta ut sine deo regi non posset, ipsa res deorum nomen obtinuit) (2.23.61). In this account, the divinization of abstractions allows the Roman people to come to terms with, indeed to regulate or manage, the real and potentially overwhelming forces affecting their individual and collective lives. Faith and Mind, then, are simultaneously gods and thinking machines insofar as they allow their worshippers to conceptualize and even manipulate forces that would otherwise be beyond their knowledge or control. Balbus argues that since these "things" have such great power over human life, it is both right and rational to treat them as divinities.

So central are deified virtues to Balbus's account that he treats them as the paradigm for other forms of divinity. The virtues thus serve as models for the more controversial deified vices, whose worship Cicero roundly condemns in *On the Laws*. For Balbus, even "vicious and unnatural things" (vitiosarum rerum neque naturalium) such as Voluptas (Pleasure), Cupido (Cupid/Desire), and Lubentina Venus (Sensual Venus) should be deified—as they in fact were in the Rome of his day—because "the urge of these vices often overpowers natural instinct" (ipsa vitia natura vehementius saepe pulsant) (2.23.61). Again, the prerequisite for deification is not virtue but raw, overwhelming power. For Balbus, deifying sexual desire both recognizes it and regulates it, making it part of the social fabric—and so is a rational act, despite or even because of the irrationality of desire itself. Balbus applies a similar logic to named deities, as we have begun to see with his conflation of Voluptas, Cupido, and Lubentina Venus. Where the first is a personified abstraction, the second is simultaneously a personified abstraction and a personalized deity, and the third is an aspect of a personalized Olympian deity, Venus in her capacity as giver of pleasure. In the same section of the dialogue, Balbus describes the named gods as personifications of the benefits they provide to humankind, offering a series of etymological allegories whereby Saturn (in Greek, Chronos) represents the regular passage of time, Jupiter or Jove is a "helping father (iuvans pater)," Juno is the air, and so on (2.25.64). Dismissing the Homeric accounts of vain, angry, and jealous gods as "immoral fables" (impias fabulas), he argues for the personal deities as rational, animate beings who demonstrate virtues such as *mens*, *fides*, and *concordia*, thus assimilating them to the personified virtues (2.24.64). All of these divinities dwell harmoniously in a perfected version of the classical polis, "united together in a sort of social community or fellowship, ruling the one world as a united commonwealth or state" (compotes inter seque quasi civili conciliatione et societate coniunctos, unum mundum ut communem rem publicam atque urbem aliquam regentis) (2.31.78). To worship these gods through their "majestic and holy images" (augusta et sancta simulacra), as part of the prescribed course of the Roman state religion, is accordingly to conform one's self to their virtues, even as those same images, in representing both personalized and abstract deities in human form, conform the gods to us (2.31.79).

The Academician Cotta, as one would expect, vehemently disagrees with Balbus, offering a critique of religious personification that anticipates many of the arguments of his twentieth-century counterparts. To begin with, Cotta first simplifies then dismisses Balbus's argument that cult practices constitute evidence of divinity. Where Balbus seeks to distinguish between superstitious and religious cult practices, coding the former as primitive, feminine, and slavish and the latter as traditional, masculine, and rational, Cotta admits no such distinction. The "stupidity of the vulgar and the ignorant" (volgi atque imperitorum inscitiam) generates a staggering array of superstitions, not only in Syria and Egypt but also in Greece and Rome (3.15.39). Men have deified animals, things, and each other without discrimination, and indeed continue to do so, believing these new gods "to have been admitted to celestial citizenship in recent times, by a sort of extension of the franchise" (quasi novos et adscripticios cives in caelum receptos) (3.15.39).[18] Rather than serving as a check on the irrationality of the masses, governments pursue their secular interests by licensing the deification of heroes:

> It is easy to see that in most states the memory of brave men has been sanctified with divine honours for the purpose of promoting valour, to make the best men more willing to encounter danger for their country's sake.
>
> In plerisque civitatibus intellegi potest augendae virtutis gratia, quo libentius rei publicae causa periculum adiret optimus quisque, virorum fortium memoriam honore deorum immortalium consecratam. (3.19.50)

Cotta here anticipates the arguments of the medievalists critiqued by Justice, explaining away large swathes of religious practice as the collusion of cynical, secular elites and hopelessly credulous, ovine masses. In singling out deification for particular scorn, he also presents an understanding of divinity itself that differs sharply from that of Balbus. If for Cotta deification is patently absurd, a logical impossibility, it follows that he considers divinity to be an ontological state that exists outside of time. True deities always have been and always will be divine. In contrast to Balbus, then, Cotta understands the difference between men and gods as absolute. He sees Balbus's attempt to philosophize about the gods as not just erroneous but fundamentally misguided. Men cannot philosophize about the gods because the gods are inaccessible to human reason; instead, they transcend it.

Cotta rejects deified personifications on grounds similar to those he adduces for rejecting deified heroes such as Hercules and Asclepius. They are so closely associated with humanity that they cannot possibly be divine:

> We see that mind, faith, hope, virtue, honor, victory, safety, concord and the other things of this type are in essence abstractions, not gods. For they are either properties inherent in ourselves, for instance mind, hope, faith, virtue, concord, or things we should desire, for instance honor, safety, victory. I see that they have value, and I am also aware that statues are dedicated to them; but why they should be held to possess divinity is a thing that I cannot understand without further enlightenment.
>
> Nam mentem fidem spem virtutem honorem victoriam salutem concordiam ceteraque eius modi rerum vim habere videmus, non deorum. Aut enim in nobismet insunt ipsis, ut mens ut spes ut fides ut virtus ut concordia, aut optandae nobis sunt, ut honos ut salus ut victoria; quarum rerum utilitatem video, video etiam consecrata simulacra, quare autem in iis vis deorum insit tum intellegam cum cognovero. (3.24.61)

Cotta goes on to point out that although men rightly and spontaneously thank the gods for abundant harvests and other external benefits, they do not feel grateful for the virtues because they consider them to be their own accomplishments, or their own internal qualities. At the same time, he cautions that there is no clear distinction between the personified virtues on the one hand and negative or ambivalent cult figures such as Fever and Fortune on the other, whose inconstancy and haphazard action "are certainly unworthy of a god" (digna certe non sunt deo) (3.24.61). Even more fundamentally, Cotta claims that when the Stoics seek divine referents for words such as faith, hope, and virtue, they fail to understand the nature of language itself. He maintains that "when we speak of corn as

Ceres and wine as Liber, we employ a familiar figure of speech, but do you suppose that anybody can be so insane as to believe that the food he eats is a god?" (cum fruges Cererem, vinum Liberum dicimus, genere nos quidem sermonis utimur usitato, sed ecquem tam amentem esse putas qui illud quo vescatur deum credat esse?) (3.16.41). Whether in literary works or everyday conversation, language refers back to itself rather than to underlying truths about gods and men. Cotta likewise charges that in offering allegorical interpretations of the stories of the Olympian gods, Balbus fails to understand their status as "fabulous inventions" (commenticiarum fabularum) (3.24.63). For Cotta, the Homeric myths, like the deified heroes they recount, are not veiled representations of truth but outright fabrications. The personified abstractions in such texts are entirely fictional, while personification itself is purely a rhetorical trope.

The debaters in *On the Nature of the Gods* fall silent without reaching a resolution. Although Cotta offers the final sustained argument, Balbus vows to continue the debate beyond the text's narrative frame, to continue fighting "on behalf of our altars and hearths, of the temples and shrines of the gods, and of the city-walls . . . so long as I yet can breathe" (pro aris et focis certamen et pro deorum templis atque delubris proque urbis muris . . . dum quidem spirare potero) (3.40.94). Among the bystanders, Velleius, the discredited Epicurean, favors Cotta, while Cicero offers very tentative support for Balbus, describing his position as "nearer to a semblance of the truth" (ad veritatis similitudinem . . . propensior) (3.40.95). To the extent that Cicero synthesizes the debaters' positions he does so not in *On the Nature of the Gods* but in *On the Laws*, where he imagines the laws of an ideal polis based on the early Roman Republic. As for Balbus, this polis is in some sense common to gods and men, who jointly possess the divine capacity for reason and its corollaries: right reason, law, justice. Since these qualities, in turn, define the *res publica*, Cicero argues that "we must now conceive of this whole universe as one commonwealth of which both gods and men are members" (iam universus hic mundus sit una civitas communis deorum atque hominum existimanda) (1.7.23). Following Balbus in stressing humans' capacity for reason rather than their frequent ignorance and vulgarity, he claims a concordance or continuity between gods and men that renders the process of divinization, if not routine, then at least plausible and natural. Human beings who pursue right reason, law, and justice make themselves godlike while, as we will see, those who actually achieve these qualities make themselves gods.

In *On the Laws*, the first order of business for Cicero's ideal government is to incorporate the gods into its cities, building temples in which they can dwell side by side with mortal citizens. These temples afford the gods a physical presence in the polis, rendering them perceptible as well as thinkable, "for it is believed that perception of the gods is possible to our eyes as well as to our minds" (est enim quaedam opinione species deorum in oculis, non solum in mentibus) (2.11.27). They also teach citizens to understand the gods as part of the body politic and as taking an especially active role in the administration of justice. As Cicero exclaims, "How sacred an association of citizens becomes when the immortal gods are made members of it, either as judges or as witnesses!" (Quamque sancta sit societas civium inter ipsos diis inmortalibus interpositis tum iudicibus, tum testibus!) (2.7.16). *On the Laws* thus draws up plans for a civic religion in multiple senses of the term. In its ideal polis, men are bound to the gods specifically as fellow citizens, thereby sacralizing the polis and politicizing the sacred. To perform one's civic duty is also to honor the gods, while to honor the gods is also to perform a civic duty. This virtuous cycle, in turn, strengthens precisely those qualities of right reason, law, and justice that men share with the gods and so has the effect of deifying them, either in whole or in part. Cicero goes so far as to argue that to become a civic hero is simply to become a god, for "while the souls of all men are immortal, those of good and brave men are divine" (omnium quidem animos inmortalis esse, sed fortium bonorumque divinos) (2.11.27–28). Not only are humanity and divinity continuous, but civic virtue—that is, virtue in the service of the ideal state, though not necessarily in accordance with its empirical manifestations—is the means of ascending from the first condition to the second.

This conception of divinity leads Cicero to call for an extensive program of deification. He prescribes the worship not only of *"those who have always been regarded as dwellers in heaven"* (*qui caelestes semper habiti*) but also *"of those of the human race who have been deified, such as Hercules and the rest"* (*ex hominum genere consecratos, sicut Herculem et ceteros*) (2.8.19, 2.11.27).[19] Rather than being limited to an established canon of heroes, this latter category remains open ended, so that any virtuous mortal whom the state consecrates can appropriately receive divine honors. The same logic leads to the worship of personified abstractions:

> It is a good thing also that *Intellect, Piety, Courage, and Faith should be deified by the hand of man* [*consecratur manu*] and in Rome temples have been dedicated by the State to all these qualities, the purpose being that those who possess them (and all good men do) should believe that the gods themselves are established within their own souls.

> For that was a bad thing which was done at Athens on the advice of Epimenides the Cretan, when, after the crime of Cylon had been expiated, they established a temple to Disgrace and Insolence, for it is proper to deify the virtues *but not the vices*. The ancient altar to Fever on the Palatine and the one to Bad Fortune on the Esquiline as well as all other abominations of that character must be done away with. But if we must invent names for gods [*quodsi nomina fingenda*], we ought rather to choose such titles as Vica Pota, derived from Victory and Power, and Stata, from the idea of standing firm, and such epithets as those of the Strengthener and the Invincible, which are given to Jupiter; also the names of things which we should desire, such as Safety, Honour, Wealth, and Victory. And since the mind is encouraged by the anticipation of good things, Calatinus was right in deifying Hope also.
>
> Bene vero, quod *Mens, Pietas, Virtus, Fides* consecratur manu; quarum omnium Romae dedicata publice templa sunt, ut, illa qui habeant (habent autem omnes boni), deos ipsos in animis suis conlocatos putent. nam illud vitiosum, Athenis quod Cylonio scelere expiato Epimenide Crete suadente fecerunt Contumeliae fanum et Impudentiae; virtutes enim, *non vitia* consecratur decet. araque vetusta in Palatio Febris et alter Esquiliis Malae Fortunae detestataque omnia eius modi repudianda sunt. quodsi fingenda nomina, Vicae Potae potius vicendi atque potiundi, Statae standi cognominaque Statoris et Invicti Iovis rerumque expetendarum nomina, Salutis, Honoris, Opis, Victoriae. quoniamque expectatione rerum bonarum erigitur animus, recte etiam Spes a Calatino consecrata est. (2.11.28; italics in original)

Where Cotta considers the category of the divine to be eternal and unchanging, so that any new god is by definition illegitimate, Cicero considers it self-evident that gods are human creations. Indeed, he emphasizes that the gods are deified artefactually rather than naturally—literally "consecrated by hand" (consecratur manu)—in order to establish guidelines for doing so appropriately.[20] Cicero likewise sees nothing wrong with fashioning names for gods. The verb *fingere* means to touch or handle, and more broadly to form or represent, either artistically or intellectually. Cicero thus suggests that lawmakers should craft names for the gods much as artists craft cult statues for their temples. Indeed, the past participle of Cicero's verb *fingere* is *fictum*, the root of the English word *fiction*. While Cicero uses *fingere* in its positive sense of forming or representing something, rather than in its negative sense of feigning or pretending, his choice of terms suggests an intense awareness that abstractions do not exist as gods until humans deify them through religious observance.

It follows that for Cicero deification is also contingent, as the Romans craft new gods to respond to new civic needs. We have seen that Cotta condemns deification as arbitrary, with humans deifying things, animals, and each other irrationally and seemingly at random. For Balbus, in contrast, humans rationally choose to deify those things that exert the greatest force on their lives—that is to say, those things that demonstrate divine power (*vis deorum*). Balbus accepts the worship of negative figures such as Fever and Bad Fortune because they are powerful as well as because they are venerated in the Rome of his own day. When Cicero writes in propria persona, he adopts an intermediate position, sanctioning only the deification of virtues. As the defining qualities of divinity, as well as the means by which humans become divine, the virtues have a claim to deification that other abstractions do not. While Cicero has a higher opinion of human rationality than Cotta does, he acknowledges that even the Romans can make mistakes, resulting in the veneration of "abominations" such as Fever. When Cicero rejects deification on the basis of power and popularity, however, he loses the ability to explain why some virtues are gods while other virtues, seemingly equally worthy, are not. Since all virtues are by definition virtuous, why are they not all divine? Cicero's answer seems to be that they all *could* be. That is to say, he permits mortals to "invent names for gods" as long as their choices are both rational and decorous, much as his ancestors invented names for Vica Pota, a victory goddess, and Stata Mater, a goddess of fire protection. The virtues not yet chosen for deification thus constitute something like a reserve army, standing ready to be called into action. Their mobilization implicitly depends on the challenges faced by Cicero's ideal polis, or indeed by the empirical Roman Republic. In recognizing the contingency of erecting a temple in honor of one facet or formulation of virtue rather than another, Cicero allows for the possibility of erecting new temples to new facets and formulations of virtue, either because the polis has begun to understand virtue somewhat differently or because new times demand new emphases. In deciding which virtues to deify, the Roman people, through their state representatives, exercise a degree of what we might call artistic control. While in Balbus's account worshippers simply ratify power, in Cicero's they choose to form or craft (*fingere*) one god rather than another.

In making this argument, Cicero goes out of his way to counter Cotta's contention—echoed by many modern critics—that deified abstractions are the products of elite manipulation on the one hand and popular credulity on the other. As his repeated use of the first-person plural indicates, Cicero emphatically includes himself among those who must cultivate the virtues through worship:

> The Greeks and Romans have done a better thing: for it has been our wish, to the end that we may promote piety toward the gods, that they should dwell in [*incolere*] our cities with us. For this idea encourages a religious attitude that is useful to communities [*civitatibus*], if there is truth in the saying of Pythagoras, a most learned man, that piety and religious feeling are most prominent in our minds while we are performing religious rites.
>
> Melius Graii atque nostri, qui ut augerent pietatem in deos, easdem illos urbis quas nos incolere voluerunt; adfert enim haec opinio religionem utilem civitatibus, siquidem et illud bene dictum est a Pythagora, doctissimo viro, tum maxume et pietatem et religionem versari in animis, cum rebus divinis operam daremus. (2.11.26)

Cicero's religious rites and the temples in which they occur function in much the same way as Gregory the Great's "machines of the mind," bringing their users into harmony with the divine. Where Gregory's machines lift their users toward a transcendent divinity, however, Cicero's act upon the users themselves, inculcating in them the virtues of *religio* and *pietas*. That is to say, they bring their users into harmony with an immanent divinity, to be found both within themselves and within the community or the state. Tellingly, Cicero defines *pietas* as justice with regard to the gods ("est enim pietas iustitia adversus deos") and *religio* as the cultivation of the gods ("cultu deorum") (*On the Nature of the Gods* 1.41.116, 117–18; 2.3.8). Both are reciprocal social virtues, involving what Emile Durkheim calls "an exchange of mutually invigorating good deeds between the divinity and his faithful."[21] Just as worshippers cultivate the gods through ongoing ritual practice, the gods in turn cultivate their worshippers—another sense of *incolere*—by making them more godlike. This same dynamic implicitly holds true for the divine abstractions around whom a significant proportion of Roman rites were organized. From Cicero's point of view, it is certainly good to know, in an abstract way, that faith, hope, honor, and so on are divine virtues. It is far superior, however, to grant them a material and bodily presence in moral and political life by "forming" them as deities, erecting temples and offering sacrifices in their honor as an almost mechanical way of keeping them in mind. Indeed, the veneration of such divinized Virtues renders the worshippers themselves more divinely virtuous—and thus true co-citizens with the gods in Cicero's ideal republic. In exchange for ritual observance, gods such as Faith and Mind help their worshippers to attain both conceptual purchase on and practical mastery of their respective virtues. Although Saint Paul dismisses such exchanges as "mere business transaction[s]," in contrast to the Christian God's unilateral grace, Cicero considers divinized abstractions to be simultaneously numinous and useful.[22]

Cicero, then, complicates, if he does not vitiate, Whitman's claim of a clear distinction between "giving an *actual* personality to an abstraction" and "giving a consciously *fictional* personality to an abstraction, 'impersonating' it." The divine abstractions in *On the Nature of the Gods* and *On the Laws* do not receive their personalities through an unconscious and implicitly primitive process but rather openly and deliberately, at the hands of highly educated, socially powerful men. Cicero's personifications are also "fictional" in the sense that the past participle of his *fingere* is *fictum*, the root of the English *fiction*. His gods are artfully formed, first as thoughts, then in speech, and finally by hand, through the crafting of statues and other cult objects. This process of deification is self-consciously contingent, as the Romans choose to deify some virtues but not others, prioritizing those who align with their evolving politico-religious values. As they cultivate and are in turn cultivated by these new gods, the citizens of Rome at least ideally become more godlike, developing precisely those qualities needed for individual and collective prosperity. Simultaneously realist and man-made, Cicero's gods help to create yet more gods in a virtuous cycle.

Both *On the Laws* and *On the Nature of the Gods* were read and copied during the Middle Ages, but neither circulated widely. *On the Nature of the Gods*, in particular, had an ambiguous reputation, with Cicero's general authority offset by Augustine's criticism of his depiction of the Skeptic Cotta.[23] Their formative model of personification was more frequently transmitted to the Middle Ages indirectly, through literary personifications and rhetorical manuals produced within the same discursive milieu. The first of these will be the subject of chapter 2, which examines Prudentius's efforts to adapt the classical tradition of formative personification to Christian ends. It is to the second that I now turn.

THE RELIGION OF RHETORICAL PERSONIFICATION

We have seen that critics generally understand religious personification as diametrically opposed to rhetorical personification. The first half of this chapter has argued that religious personification is in fact more rhetorical than usually imagined, treating deified abstractions such as Mind and Faith as self-conscious human creations. The second half will argue, conversely, that rhetorical personification is more religious than is usually imagined. Although the concept of rhetorical personification does not necessarily involve religion, the examples authors reach for often do. In the classical rhetorical tradition, the paradigmatic examples of personification, transmitted from one treatise to the next, are ancestor and country. These examples have frequently been discussed in terms of their difference: the former is animate and traditionally masculine, while the latter is inanimate and traditionally feminine. The latter also coincides more neatly with our modern understanding of prosopopoeia, insofar as we think of personification as inventing a body for an abstraction rather than imaginatively revivifying the dead. In Greek and Roman religion, however, both examples represent divine, semidivine, or potentially divine beings. That is to say, they represent beings who were understood as susceptible to religious veneration, even when we do not know whether a particular ancestor or locality was empirically venerated. When ancient and classical orators personify these powers, they invoke them as witnesses to, and potentially as guarantors of, the actions they urge and the agreements they record. As a rhetorical act, personification thus resembles a vow or an oath. It is carefully crafted but also speaks in the name of a higher power, claiming truth if not facticity. These examples dominate the influential discussion of prosopopoeia in Demetrius's *On Style* and are translated into Latin texts that circulated widely during the Middle Ages, including the pseudo-Ciceronian *Rhetorica ad Herennium* and Cicero's own oratory. Although Quintilian's *Institutes of Oratory* expands the range of personification to include orators' speeches on behalf of their clients, he continues to treat it as sacralized discourse, instructing his clients to dress in mourning clothes to mark the deadly seriousness, even otherworldliness, of the occasion. The orator can speak on behalf of the client because the client's clothes mark him as civically or politically dead, a figure akin to Agamben's *homo sacer*, both sacred and profane, subject to the law and somehow outside it. Like classical religious personification, classical rhetorical personification thus functions, at least ideally, not just as a tool for forming the orator and his audience to virtue but more specifically as a tool for conforming them to divinity. Both are what we might call civic performances, artful and highly self-conscious attempts to guide civic audiences, and ultimately the state as a whole, toward embodying divine virtue.

Given these commonalities, one might wonder whether it continues to make sense to distinguish between religious and rhetorical personification. I find the categories useful as heuristics, if not absolutes, because despite their shared goals, religious and rhetorical personification differ in the process, and ultimately the agency, by which they are produced. Where religious personification is authorized and institutionalized by the state, or at least is imagined as achieving such authorization in an ideal polis, rhetorical personification is largely *ex tempore*, produced within the give and take of civic life and adversarial judicial proceedings. Its truth claims are almost by definition more provisional, even when not subject to formal adjudication. Within the structure of a debate, accepting one orator's personifications as truthful generally means rejecting another orator's personifications as distortions or falsifications, or simply empty nothings. Perhaps for this reason, rhetorical personification tends to be more modest in the kinds of beings it represents. Ancestors and countries are overwhelmingly familial and local deities. They tend to dwell on earth or in the underworld rather than in the heavens, and, within a religious system that allows for multiple kinds and degrees of divinity, generally have a lower ontological status than the celestial gods. Ancestors and countries may be susceptible to rhetorical personification—that is, to impersonation by an orator who speaks on their behalf—because they are already closer to humans and human concerns. Religious and rhetorical personification are also worth distinguishing because, historically, they have been associated with different discourses. We have seen that twentieth-century medievalists treat religious and rhetorical personification as belonging to wholly different academic disciplines, the first pertaining to anthropology or the history of religion, the second to rhetoric or literary studies. Although I have argued that this distinction is overdrawn, it has roots in the medieval reception of classical texts, which privileged rhetorical handbooks over discussions of pagan theology. Classical rhetorical theory is thus worth examining in its own right for its influence on medieval personification, both directly through widely copied rhetorical treatises and indirectly through important works of personification allegory.

The Greek treatise *On Style*, attributed to an unidentified Demetrius and dated between the third and first centuries BCE, establishes the paradigm for classical rhetorical personification:[24]

> Another figure of thought which may be used to produce force is the figure called prosopopoeia, for example, "Imagine that your ancestors are rebuking you and speak such words, or imagine Greece, or

> your country in the form of a woman." This is what Plato uses in his Funeral Speech, "Children, that you are the sons of brave men. . . ." He does not speak in his own person but in that of their fathers. The personification makes the passage much more lively and forceful, or rather it really turns into a drama. (265–66)

In describing prosopopoeia as a figure of speech which "makes the passage much more lively" and "may be used to produce force," Demetrius anticipates Gregory the Great's characterization of the trope as a builder's tool that multiplies human effort in order to lift otherwise unmanageable loads. Indeed, Demetrius goes on to note that skillful orators achieve their best results by combining a number of figures of speech to produce a single, more powerful utterance, much as simple machines such as pulleys and levers can be combined to produce a builder's hoist. Demetrius's examples suggest that prosopopoeia achieves its multiplication of force in part by eliciting an emotional response from its audience. The funeral oration in Plato's *Menexenus*, from which Demetrius draws his second illustration, was recited yearly in Athens as the foremost instance of its genre, the "epitaphios par excellence."[25] Its use of personification is thus "lively" not only because it contributes to a larger pattern of rhetorical variation but also because it brings the dead to life in the highly charged context of a funeral oration. Prosopopoeia gives the orator access to the intimate relationship between father and son, allowing him to imagine the words that the fathers, recently fallen in Athens's wars, might have spoken to their sons from their deathbeds. At the same time, the speech's collective address, together with the fact that it personifies those who have died on the battlefield on behalf of the polis, treats the dead as civic heroes. According to the *Menexenus*, the purpose of an *epitaphios* is to yoke the city's ancestors, its recent war dead, and its living citizens into a single community—an enterprise that the dialogue's Socrates figure regards with skepticism, but which later Athenians seem to have treated as partially constitutive of their city-state.[26] As recited at each year's Epitaphia festival, Plato's invocation of Athens's heroic war dead serves as a model of civic performance, blurring the line between rhetorical ornament and religious ritual.

Instead of illustrating the trope's range, Demetrius's other examples deepen this connection between prosopopoeia and civic ritual. Demetrius's personifications of "your ancestors . . . rebuking you" and "your country in the form of a woman" are rhetorical ornaments, but they also invoke spirits understood as both invested in and having power over the orator's local audience.[27] An orator who misrepresents an ancestor implicitly invites his (or, in a substantial minority of attested cases, her) displeasure.[28] So, too, does a listener who disregards the orator's legitimate representation of the ancestor's will or interests. Presumably, both of these effects are magnified when the personified ancestor is not only deifiable but deified: the object of one of the many local hero and ancestor cults attested in Greece in this period. The same holds true for personified localities, whose cult statues have been found in temples alongside those of recognized gods. Even localities who were not worshipped are depicted on wedding vases and civic monuments at a scale intermediate between gods and humans, seemingly indicating a state of semidivinity or potential divinity.[29] In all of these contexts, prosopopoeia is a religiously heightened as well as a rhetorically heightened mode of address.[30]

Comparisons to civic monuments and wedding vases, however, can only take us so far. When a visual artist personifies a city or ancestor, he produces an image or an object, separate from himself, made of paint or stone or clay. When an orator personifies the same city or ancestor, he asks his audience to juxtapose the personification's imagined body and his own empirical one. Demetrius highlights this dynamic when he specifies that the trope "makes the passage much more lively and forceful, or rather it really turns into a drama." The *prosopon* at the root of prosopopoeia here becomes specifically the mask worn by an ancient Greek actor. Implicitly, the orator who speaks on behalf of a personification "speaks through" its represented body in the same way that an actor projects his voice through the mouth of a mask. Or does the personified divinity "speak through" the superimposed body of the orator, who in turn becomes the mask?[31] In each of these scenarios, personification is dynamic rather than static, the product of an ongoing, potentially highly charged relationship between the material body of the orator and the imagined body of the ancestor or abstraction in whose name he speaks. Already ambiguous insofar as it is unclear whether the personification serves the rhetorician or the rhetorician serves the personification, this relationship has the potential to become even more complex as the two bodies become more disparate. How does an orator, almost by definition a mature, city-dwelling male of elite social status, speak differently on behalf of a young woman? A child? A rustic? As we shall see, these questions proved controversial in Latin classical rhetorical treatises, as well as in literary works like the *Psychomachia*.

The earliest Latin account of personification occurs in the *Rhetorica ad Herennium* (90–80 BCE), attributed during the Middle Ages to either Cicero or Cornelius. Widely circulated, it survives in more than one hundred manuscript copies and a number of complete commentaries, as well as in thirteenth-century Italian and French translations. The *Rhetorica* translates Demetrius's *prosopopoeia* into Latin as *conformatio*, referring to the formation or fashioning of something to be congruent with something else, as when for instance the body is formed to be congruent with the soul. In doing so, it offers variations on Demetrius's paradigmatic examples:

> Personification consists in representing an absent person as present, or in making a mute thing or one lacking form articulate, and attributing to it a definite form and a language or a certain behaviour appropriate to its character, as follows: "But if this invincible city should now give utterance to her voice, would she not speak as follows? 'I, city of renown, who have been adorned with numerous trophies, enriched with unconditional triumphs, and made opulent by famous victories, am now vexed, O citizens, by your dissensions. Her whom Carthage with her wicked guile, Numantia with her tested strength, and Corinth with her polished culture, could not shake, do you now suffer to be trod upon and trampled underfoot by worthless weaklings?'" Again: "But if that great Lucius Brutus should now come to life again and appear here before you, would he not use this language? 'I banished kings; you bring in tyrants. I created liberty, which did not exist; what I created you do not wish to preserve. I, at peril of my life, freed the fatherland; you, even without peril, do not care to be free.'" Personification may be applied to a variety of things, mute and inanimate.

> Conformatio est cum aliqua quae non adest persona confingitur quasi adsit, aut cum res muta aut informis fit eloquens, et forma ei et oratio adtribuitur ad dignitatem adcommodata aut actio quaedam, hoc pacto: "Quodsi nunc haec urbs invictissima vocem mittat, non hoc pacto loquatur? 'Ego illa plurimis tropaeis ornata, triumphis ditata certissimis, clarissimis locupletata victoriis, nunc vestris seditionibus, o cives, vexor; quam dolis malitiosa Kartago, viribus probata Numantia, disciplinis erudita Corinthus labefactare non potuit, eam patimini nunc ab homunculis deterrimis proteri atque conculcari? Item: "Quodsi nunc Lucius ille Brutus revivescat et hic ante pedes vestros adsit, is non hac utatur oratione? Ego reges eieci; vos tyrranos introducitis. Ego libertatem, quae non erat, peperi; vos partam servare non vultis. Ego capitis mei periculo patriam liberavi; vos liberi sine periculo esse non cura-

> tis.'" Haec conformatio licet in plures res, in mutas atque inanimas transferatur. (4.53.66)

Where Demetrius instructs his readers to "imagine . . . your country in the form of a woman," the author of the *Rhetorica* actually does so, depicting a personified Rome who seeks to maintain her preeminent position within a group of rival city-states. Like Demetrius, the *Rhetorica* author represents Rome as not only distinct from but also in conflict with her citizens, whom she apostrophizes in strongly gendered terms. Rome claims that, instead of protecting her as they should, the Romans have exposed her to public dishonor, subjecting her to maltreatment and abuse by weaklings, literally "little men" (homunculis), who are unfit partners for her greatness. Indeed, the *Rhetorica* hints that Rome assumes a human body precisely because the citizens who should constitute a unified body politic have given themselves over to civil discord. Someone must speak for, and in the interests of, the collectivity that is Rome, and since the men who should do so have failed in their office, the task is left to a feminine personification of the city. The fact that Rome speaks at all accordingly testifies to a breakdown in civic order, while the language she uses suggests that she speaks simultaneously as a place and a woman, with the verbs *proteri* and *conculcari* signifying both to tread underfoot and, in an extended sense more appropriate to persons, to abuse or treat with contempt. In personifying Rome, the *Rhetorica* author tries to rouse his audience by making the political personal, treating a geopolitical setback as a gender-inflected crime.

Like Demetrius, the *Rhetorica* author offers his readers what amounts to a choice between masculine and feminine personifications of the same body politic. Immediately after Rome offers the lament of a wronged woman, the personified founder of the Roman Republic, Lucius Junius Brutus, offers a parallel, if more masculine, rebuke. Where Rome speaks for the city as a place, Brutus speaks on behalf of its ongoing history as a republic, which he cautions has now come under threat. As befits his role as a heroic ancestor, Brutus warns of the imminent collapse of patriarchal and governmental continuity, with Rome's current citizens not only failing to live up to the example of their illustrious predecessor but also dishonoring his memory by making no effort to do so. In parallel to his feminine counterpart, Brutus apostrophizes the Roman *cives*, juxtaposing his past deeds with their present-day inertia, which threatens to reverse his accomplishments. Despite their gender and category differences, both personifications are thus brought to life, or at least given voice, by outraged dignity. They represent themselves not as initiating an exchange with the Roman *cives* but instead as responding to a provocation, even though in both cases this provocation ultimately reveals itself to be one of omission, a failure of the *cives* to act as they should. Both personifications, moreover, gain the attributes of personhood at the same time as, and in proportion to, the personhood of the *cives* is reduced through inaction, becoming so diminished that even *homunculi* can defeat them. Both of the *Rhetorica*'s exemplary personifications accordingly gain strength from, or in response to, the citizens' weakness. They speak the words the *cives* themselves should have spoken in order to redress an imbalance of power, lending their voices to what the *Rhetorica* author considers to be a just but unpopular cause.

The *Rhetorica*, then, teaches orators to use the rhetorical "force" of prosopopoeia to persuade listeners to do the right thing. But do its personifications also exert force in a religious sense, threatening those who fail to offer them due honor? In the case of Brutus, this seems a distinct possibility. In Roman religion, the dead were deified as *manes* or *di manes* (divine *manes*) and worshipped publicly in festivals such as the *Parentalia* and *Lemuria* as well as privately in domestic shrines.[32] Inhabiting the human world either instead of or in addition to the underworld realms of Elysium and Tartarus, the deified dead held direct power over the living. While some *manes*, mainly the spirits of wicked men, were warded off as malevolent, most were considered helpful to humans as long as they were offered proper honor. Cicero's *On the Laws* thus offers a set of rules governing the cult of *manes*, connecting the obligation of worship to financial inheritance (2.18.45–2.27.68). Other authors describe worship as continuing a reciprocal relationship begun while the person was still alive. As such it could extend a family tie, friendship, or political alliance into the afterlife, blending into the larger virtue of *pietas*.[33] Since *manes* had the power both to shorten and to extend lives, prayers to them typically asked for either the gift of years or the death of enemies. When a soldier, swearing that he had fought courageously, invoked as witnesses the *manes* of his dead comrades, he invited them to end his life if he was not telling the truth. In this context, the Brutus of the *Rhetorica* arguably speaks as one of the *manes*, especially entitled to widespread honor as the founder of the Roman Republic. Indeed, in a religious system that admitted many degrees of divinity, Brutus may have belonged to the class of civic heroes whose *manes* Cicero considered to be worthy of individual public worship.

In personifying Brutus, the *Rhetorica* author speaks through a rhetorical *prosopon* that evokes the ancestral funerary masks worn by mourners in funeral processions and during the public elegies of prominent men. Displayed prominently in the home when not in use, these masks represent the presence of the *manes* in the world of the living in a manner similar to the orator's act of *conformatio*. While *conformatio* remains a rhetorical trope, in the sense of attributing a fictional rather than an actual speech to Brutus, it gives voice to a divinity understood as capable of exerting force in the world of the living.

The status of the *Rhetorica*'s personification of Rome is less clear. In Roman religion, every locality was governed by a *genius loci* (spirit of the place), but it is not obvious that this spirit corresponds to the text's feminine personification. Later records characterize the *genius* of the city of Rome (Genius Urbis Romae) as of unknown or ambiguous gender ("sive mas sive femina").[34] There was also a full-fledged *dea* Roma, a goddess venerated in the Greek-speaking east as part of a larger practice of city worship, but there was no temple in her honor within Rome itself until the reign of Hadrian. The classicist Ronald Mellor traces the earliest images of a divinized Roma to Augustus's return from the battle of Actium, noting that while Augustan poetry regularly plays on the triple status of Roma as goddess, city, and representation of the Roman people, in earlier writings the term refers either to the city alone or to a personification of the *patria* or the state.[35] Numismatists, in contrast, generally identify the female figure depicted on Republican coins from the third century BCE as a divinized Roma, comparing her to the protective goddesses depicted on the coins of rival Mediterranean city-states.[36] If they are correct, it is tempting to see the *Rhetorica*'s personification of Rome—who compares herself to Carthage, Numantia, and Corinth—in relation to this iconography. In any case, these traditions cumulatively suggest that the contemporary audience of the *Rhetorica* was unlikely to have understood its feminine personification of Rome as a mere fiction. If not yet a full-fledged *dea*, she still would have represented the spirit of the place, capable of protecting or withholding protection from its inhabitants. In personifying Rome in conjunction with Brutus, the *Rhetorica* author implicitly pays homage to the masculine and feminine spiritual forces protecting the city in a manner evocative of the ritual formula *sive mas, sive femina*.[37] As one would expect in a context in which both oratory and religious observance are fundamentally civic practices, they are closely intertwined with one another. The orator persuades his audience, in part, by invoking divinities who by their nature are intimately concerned with the matter at hand, having both the power to reward just responses and punish unjust ones and the force to move the orator's audience.

The accounts of personification in *On Style* and the *Rhetorica* define personification in terms at once broader and narrower than those we use today. On the one hand, as already mentioned, both Demetrius's prosopopoeia and the *Rhetorica* author's *conformatio* join "representing an absent person as present" to the modern understanding of personification as "making a mute thing or one lacking form articulate." On the other hand, the entities they represent occupy a relatively narrow range. In both works, personification is closely associated with the "lower" gods, dwelling on earth or in the underworld, rather than with either mortal beings or heavenly divinities. Cicero does not hesitate to apostrophize the heavenly gods during legal proceedings or to introduce their testimony through various types of signs, auguries, and oracles, but he always makes it clear that they participate in absentia: "Ye immortal gods! how could ye speak with us more clearly, if ye were with us and moving in our midst?" (Pro di immortales! qui magis nobiscum loqui possetis, si essetis versareminique nobiscum?)[38] These examples highlight the intimate relationships among apostrophe, religious invocation, and personification, as theorized by Paul de Man and J. Hillis Miller. Indeed, we can think of apostrophe as personification in absentia, since "the linguistic structure of the apostrophic utterance presumes or predicates a responsive human consciousness in inanimate objects."[39] At the same time, these examples treat personification as a more extreme version of apostrophe or invocation, one that can take the process of person making a bit too far. It seems to have been indecorous, if not irreligious, for an orator to speak on behalf of the heavenly gods via personification rather than apostrophe. Ancestors and cities, in contrast, were available for personification because they were already intermediate figures, powerful enough to be authoritative but still dwelling on earth, and so more accessible and closely connected to the daily rhythms of human affairs.

Subsequent generations of orators repeat Demetrius's paradigmatic examples while pushing the "force" of personification to its limits. Where Demetrius asks his readers to imagine themselves rebuked by "Greece, or your country in the form of a woman," Cicero represents himself as called to account by Italy, his fatherland, and the Republic. Toward the end of his first oration against Cataline, he asks, "What if my fatherland . . . if the whole of Italy, if all the Republic were to speak thus to me: 'Marcus Tullius, what are you doing?'" (Etenim si mecum patria . . . si cuncta Italia, si omnis res publica sic loquatur: "M. Tulli, quid agis?") (27). In this politico-religious speech, delivered to the Senate in the temple of Jupiter Stator (Jupiter the Stayer), Cicero plays on his audience's sensibilities with the skill of a seasoned lawyer. But his rhetoric works, in part, because in giving voice to the "most sacred utterances of the Republic" (sanctissimis rei publicae vocibus) he sacralizes his own discourse (29). If Cicero misrepresents the Republic or fails to carry out his promises to her, he invites her retribution as well as that of Jupiter Stator. Cicero likewise imagines the personified patria speaking to Cataline, but in much harsher terms:

> Now your fatherland [*patria*], the common parent of us all, hates and fears you, and for a long time now judges you to think of nothing but her destruction [*parricidio*]. Will you not revere her authority, nor follow her judgment, nor fear her power? She addresses you, Cataline, and speaks in a certain silent fashion: "For some years now, no crime has occurred but through you."

> Nunc te patria, quae communis est parens omnium nostrum, odit ac metuit et iam diu nihil te iudicat nisi de parricidio suo cogitare: huius tu neque auctoritatem verebere nec iudicium sequere nec vim pertimesces? Quae tecum, Catalina, sic agit et quodam modo tacita loquitur: "Nullum iam aliquot annis facinus exstitit nisi per te." (17–18)

Cicero suggests that he does not compose the fatherland's words as much as amplify them, allowing her to speak through him to repeat, in a public forum, what she has been telling Cataline privately and silently for years. Although the fatherland speaks with Cicero's voice, the authority, judgment, and power to which she alludes are her own—and specifically the qualities of a goddess. Indeed, as represented by Cicero she is simultaneously goddess and personification, country and ancestor, even feminine and masculine. A feminine embodiment of a masculine concept—and thus, perhaps, another instantiation of the formula *sive mas, sive femina*—she accuses Cataline of contemplating not insurrection but parricide, the killing of a parent. Cicero calls upon his fellow senators, as the fatherland's other sons, to forestall this unnatural crime.

Later rhetorical treatises continue to understand personification in similar terms but begin to express ambivalence about the degree to which prosopopoeia renders speech "much more lively and forceful, or rather it really turns into a drama." Cicero's *Orator*—written three years before the author's death and not to be confused with his earlier *On the Orator*

(*De Oratore*)—repeats Demetrius's paradigmatic examples but treats them with suspicion, promising that its ideal orator

> will not represent the state as speaking or call the dead from the lower world, nor will he crowd a long series of iterations into a single period. This requires stronger lungs, and is not to be expected of him whom we are describing or demanded from him. For he will be rather subdued in voice as well as in style.

> non faciet rem publicam loquentem nec ab inferis mortuos excitabit nec acervatim multa frequentans una complexione devinciet. Valentiorum haec laterum sunt nec ab hoc quem informamus aut exspectanda aut postulanda; erit enim ut voce sit etiam oratione suppressior. (25.85–86)

In contrasting the "stronger lungs" required by personification with the "subdued" voice of the ideal orator, Cicero suggests that Roman orators spoke the words attributed to personifications in a distinctive tone of voice, louder and implicitly more dramatic than their usual one—perhaps, as Hamlet says, "tear[ing] a passion to tatters" (3.2.8–9).[40] Personification, then, may have begun to feel unseemly in part because orators imitated the voices of the deified dead and local divinities, speaking for them in a more literal sense than we usually imagine. Although Quintilian allows personification somewhat more latitude in his *Institutes of Oratory*, he too is defensive: "In this form of speech we are even allowed to lead forth the gods or raise the dead; cities and nations even acquire a voice" (Quin deducere deos in hoc genere dicendi et inferos excitare concessum est. Urbes etiam populique vocem accipiunt) (9.2.31–32). He also expands personification's range by linking it explicitly to stage performance, cautioning, "Nor do I think that prosopopoeiae, as some advise, should be pronounced in the manner of the comic stage, though there should be some inflection of the voice to distinguish them from passages in which the poet speaks in his own person" (Nec prosopopoeias, ut quibusdam placet, ad comicum morem pronuntiari velim, esse tamen flexum quendam quo distinguantur ab iis in quibus poeta persona sua utetur) (1.8.3). Like comic actors, whose masks (in Latin, *personae*) designated a series of stock characters such as the miserly *senex*, the amatory *adulescens*, and the venal procurer, orators must play a wide range of roles (3.8.50–52). At the same time, they must modulate their voices as befits the greater dignity of their office.[41] Prosopopoeia involves performance, but it should never be treated as *mere* performance.

In the *Institutes of Oratory*, the most important site of personification is arguably the court of law, where Quintilian emphasizes that—again like one of Gregory the Great's machines of the mind—it moves its hearers more effectively than the facts alone:

> It is in these places particularly that good service is done by prosopopoeiae, that is to say fictitious speeches of other persons. When an advocate speaks for a client, the bare facts move [*movent*] the hearer; but when we pretend that the victims themselves are speaking, the emotional effect is drawn also from the persons. The judge no longer thinks that he is listening to a lament for somebody else's troubles, but that his ears seem to receive the feelings and voice of the afflicted, whose silent appearance [*mutus aspectus*] alone moves [*movet*] him to tears; and, as their pleas would be more pitiful if only they could make them themselves, so to a certain extent the pleas become more effective by being as it were put into their mouths, just as the same voice and delivery of the stage actor produces a greater emotional impact [*ad movendos adfectus*] because he speaks behind a mask [*sub persona*].

> His praecipue locis utiles sunt prosopopoeiae, id est fictae alienarum personarum orationes. Quando enim pro litigatore dicit patronus, nudae tantum res movent: at cum ipsos loqui fingimus, ex personis quoque trahitur adfectus. Non enim audire iudex videtur aliena mala deflentis, sed sensum ac vocem auribus accipere miserorum, quorum etiam mutus aspectus lacrimas movet: quantoque essent miserabiliora si ea dicerent ipsi, tanto sunt quadam portione ad adficiendum potentiora cum velut ipsorum ore dicuntur, ut scaenicis actoribus eadem vox eadem pronuntiatio plus ad movendos adfectus sub persona valet. (6.1.25–27)

Quintilian concentrates on the auditory experience of prosopopoeia, as the judge's "ears seem to receive the feelings and voice of the afflicted" transmitted through the mouth of the orator. But the judge's eyes also perceive—and respond tearfully to—the victims' "silent appearance" as they stand beside the advocate who speaks on their behalf. This spectacle was moving in part because during Roman trials the accused and his or her close supporters generally dressed in *sordes*, clothes that were either purposely dirtied or allowed to become dirty, while allowing themselves to become *squalidus* by neglecting personal hygiene. Associated with mourning, *sordes* by the late Republic had become a visual form of protest against injustice, intended to call attention to a sufferer's plight while inciting indignation against his or her oppressor.[42] In counseling his clients to attend court with "mourning clothes, and unkempt appearance, and relatives similarly attired" (sordes et squalorem et propinquorum quoque similem habitum), Quintilian expects their bodies to send a powerful, if silent, message, to constitute a silent chorus (6.1.33). Here again, Quintilian compares the orator's act of "speaking through" his client's silent body to an actor speaking through a mask. Implicitly, the defendant's theatrically costumed body is superimposed on the orator's conventionally dressed one to such an extent that the orator's voice becomes the client's voice, at least in the heat of the moment.

The defendant's *sordes* are not merely a costume, however. Quintilian describes those dressed in *sordes* as "dirty and deformed" (squalidos atque deformes), assimilating them to the "res . . . informis" personified in the *Rhetorica* (6.1.30). Given the association between *sordes* and mourning, a person wearing *sordes* also occupied a liminal space between the living and the dead. Roman funeral customs dictated a nine-day period of full mourning, during which men did not wash, wore dark or dirty clothing, allowed their hair, beards, and nails to grow, and refrained from engaging in public life.[43] Until they bathed at the end of this period, washing off the pollution of death, they did not fully belong to the polis, or indeed to the world of the living. Instead, their primary connection was to the person who had just died. This abnegation of political personhood is underscored by cases in which senators and *equites* discarded their signs of rank when they put on *sordes*, as well as by the more general way in which *sordes* mimic the squalor of the disenfranchised. In the courtroom, the political mourning undertaken by defendants dressed in *sordes* placed them in a similarly suspended state, as exiles from the world of the living.[44] In contrast to the nine-day period of purification after a death, however, legal defendants and their supporters continued to wear *sordes* throughout the trial, leading some accusers to prolong cases in order to force their opponents "into mourning attire (and increased humiliation) for an extended period of time."[45] In these conditions, the accused and their supporters become a kind of living dead, as close to outraged *manes* as it is possible for living human beings to be. By putting on *sordes*, they render themselves at once politically powerless and spiritually powerful, at once voiceless and eloquent. Quintilian's orator thus speaks on behalf of a client dressed in *sordes* in much the same way that the *Rhetorica* author speaks on behalf of the *manes* of Brutus. All of these classical examples of personification differ in kind from those commonly cited in twenty-first-century definitions of literary terms, such as the sun, the wind, a bridge, a car, the smell of baking muffins.[46] They characterize personification as a graver, more consequential endeavor. Although a rebuke from one's country, or from a man on trial for his life, is undeniably rhetorical, it cannot easily be dismissed as mere rhetoric.

CONCLUSION

In these circumstances it seems clear that, at least in the classical tradition, religious and rhetorical personification are overlapping rather than opposed categories. They have much in common, beginning with a shared moral seriousness and a central concern with the well-being of the public sphere. Like religious personification, rhetorical personification seeks to mediate between the human world and a transcendent or at least otherworldly one, conveying truths that in Quintilian's terms "surpass the facts" (supra vera sunt) (9.2.33). Because both kinds of personifications are products of self-conscious human craftsmanship, they are also capable of going wrong, resulting in "abominations" on the one hand and what Quintilian calls "empty nothings" (vanis) on the other (9.2.33). Their power means that they must be handled not only with great skill but also with great discretion, since an abstraction wrongly deified or person wrongly personified can lead an entire people toward vice. Religious and rhetorical personification also share an overlapping cast of characters, traditionally the deified dead and local *genii*. Although Quintilian pushes these boundaries by defining orators who speak on behalf of clients as practicing prosopopoeia, he expects these and other victims of injustice to dress in *sordes* and so represent themselves as having experienced a social and political death, indeed as living dead. While religious personification remains "higher" than rhetorical personification according to most measures—including in its representation of heavenly rather than chthonic deities—the continuities between them are as important as the differences.

In fact, the most salient difference between religious and rhetorical personification may be quantitative rather than qualitative. For Cicero, the institutions of Roman religion do a reasonably good job of regulating the process of deification, so that it is neither overly restrictive nor overly permissive. His greatest concern is with illicit acts of deification within the private sphere, the *res privata*, which are not subject to the same kind of public and collective deliberation (*On the Laws* 2.8.19). In contrast to these unlicensed deifications, rhetorical personification takes place in public, usually in a political speech or as part of a legal proceeding. It resembles private deification, however, in being the act of an individual orator rather than a civic institution, and so entirely dependent on his moral judgment and rhetorical skill. Even Quintilian acknowledges that not every orator possesses "all the virtues of character" (omnis animi virtutes) required for personification, leaving them open to the charge of using their rhetorical skill for private gain rather than the public good (1.Pro.9). At best, legal prosopopoeia allows orators to speak for individual and collective victims of injustice who cannot speak effectively on their own behalves. At worst, it suffers from the vices we still associate with the legal profession, including insincerity and venality. As Paxson points out, the modern slang terms "mouthpiece" and "mask" connect present-day lawyers to personification via the sense of *persona* (and, earlier, *prosopon*) as a theatrical mask.[47] These two sides of rhetorical personification necessarily coexist. In an adversarial legal system, when one advocate's *ex tempore* acts of personification "surpass the facts," the other's are almost inevitably dismissed as "empty nothings." It falls to the orator's audience to decide which is which, and it may well be this hermeneutic of suspicion, rather than any ontological difference, that most strongly distinguishes rhetorical from religious personification. Although in their ideal state religious and rhetorical personification have much in common, rhetorical personification attains this ideal state more rarely.

While religious and rhetorical personification remain distinct phenomena, then, they are much more consonant with each other than is generally recognized. Together, they define my category of formative personification allegory, which treats personification as simultaneously numinous and the product of self-conscious human craftsmanship. Both religious and rhetorical personifiers take care to form or shape their personifications, often using the same verb—*fingere*—to describe their work.[48] And they, in turn, are shaped by the entities they have brought into being, in a virtuous cycle of mutual formation. For Cicero in *On the Nature of the Gods* and *On the Laws*, this reciprocity is the central mechanism of Roman religion, the means by which individuals and communities become more virtuous, and thus more godlike. In the classical rhetorical tradition, orators "speak through" a personified place or ancestor—or even a client dressed in *sordes*—in order to score a political or legal point. But they also lend their voices to these localized divinities and, at least in theory, become more like them, speaking on behalf of the public good rather than private interests. Both kinds of formation occur through repeated practice, through repeated engagement with the personification as *machina*. Quintilian captures this dynamic when he declares that "for posterity Cicero has become the name not of a man, but of Eloquence itself" (apud posteros vero id consecutus ut Cicero iam non hominis nomen sed eloquentiae habeatur) (10.1.112). As an ancestor, Cicero has become one of the *manes*, with special jurisdiction over those who follow him within the discipline of rhetoric. But he has also served the virtue of eloquence so assiduously, and for such a long time that, at least in Quintilian's estimation, he has become a personified abstraction. Quintilian thus "deifies" Cicero by acknowledging the magnitude of his contribution to rhetoric and its central value to the Roman state, much as that state had earlier deified Asclepius in recognition of his pioneering role in the discipline of medicine. At the same time, in recognizing Cicero as Eloquence, and paying tribute to him in his own work, Quintilian seeks to become more like him, and perhaps to someday attain the same divine status. This act of rhetorical deification not only blurs the distinction between religion and rhetoric but also emphasizes their joint role in forming persons and personifications.

Looking beyond the ancient world, the category of formative or Prudentian personification enables a revised understanding of certain medieval allegorical figures. Prudentius's adaptation of classical personification for a Christian milieu inaugurates a tradition of understanding the Virtues and Vices as formative personifications. As discussed in chapter 2, his personifications are not simply mnemonic or schematic but instead function as machines of the mind, fostering readers' own work of moral reformation. Readers reform or re-create the poem's personification as they read, and are in turn reformed by them, remade first as virtuous readers and ultimately as personifications of virtue. This dynamic extends to medieval allegories such as *Piers Plowman* where—as explored in chapter 7—those who "putten hem to þe plouȝ" and "putten hem to pride" are transformed, respectively, into plowmen and pride-men. The pride-men and their fellows not only bring the personified sins into being but also become the Vices they serve in much the same way that Cicero, for Quintilian, becomes the virtue of Eloquence. Elsewhere, ancestral spirits encourage or chastise their descendants as a means of forming them to virtue. In *Piers*, ancestors such as Cato and Trajan rub shoulders, seemingly as ontological equals, with abstractions such as Reason and Recklessness. When Trajan bursts out of hell to rebuke the dreamer, he does so as the personification of an ethical or political imperative. In this he resembles not only the *Rhetorica ad Herennium*'s Brutus but also the Nine Worthies who, beginning in the fourteenth century, embody the virtues of chivalry in miniatures, paintings, tapestries, and sculpture, as well as in texts such as the *Parliament of the Three Ages*.[49] Formative personification also intersects productively with the trope Fiona Somerset identifies as "speaking in person." Just as, for Quintilian, prosopopoeia involves speaking not only on behalf of but also in the voice of another person, so "speaking in person" involves a speaker implicitly or explicitly speaking as someone else in an act of identification or disidentification. The lollard who responds to the authorities in the voice of a saint or prophet has obvious resonances with the orator who castigates the *cives* as Brutus. But the trope also encompasses the psalmist momentarily speaking as a wicked man, producing himself in part through contrast.[50] In all of these cases, persons form personifications who in turn form persons, generating either a virtuous or a vicious cycle.

CHAPTER TWO

How to Fight like a Girl: Christianizing Personification in the *Psychomachia*

For better and for worse, Prudentius's *Psychomachia* has long served as "a paradigm of the allegorical poem."[1] Written at the turn of the fifth century, it is generally considered the first work of full-fledged personification allegory, expanding the rhetorical trope of prosopopoeia into a literary genre in which personifications are the primary agents.[2] Eulogized by Theodulf of Orléans as "a most eloquent and Christian poet" (disertissimus atque Christianissimus poeta), Prudentius was admitted to the Christian literary canon soon after his death, with his poems surviving in over three hundred manuscripts and a plethora of early printed editions.[3] Beginning in the eighth century, the *Psychomachia* was increasingly singled out from the rest of Prudentius's works, appearing alone or with non-Prudentian texts in sixty manuscripts as well as curricula, reading lists, and inventories.[4] Programs of annotation and illustration indicate that the poem was read intensively as well as extensively, with twenty surviving manuscripts containing between two and ninety illustrations each.[5] These illustrations are associated with a broader iconographic tradition that depicts the *Psychomachia*'s battles between personified Virtues and Vices in paintings and sculpture.[6] Beyond its historical status as the first extended personification allegory, then, the *Psychomachia* would have been among the first allegorical works read by generations of medieval schoolboys, while a broader public would have encountered Prudentius's personifications in church wall paintings and archivolt sculptural decorations, carved capitals, and baptismal fonts.

For modern critics, the *Psychomachia*'s pathbreaking status and early success serve, paradoxically, as evidence for its aesthetic failure. For C. S. Lewis, the *Psychomachia* was "the crudest allegory," a form of automatic writing produced by the zeitgeist with scarcely any human intervention. More recently, Carolynn Van Dyke has described it as "the earliest and simplest allegory," while Mary Carruthers finds it to be suited only to "novice, schoolboy minds."[7] For many, the most telling mark of primitivism is the brutality with which Prudentius's personified Virtues annihilate his personified Vices. For Lewis, this violence renders the poem a remnant of the pagan past despite its overtly Christian content: "How is Patience to rage in battle? How is Mercy to strike down her foes, or Humility to triumph over them when fallen?"[8] Others admit that their "aesthetic embarrassment" is derived from the Virtues' transgression of gender norms, with A. D. Nuttall recording the "shock" of finding the "sweetly modest *virgo Pudicitia*" running through her opponent with a sword.[9] Maurice Lavarenne bemoans the Virtues' unladylike conduct at length:

> It is not without a certain scandalized astonishment that we read of the Christian Virtues, who ought, in our eyes, to be pure and modest virgins, perpetrating more or less savage murders and greatly intensifying them by exclamatory tirades. We expect mildness in their actions, modesty in their words, and behold they present themselves as amazons, destitute of all timidity, who strangle their opponents at will, who slit their throats, who tear them to pieces, who pierce them all the way through, who ferociously insult their enemies once they have fallen, who reveal themselves to be devoid of mercy, that most human of sentiments. . . . Is it really necessary that these daughters of the God of love and humility attack with such ardor, kill with such joy, insult with such sarcasm, and speechify with such pretension?[10]

For these critics, such unnatural behavior can only arise from authorial weakness, whether an excessively literal interpretation of internal psychological struggle or more simply a "terrible lack of taste."[11] If Prudentius had just been a better poet, he would have written something closer to Boethius's *Consolation of Philosophy* or Bernardus Silvestris's *Cosmographia*.

A problem with this line of argumentation is that Prudentius is perfectly capable of producing refined, ladylike personifications when he so chooses. The *Psychomachia*'s culminating personification neither insults her enemies nor slits their throats but rules, majestic and serene, from within a jeweled temple whose textual details are borrowed from the book of Revelation:

> Here mighty Wisdom sits enthroned and from her high court sets in order all the government of her realm, meditating in her heart laws to safeguard mankind. In the sovereign's hand is a scepter, not finished with craftsman's skill but a living rod of green wood; severed from its stock, it draws no nurture from moist earthly soil, yet puts forth perfect foliage and with blooms of blood-red roses intermingles white lilies that never droop on withering stem.

> Hoc residet solio pollens Sapientia et omne
> consilium regni celsa disponit ab aula,
> tutandique hominis leges sub corde retractat.
> in manibus dominae sceptrum non arte politum
> sed ligno vivum viridi est, quod stirpe recisum,
> quamvis nullus alat terreni caespitis umor,
> fronde tamen viret incolumi, tum sanguine tinctis
> intertexta rosis candentia lilia miscet
> nescia marcenti florem submittere collo. (875–83)

Thus described, Wisdom serves as a textbook example of Neoplatonic allegory, satisfying nearly all of Barbara Newman's "key guidelines for detecting a Platonic personification": she is serious rather than satiric; she is rendered numinous through scriptural quotation; she elicits awe and reverence; and her femininity affords her an intimate, yet subordinate, relationship with God.[12] Indeed, given the early date of the *Psychomachia*, Wisdom not only conforms to Newman's paradigm but also helps to create it. Building on the biblical representations of a personified Wisdom in Proverbs and Ecclesiasticus, Prudentius helps to define Wisdom both as an extrabiblical literary character and as a model for Neoplatonic personification more generally. In specifying that Wisdom's blooming scepter "draws no nurture from moist earthly soil," however, Prudentius carefully separates her from the material world and the more mundane personified Virtues who inhabit it. Although the *Psychomachia*'s other Virtues make Wisdom's reign possible by defeating her enemies and building her temple, they conspicuously do not set foot in it. Wisdom occupies a distinctly "higher" domain, one more scriptural, more numinous, and more timeless—indeed, as the association with the book of Revelation suggests, one located outside of time altogether.

In these circumstances, it does not seem fair to blame the other personifications' lack of refinement on authorial incompetence. Instead, it seems clear that, for Prudentius at least, they represent a different kind of personification, one that has been consistently misrecognized. In most histories of the *longue durée* of personification allegory, transcendent personifications gradually give way to more worldly ones marked by an abundance of verisimilar detail. This narrative depends, however, on understanding the personifications in the main body of the *Psychomachia* as exceptional or even aberrant. I argue, on the contrary, that the one-on-one battles between the Virtues and Vices inaugurate a tradition of Prudentian personification that remains distinguishable, if not always empirically distinct, from the Neoplatonic and Aristotelian traditions. These personifications borrow their basic operating mechanism from the classical world. Like the religious and rhetorical personifications discussed in chapter 1, they are simultaneously supernatural powers and the products of self-conscious human craftsmanship. Formed by their creators, they also form their creators in an ongoing, reciprocal relationship.

In drawing on the classical tradition of personification, Prudentius adapts it for his own Christian milieu. His first step, repeated again and again over the course of the poem, is to do away with the negative aspects of the classical tradition, represented by the personified Vices. We will see that, although Prudentius compares his Vices to the "spirits of wickedness" of Saint Paul's letter to the Ephesians, they also bear a striking resemblance to the negative abstractions whose deification Cicero condemns in *On the Laws*. Where Cicero treats these wrongly deified abstractions as aberrations, however, Prudentius treats them as part of the larger blindness of paganism. He includes within their number not only personifications universally understood to be negative—such as Wrath (Ira) and Discord (Discordia)—but also personifications that, in his judgment, the Romans mistakenly understood to be positive. Prudentius's most interesting Vices, in other words, believe themselves to be Virtues. When these self-deluded Vices fight Prudentius's actual Virtues, they fight over what we might call the content of virtue, over the traits to which humans should aspire. But they also fight over the form virtue takes, contesting what it means to be a virtuous personification.

While the conflicts over the content of virtue are generally resolved within the poem's individual battles between Virtue and Vice, the conflict over the personified form of virtue extends through the poem as a whole. Indeed, it determines the *Psychomachia*'s overall structure, as successive aspects of formative Christian personification come into view in the poem's successive battle scenes. Prudentius begins to define this new form of personification in his prologue, where he associates the personified Virtues with the Christian tradition of allegorical exegesis and specifically with Abraham as a site of allegorical self-formation. This genealogy authorizes him first to rewrite the traditional type of faithfulness as the feminine personification Faith, then to invite his normatively masculine readers to imagine themselves as Faith, divesting themselves of their gender in the process.[13] Prudentius's next step is to define this virtuous personification specifically as a Marian performance. Departing from the classical tradition's flexible approach to the gender of personifications, he characterizes his Virtues as inherently feminine and virginal so that they can conceive the Word. For the poem's male readers, virtue becomes a specifically transgender act of self-allegoresis—one in which, as we will see, the Virtues revert to their natural male bodies as soon as they slacken in their fight against Vice. Finally, Prudentius emphasizes that personification must be understood as a formal practice rather than a stable identity or collection of attributes. Since his Christian personifications are defined by what they do rather than by what they are, they do not invite worship in the manner of pagan idols. Instead, they inculcate in readers a *habitus* of virtue, understood as an ethical disposition, a monastic habit, and perhaps even "an acquired perfect state or condition."[14] Collectively, Prudentius's Virtues resemble their classical predecessors as divine forces and carefully constructed machines for self-reformation but differ from them in their gender dynamics as well as in being sites for performance rather than objects of worship.

DOING AWAY WITH ABOMINATIONS

Critics have long located the starting point for the *Psychomachia* as a whole—what Mary Carruthers calls "the preamble to the preamble"—in Saint Paul's epistle to the Ephesians.[15] The passage was popular in the late-classical period, often cited in support of the influential tradition of the Christian as a *miles Christi*. Prudentius aligns himself with that tradition while drawing on Paul's allegorical language to authorize his own development of Christian personification allegory:

> Put you on the armour of God, that you may be able to stand against the deceits of the devil, for our wrestling is not against flesh and blood; but against principalities and powers, against the rulers of the world of this darkness, against spirits of wickedness in the high places. Therefore take unto you the armour of God, that you may be able to resist in the evil day, and to stand in all things perfect. Stand therefore, hav-

ing your loins girt about with truth, and having on the breastplate of justice. And your feet shod with the preparation of the gospel of peace: in all things taking the shield of faith, wherewith you may be able to extinguish all the fiery darts of the most wicked one. And take unto you the helmet of salvation, and the sword of the Spirit (which is the word of God).

Induite vos arma Dei / ut possitis stare adversus insidias diaboli / quia non est nobis conluctatio adversus carnem et sanguinem / sed adversus principes et potestates / adversus mundi rectores tenebrarum harum / contra spiritalia nequitiae in caelestibus / propterea accipite armaturam Dei / ut possitis resistere in die malo / et omnibus perfectis stare / state ergo succincti lumbos vestros in veritate / et induti loricam iustitiae / et calciati pedis in praeparatione evangelii pacis / in omnibus sumentes scutum fidei / in quo possitis omnia tela nequissimi ignea extinguere / et galeam salutis adsumite / et gladium Spiritus / quod est verbum Dei. (Ephesians 6:11–17)

The passage's general congruence with the *Psychomachia* is self-evident, although Paul's "breastplate of justice" and "helmet of salvation" have no direct counterparts in Prudentius's poem. Instead, the passage issues an allegorical call to arms to which the *Psychomachia* responds, asking its readers to transform themselves into personified Virtues to fight against the powers of darkness. No such translation is required, however, to understand Paul's "principalities and powers" and "spirits of wickedness" as Prudentius's Vices. These evil spirits are at once very real, minions of the devil who have ruled the earth since the Fall, and spiritual rather than earthly powers, susceptible to allegorical rather than literal weaponry. The passage in Ephesians, like the *Psychomachia* as a whole, marks the moment their long, uncontested reign comes to an end with the rise of Christianity.

At the same time, Prudentius's Vices are enmeshed in pagan Roman religion. Kenneth Haworth links the *Psychomachia*'s battles between Vice and Virtue to Cicero's representation of inner struggle in the *Tusculan Disputations* (*Tusculanae Disputationes*) as well as to his broader opposition to the deification of Vices.[16] In *On the Laws*, Cicero argues that "it is proper to *deify the virtues* but not the vices," holding that "the ancient altar to Fever on the Palatine and the one to Bad Fortune on the Esquiline as well as all other abominations of that character must be done away with." Prudentius repudiates his own personified Vices in similar terms, attacking them not just as negative character traits but also as false gods. We see this dynamic most intensely in his description of the followers of Avarice (Avaritia), whom he assimilates to the Eumenides or Furies, the classical world's chthonic goddesses of vengeance:

> Care, Hunger, Fear, Anguish, Perjuries, Pallor, Corruption, Treachery, Falsehood, Sleeplessness, Meanness, diverse fiends [*Eumenides variae*] go in attendance on the monster; and all the while Crimes, the brood of their mother Greed's black milk, like ravening wolves go prowling and leaping over the field.
>
> Cura, Famis, Metus, Anxietas, Periuria, Pallor,
> Corruptela, Dolus, Commenta, Insomnia, Sordes,
> Eumenides variae monstri comitatus aguntur.
> nec minus interea rabidorum more luporum
> Crimina persultant toto grassantia campo
> matris Avaritiae nigro de lacte creata. (464–69)

The entire scene borrows heavily from book 6 of the *Aeneid*, in which the Furies perch malevolently at the entrance to the underworld, attended by Care, Hunger, and Fear (6:273–81). Their companion Discord closely resembles Prudentius's personification of the same name, who is attended and eventually betrayed by Pallor and Panic, companions of Mars whose worship was said to have been established by the early Roman king Tullus Hostilius.[17] For Prudentius these abstractions must be unmade or undone not only as negative moral qualities but also as religious "abominations."

It follows that in the *Psychomachia* each Vice receives two sets of fatal injuries: one as a particular sin and the other as a false god or illegitimate personification. As both James Paxson and S. Georgia Nugent note, the Vices almost always die, at least in part, from defacement. They are repeatedly, not to say ritually, injured in the eyes, mouth, and throat. Paxson links this pattern of injury to prosopopoeia's history as a classical rhetorical trope, derived from *prosopon* + *poiein*, to make a face or mask. In killing the Vices, Paxson argues, the Virtues symbolically dismantle "the trope by which the text invents the figural characters who inhabit its actantial narrative," marking "the inception of self-reflexive personification fabulation."[18] This pattern of destruction likewise evokes the historical defacement of cult statues in Roman temples, which Prudentius may have directed as a senior official under the Christian emperor Theodosius.[19] For her part, Nugent reads the injuries to the Vices' faces and necks as a violent repudiation of their female sexuality.[20] She points out that Greek and Roman medical discourses consistently link the upper *stoma*, the mouth and throat, to the lower *stoma*, the uterus, leading physicians to believe that women's necks and voices changed in response to sexual activity.[21] The ritualized destruction of one *stoma*, with its associated lips and neck, thus destroys the other literally as well as symbolically, foreclosing at once upon female speech and female sexuality. Together these analyses suggest that to obliterate the Vices' faces and stop up their throats—to put an end to their seeing and their speaking—is to stifle their ability to deceive and entice, and therefore to destroy them specifically as feminine personifications.

When the Vices die, their personifying power passes to the Virtues who kill them. Lavarenne complains that after "attack[ing] with such ardor" and "kill[ing] with such joy," Prudentius's Virtues invariably go on to "insult with such sarcasm, and speechify with such pretension." Stripped of Lavarenne's objections to unladylike conduct, this pattern implies that when Faith or Chastity destroys her opponent's speech apparatus, the Vice's ability to speak is transferred to her conqueror. While the personified Vices have existed in one form or another since the Fall, the personified Virtues are brought into being through combat with their vicious counterparts. Prudentius offers a theological justification for this dynamic in his *Hamartigenia* (*The Origin of Sin*), asserting that "it is not virtue unless it spring forth in the act of rejecting the worse and seek the right path because its nature is better" (nec tamen est virtus, ni deteriora refutans / emicet et meliore viam petat indole rectam) (695–96). This struggle demonstrates that virtue is an act of free will, since "he who is not good of his own will is neither good nor praiseworthy" (nec bonus est nec conlaudabilis ille / qui non sponte bonus) (692–93). It also suggests, however, that virtue is in a fundamental sense both subsequent to and consequent upon vice. In the *Psychomachia*, the Virtues are likewise "second order" personifications by historical necessity rather than happenstance, gaining power through confrontation with, and at the expense of, the reigning Vices. They come into being through, and are defined by, moral struggle and are associated with, even animated by, the human will as it turns from vice to virtue.

This pattern of defacement, however, does not account for all the violence in the *Psychomachia*. In addition to striking Discord in the mouth with a javelin, "driving its hard point through the foul tongue" (pollutam rigida transfigens cuspide linguam), Faith leads the virtuous army in tearing her limb from limb as a collective act of retribution (718). Whereas the first injury "stopped her speech and blocked the passage of her voice" (verba loquentis / inpedit et vocis claudit)," enabling Faith's own victory speech, the second subjects Discord, who had sought to divide the body of the virtuous army, to her own logic of division (716—17). Worship of the Old Gods (Veterum Cultura Deorum) both suffocates and has her eyes gouged out in token of her spiritual blindness, while Indulgence (Luxuria) is fatally mangled by her own chariot before being finished off by a stone that "smashed the breath-passage in the midst of the face and beat the lips into the arched mouth. The teeth within are loosened, the gullet cut, and the mangled tongue fills it with bloody fragments" (medii spiramen ut oris / frangeret, et recavo misceret labra palato. / dentibus introrsum resolutis lingua resectam / dilaniata gulam frustis cum sanguinis inplet) (421–24). In addition to perishing as a representative of idolatrous personification, each Vice also brings destruction upon herself through the logic of *contrapasso*, in which the punishment fits the crime.[22] In doing so, she cedes her place to a particular Virtue. Indulgence, advancing mindlessly in her chariot, still drunk from the night before, provokes the carefully reasoned stability of Sobriety (Sobrietas), while Discord energizes Concord (Concordia), understood as deliberate and hard-won agreement rather than unthinking unanimity. While the violence of the *Psychomachia* may seem gratuitous, it actually obeys a rigorous logic. Each Vice is destroyed both as a personification and as the sinful content represented by the personification. Each Virtue emerges not only as a representation of virtuous content but also as a legitimate and efficacious representative form.

The battle between Pride (Superbia) and Humble Mind (Mens Humilis) perhaps best illustrates this dynamic. As one would expect, Pride's death is overdetermined: she receives one fatal injury according to the logic of *contrapasso* and another to her neck, specifically designed to stop her speech. She receives the first of these wounds when she charges into enemy territory to show off her sumptuous battle array and humiliate her foes, but instead falls into a trench dug by Deceit (Fraus) to trap the advancing Virtues:

> Into the snare has fallen that rider as she galloped in swift career, and suddenly revealed the secret gulf. Thrown forward, she clings around the horse's neck in its tumble; the weight of its breast comes down on her and she is tossed about among its broken legs.
>
> Hunc eques illa dolum, dum fertur praepete cursu,
> incidit, et caecum subito patefecit hiatum.

prona ruentis equi cervice involvitur, ac sub
pectoris inpressu fracta inter crura rotatur. (270–73)

Just as the Vices' collective defeat enacts Romans 6:23, "the wages of sin is death" (stipendia enim peccati mors), so Pride's individual downfall acts out Proverbs 16:18, "Pride goeth before destruction: and the spirit is lifted up before a fall" (contritionem praecedit superbia et ante ruinam exaltatur spiritus).[23] As often in the *Psychomachia*, however, the wordplay is intertextual, with readers asked to supply the biblical truth blindly illustrated by Pride, who can see neither the "caecum . . . hiatum" that lies open before her nor the workings of her own self-destructive nature. Immobilized at the bottom of the pit, a "vain monster crushed and lying at the point of death" (levitatem . . . obtritam monstri sub morte iacentis), Pride becomes a perverse version of the Word of God made flesh, the mechanical enactment of a biblical text that she either has not read or cannot understand (274–75). Although Pride proudly believes that she controls her own destiny, she is in fact a slave to sin and its consequences, a puppet who acts out with particular literalism, and thus particular clarity, the truths of Proverbs and the Pauline epistles. In contrast to the Virtues' deliberate decision making, which sees Humble Mind pause and consult with her colleague Hope (Spes) before determining to slay Pride, Pride and her sisters act unburdened by thought, and so almost as automata. They lack the intellectual purchase on their own actions that the *Psychomachia* seeks to impart to its readers, who are asked to understand this scene as a dramatized instantiation of scriptural truth.

Prudentius links Pride's inability to read or understand scripture specifically to her feminine sexuality, defined in traditionally misogynist terms as a mixture of garrulousness and sexual excess. In describing Pride as "puffed up" (inflata) and a "windbag she-man" (ventosa virago) filled with "swelling disdain" (tumido . . . fastu), Prudentius associates her with yet another aphoristic expression of Christian truth, Cyprian of Carthage's widely cited tag "pride puffs up" (inflat superbia) (178, 194, 182).[24] Implicitly, the wind that inflates Pride and lends her a false sense of importance is her vain speech, by which she falsely claims masculine authority. Talking when she should be reading, and with nothing substantive to say, Pride's speech is a purely physical phenomenon with no relationship either to authority or to deliberation. It lends a false sense of solidity to her elaborate bodily display, when in fact she is nothing but sumptuous surface. Prudentius's representation of Pride, with her hair piled high on her head and her neck and bosom accentuated by a filmy scarf and elegant mantle, intimates that the splendidly dressed, sexually alluring female body is almost intrinsically that of a braggart, while to indulge in *braggadocio* is to speak as, or as if, a sexually active woman. While this quality is proper to Pride, it is common, in a less dramatic form, to all the personified Vices. All are feminine and at least incipiently sexual, with even Pride's own sexuality in a sense borrowed from Sodomitic Lust (Sodomita Libido), the Vice who immediately precedes her. All likewise presume their own superiority, only to be proved wrong by the course of battle. Pride embodies pride, then, because her actions exemplify it so clearly, rather than because she is the only Vice to act pridefully. It is her dominant logic, but also part of the general, deformative logic of vice itself.

Pride's second set of fatal wounds are inflicted by Humble Mind, whose name conspicuously revises the name of the classical deified abstraction Mind. (In many medieval *Psychomachia* manuscripts, the Virtue is instead named Humility [Humilitas], presumably because the reference to Mind was no longer legible.) Humble Mind severs Pride's throat, according to Greco-Roman medicine simultaneously foreclosing upon her sexuality and cutting off her speech in midstream:

> Grasping her blood-stained enemy by the hair, she drags her out and with her left hand turns her face upwards; then, though she begs for mercy, bends the neck, severs the head, lifts it and holds it up by the dripping locks.

> Illa cruentatem correptis crinibus hostem
> protrahit et faciem laeva revocante supinat,
> tunc caput orantis flexa cervice resectum
> eripit ac madido suspendit colla capillo. (280–83)

M. Clement Eagan notes that Humble Mind here reenacts Aeneas's killing of the Rutulian warrior Magus in *Aeneid* 10.536.[25] Even as this allusion furnishes Humble Mind with a distinguished heroic lineage, it emphasizes the seeming excess of Pride's second wound. In contrast to the uninjured Magus, who grasps Aeneas's knees and pleads eloquently for his life, Pride is already "crushed and lying at the point of death." Humble Mind's decapitation of Pride renders any further speech categorically impossible, however, and so serves as an appropriate hinge between Pride's long, hectoring battle challenge and Hope's victory oration. This speech—which begins with the exclamation, "An end to thy big talk!" (Desine grande loqui!)—suggests that the power of speech is itself the most important spoil of war, migrating from the mutilated throat of the Vice to the intact throat of her conqueror (285).

But what does Pride say that must be so vigorously, and so completely, silenced? Ironically, she presents herself as a Virtue rather than a Vice, as the embodiment of a healthy and appropriate pride in self, family, and country. Indeed, she allies herself with *virtus* itself, interpreted in the classical world as courage or military valor. She defines *virtus* as etymologically indissociable from *vir* (man), arguing that to use it otherwise is to commit a moral as well as a grammatical solecism:

> What shame it is, O Mars, O conscious valor [*virtus*], to face such an army as this, to take the sword against such trumpery, and engage with a dance troupe full of girls, among them beggarly Justice and poverty-stricken Honesty, dried-up Sobriety and white-faced Fasting, Modesty with scarce a tinge of blood to color her cheeks, unarmed Simplicity exposed with no protection to every wound, and Humble Mind humbling herself to the ground, with no freedom even in her own eyes, and whose agitation betrays her ignoble spirit! I shall have this feeble band trodden down like stubble; for we disdain to shatter them with our stark swords, to dip our blades in their frigid blood, and disgrace our warriors with a triumph that needs no manhood.

> Quam pudet, o Mavors et virtus conscia, talem
> contra stare aciem ferroque lacessere nugas,
> et cum virgineis dextram conferre choreis,
> Iustitia est ubi super egens et pauper Honestas,
> arida Sobrietas, albo Ieiunia vultu,
> sanguine vix tenui Pudor interfusus, aperta
> Simplicitas et ad omne patens sine tegmine vulnus,
> Et prostrata in humum nec libera iudice sese
> Mens Humilis, quam degenerem trepidatio prodit!
> faxo ego, sub pedibus stipularum more teratur
> invalida ista manus; neque enim perfringere duris
> dignamur gladiis, algenti et sanguine ferrum
> inbuere fragilique viros foedare triumpho. (240–52)[26]

Pride's understanding of courage is rooted in the ideology and practices of the Roman army and associated with the worship of the deified abstraction Virtus.[27] As such, it is strongly linked to masculine sexuality and formally excludes women.[28] Historically, soldiers in the Roman army were long forbidden to marry, while officers were encouraged to leave their wives at home. Pride defends this ban by evoking the medical model whereby, to quote Galen, "the man is more perfect than the woman, and the reason for his perfection is his excess of heat."[29] Women cannot fight because they are cold blooded, with Pride's adjective *algens* denoting the chilliness of something that is usually or normatively hot. This same adjective suggests that Mars *should* be dipping his sword in the hot blood of other men, a sexually symbolic act that evokes the war rape perpetrated by victorious Roman armies against their opponents. In this scenario, military victory renders men simultaneously virtuous and virile while imposing femininity upon defeated opponents.[30] The female Virtues are pushed so far down the great chain of being that they are not even human, with Pride promising that they will be "trodden down like stubble," at once objectified and obliterated. Pride's fantasy of depersonifying her opponents, of doing to them what they ultimately do to her, emphasizes that the battle between Vice and Virtue is a battle over personification itself.

In Pride's boast, the Virtues' gender-based violation of social and literary decorum is compounded by their commitment to virginity, which challenges the traditional Roman pride in lineage. Using "virgineis . . . choreis," a troupe of dancing maidens, as a term of opprobrium, Pride articulates traditional Roman sexual mores in suggesting that the Virtues' virginity consigns them to perpetual adolescence.[31] Their virginity disrupts the elite patriarchal succession in which "bellica virtus," virile military virtue, is passed from generation to generation through aristocratic marriage and service in the Roman army. Pride claims that because the Virtues' army fails to adhere to this model, it is vulgar and disorganized, even vicious:

> Are ye not ashamed, ye poor creatures, to challenge famous captains with troops of low degree, to take the sword against a race of proud distinction, whose valor in war has long won wealth for it, and given it power to impose its rule on hills where rich grass grows? And now—can it be?—a newcomer with nothing is trying to drive out the ancient princes! . . . Absurd mob [*O ridiculum vulgus*]! Why, in the hour of birth we embrace the whole man, his frame still warm from his mother, and extend the strength of our power through the body of the new-born child, we are lords and masters all within the tender bones.

> Non pudet, o miseri, plebeio milite claros
> adtemptare duces ferroque lacessere gentem

> insignem titulis, veteres cui bellica virtus
> divitias peperit, laetos et gramine colles
> imperio calcare dedit? nunc advena nudus
> nititur antiquos, si fas est, pellere reges!
>
> . . .
>
> nempe, o ridiculum vulgus, natalibus horis
> totum hominem et calidos a matre amplectimur artus,
> vimque potestatum per membra recentis alumni
> spargimus, et rudibus dominamur in ossibus omnes. (206–11, 216–19)

For Pride, the abstract names of the personified Virtues—she has just listed Chastity, Piety, Justice, Honesty, Sobriety, Fasting, Modesty, Simplicity, and Humble Mind in a scornful litany—become shameful alternatives to the aristocratic Roman *nomen* and *cognomen*, while Christianity itself becomes a pretentious upstart, dwarfed by the long history of Roman military success. At the same time, Pride associates the historical Roman Empire with the Vices' reign over the human body, which she dates to Adam and Eve's expulsion from Eden.[32] She thus weaves all pre-Christian history into a single genealogical chain, defining virtue through a combination of patrilineal succession and military valor. The Virtues' challenge to this order stems from their nature as feminine and virginal personifications. Even as their femininity undermines Roman virtue's association with virility, their virginity and abstract names sever merit and accomplishment from lineage. It follows that when Humble Mind defeats Pride on the field of battle, she not only discredits the classical conception of *virtus* but also defines Pride herself as one of Cicero's "abominations," something that was personified but should not have been.

While Pride depicts pagan Roman *virtus* quite explicitly, the embodied Christian virtue that replaces it remains a work in progress. Indeed, describing it becomes the work of the poem as a whole. A few characteristics are clear, however, despite Humble Mind's resolute silence, which inverts Pride's verbosity. The ritual victory speech in this case is delivered by Hope, whose aid to Humble Mind fittingly contrasts with Fraud's unwitting sabotage of Pride. Whereas Pride ignorantly enacts the proverb that pride goes before a fall, Hope deliberately constructs her victory speech from biblical paraphrase. Recognizing the allusion that Pride misses, she warns the proud, "Learn to beware the pit beneath your feet" (Disce cavere / ante pedes foveam) before restating Matthew 23:12 and 1 Peter 5:5

and summarizing David's defeat of Goliath in 1 Kings 17 (287–88).[33] Her paraphrase of Matthew 23:12, in particular, is carefully marked, allowing her to pay homage to the power of Christ's own words: "Well known and true is the saying of our Christ that the lowly ascend to high places and the proud are reduced to low degree" (Pervulgata viget nostri sententia Christi / scandere celsa humiles et ad ima redire feroces)" (289–90). As presented here, the "sententia Christi" itself seems to have defeated Pride, with Humble Mind and Hope serving merely as instruments of biblical truth. More precisely, where Pride acts unilaterally, not even conferring about strategy with her fellow Vices, Hope and Humble Mind knowingly and voluntarily align themselves with "our Christ" so that their victory is inseparable from his. The "sententia Christi" triumphs not by military conquest but by spreading and flourishing until it is widely acknowledged by the very *vulgus* that Pride disdains ("pervulgata viget"). Implicitly, as Christ's sayings become more widely known, they also become more widely true, with Christians becoming the sayings' earthly agents. In this context, Hope and Humble Mind are, if not full-fledged goddesses, then at least powerful spiritual forces who simultaneously recall, critique, and supersede the classical deified abstractions Hope and Mind. Instead of descending from on high, they are divinized by ordinary believers who, like Prudentius, read, internalize, and seek to enact Christ's teachings. This process reaches its local culmination when Hope, "striking the air with her gilded wings . . . flies off to heaven" (auratis praestringens aëra pinnis / in caelum se . . . rapit)—the only one of the Virtues to achieve transcendence within the main body of Prudentius's poem (305–6).

REFORMING VIRTUE

By depicting the deaths of the Vices in gory detail, Prudentius distances his own use of personification from the practice of Roman state religion. Although he follows Cicero in condemning the deification of negative qualities, he also redefines classical virtues such as Virtus and Mens as themselves vicious "abominations." Not all of the classical virtues, however, can be dismissed so easily. Since virtues such as Faith, Chastity, and Patience feature prominently in Christian morality, Prudentius instead sets out to reform them, both literally and figuratively, in order to make them fit for purpose. He provides them with a Jewish rather than pagan genealogy via allegorical exegesis, linking Faith to Abraham, Chastity to Judith, and Patience to Job. In doing so, he uses exegetes' rewriting of Abraham as the father of the Christian faithful to justify his own rewriting of

Abraham as the feminine personification Faith—and thus as a paradigm for Christian personification more broadly. Although Prudentius does not explicitly link this paradigm to the tradition of formative personification discussed in chapter 1, the resemblance is striking. His Virtues are simultaneously divine forces and carefully crafted machines for personal and collective moral reformation. Indeed, when Prudentius "resculpts" the Virtues in his poem and invites his readers to do the same in the medium of their own lives, we can almost hear an echo of Cicero's *On the Laws*: "It is a good thing also that *Intellect, Piety, Courage, and Faith should be deified by the hand of man* . . . the purpose being that those who possess them (and all good men do) should believe that the gods themselves are established within their own souls." In this context, the primary difference between pagan and Christian formative personifications may be their gender. While the Romans placed relatively little emphasis on the gender of their deified abstractions—and some, like Virtus, could be represented as either masculine or feminine—the Christianity of Prudentius's personifications is defined in part by their virginal femininity.

Although critics concerned with medieval and postmedieval allegory sometimes argue for a strong separation between personification allegory and allegorical exegesis, studies of the *Psychomachia* overwhelmingly follow Henri de Lubac in appreciating a close connection between the two: "Does not one recognize, discreetly sketched beneath the figures of Chastity, Patience, and Sobriety, the characters of Judith, Job, David, and Samuel?"[34] Writing some twenty years before de Lubac, Laura Cotogni sketched a similar dynamic in the relationship between the *Psychomachia*'s typological preface and the main body of the text, characterizing the latter as "a poetic elaboration of allegorical exegesis."[35] She argues that the preface's portrait of the Old Testament Abraham as the type of faith anticipates the feminine personification Faith, the first Virtue elaborated in the main body of the poem. The allegorization of Abraham begins in the Pauline epistles, which reinterpret Abraham as justified by faith rather than works and therefore as the spiritual rather than literal forefather of the Christian faithful (Romans 4). Ambrose's *On Abraham*, which Cotogni identifies as the primary source for the *Psychomachia*'s preface, develops this reading into a line-by-line interpretation of the Abrahamic section of Genesis as a guide to cultivating Christian virtue.[36] Troubled by elements of the narrative such as Abraham's relationship with Hagar, Ambrose represents Abraham as a sinner who must raise himself up in order to follow God and thus as a model for all Christian sinners. He emphasizes Abraham's battle to rescue his nephew Lot from captivity, interpreting the five kings with whom Lot mistakenly aligns himself and the four who capture him as the five bodily senses and the four material elements.[37] In opposing these kings, Abraham fights his way from fleshly to spiritual understanding in what is essentially an act of self-allegoresis. Prudentius and his early readers thus would have understood Abraham both as a figure for allegory itself and as a tool for becoming allegorical, even as he continued to represent the paradigmatic Christian virtue of Faith.[38]

The *Psychomachia*'s preface retraces this trajectory in a highly compressed form, introducing Abraham as the "senex fidelis" (faithful old man) rather than by name (preface 1). As in *On Abraham*, the patriarch's battle against the nine kings, allegorized as sins, becomes the most important event in his biography. In Ambrose's account, Abraham's victory allows him to progress from being the Jewish father of Ishmael, his child of the flesh with his handmaid Hagar, to being the Christian father of Isaac, his child of the spirit with his wife, Sarah. Prudentius, seemingly uncomfortable with even married sexuality, takes this logic a step further. He refrains from describing Abraham and Sarah as husband and wife, or even associating them with each other. Instead, Sarah becomes the spouse of the Holy Ghost, while Abraham is married to a personification of Virtue:

> [Abraham] has counseled us to war against the ungodly tribes, himself giving us an example of his own counsel, and shown that we beget no child of wedlock pleasing to God, and whose mother is Virtue, till the spirit, battling valorously, has overcome with great slaughter the monsters in the enslaved heart.

> [Abraham] pugnare nosmet cum profanis gentibus
> suasit, suumque suasor exemplum dedit,
> nec ante prolem coniugalem gignere
> Deo placentem, matre Virtute editam,
> quam strage multa bellicosus spiritus
> portenta cordis servientis vicerit. (preface 9–14)

In these lines, Abraham's only divinely sanctioned marriage seems to be his figurative union with Virtue. This marriage is enabled by his battle against sin and especially by his victory over sexual desire. By spiritualizing himself, Abraham raises himself to the same plane as his wife and so becomes a kind of proto-personification. As he subjugates his fleshly desires, he is defined more and more completely by his faithfulness and so becomes, for Prudentius, a suitable partner for Virtue.

Prudentius encourages similar acts of self-allegorization by characterizing Abraham as a verbal sketch that his readers must elaborate and animate. Near the end of the preface, he remarks,

> This figure has been inscribed beforehand to be a model for our life to trace out again with true measure, showing that we must watch in the armour of faithful hearts, and that every part of our body which is in captivity and enslaved to foul desire must be set free by gathering our forces at home.

> Haec ad figuram praenotata est linea,
> quam nostra recto vita resculpat pede:
> vigilandum in armis pectorum fidelium,
> omnemque nostri portionem corporis,
> quae capta foedae serviat libidini,
> domi coactis liberandam viribus. (preface 50–55)

Prudentius here commits to rewriting or redrawing the figure of Abraham, first in his poem, then in the medium of his life, and asks his readers to do the same.[39] For Carruthers, who sees these lines as central to the poem as a whole, "lineae" denote "the richly textured lineaments of an educated and well-stocked memory." As readers of the poem, we should allow the text "to paint its synaesthetic pictures in our own minds, and transfer that picture to our memories where it will always be available to us . . . as a sort of ethical device, part of the furnishing of our soul."[40] For Prudentius, however, retracing the figure of Abraham seems to involve projecting one's self into the text rather than extracting images from it. In the first of a series of acts of self-personification, readers are to imagine themselves in the role of Abraham as a step toward remaking themselves as an embodiment of faith. They must strive against the vices so that, like Abraham, they can beget allegorical children who are "pleasing to God."

But how, exactly, does this act of self-formation or self-personification work? Insofar as Prudentius asks readers to remake themselves in the image of Abraham, he courts idolatry. Man is explicitly, and exclusively, an *imago dei*. Prudentius specifies, however, that as a "figura" Abraham is himself a visual figure or rhetorical trope. He is a "way of believing" (credendi via) that stands for and leads to truth rather than truth itself (preface 1). As a figure, moreover, Abraham is usefully incomplete, "praenotata." The prefix *prae-* denotes temporal or logical priority, pointing at once to Abraham's status as an Old Testament patriarch and to his position in the preface to the *Psychomachia*, while *notare* means to summarize, to write in shorthand, even to write in cipher. In the Latin lexicon, *praenotare* is logically opposed to *perscribere*, to write in full or at length. From Prudentius's Christian perspective, Abraham is necessarily a sketch or a summary, exemplary and yet incomplete, because he lived and died before the Incarnation. For that very reason, he is also pedagogically useful. To rewrite Abraham's life "recto . . . pede"—at once with correct measurements, with metrically correct verse, and with moral rectitude—requires both good intentions and technical skill. Implicitly, virtue is a craft that can be learned by diligently imitating good models. Since Abraham is incomplete, however, he leaves room for Prudentius and his readers to move beyond reproduction to interpretation and embellishment, both in writing the *Psychomachia* and in writing their own lives. They must exercise creativity to write out in full what has only been summarized and ingenuity to puzzle out what is written in cipher.

While Abraham presides over the first stage of self-reformation in the preface, the process can only be completed under Christ's aegis in the main body of the text. In the poem's opening lines of dactylic hexameter, where we might otherwise expect the invocation of the Muse, the Prudentian narrator instead addresses Christ directly: "Thou thyself dost command relieving squadrons to fight the battle in the body close beset, Thou thyself dost arm the spirit with pre-eminent kinds of skill" (Ipse salutiferas obsesso in corpore turmas / depugnare iubes, ipse excellentibus armas / artibus ingenium) (14–16). Although the poem has already referred to virtues, they become embodied only as agents of Christ, acting at once on his authority and on his behalf:

> The plan for victory is right here if we may mark [*notare*] at close quarters the very faces of the Virtues, and the evil forces that close with them in deadly struggle.
>
> Vincendi praesens ratio est, si comminus ipsas
> Virtutum facies et conluctantia contra
> viribus infestis liceat portenta notare. (18–20)

The verb "notare" links the newly personified Virtues to the "praenotata linea" of the preface, promising that they will complete the figure of Abraham, "reengraving" him for the New Dispensation. As in the preface, "notare" demands the active participation of the *Psychomachia*'s readers: the plan for victory is right here, in the very faces of the personified Virtues, if "we" will only notice it. For Carruthers, "ratio" in this passage refers to a memory scheme that organizes ethical material for memorial "inventio." Each battle becomes a "background cell" that allows Prudentius to arrange the dominant characteristics of the vices and virtues, their typical manifestations, other virtues and vices associated with the principle ones, and biblical episodes that show the vices and virtues in action.[41] Prudentius, however, specifically instructs his readers to reform themselves by looking at the "very faces" of the Virtues, person to personification. The Virtues' primary function is identification—and ultimately allegorical self-formation—rather than schematic organization.

The first personified Virtue "we" confront, face to face, is Faith. On the one hand, she is clearly Abraham's alter ego, both the culmination of his transformation from type to personification and a resculpting of his *figura*. On the other hand, she can take Christ's place as an epic protagonist because she is his subordinate in Prudentius's imagined military hierarchy, bearing his arms and obeying his orders. She complements both figures because, as a feminine personification, she occupies a differently gendered field of action. The battle seems to take place at once within "the body close beset" and, as Paula James points out, within the blank and delimited space of the Roman arena.[42] When Faith defeats Worship of the Old Gods, she is suddenly joined by a host of Christian martyrs, whom she "crowns with flowers and bids clothe themselves in flaming purple in proportion to the glory they have won" (pro laude coronat / floribus ardentique iubet vestirier ostro)" (38–39). As part of a military chain of command, Faith fights on behalf of the present yet invisible Christ as his subordinate and on behalf of the present yet (at least initially) invisible martyrs as their chief. In doing so, James argues, she acts out the spiritual significance of martyrdoms like that of Saint Perpetua, who understands herself to be defeating the devil in single combat even as her body is torn apart by beasts as a public spectacle.[43] These allusions lend a degree of historical specificity to Faith's battle, suggesting that her status as a personification allows her to link Christ outside of time to his followers within it. Simultaneously, her femininity helps to define her military victory as spiritual rather than literal, even as it distinguishes her from Abraham and Christ on the one hand and Prudentius's normatively masculine, classically trained readers on the other. Operating at a remove from both revealed truth and empirical reality, Prudentius's feminine personification of Faith enjoys an important degree of speculative or experimental leeway.[44]

Faith's femininity likewise helps to define the *Psychomachia* as a Christian *Aeneid*. Her battle against Worship of the Old Gods transforms yet another classical virtue—the Romans described their religious practice as the cult of the "old gods"—into a vice that must be overcome.[45] In doing so, Faith simultaneously recalls and reverses the final battle between Aeneas and Turnus in the *Aeneid*. "Rising higher" (altior insurgens) like Turnus, she succeeds where he fails, knocking down her opponent in a display of pure strength before gouging out her eyes as she lies choking to death in the dust (31, cf. *Aeneid* 12.902). In the process, Faith effectively overwrites the *Aeneid*, defining a new, specifically Christian model of epic heroism. Carruthers argues that such overwriting was widespread: since major classical landmarks were too well known to be erased from Christians' communal memories, they were instead assigned new Christian significance.[46] In the *Psychomachia*, Faith's femininity is crucial to this process because it established the poem's irreducible difference from its most prominent classical source. No matter how close its verbal echoes, the underlying nature of the *Psychomachia* is as different from that of the *Aeneid* as woman is from man. Indeed, as we have begun to see, Prudentius identifies Christianity with a virginal femininity that occupies a qualitatively different sphere from that of the *Aeneid*.

In particular, Faith's femininity means that the nudity traditionally associated with epic heroes ceases to be a mere generic convention:

> Faith first takes the field to face the doubtful chances of battle, her rough dress disordered, her shoulders bare, her hair untrimmed, her arms exposed; for the sudden glow of ambition, burning to enter fresh contests, takes no thought to gird on arms or armour, but trusting in a stout heart and unprotected limbs challenges the hazards of furious warfare, meaning to break them down.
>
> Prima petit campum dubia sub sorte duelli
> pugnatura Fides, agresti turbida cultu,
> nuda umeros, intonsa comas, exerta lactertos;
> namque repentinus laudis calor ad nova fervens
> proelia nec telis meminit nec tegmine cingi
> pectore sed fidens valido membrisque retectis
> provocat insani frangenda pericula belli. (21–27)

In the classical cannon, a woman's bare shoulders, unkempt hair, and bare upper arms generally denote sexual rather than martial readiness, as when Daphne inflames Apollo in Ovid's *Metamorphoses*. Nugent argues that the *Psychomachia* "sublimates each of these potentially erotic signs of undress, immediately diverting them to the signification of *heroic* nudity."[47] For masculine readers trained in the classical tradition, however, this sublimation likely required some effort. As such readers struggle to imagine Faith's breast as a site of martial courage rather than décolletage, they begin to fight in solidarity with her—and so embark upon their own battles as *milites Christi.* Prudentius's description of Faith's half-naked body thus invokes and rewrites the story of Daphne and Apollo at the beginning of the *Metamorphoses.* As a trial for admittance to the main body of the *Psychomachia,* it separates authorized readers who fight alongside and ultimately identify with Faith from unauthorized readers who approach the poem voyeuristically. Faith challenges the poem's classically educated audience to read against the grain of their training, indeed to convert their entire mode of reading from masculine to feminine and from pagan to Christian.

Given that Faith's battle seems to be set in a Roman arena, it is not surprising that this reading process echoes one Sarah Salih identifies in many early saints' lives.[48] In virgin martyr legends, the young female protagonist typically chooses Christ as her bridegroom in place of a high-ranking pagan suitor. Brought to trial on all but indistinguishable charges of being a Christian and refusing to marry, she is ordered to appear naked in the arena as a form of sexual humiliation. Her execution becomes a public and punitive version of the sexual consummation she has refused, with the penetration of the virgin's body by wild beasts or instruments of torture substituting more or less explicitly for sexual penetration. As critics have observed, these legends' often graphic descriptions of torture have significant pornographic elements.[49] Salih argues, however, that the saints' lives also challenge their male readers to distance themselves from the persecutor's voyeuristic perspective, indeed to understand it as a temptation to be overcome. In order to read as Christians rather than pagans, they must train themselves to see the virgin martyrs' nudity as heroic rather than sexual—in the process reframing their own identities in differently gendered terms. In other words, an individual reader's struggle to see the saint as a solider of Christ rather than a sex object parallels the martyr's struggle in the arena and ultimately shares its meaning. When the life of a virgin martyr is read properly, the persecutor's strategy of humiliation backfires. By learning to interpret the virgin's martyrdom as heroic rather than sexual, the male reader triumphs with her, with his conversion from a sexualized masculinity to holy chastity paralleling the arena audience's conversion from paganism to Christianity within the story. In juxtaposing the setting and generic conventions of classical epic with those of hagiography, Prudentius invites his readers to embark upon a similarly virtuous transformation, using Faith and her sisters as instruments or machines for doing so.

The *Psychomachia*'s succession of personified Virtues, therefore, becomes a kind of syllabus, a series of opportunities for male readers to test and refine their renunciation of masculine sexuality by reforming themselves as feminine personifications of Virtue. Like Faith, these other personifications come into being because the *figurae* of Abraham and other Old Testament heroes are incomplete and must be supplemented. Indeed, as a sketch or summary, Abraham provides the *Psychomachia* with a model of rhetorical composition that is almost infinitely expandable. Carruthers emphasizes that, over the course of the Middle Ages, the organizational schema of the *Psychomachia* would develop into a more or less standard pairing of seven deadly sins with seven countervailing virtues. For Prudentius himself, however, the number of virtues is much more fluid. Depending on how one counts, Prudentius "fleshes out" eight or nine or ten principal Virtues by imagining them fighting against Vice, often in seemingly ad hoc coalitions such as Hope and Humble Mind against Pride, or Reason (Ratio) and Works (Operatio) against Avarice. Beyond them stand a mass of personifiable if not personified Virtues that Macklin Smith dubs the "ready reserves," available to join the fight at any moment.[50] These reserves include those principal Virtues not currently fighting, nonce personifications such as Justice, Honesty, and Fasting, and the unnamed Virtues who fill out the ranks of the "health-bringing squadrons" (salutiferas . . . turmas) sent by Christ to aid the besieged soul (14).[51] Pride's listing of Justice, Honesty, and Fasting alongside the protagonists Chastity and Sobriety suggests that each of these Virtues is ready to step to the fore as needed to become her army's champion. Prudentius's model of virtuous personification thus has much in common with Cicero's understanding of virtuous deification. As we have seen, Cicero permits mortals to "invent names for gods" as long as their choices are both rational and decorous, with the virtues not yet chosen for deification standing ready to be called into action as the polis faces new challenges. Both Cicero and Prudentius, then, recognize the contingency of personifying one facet or formulation of virtue rather than another and so extend to their audiences a degree of what we might call artistic control. They not only craft their own divinities but also choose to craft one divinity rather than another as they seek to form selves capable of overcoming vice.

TRANSGENDER IDENTIFICATION

Prudentius's personifications resemble those of Cicero in being consecrated or deified by hand—that is, formed by the very humans whom they form in turn. They differ from them most visibly, and most radically, in their gendered relationship with those same followers. Where classical religious and rhetorical personifications can be either masculine or feminine, Prudentius's Christian Virtues are exclusively feminine and virginal. Their status as maiden warriors renders them figurative rather than literal, spiritual rather than historical. It also defines them as sites of transgender identification, insofar as the masculine readers of the *Psychomachia* align themselves with, and even imagine themselves as, feminine personifications of Virtue. While we saw this dynamic at work in a limited way in Prudentius's treatment of Abraham and Faith, it plays a central role in Chastity's defeat of Sodomitic Lust and Sobriety's defeat of Indulgence. Both battles are especially concerned with the form—as contrasted with the content—of Christian formative personification. The first characterizes Christian personification as inherently rather than accidentally feminine, at once enabled by and modeled on Mary's conception of the Word. The second reveals that the Virtues are themselves transgender personifications who revert to their male bodies as soon as they slacken in their fight against Vice. Together these battles invite Prudentius's readers to renounce their masculine sexuality and transform themselves into—that is to say, allegorize themselves as—feminine personifications of virtue.[52]

The *Psychomachia*'s second battle, between Chastity and Sodomitic Lust, represents Christian personification as a reenactment of Mary's conception of the Word that is intrinsically virginal yet fecund, female yet virtuous. Chastity anticipates Pride's claims on behalf of traditional Roman *virtus* and seeks to inoculate readers against them by defining its Christian counterpart. Striking Sodomitic Lust in the throat, she delivers one of the victory tirades so despised by Lavarenne:

> "A hit!" cries the triumphant princess. "This shall be thy last end; for ever shalt thou lie prostrate; no longer shalt thou dare to cast thy deadly flames against the male and female servants of God; the inmost fibre of their pure heart is kindled only from Christ's wedding torch. Shalt thou, O troubler of mankind, have been able to resume thy strength and grow warm again with the breath of life that was extinguished in thee, after the severed head of Holofernes soaked his Assyrian cham-

ber with his lustful blood, and the unbending Judith, spurning the lecherous captain's jeweled couch, checked his unclean passion with the sword, and woman as she was, won a famous victory over the foe with no trembling hand, maintaining my cause with boldness heaven-inspired? But perhaps a woman still fighting under the shade of the law had not force enough, though in doing so she prefigured our times, in which true power [*vera virtus*] has passed into earthly bodies to sever the great head by the hands of feeble agents?

"Hoc habet," exclamat victrix regina, "supremus
hic tibi finis erit, semper prostrata iacebis,
nec iam mortiferas audebis spargere flammas
in famulos famulasve Dei, quibus intima casti
vena animi sola fervet de lampade Christi.
tene, o vexatrix hominum, potuisse resumptis
viribus extincti capitis recalescere flatu,
Assyrium postquam thalamum cervix Olofernis
caesa cupidineo madefactum sanguine lavit,
gemmantemque torum moechi ducis aspera Iudith
sprevit et incestos conpescuit ense furores,
famosum mulier referens ex hoste tropaeum
non trepidante manu vindex mea caelitus audax!
at fortasse parum fortis matrona sub umbra
legis adhuc pugnans, dum tempora nostra figurat,
vera quibus virtus terrena in corpora fluxit
grande per infirmos caput excisura ministros. (53–69)

For Prudentius, just as Faith "translates" the Jewish Abraham into a Christian personification, so Chastity and Sodomitic Lust "translate" the Old Testament combat between Judith and Holofernes into a new arena. Chastity gives credit to Judith as a historical exemplar whose "famosum . . . tropaeum"—famous trophy or victory monument—serves as an inspiration to future generations. She represents herself, however, as a distinct phenomenon of the New Dispensation, in which "vera . . . virtus" flows into weak earthly bodies, implicitly as divine grace. Where Judith slays Lust in the body of Holofernes, extinguishing lust in a particular time and place, Chastity claims to slay Lust once and for all, in the bodies of all of God's servants. And where in Judith's time lust returns as long as life continues, with both life and lust imagined in terms of vital warmth, Chastity declares that her victory will allow Christians to burn only with the light of Christ, catching fire from his wedding torch. As Marc Mastrangelo notes, she likens Christ's servants to the wise virgins of Matthew 25 who have prepared their lamps for the arrival of the bridegroom.[53] Even in the idealizing terms of this victory speech, Chastity does not eliminate lust from the world any more than the wise virgins change the conduct of the foolish virgins who bring no oil for their lamps: she does not do away with the human freedom to do well or ill. But she does offer God's servants the possibility of freeing themselves from lust so that they may be united with their bridegroom. In the process, she distinguishes her own status as a Christian personification from that of her typological predecessor.

Continuing the Prudentian narrator's use of the first-person plural to invoke "our times," Chastity goes on to suggest that in the New Dispensation all human beings can become virtuous personifications if they follow Christ. Still addressing Sodomitic Lust, she asserts that "all flesh" can wield divine power because it participates in the mystery of the Incarnation:

> Since a virgin immaculate has borne a child, has thou any claim remaining—since a virgin bore a child, since the day when man's body lost its primeval nature, and power from on high created a new flesh, and a woman unwedded conceived the God Christ, who is man in virtue of his mortal mother but God along with the Father? From that day all flesh is divine, since it conceives Him and takes on the nature of God by a covenant of partnership. For the Word made flesh has not ceased to be what it was before, that is, the Word, by attaching to itself the experience of the flesh; its majesty is not lowered by the experience of the flesh, but raises wretched men to nobler things. . . . It is his gift that thou liest conquered, filthy Lust, and canst not, since Mary, violate my authority.

> Numquid et intactae post partum virginis ullum
> fas tibi iam superest? post partum virginis, ex quo
> corporis humani naturam pristina origo
> deseruit carnemque novam vis ardua sevit,
> atque innupta Deum concepit femina Christum,
> mortali de matre hominem, sed cum Patre numen.
> inde omnis iam diva caro est quae concipit illum
> naturamque Dei consortis foedere sumit.
> Verbum quippe caro factum non destitit esse
> quod fuerat, Verbum, dum carnis glutinat usum

maiestate quidem non degenerante per usum
carnis, sed miseros ad nobiliora trahente. . . .
dona haec sunt, quod victa iaces, lutulenta Libido
nec mea post Mariam potis es perfringere iura. (70–88)

Although a number of critics have linked the *Psychomachia*'s personifications to the Incarnation in general terms, they align Chastity and her sisters directly with Christ's dual nature, at once fleshly and numinous.[54] Chastity, however, takes as her model not Christ but the Virgin Mary at the moment of the Annunciation. This is perhaps to be expected from a personification of Chastity, especially given the established typological link between Judith and Mary. Just as Pride embodies a pride that is common to all the Sins, however, so Chastity speaks inclusively on behalf of all the Virtues, as well as on behalf of humanity writ large. Prudentius, usually so careful to vary his diction, uses the crucial verb *concipere* twice in the space of three lines. First Mary and then all human flesh conceive Christ and are thereby filled with the "vera . . . virtus" that allows them to defeat personified Sin. Like its English cognate, the Latin *concipere* means both to become pregnant and to grasp something intellectually, so that each of these figures conceives the Word mentally and morally as well as physically.[55] Prudentius's use of the term implies that readers of the *Psychomachia* can themselves become personifications if they conceive the Word as Chastity and her sisters have done, reading scripture either directly or as enacted and commented upon in the *Psychomachia*.[56] Becoming a virtuous personification is thus the result of a carefully conceived program of reading and study. Indeed, a further sense of the Latin *concipere*—to compose—suggests that for Prudentius writing the *Psychomachia* is itself a Marian activity and therefore a work of self-personification. Prudentius's personification allegory is not merely an incarnational poetics, a new mode of writing and reading made possible by the coming of Christ. It is also intrinsically rather than accidentally a poetics of female bodies, which become both powerful and virtuous by conceiving the Word.

By using Mary's rather than Christ's experience of the Incarnation as his paradigm for virtue, Prudentius instructs his normatively masculine readers to turn themselves into feminine personifications. In doing so, he builds upon a biblical foundation: as we have just seen, the parable of the wise and foolish virgins asks men as well as women to imagine themselves as brides of Christ. He also builds upon the patristic understanding of the virginal female body as inherently transgender. As Jerome puts it in his often cited commentary on Ephesians, "As long as woman is for birth and children, she is different from man as body is from soul. But if she wishes to serve Christ more than the world, then she will cease to be a woman and will be called man" (Quamdiu mulier partui servit et liberis, hanc habet ad virum differentiam, quam corpus ad animam. Sin autem Christo magis voluerit servire quam saeculo, mulier esse cessabit, et dicitur vir)."[57] As the embodiment of chastity, Chastity is the most masculine of the Virtues. More directly than any of the others, she struggles against and ultimately purges the dangerous female sexuality that characterizes personified Vice, slaying her opponent with a conspicuously phallic sword. When she pierces Sodomitic Lust through the throat, the classical association between the neck and the cervix suggests a horrifying *contrapasso* in which the personification of Lust is raped to death. This transgendering continues, albeit in a different form, when Chastity figuratively conceives "vera . . . virtus." As Stephen Barney points out, *verus* is "the technical term in the Vulgate for describing Christ's fulfillment of ancient figure: Christ is the 'true' manna or 'true' vine."[58] It is consequently the masculine Christ, acting in or through Chastity's feminine body, who gives her the power to triumph over vice. Once again, we can hear an echo of classical medical discourse. Just as writers from Hippocrates to Galen to Rufus understand the inherently disordered female body to be "cured" by intercourse and pregnancy, so Prudentius suggests that inherently sinful human flesh, figured as generically feminine, is cured by conceiving the Word. As virginal bodies purged of sexuality but metaphorically pregnant with the male Christ child, Chastity and her sisters are safe spaces for masculine projection. Chastity can serve as their spokeswoman, defining Christian personification as such, precisely because she is the most virginal of the virgins and the most direct opponent of all sexuality.

After she has slain her opponent, Chastity performs a ceremony akin to Faith's crowning of the martyrs. Celebrating Sodomitic Lust's death, she commemorates the extinction of feminine sexuality that, for Prudentius, serves as a condition of possibility for transgender personification. Seen this way, Chastity represents transgender personification, and the sacrifice of masculine sexuality that accompanies it, as a quasi-sacramental act. Having polluted her phallic sword with the symbolic rape of Sodomitic Lust, she purifies it before offering it on the altar of a "Catholic temple":

> So spake Chastity, and rejoicing in the death of Lust, whom she had slain, washed her stained sword in the waters of Jordan; for a red dew of gore had clung to it and befouled the bright steel from the wound. So the conqueress deftly cleanses the conquering blade by bathing it

in the stream, dipping it in to wash away the stain of blood that came from her foe's throat; and, no longer content to sheathe the purified sword, lest rust unseen engross the clean, bright surface with its dirty scurf, she dedicates it by the altar of the divine spring in a Catholic temple, there to shine and flash with unfading light.

Dixerat haec et laeta Libidinis interfectae
morte Pudicitia gladium Iordanis in undis
abluit infectum, sanies cui rore rubenti
haeserat et nitidum macularat vulnere ferrum.
expiat ergo aciem fluviali docta lavacro
victricem victrix, abolens baptismate labem
hostilis iuguli; nec iam contenta piatum
condere vaginae gladium, ne tecta rubigo
occupet ablutum scabrosa sorde nitorem,
catholico in templo divini fontis ad aram
consecrat, aeterna splendens ubi luce coruscet. (98–108)

These lines' primary intertextual referent is Matthew 19:12, which urges those unmarried men who can do so to make themselves eunuchs for the kingdom of heaven. Prudentius, however, represents this step as a universal Christian duty rather than an elite vocation, redefining the Roman virtue of married chastity as complete sexual abstinence. By washing her sword in the Jordan, Chastity defines the renunciation of masculine sexuality as the completion or perfection of baptism.[59] Implicitly, all true Christians are celibate. At the same time, the *Psychomachia* recognizes the magnitude of the celibate's loss by depicting the phallus in exalted terms, "shin[ing] and flash[ing] with unfading light." While the penis is flesh, and must be despised as such, the phallus, once separated from it, can shine eternally as a gift to God; this gift recalls and fulfills Abraham's circumcision and sacrifice of Isaac. It is through this shared sacrifice, moreover, that the masculine reader of the *Psychomachia* joins Chastity in her victory. In doing so, he changes not only his gender identity but also his status, from person to personification. In understanding himself as feminine, he achieves the virtue of chastity, while in becoming a personification he internalizes the paradigm of virtue in general. Importantly, this dynamic obtains whether the imagined object of the reader's desire is feminine, as suggested by the gender of the personification Sodomitic Lust, or masculine, as suggested by her unusual double name, with its reference to the destruction of Sodom in the Abrahamic section of Genesis.

Prudentius thereby figures transgender self-personification as an inclusive antidote to all forms of masculine sexuality, including same-sex desire.

The combat between Sobriety and Indulgence (Luxuria) replays, either ritually or obsessively, important aspects of the battle between Chastity and Sodomitic Lust. Although Lewis defines Luxuria as "the sin of the profiteer," seeking to distinguish her from medieval personifications of Lust with the same name, she in fact represents all forms of sensual indulgence.[60] As such, she wages a "new kind of warfare" (nova pugnandi species), riding onto the battlefield in a chariot that—like the arena in which the Virtues fight—evokes a historically specific *Romanitas* (323). As Nugent points out, Indulgence's appearance parodies a Roman triumphal procession even as, by throwing flowers at the Virtues, she seduces them into believing they have already defeated the Vices and can relax their guard.[61] Her attack takes place simultaneously on the field of battle and in a "ganea" or "lupanar," the former ambiguously an eating house or house of ill repute, the latter explicitly a brothel (343, 378). When the Virtues enter Indulgence's "madidum . . . lupanar," her moist or drunken den, they are not only seduced into laying down their arms but also startlingly assume male bodies, undergoing what Van Dyke calls "sex change on the battlefield."[62] As they prepare to abandon their vows of chastity, the Virtues abandon their figurative female bodies in favor of literal male ones. In doing so, they cease to be Virtues, both because they are no longer virtuous and because they are no longer feminine personifications. In contrast to the weak and generically feminine flesh described by Chastity, which allowed them to channel divine *virtus*, the ex-Virtues are suddenly powerful in a way that Pride would recognize, with "bulging, iron-hard muscles" (ferratos . . . toros), "stout arms" (rigidas . . . ulnas), and even "manly hair" (caesariem . . . virilem) (331, 357, 358). This metamorphosis suggests that, in retrospect, we must understand the Virtues' female bodies as having been voluntarily assumed, a product of the willed renunciation of masculine sexuality commemorated by Chastity. Prudentius's feminine personifications of Virtue represent the better selves, the consciously reformed second natures, of men who revert to their first natures as they fall into sin.

In a seeming paradox, Sobriety condemns this abandonment of voluntary femininity as itself feminizing. Even as the erstwhile Virtues' stout arms and manly hair become visible, Sobriety warns that they are being softened by Indulgence's blandishments:

> What bonds are these (for shame!) you long to bear on arms that were meant for weapons, these yellow garlands interspersed with bright lil-

> ies, these wreaths blooming with red-hued flowers? Is it to chains like these you will give up hands trained to war, with these bind your stout arms, to have your manly hair confined by a gilded turban with its yellow band to soak up the spikenard you pour on?

> Quae vincula tandem,
> pro pudor, armigeris amor est perferre lactertis,
> lilia luteolis interlucentia sertis
> et ferrugineo vernantes flore coronas?
> his placet adsuetas bello iam tradere palmas
> nexibus, his rigidas nodis innectier ulnas,
> ut mitra caesariem cohibens aurata virilem
> conbibat infusum croceo religamine nardum. (352–59)

Nugent notes that these taunts are derived from the accusations of eastern effeminacy hurled against Aeneas and his son Ascanius in the *Aeneid*.[63] Here, they suggest that the gender identity of the ultramasculine warrior—the possessor of *virtus* as defined by Pride—is inherently unstable. Because this seeming *virtus* is located in the body, it easily succumbs to Indulgence's sensual pleasures. Leading the ex-Virtues into her *lupanar*, and offering up her body as if it were the spoils of war, Indulgence contaminates Roman masculinity with an exotic femininity that spreads through the opposing army in the manner of a sexually transmitted disease, first changing feminine personifications into virile males, and then changing those virile males into effeminate ones. This dynamic paradoxically implies that the only true and stable masculinity is the voluntary assumption of a figuratively female body. From Prudentius's point of view, such transgendering appropriately subordinates feminine flesh to masculine spirit even as it piously recognizes humanity's weakness—and thus femininity—relative to Christ's *vera virtus*. Less piously, Indulgence facilitates a sneak peek at the Virtues' hypermasculine bodies that might reassure anxious readers. The Virtues' "iron-hard muscles" make it clear that they renounce their robustly physical masculinity as an act of piety rather than because they are "naturally" effeminate men for whom transgender identification represents no great sacrifice. This same logic underlies the earlier suggestion that Sodomitic Lust is raped to death: Chastity demonstrates the potency of his/her sword before renouncing it.

While Indulgence allows readers a voyeuristic glimpse of the Virtues' male bodies, Sobriety's countermeasures suggest practical steps for becoming—or becoming once again—a feminine personification of virtue.

Although all of the Vices are characterized by thoughtlessness, and especially by a lack of self-awareness, Indulgence carries this trait so far that she is virtually a somnambulist or automaton. As described by Sobriety, "The purpose of [Indulgence's] life is . . . to weaken her nerveless intellect . . . and to disperse her fractured understanding" (Vitae cui causa . . . elumbem mollire animum . . . et fractos solvere sensus), so that she rides to war, still drunk from the night before, in a chariot she cannot control (313–15). Fittingly, Sobriety's antidote to this mindless Vice is memory. Lamenting that with their "disordered minds" (insanas . . . mentes) the former Virtues have already come to resemble Vices, she exhorts them, "Remember who you are, and remember Christ too!" (Vestri memores, memores quoque Christi!) (351, 381). Sobriety seeks to reintegrate her allies' selves, to reestablish the supremacy of their minds over their bodies, by asking them to remember their own personal histories, and especially their own baptisms (351–70). Inseparably, she demands that they remember what they have read, a sacred history of sober living and divine reward that stretches back to Exodus (371–76). In order to regain their status as personified Virtues, Sobriety's allies must recollect and collate Old Testament examples that can recall them to their better selves, not only Moses but also David, Samuel, and Jonathan. These extracts or summaries are to become part of the warriors' selves, reordering their minds and making them good sons to their textual "fathers" (patribus) (372). For Sobriety herself, this integration is so thorough that biblical history is no longer distinguishable from personal or family history, with the newly baptized entering the textual order "after signs are inscribed on their brows with oil" (post inscripta oleo frontis signacula) (360). The formation of a textual self, in which scriptural tradition has the same intimate status as personal memory, becomes a prerequisite for self-personification.

The fact that all of this occurs while Sobriety's allies are still men suggests, however, that it is merely a beginning—as does the ultimately unstable virtue of the Old Testament exemplars she invokes. By this point in the poem, genealogy is an inherently suspect model for the transmission of virtue, associated with both Judaism and pagan *Romanitas*—and so, too, is exemplarity. Neither the Israelites who grumble in the wilderness nor David who covets Bathsheba nor Jonathan who tastes the honeycomb can uncomplicatedly represent sobriety. Sobriety's allies do not actually regain their status as "Virtues" (Virtutibus) until she defeats Indulgence with her jeweled cross, holding it before her horses so that they panic, overturn their chariot, and crush their mistress (404). The cross recalls the baptismal "signaculum" that supersedes the Old Testament "signaculum" of circumcision, once again associating virtuous personification with the New Dispensation.

PERFORMING PERSONIFICATION

The Virtues' reversion to male bodies in the Indulgence episode suggests an important quality of Prudentius's formative personifications: they are not fixed identities but ongoing operative pursuits. The ensuing battle between Avarice and Works invites readers to consider the practical, active dimension of personification in greater detail. The Virtues' attention to process enables them to counter the Vices as they change over time, including when they disguise themselves as Virtues. More fundamentally, it defends them against accusations of idolatry by defining them as models to be emulated rather than images to be worshipped. This lesson is particularly appropriate to the battle between Avarice and Works because, as we have seen, Prudentius depicts Avarice as a Ciceronian "abomination," strongly associated with Bellona and the Furies, who stands at the head of a troupe of wrongly deified abstractions. Her characteristic hoarding is itself a form of idolatry, as she accumulates wealth for its own sake rather than for use. Works, in contrast, cannot be worshipped as an idol because she is what she does, and she cannot be idolatrous because she assigns no fetishistic value to material objects. By clarifying this crucial distinction between Prudentius's Christian formative personifications and their classical predecessors, Works sets the stage for Wisdom's triumphant enthronement at the end of the poem.

Avarice owes her rise to Sobriety's slaying of Indulgence. When Indulgence's followers flee the battlefield, they leave behind a series of material signs of self-indulgence: "a hairpin, ribbons, fillets, a brooch, a veil, a breast-band, a coronet, a necklace" (crinalis acus, redimicula, vittae, / fibula, flammeolum, strophium, diadema, monile) (448–49). In obedience to the Old Testament strictures against plunder she has just cited, Sobriety lets these fripperies lie. Because she operates according to a relatively simple logic, understanding the spoils left by Indulgence's army exclusively as vain personal ornaments, she cannot anticipate their conversion into economic assets. Avarice, in contrast, cannot see the spoils as anything else. Her own governing logic understands everything, including family relationships, in economic terms. Under her aegis one brother slays another to steal his armor, a son strips his father's corpse of valuables, and the parents Love of Possession (Amor Habendi) and Unnatural Hunger (Famis Inpia) rob their own offspring. While Indulgence prizes wealth because it furnishes her with material comforts and personal adornments, Avarice prizes it for its own sake, hoarding it rather than using it and valuing it more highly than any human relationship.

This single-minded devotion to wealth allows Avarice to elude Reason, the first Virtue to take to the field against her, by disguising herself as Thrifty. Having already sponsored fratricide and poisoned her own children, Avarice does not hesitate to slough off her identity:

> She puts off her grim look and her fiendish weapons, and changes to a noble appearance [*habitus*]; in her deportment, with austere mien and dress, she becomes the Virtue men call Thrifty, whose pleasure is to live sparingly and save what she has; she looks as if she never snatched aught with greedy hands, and with her air of carefulness she has gained repute for the quality she counterfeits.

> Torvam faciem furaliaque arma
> exuit inque habitum sese transformat honestum;
> fit Virtus specie vultuque et veste severa
> quam memorant Frugi, parce cui vivere cordi est
> et servare suum; tamquam nil raptet avare,
> artis adumbratae meruit ceu sedula laudem. (551–56)

Habitus—from *habere*, to have—can be either superficial or existential; it can refer either to one's usual garment or to one's moral character, even one's "acquired perfect state or condition."[64] Avarice understands the term in the former sense. She "has" one set of clothing and accouterments as Avarice and exchanges them for the distinctive garments of the Roman matron in order to redefine herself as Thrifty. Reduced to commodities, clothes no longer have any special or habitual relation to their wearer and can be donned and doffed at will. The marks of matronly respectability thus become a mere costume, while Avarice's maltreated children become stage props, allowing her to "hide her snaky tresses with a delicate covering of motherly devotion" (tenero pietatis tegmine crines / obtegit anguinos) and "display her plundering and thieving and greedy storing of her gains under the pleasing name of care for her children" (quod rapere et clepere est avideque abscondere parta, / natorum curam dulci sub nomine iactet) (559–60, 562–63).[65] By so disguising herself, Avarice confounds Reason and the rest of the Virtuous army. With even the names and attributes that traditionally define personification allegory no longer to be trusted, "the Virtues' line falters; for they are misled by the monster's bi-form figure" (nutabat Virtutum acies errore biformis / portenti) (569–70). As in their earlier encounter with Indulgence, the Virtues lose the ability to distinguish virtue from vice and so cease to function as personifications. There, they followed Indulgence by abandoning willed action in favor of passive pleasure, relinquishing their feminine personified bodies in favor of literal male ones. Here, the conflict turns on the definition of personification itself. Is it a matter of accouterments, or of actions?

Prudentius's response to the Virtues' paralysis is the specifically Christian Works (Operatio), who succeeds and punningly subsumes within herself the lesser and more ecumenical Reason (Ratio).[66] Where H. J. Thompson translates Operatio as "Good Works," Van Dyke prefers the more neutral "conduct," suggesting that, as "the practical fulfillment of principles," Operatio is qualitatively different from her sisters.[67] I see Works as the *Psychomachia*'s most focused representation of virtuous action just as Chastity is its most focused representation of virginity—even as, for Prudentius, both qualities remain essential components of virtue in general. Works, therefore, should be seen as clarifying the distinction between Prudentius's newly personified Virtues and the older form of personification represented by his Vices. Whereas Avarice understands *habitus* as the things she has, Works represents it as a moral disposition arising from repeated acts. Specifically, the repeated act of distributing her possessions to the poor has rendered Works at once thoroughly virtuous and—like Faith—heroically naked:

> Every load she had cast off from her shoulders, and she moved along naked of all coverings; of many a burden had she lightened herself, for once she had been borne down by riches and the weight of money, but now had freed herself by taking pity on the needy, whom she had cared for with kindly generosity, lavishing her patrimony with a wise prodigality.
>
> Omne onus ex umeris reiecerat, omnibus ibat
> nudata induviis multo et se fasce levarat,
> olim divitiis gravibusque oppressa talentis,
> libera nunce miserando inopum, quos larga benigne
> foverat effundens patrium bene prodiga censum. (577–81)

For Avarice, *habitus* is a superficial covering, indeed a disguise, while for Works it is produced by action, and so irreducibly personal. Because Works' *habitus* is precisely her lack of clothing, there is no way for Avarice to imitate it without revealing her true nature, the "naked truth" of her identity. Works defines herself as Avarice's opposite, regardless of appearance, because the former rakes in wealth, concentrating it in her person, while the latter gives it away, distributing it to the poor. Clothing and even demeanor can be falsified, but Works' consistent pattern of action—and the heroic nudity that results from it—cannot be.

This definitive representation of the form of Christian personification has immediate repercussions. Works' appearance on the battlefield paralyzes Avarice, confounding her just as she earlier confounded the Virtues. Indeed, Avarice and Works are so strongly antithetical that Avarice all but ceases to exist before Works strikes a single blow: "Cold with terror, no longer mistress of herself, her senses benumbed, Avarice could not move, and knew her doom had come" (Inpos / mentis Avaritia stupefactis sensibus haesit / certa mori) (584–86). When Works does finally engage her opponent, this "strongest Virtue" (Virtus fortissima), made powerful through constant exercise, simply "sets upon her with the iron grip of her arms and strangles her" (duris / ulnarum nodis, obliso et gutture frangit), depersonifying her through the sheer force of her being (589–90). Works disposes of the spoils that baffled Sobriety just as she disposed of her own patrimony, stripping them of their vicious power by transforming them into alms. Then she urges the rest of the virtuous army to follow her example, citing an array of gospel verses in support of her position. Christians who give away their wealth until they have no more will become Works and defeat Avarice, in the process acquiring a *habitus* of charity to replace the garments and ornaments they relinquish. For Prudentius, this "wise prodigality" goes to the heart of the difference between pagan and Christian virtue, as well as between pagan and Christian personification allegory. Where generous pagans plan a stable program of giving, balancing income and expenditures, generous Christians give until, having nothing left, they become personifications of Virtue. This genuine transformation into personified Virtue at once replicates and puts to shame Avarice's seeming transformation into Thrifty. As a Ciceronian abomination disguised as a Virtue, Avarice attempts to trick her followers into idolatrous worship. As a true Virtue, in contrast, Works derives both her power and her identity from repeating virtuous acts until she has, and is, nothing else. In so doing, she teaches the rest of the Virtues how to regain their status as full-fledged personifications, while promising readers of the *Psychomachia* that they, too, can form themselves as virtuous personifications by repeating virtuous acts.

Although in the main body of the *Psychomachia* each Virtue is defined by its own distinctive moral *habitus*, at the very end of the poem, just as allegorical action gives way to transcendent vision, at least one figure follows Works' advice. When Faith slays the first vice, Worship of the Old Gods, she appears to be first among equals, establishing the poem's pattern of individual battles between logically opposed pairs of Virtues and Vices. When she returns at the end to destroy Discord, however, she is abruptly characterized as "queen of the Virtues" (Virtutum . . . regina) (716). Just as Abraham prospectively generates a conceptual framework for the Virtues, so Faith does the same retrospectively, as Prudentius reveals all the Virtues to be, twice over, consequences or ramifications of faithfulness. At the same time, the victories of the individual, lesser Virtues elevate Faith to her new position, completing her just as she, in the final building of a temple to the Christlike Wisdom, completes the work of Abraham. While the logic of Abrahamic "resculpting" might initially seem to be diffuse, producing a potentially infinite array of personified Virtues, it ultimately generates a newly powerful and unified self that is prepared to welcome Christ. We see this unity most clearly at the very end of the poem, when Prudentius specifies that the temple to Wisdom is adorned with "a great pearl costing a thousand talents, to buy which Faith had boldly sold at auction all her substance and her property" (mille talentis / margaritum ingens, opibusque et censibus hastae / addictis, animosa Fides mercata pararat) (872–74). Just as Works incorporates or subsumes Reason into her more powerful vice-fighting logic, so Faith would seem to incorporate or subsume Works. Already allied with Works through shared heroic nudity, Faith becomes Works, according to Works' own definition of virtue, when she divests herself of all her property. On a doctrinal level, this act joins faith with works as a prerequisite to salvation, in keeping with James 2:26: "Faith without works is dead" (Fides sine operibus mortua est).

On a rhetorical level, it transforms the poem's personification allegory. Faith is the last of the militant Virtues to remain "on stage" at the end of the *Psychomachia*, and divesting herself of her possessions is her last act as a personification. But her disappearance (or her union with Works and the other Virtues) coincides with the sudden appearance of another queen of the Virtues, who reigns from the throne that Faith has just constructed. Van Dyke suggests that Wisdom is the key to understanding all of Prudentius's personifications: "If Sapientia is a name for Christ, perhaps all the virtues are ultimately versions of him."[68] This characterization, however, equates what I have been arguing are two distinct types of personification. Although the *Psychomachia*'s Virtues are generated by the typological allegory of its preface and culminate in the Neoplatonic allegory of its conclusion, they collapse into neither. Wisdom's almost architectural stability would be fatal to the personified Virtues, who devolve into mere persons as soon as they cease struggling against Vice. Moving between foreground and background, their power and authority confined to a particular, delimited sphere, the Virtues are also partial, even unstable, in a way that the Christlike Wisdom is not. They are engines for the active performance of virtue rather than representations of virtue as a fait accompli. Prudentius's formative personifications resemble Barbara Newman's Platonic ones insofar as their obligatory femininity marks them as a subordinate form of divinity, affording them latitude for experimentation within "a comparatively safe space for the imaginative exploration of Christian faith."[69] In the *Psychomachia*, however, this femininity is visibly assumed or performed, falling away to reveal "manly hair" and "bulging, iron-hard muscles" as soon as the Virtues slacken in their fight against Vice. Although Prudentius's Virtues come into being with the Incarnation, they are not primarily brides or daughters of God: their formal relation to Christ is of deployed subordinates to an absent military commander. They read scripture carefully and invoke it polemically but are not constructed from it as Wisdom is. Instead, they are heroic in the manner of the lower deities of the classical world, larger than life but not set apart from humanity in a transcendent realm. Indeed, humans can become virtuous personifications and virtuous personifications can become human, depending on their spiritual condition. Prudentius even suggests that one cannot become a full-fledged Christian without also becoming a feminine personification of virtue, repeating virtuous actions in the manner of Works until they become a *habitus*.

Although Prudentius's formative personifications ultimately turn into or are subsumed within the Neoplatonic Wisdom, this transformation occurs outside of historical time. As we have seen, the main action of the *Psychomachia* takes place within an arena that is specifically and historically Roman. Faith fights alongside martyrs whom she crowns in victors' purple; Indulgence in her chariot parodies a Roman triumph; Discord—or, to use her full Roman *nomen* and *cognomen*, Discord Heresy (Discordia Heresis)—threatens both the unity of the human self and the unity of the church as a historically embedded institution. When the Virtues falter, they become ordinary human males, wearing ordinary human clothing. Wisdom's temple, in contrast, is quite literally built out of prophecy, woven together from verses in the book of Revelation describing the New Jerusalem. The collective victory of the Virtues, represented in linear terms in the body of the poem, with plenty of dramatic reversals and opportunities for mutual aid, does not become Wisdom's unitary triumph until the end of time. Within time, the individual Virtues are specifically designed to facilitate the human performance of virtue. As engines of struggle rather than stable representations of eternal verities, they allow for adaptation and experimentation in response to culturally specific, and thus ever-shifting, enticements to sin. The Virtues accordingly function, both individually and collectively, as affective and cognitive machines of the mind. They are dynamic thought experiments or moral prostheses—and it is precisely this dynamism that sets them apart from Wisdom and allows them to prevail over the personified Vices in this world.

As formative personifications, the *Psychomachia*'s Virtues and Vices have their roots in classical religious and rhetorical personification. As we have seen, Prudentius's Vices are modeled on the negative deified abstractions of the Greco-Roman world. Like Cicero, Prudentius seeks to undo their wrongful deification, attacking them not only as representations of Lust, Pride, Avarice, and the like, but also as personifications. I have argued that these two-pronged attacks produce the *Psychomachia*'s distinctive pattern of violence, with each Vice suffering the consequences of her particular sin alongside depersonifying injuries to her face and vocal apparatus. When she dies, the power of speech that marks her status as a personification passes to the Virtue who defeats her, signaling the ascendance of a new, specifically Christian, variety of formative personification allegory. Prudentius assembles and defines this new form of personification over the course of his poem. As we have seen, his Virtues borrow their basic mode of operation from their classical predecessors: formed through self-conscious human rhetorical craftsmanship, they also form their followers to virtue. He attaches them, however, to the Christian tradition of allegorical exegesis, and specifically to the biblical Abraham as a site for allegorical self-formation. This genealogy authorizes Prudentius to "resculpt" the traditional type of faithfulness into the feminine personification Faith—and to invite his normatively masculine readers to imagine themselves as Faith, divesting themselves of their gender in the process. Prudentius goes on to define virtuous personification as specifically feminine and virginal, enabled by Mary's conception of the Word. Finally, he emphasizes that virtuous personification must be understood as a habitual practice rather than an essentialist identity or collection of attributes. Prudentius's Virtues thus resemble their classical predecessors insofar as they are both divine powers and carefully constructed machines for self-reformation but differ from them in their gender dynamics as well as in being habitual performances but not objects of worship.

This understanding of personification as an ongoing work of self-formation enables Prudentius's Virtues to combat a changing roster of Vices. The poem invites its readers to personify the Virtues they most need at any given moment and to shift from one to another as they fight to come to grips with new temptations. This flexibility recalls Cicero's approach to religious personification in *On the Laws,* which licenses the deification of new Virtues to meet new challenges. It also both anticipates and authorizes the medieval reception of the *Psychomachia,* in which authors routinely invent new personifications of Virtue in order to meet new religious needs.

PART II

Neoplatonic Personification

CHAPTER THREE

Ex Uno Omnia: Plato's Forms and Daemons

We have seen that, for most of the twentieth century, critics treated Platonic realism as the condition for all personification allegory. Although this stance is most strongly associated with early- and mid-century scholars such as Johan Huizinga, Angus Fletcher, and Owen Barfield, it also features prominently in more recent work by Sheila Delany and Gordan Teskey. In 2014, Jill Mann articulated an updated version of their position:

> Personification allegory . . . quasi-inevitably embodies a 'Platonizing' tendency. That is, it assumes or implies that abstractions such as Truth, Justice, Love, Hate, Pride, Avarice and the like are not mere words, but reflections of Ideas that have a real, albeit supra-sensible, existence. (Indeed in the Platonic view they have a *more* real existence than the phenomena of the concrete world that reflect them.) Personification allegory treats the linguistic existence of these entities as evidence of their *actual* existence, and makes their operation in the sensible world visible by linking these abstract nouns with concrete verbs.[1]

Insofar as Mann argues that the majority of medieval writers understood universals to be real rather than merely rhetorical, she is certainly correct. As we will see in chapter 5, even medieval *nominalistae* held that mental words refer naturally, rather than merely conventionally, to an objective reality. But insofar as she argues that all medieval personification allegory is specifically Platonic—and, even more precisely, refers directly to the Platonic forms—I believe she is mistaken. Her argument not only subsumes all personification under the banner of Platonic realism but also fails to interrogate Platonic realism itself. Throughout this book I take issue with the notion of an inevitable connection between the Platonic forms and personification, arguing that serious-minded personification allegory can imply a different metaphysics. While later chapters will make the case for a vibrant tradition of Aristotelian personification, the present chapter challenges the claim that Platonic personification necessarily seeks to represent the Platonic forms. Exploring the range of Neoplatonisms available to medieval authors, it argues for a greater diversity of Platonic personifications than has heretofore been acknowledged.

This chapter examines two main kinds of Platonic personification: those modeled on Plato's forms or ideas and those modeled on his daemons. Even the first of these categories, which I call "formal personification," admits a surprising degree of variety, corresponding to different strands of Platonic thought. Augustine, for instance, interprets the forms as attributes of God or ideas in the divine mind. He holds that, given the corruptibility of the senses in the postlapsarian world, humans can only attain knowledge insofar as their minds are illuminated by these ideas. I argue that these ideas correspond to a subset of formal personifications that are numinous rather than phenomenal and often explicitly the product of visionary experience. As one would expect, these numinous personifications are much better suited to representing positive qualities such as truth, justice, and love than negative qualities such as hate, pride, and avarice. Indeed, it is not clear that numinous personifications *can* represent negative qualities. As we will see, Augustine does not recognize hate, pride, and avarice as forms because he does not recognize them as attributes of God or ideas in the divine mind. He does not, in other words, treat "the linguistic existence of these entities as evidence of their *actual* existence." Another important strand of medieval Neoplatonism follows Cicero in holding that humans can gain knowledge of universals through philosophical dialectic. The corresponding subset of formal personifications likewise tends to be philosophical rather than mystical, associated with disputation rather than awe-inspiring visions. While still generally positive, these dialectical personifications tend to embody relatively worldly virtues such as eloquence rather than transcendent ones such as blessedness. Even though the two kinds of personification refer to Plato's forms, they represent both the forms themselves and their own truth claims in very different ways.

The second major group of Platonic personifications I consider does not refer to the forms at all but rather to daemons, figures intermediate between humans and the supreme deity in the Neoplatonic hierarchy of being. While Platonic writers usually associate the forms with the highest level of divinity—the *artifex* of Plato's *Timaeus*, the One of Plotinus's *Enneads*, Augustine's Christian God—the daemons' sphere of activity is decidedly more modest. As low-level divinities, they act as guardian spirits to individual human beings, accompanying them through life and leading them to judgment after death; they also exhibit a penchant for the ridiculous that originates with Plato himself. The figures I call "daemonic personifications" possess many of these same qualities. They tend to have an intimate, tutelary relationship with their human interlocutors, often claiming to have known them their entire lives and sometimes—as we will see in the next chapter with Boethius's Philosophy—standing ready to accompany them in death. While formal personifications are perfect like the forms themselves, daemonic personifications are frequently flawed and subject to vagaries. Because daemons are enmeshed in the classical pantheon in ways the Platonic forms are not—often rubbing shoulders with Olympian gods, deified heroes, and other classical divinities—they can also pose interpretive challenges for Christian writers. Where Augustine condemns daemons as agents of the devil, later Platonists such as William of Conches subject them to integumental allegorical reading. Although daemonic personifications have the same deep roots in the Platonic tradition as formal personifications, they do not look or behave in the ways most moderns expect.

PLATONIC FORMS AND PROSOPOPOEIA

The Platonic forms play a curious role in histories of medieval personification allegory. They are the grounds on which all medieval personifications are ostensibly built, yet they receive little critical attention. Although Huizinga and his immediate successors expressed considerable respect for classical traditions, they assumed that the medieval reception of those traditions was naïve and simpleminded. As a result, they concerned themselves with a naïve and simpleminded version of the Platonic forms rather than with their empirical reception. Later critics, including Delany and Teskey, dismissed both classical Platonism and its medieval inheritance as mere ideology—and therefore as something to be read past rather than investigated. One of this chapter's goals is to address this lacuna by offering a more detailed account of the history of the Platonic forms and their relationship to personification allegory. In tracing the paths by which medieval writers gained knowledge of the forms, I identify two distinct subtypes of formal personification. The first path, which descends to the Middle Ages via Augustine, produces the numinous personifications Barbara Newman discusses in *God and the Goddesses*. The second, which descends via Cicero, produces the less exalted, more philosophical personifications of medieval debate poetry. Even when these strands are reunited in the complex narrative allegories of the later Middle Ages, they remain distinguishable if not always distinct.

In the introduction to this book I argued that the stereotyped portrait of the "man of the Middle Ages" as a naïve realist is a modern invention. This argument certainly extends to the reception history of the Platonic forms. Awareness of the difficulties inherent in the doctrine of the forms begins with Plato himself. In his late dialogue *Parmenides*, Plato depicts Socrates as a promising young student who seeks to explain the doctrine of the forms to the renowned Eleatic philosophers Parmenides and Zeno of Elea. When Socrates cannot respond to Parmenides's searching questions, Parmenides outlines a pedagogical program designed to allow Socrates to defend the forms more successfully in the future. While the dialogue is not dismissive of the forms, it gives them the status of a promising hypothesis rather than patent truth. It also gives serious weight to Parmenides's unanswered questions, which go on to serve as the genesis for both Aristotle's critique of the forms in his *Metaphysics* and the influential series of questions at the beginning of Porphyry's *Isagoge*—both of which I will discuss in chapter 5. Although the *Parmenides* was available to the Middle Ages only indirectly, through William of Moerbecke's thirteenth-century translation of Proclus's commentary, Aristotle's *Metaphysics* was translated into Latin in the twelfth century, and throughout the Middle Ages Boethius's translation of and commentary on the *Isagoge* served as the standard introduction to the study of logic. Even the most ardent medieval realists, then, were familiar with *both* the Platonic theory of forms *and* the established classical critique of that theory. Nothing is more medieval than probing the problems and limits of realism.

This is not to deny that Plato's forms were profoundly influential or that they offer an important model for personification. The *Phaedo*, for instance, takes as its starting point precisely those ethical abstractions that predominate in personification allegory. This time speaking through the persona of a more mature Socrates, Plato emphasizes that these abstractions really exist even though they cannot be grasped by the senses:

> What about the following, Simmias? Do we say that there is such a thing as the Just itself, or not? / We do say so, by Zeus. / And the Beautiful, and the Good? / Of course. / And have you ever seen any of these things with your eyes? / In no way, he said. / Or have you ever grasped

> them with any of your bodily senses? I am speaking of all things such as Bigness, Health, Strength and, in a word, the reality of all other things, that which each of them essentially is. (65d–e)

Plato goes on to contrast these entities, which he calls *eide* (forms) or *ideai* (ideas), with the sensible things that resemble or partake of them. While the Just is a perfect paradigm, simple and changeless, each just man is an imperfect copy of that paradigm, both because he is made of imperfect matter and because he is subject to change and decay. Thus, where a form, in its simplicity, can only be predicated of itself (e.g., "Justice is just," "Largeness is large"), a particular can be predicated of many things (e.g., "Socrates is both just and mortal"). Even these statements are deceptive, however, because Justice "is" just differently than Socrates "is" just. Where Justice is inherently just, or just in its being, Socrates is just only insofar as he partakes of the form of Justice. As a result, Socrates's justice never perfectly coincides with the form.

Given this gulf between particular and universal, how do the two relate to each other?[2] In the *Phaedo*, Socrates uses the metaphors of paradigm and example, model and copy, original and image, with the particular in each case striving and yet failing to fully instantiate the universal. He does not, however, explain exactly what it *means* for a particular to participate in a universal, and this is a point on which the Socrates of the *Parmenides* also falters. To the extent that Plato answers this question, he does so in his *Timaeus*. Even here, however, he attributes his answer not to Socrates but to the narrator Timaeus of Locri, who carefully characterizes his explanation as speculation rather than truth: it is merely an account "no less likely" than any other (29c). With this caveat in place, Timaeus posits what he calls the "Receptacle":

> Not only does it always receive all things, it has never in any way whatever taken on any characteristic similar to any of the things that enter it. Its nature is to be available for anything to make its impression upon, and it is modified, shaped and reshaped by the things that enter it. These are the things that make it appear different at different times. The things that enter and leave it are imitations of those things that always are, imprinted after their likeness in a marvelous way that is hard to describe. (50b–c)

Marvelous and mysterious, the Receptacle is knowable primarily through its effect, its ability to produce material copies of immaterial forms. It follows that it is itself neither form nor instantiation but situated in every way between them. Timaeus goes on to liken "the receiving thing to a mother, the source to a father, and the nature between them to their offspring," transforming the dyad of universal and particular into a family triangle (50d). This metaphor insinuatingly domesticates the relationship between universal and particular, aligning the indescribable Otherness of the Receptacle with the more familiar Otherness of the wife and mother.

While Plato acknowledges, in both the *Timaeus* and the *Parmenides*, that the relationship between particulars and universals represents the weak link in his theory of forms, he does define concrete ways in which individuals can come to know the forms. The first and most fundamental path is through recollection: having dwelt in the separate realm of the forms before being incarnated into a human body, the soul can remember this early experience if it systematically frees itself from earthly attachments (*Phaedo* 73–80). In the *Republic,* members of the elite guardian class also achieve knowledge of the forms through a disciplined program of study. In the first stage of higher education, the guardians investigate from hypotheses, using particular images to understand forms such as Square and Diagonal. From here, their souls proceed to the final stage of knowledge, defined as "that which reason itself grasps by the power of the dialectic" (511b). The soul uses these hypotheses to "reach the unhypothetical first principle of everything," then "comes down to a conclusion without making use of anything visible at all, but only of forms themselves, moving on from forms to forms, and ending in forms" (511b–c). Members of the guardian class accordingly come to know the forms through a philosophical practice modeled on that of Socrates and enacted in the dialogic structure of Plato's own works.

While in the *Republic* this knowledge of the forms requires a complete rejection of the visible world, in the *Timaeus* it depends to an important extent on empirical observation. The dialogues' different approaches to astronomy are a case in point. The *Republic* characteristically recommends the study of astronomy as a mathematical discipline, instructing budding astronomers to "leave the things in the sky alone" (530b–c). In the *Timaeus,* in contrast, observational astronomy offers a privileged route to knowledge of the forms:

> As my account has it, our sight has indeed proved to be a source of supreme benefit to us, in that none of our present statements about the universe could ever have been made if we had never seen any stars, sun or heaven. As it is, however, our ability to see the periods of day-and-

> night, of months and of years, of equinoxes and solstices, has led to the invention of number, and has given us the idea of time and opened the path to inquiry into the nature of the universe. These pursuits have given us philosophy, a gift from the gods to the mortal race whose value neither has been nor ever will be surpassed. (47a–b)

Here the celestial bodies do not distract from the forms but rather lead the way to them via a step-by-step ascent that passes through the forms of number and time on the way to an investigation of the nature of the universe. Instead of resting on a rejection of the senses, this sequence of increasingly intellectual perceptions begins with physical sight, and indeed constitutes "the supreme good our eyesight offers us" (47b). It also represents a progressive awareness of a person's place in the world. For Timaeus, the spherical human head reproduces the perfect shape of the celestial bodies, while the eye, which emits beams of fire, is specifically modeled after the sun. To study the skies is thus to come to see oneself as a microcosm of the heavenly macrocosm, and eventually to see the heavens themselves as copies of the invisible forms. Such study progresses, seemingly naturally, to the contemplation of divine gifts, and ultimately to the contemplation of divinity itself. In the *Timaeus*, observation of the natural world thus leads, in a series of upward steps, first to knowledge of the forms, then to knowledge of oneself, and finally to knowledge of the Demiurge, or Craftsman God. While in this account the forms are perhaps easier to know than in the *Phaedo* or the *Republic*, they have also ceased to be the highest object of human knowledge. This discrepancy can be explained in part by the fact that the *Timaeus* concerns itself only with the forms of material objects, making no mention of forms of immaterial things such as Justice, Beauty, and the Good.

I have emphasized the *Timaeus* in part because of its relative accessibility to medieval writers, via Calcidius's partial translation. Plato's other accounts of the forms were transmitted primarily through a tradition of oral teaching, philosophical digests, and commentaries. Since these later Platonists treat Plato's work as a means of discovering truth rather than a historical artifact, their accounts mix Stoic and Aristotelian elements with various strands of Platonism.[3] Nevertheless, Latin writers including Cicero, Augustine, and Calcidius define universals within a clearly recognizable Platonic tradition. In a wide-ranging study of the sources of medieval Neoplatonism, Stephen Gersh describes Cicero's philosophy as a synthesis of the teachings of the New and Old Academies, both of which claimed Plato as their founder.[4] During Cicero's lifetime, the New Academy dominated, having developed Plato's insistence on the unreliability of sense perception into the full-blown Skepticism embodied by Cotta in *On the Nature of the Gods*. For these Skeptics, neither empirical observation nor philosophical dialectic could lead to knowledge. When studying in Athens, Cicero also attended the lectures of Antiochus of Ascalon, who sought to revive the Platonism of the ancient Academy, understood as largely consonant with the Stoic and Peripatetic schools. This study seems to have motivated Cicero's translations of Plato's *Protagoras* and part of the *Timaeus* into Latin.[5] The approaches of the two Academies were compatible to a certain extent. Although Skeptics denied the possibility of certain knowledge, they did recognize the possibility of true belief and understood some doctrines to be more probable than others. Cicero himself seems to have placed the greatest faith in a synthesis of Platonism and Stoicism. We have seen that, at the end of *On the Nature of the Gods*, his authorial persona endorses the doctrine of the Stoic Balbus with a suitably skeptical disclaimer of certainty: "I felt [the discourse] of Balbus approximated more nearly to a semblance of the truth." Compared to Plato's, Cicero's account of the forms is generally more provisional and less certain that it is possible to know, rather than merely approximate, a given form.

Cicero's most sustained and explicit treatment of universals occurs in his *Orator*. In this late work, addressed to an audience of young men who criticize his rhetorical style, Cicero shifts from the religious and rhetorical model of personification discussed in chapter 1 to a model based on the Platonic forms, as I will discuss below. His initial discussion of the forms is worth quoting at length because it captures a number of important developments within the Platonic tradition:

> In delineating [*fingendo*] the perfect orator I shall be portraying such a one as perhaps has never existed. . . . But I am firmly of the opinion that nothing of any kind is so beautiful as not to be excelled in beauty by that of which it is a copy, as a mask is a copy of a face. This ideal cannot be perceived by the eye or ear, nor by any of the senses, but we can nevertheless grasp it by the mind and the imagination. For example, in the case of the statues of Phidias, the most perfect of their kind that we have ever seen, and in the case of the paintings I have mentioned, we can, in spite of their beauty, imagine something more beautiful. Surely that great sculptor [*artifex*], while making the image of Jupiter or Minerva, did not look at any person whom he was using as a model, but in his own mind there dwelt a surpassing vision of beauty [*species pulchritudinis*]; at this he gazed and all intent on

> this he guided his artist's hand to produce the likeness of the god. Accordingly, as there is something perfect and surpassing in the case of sculpture and painting—an intellectual ideal [*speciem*] by reference to which the artist represents those objects which do not themselves appear to the eye, so with our minds we conceive the ideal [*speciem*] of perfect eloquence, but with our ears we catch only the copy. These patterns [*formas*] of things are called ιδεαι or ideas by Plato, that eminent master and teacher both of style and of thought; these, he says, do not "become"; they exist for ever, and depend on intellect and reason; other things come into being and cease to be, they are in flux and do not remain in the same state. Whatever, then, is to be discussed rationally and methodically, must be reduced to the ultimate form and type [*formam speciemque*] of its class.
>
> Ego in summo oratore fingendo talem informabo qualis fortasse nemo fuit. . . . Sed ego sic statuo, nihil esse in ulle genere tam pulchrum, quo non pulchrius id sit unde illud ut ex ore aliquo quasi imago exprimatur. Quod neque oculis neque auribus neque ullo sensu percipi potest, cogitatione tamen et mente complectimur. Itaque et Phidiae simulacris, quibus nihil in illo genere perfectius videmus, et eis picturis quas nominavi cogitare tamen possumus pulchriora. Nec vero ille artifex cum faceret Iovis formam aut Minervae, contemplabatur aliquem e quo similitudinem duceret, sed ipsius in mente insidebat species pulchritudinis eximia quaedam, quam intuens in eaque defixus ad illius similitudinem artem et manum dirigebat. Ut igitur in formis et figuris est aliquid perfectum et excellens, cuius ad cogitatam speciem imitando referuntur ea quae sub oculos ipsa non cadunt, sic perfectae eloquentiae speciem animo videmus, effigiem auribus quaerimus. Has rerum formas appellat ιδεας ille non intelligendi solum sed etiam dicendi gravissimus auctor et magister Plato, easque gigni negat et ait semper esse ac ratione et intellegentia contineri; cetera nasci, occidere, fluere, labi, nec diutius esse uno et eodem statu. Quicquid est igitur de quo ratione et via disputetur, id est ad ultimam sui generis formam speciemque redigendum. (*Orator* 2.7–3.10)

Despite some important changes, Plato's doctrine of the forms is immediately recognizable. Transcendent, eternal, and unchangeable, available to the intellect rather than the senses, the form of Beauty—in Latin, its *forma* or *species*—serves as the paradigm for all beautiful objects, which imitate it but inevitably fall short of its perfection. The means by which people come to know Beauty, however, have shifted. Where Plato in the *Republic* dismisses mimetic art as the copy of a copy, "at the third remove from that which is," Cicero describes artists as having special access to the forms (598e). In characterizing the sculptor Phidias as an "artifex," he recalls Plato's metaphorical use of the term in the *Timaeus*, where the Craftsman God fashions the physical universe according to the paradigm of the forms.[6] Cicero's human artist thus reenacts, in microcosm, the work of the Platonic Demiurge, not creating *ex nihilo* in the manner of the Christian deity but imparting an approximation of form to inchoate matter. This valorization of the artist leads Cicero to a revised understanding of Plato himself, whom he characterizes as an artist as well as a philosopher—specifically, as a master of Cicero's own art of rhetoric. While philosophical dialectic remains a privileged route to knowledge of the forms, it shares that status with a process internal to the mind of the artist, which Cicero describes as intently gazing upon or contemplating a given form.

For Cicero, moreover, the forms do not seem to exist in a separate realm of ideas, as they do for Plato, but rather within the mind of the human *artifex* ("ipsius in mente insidebat species"). This shift, typical among later Platonists, means that Cicero's forms are no longer substantial beings—that is to say, beings with a substance of their own, independent of any mind that might perceive them—but something closer to ideas in the modern English sense of the term. It follows that Cicero's artist must look inward rather than outward to achieve knowledge. Cicero thereby elevates knowledge of the self, already important in Plato's Socratic dialogues, from a means to an end. The artist contains within himself everything he needs to know, if only he can perceive it. At the same time, the relationship between the individual human *artifex* and the divine *artifex* suggests that Ciceronian forms also exist in the divine mind—a position that Cicero adopts explicitly in *On the Laws* (2.4).[7] By looking inward, the artist discovers not objective reality but an intrasubjective truth that brings him into alignment with the mind of the divine *artifex*. We can detect in Cicero's version of the forms a vestige of the Platonic doctrine of recollection, whereby the knowledge seeker looks within his own soul for memories or impressions of the forms, along with an echo of Socrates's suggestion in the *Parmenides* that the forms might, after all, be located in the human mind (132b–c). In other respects, however, Cicero departs from the main current of Plato's thought even as he cites Plato admiringly. His portrait of the philosopher-artist as the man who most closely approaches both the form of Man and knowledge of the forms differs strikingly from Plato's portrait of Socrates as the relentless dialectician.

Cicero not only links philosophy to rhetoric in general but also ties the Platonic forms specifically to the trope of prosopopoeia. Here, too, he may be interpreting the *Timaeus*. As we have seen, the *Timaeus* treats the Demiurge and the Receptacle as quasi-personifications, assigning them gender and familial relationships. Cicero takes this logic a step further by personifying an individual form. In the passage above, he invokes the forms to defend his decision to represent an ideal rather than empirical orator. Even after acknowledging that this Orator does not exist, however, he continues to describe him in personal terms. Indeed, it is possible to boil down the *Orator* to a list of things its titular personification does and does not do. Cicero introduces this personification with the verb *fingere*—meaning to mold or model, to form or fashion by art—thereby likening him to Phidias's statues of the gods. Just as Phidias looks inward to the *species* of Beauty to produce his images of Jupiter and Minerva, so Cicero looks inward to the *species* of Eloquence in order to fashion his Orator. This comparison suggests that the Orator is in some ways like a god—not a surprising association, given Cicero's linking of religious and rhetorical personification as discussed in chapter 1. At the same time, the Orator is specifically crafted to represent the Platonic form of Eloquence, which exceeds all human orators. Cicero activates both sets of connections when he likens the relationship between empirical orators and his personified Orator to that between a mask and a face. In this context, the mask simultaneously evokes the *prosopon* (face, mask) at the root of prosopopoeia and the death masks Roman households used to represent—and, on ritual occasions, to personify—the deified dead. Even as he likens the forms to the gods, then, Cicero suggests that prosopopoeia is the most appropriate way to represent them within the human realm.

Cicero returns to this topic, making the relationship between forms and personifications somewhat more explicit, in the portion of the *Orator* that circulated during in the Middle Ages as a composite with his earlier *On the Orator*.[8] Addressing himself directly to Brutus, his chief critic, he continues:

> We have him now, Brutus, him whom we seek, but in the mind rather than at hand. . . . Who is he, then? I will describe him briefly, and then expand the description at greater length. He is in fact eloquent who can discuss commonplace matters simply, lofty subjects impressively, and

> topics ranging between in a tempered style. You will say, "There never was such a man." I grant it; for I am arguing for my ideal, not what I have actually seen, and I return to that Platonic form [*formam et speciem*] of which I had spoken; though we do not see it, still it is possible to grasp it with the mind. For it in not as eloquent *person* whom I seek, not anything subject to death and decay, but that absolute quality, the possession of which makes a man eloquent. And this is nothing but abstract eloquence, which we can only behold with the mind's eye (italics in original).
>
> Tenemus igitur, Brute, quem quaerimus, sed animo non manu. . . . Quis est igitur is? Complectar brevi disseram pluribus. Is est enim eloquens qui et humilia subtiliter et alta graviter et mediocria temperate potest dicere. Nemo is, inquies, unquam fuit. Ne fuerit. Ego enim quid desiderem, non quid viderim disputo, redeoque ad illam Platonis de qua dixeram rei formam et speciem, quam etsi non cernimus tamen animo tenere possumus. Non enim eloquentem quaero neque quicquam mortale et caducum, sed illud ipsum, cuius qui sit compos, sit eloquens; quod nihil est aliud nisi eloquentia ipsa quam nullis nisi mentis oculis videre possumus. (*Orator* 28.100–29.101)

At once an animate agent and an abstraction, embodied and visible only to the mind's eye, the Orator violates binaries almost as quickly as Cicero can establish them. The only way to reconcile these contradictions, Cicero suggests, is to understand the Orator not as *eloquens* (eloquent) but as *Eloquentia* (Eloquence), with the distinction between present participle and abstract noun marking the shift not only from instantiation to form but also from person to personification. Prosopopoeia thus becomes a potent means of representing the forms within the human realm. It also gains a crucial pedagogical function. Although Cicero evidently classes himself among the elite artists who can perceive the forms merely by gazing inward, he suggests that the best way to describe Eloquence to those who cannot yet grasp it intellectually is through prosopopoeia. The organizing conceit of the *Orator* is that its titular personification will be able to lead Brutus toward the form of Eloquence in a way that Cicero's orations and earlier rhetorical treatises have been unable to do.

In fact, Cicero's *Orator* seems to introduce formal personification—that is, personification based on the Platonic forms—as a new kind of pedagogical tool. We have seen that in the classical rhetorical tradition the paradigmatic examples of personification are the dead and the state, the former associated with Greek and Roman ancestor cults, the latter with local divinities. Cicero promises to relinquish this traditional practice in the *Orator*, assuring Brutus that his title character "will not represent the state as speaking or call the dead from the lower world . . . for he will be rather subdued in voice as in style." While the traditional prosopopoeia of an ancestor, called into the world of the living to castigate his descendants, is apparently too dramatic for the Orator's modern world, personifications based on Platonic forms seem to be more decorous. They are certainly more restrained, since by definition a personification of Eloquence can do nothing but speak eloquently. Rather than rebuke living men, Cicero's Orator furnishes them with a positive model to emulate. For Cicero, then, formal Neoplatonic personification seems to offer an alternative to traditional rhetorical personification. As the embodiment of the perfect, unchanging ideal of Eloquence, the Orator stands above the vicious political feuds of the late Republic. At the same time, he remains close enough to human concerns to provide concrete guidance.

Although Cicero suggests that his formal personifications are more decorous than his earlier personified ancestors, they are not especially transcendent. Like most abstract Latin nouns, *eloquentia* is grammatically feminine. Cicero goes out of his way, however, to craft a personification of Eloquence whose gender mirrors that of human orators, understood in the Roman world as normatively as well as empirically masculine.[9] In doing so, he represents the differences between form and instantiation as quantitative rather than qualitative. By defining the form of Eloquence as that "which seldom if ever appears throughout a whole speech but does shine forth at some times and in some places, more frequently in some speakers, more rarely perhaps in others" (quod in perpetuitate dicendi non saepe atque haud scio an nunquam in aliqua autem parte eluceat aliquando, idem apud alios densius, apud alios fortasse rarius), Cicero suggests that most Roman men of good families, trained in the Republic's signature art of rhetoric, attain eloquence at least occasionally (*Orator* 2.7–8). A smaller number do so regularly, implicitly because, like Phidias and Cicero himself, they gaze at the form within themselves as they craft their orations. The *Orator* tacitly promises its readers the same level of mastery if they proceed through the text rationally and methodically. In this respect, Cicero's theory of the forms is decidedly worldly, outlining a relatively straightforward path to knowledge of the forms and positing a fairly small ontological gap between the forms and their material instantiations. This proximity between form and instantiation means that, among the versions of Neoplatonic personification I discuss, Cicero's comes closest to the formative personification described in the preceding chapters. Even Cicero's best orators, however, participate in Eloquence only intermittently. They do not conform themselves to Eloquence as an ongoing practice, in the way that Prudentius's virtuous Christians conform themselves to his Virtues.

Augustine's widely influential accounts of the forms draw heavily on Cicero, as well as on Plotinus and the so-called doxographical tradition of philosophical digests.[10] In contrast to Cicero's attempt to balance philosophical dialectic with inner vision, however, Augustine decisively emphasizes the latter. His initial definition of the forms in his *quaestio* "On Ideas (De Ideis)," often cited during the Middle Ages, is in many respects familiar.[11] Uncreated, eternal, immutable, and self-identical, the forms are contained in the divine mind and serve as the paradigm for the formation of transitory things (46.2).[12] Augustine's account is striking, however, for its attempt to decouple the forms from their Platonic origin. Arguing in characteristically Stoic fashion for the truth of widely held propositions, Augustine asserts that wise men of all nations have recognized the forms while calling them by various names:

> Plato is said to have been the first to use the name *ideas*. However, I do not mean to imply by this that, if there was no such name before he himself instituted it, there were accordingly no such things as those which he termed *ideas*, or that they were understood by no one. . . . For it is not likely either that there were no wise men before Plato or that they did not understand those things which, as was said, Plato termed ideas (whatever they might be), since indeed so great is the importance attaching to these ideas that no one can be wise without having understood them.

> Ideas Plato primus appellasse perhibetur. Non tamen si hoc nomen antequam ipse institueret non erat, ideo uel res ipsae non erant, quas ideas uocauit, uel a nullo erant intellectae . . . nam non est uerisimile sapienties aut nullos fuisse ante Platonem aut istas quas Plato, ut dictum est, ideas uocat, quaecumque res sint, non intellexisse, siquidem tanta in eis uis constituitur, ut non his intellectis sapiens esse nemo possit. (46.1)

This claim of nearly universal recognition allows Augustine to sanction the forms as a universal truth rather than the product of a historically specific pagan philosophical tradition. By transferring authority from Plato to the forms themselves, it also lays the groundwork for their Christianization.

Augustine's emphasis on the diversity of names for the forms opens the way for him to develop a specifically Christian philosophical vocabulary, characterizing the forms as *rationes* (reasons) in preference to both the Greek *ideai* and the classical Latin *formae* and *species*.[13] For Augustine, it is a matter of faith that God created the universe and did so rationally. It follows that God created the universe by means of *rationes*:

> Now what person, devout and trained in true religion . . . would dare to say that God has created all things unreasonably [*inrationabiliter*]? But if one cannot rightly say or believe this, it remains that all things are created according to reason [*ratione*], and that Man is not created according to the same reason [*ratione*] as Horse, for it is absurd to think this. Therefore specific things are created in accord with reasons [*rationibus*] unique to them. As for these reasons, they must be thought to exist nowhere but in the very mind of the Creator. For it would be sacrilegious to suppose that he was looking at something placed outside of himself when he created in accord with it what he did create.

> Quis autem religiosus et uera religione imbutus . . . audeat dicere deum inrationabiliter omnia condidisse? Quod si *recte dici* uel credi non potest, restat ut omnia ratione sint condita, nec eadem ratione homo qua equus; hoc enim absurdum est existimare. Singula igitur propriis sunt creata rationibus. Has autem rationes ubi esse arbitrandum est nisi in ipsa mente creatoris? Non enim extra se quidquam positum intuebatur, ut secundum id constitueret quod constituebat; nam hoc opinari sacrilegum est. (46.2; italics in original)

Although Augustine echoes the creation narrative in the *Timaeus*, in which the Demiurge uses the forms to guide his creation of the natural world, he follows Cicero and the doxographical tradition in locating these forms explicitly in the divine mind. By characterizing the forms as *rationes*, he suggests that they are God's thoughts, expressions of his perfect rationality that, in turn, furnish the paradigms for the created universe. Elsewhere, Augustine associates the forms specifically with Christ as the Word of God and the divine Wisdom.[14] In doing so, he resolves in theological though not philosophical terms the problem that had shadowed the forms since the *Parmenides*. As the mediator between God and men, participating in both of their natures, Christ becomes the inner teacher who allows Christians to know the true nature of horses and men despite the unreliability of their sense perceptions.

Even as Augustine calls the forms *rationes*, then, he makes it clear that humans cannot know the forms through reason alone. We have just seen that he asks most Christians to believe in the forms rather than know them. Because "every soul but the rational is denied the power to contemplate these [ideas]" (anima uero negatur eas intueri posse nisi rationalis), the vast majority of Christians have no choice but to accept them as part of their wider belief in God's rationality (46.2). Even among the philosophical elite, only a tiny subgroup will be granted a vision of the forms:

> And indeed, not any and every rational soul is prepared for that vision, but rather, the soul which is holy and pure. It is this soul which is claimed to be fit for that vision, i.e., which has that very eye with which the ideas are seen—an eye sound, pure, serene, and like those things which it endeavors to see. . . . Now among those things which have been created by God, the rational soul is the most excellent of all, and it is closest to God when it is pure. And in the measure that it has clung to him in love, in that measure, imbued in some way and illumined by him with light, intelligible light, the soul discerns—not with physical eyes, but with its own highest part in which lies its excellence, i.e. with its intelligence—those reasons [*rationes*] whose vision makes it fully blessed [*beatissima*].
>
> Et ea quidem ipsa rationalis anima non omnis et quaelibet, sed quae sancta et pura fuerit, haec asseritur illi uisioni esse idonea, id est quae illum ipsum oculum, quo uidentur ista, sanum et sincerum et serenum et similem his rebus, quad uidere intendit, habuerit . . . anima rationalis inter eas res, quae sunt a deo conditae, omnia superat et deo proxima est, quando pura est; eique in quantum caritate cohaeserit, in tantum ab eo lumine illo intellegibili perfusa quodammodo et inlustrata cernit non per corporeos oculos, sed per ipsius sui principale quo excellit, id est per intellegentiam suam, istas rationes, quarum uisione fit beatissima. (46.2)

Plato himself restricted knowledge of the forms to the rational and virtuous, and by Augustine's day this requirement had become a feature of the generalized Platonic tradition that Jean Pépin calls "platonisme banal."[15] No philosopher can hope to understand the forms if he is distracted by worldly concerns. Indeed, one of the indirect sources for Augustine's intelligible light is almost certainly the famous comparison between the sun and the Good in Plato's *Republic*. There, Socrates explains that "what the good itself is in the intelligible realm, in relation to understanding and intelligible things, the sun is in the visible realm, in relation to sight and visible things" (508b–c). In the *City of God*, Augustine explicitly equates God with the form of the Good, while comparing the divine Wisdom to the sun (11.10). But where Plato's Good is impersonal and can be approached through moral and intellectual discipline, Augustine's Good is personal and must be approached through prayer. The rational soul can know the forms only "in the measure that it has clung to [God] in love," to the exclusion of all else.

Another important source for Augustine's beatific vision is the passage from the *Phaedrus* in which Plato describes the happiness of human souls dwelling among the forms:

> Beauty was radiant to see at that time when the souls, along with the glorious chorus . . . saw that blessed and spectacular vision and were ushered into the mystery that we may rightly call the most blessed of all. . . . That was the ultimate vision, and we saw it in pure light because we were pure ourselves, not buried in this thing we are carrying around now, which we call a body, locked in it like an oyster in its shell. (250b–c)

Augustine knew this passage through a citation in Plotinus's *On Beauty*, which retains the scene's key elements but describes them prospectively rather than retrospectively.[16] Thus mediated, the beatific vision represents not the soul's origin but its telos, which it can only achieve by freeing itself from vice and making itself similar to the forms it seeks to understand.[17] This reorientation would have been crucial for Augustine, who as a Christian rejected Plato's doctrines of reincarnation and recollection. It also defers full or continuous knowledge of the forms to the afterlife, where beatific vision becomes a state of being. In the *City of God*, Augustine describes the redeemed soul as "enlightened by the incorporeal light of God's simple wisdom, just as the corporeal air is illuminated by corporeal light" (sic inluminari . . . luce incorporea simplicis sapientiae Dei, sicut inluminatur aeris corpus luce corporea) (11.10).[18] The soul is wise insofar as it is illuminated by the divine form of Wisdom, imperfectly and intermittently in this life, and then completely and eternally in the life to come.

Although Augustine's doctrine of divine illumination bridges the gap between universals and particulars, it creates a new set of philosophical problems. A number of medieval theologians recognized that, for Augustine, God is simultaneously simple and complex, at once a form and that which contains the forms.[19] We have already seen that, in the *City of God*, Augustine identifies God with the form of the Good as described in the *Republic*. He goes on to assimilate the *Republic*'s account of the Good to both the Demiurge of the *Timaeus* and the Judeo-Christian Creation story: "There is, then, a Good which alone is simple, and therefore alone immutable, and this is God. By this Good all other goods have been created; but they are not simple, and therefore are not immutable" (Est itaque bonum solum simplex et ob hoc solum incommutabile, quod est Deus. Ab hoc bono creata sunt omnia bona, sed non simplicia et ob hoc mutabilia) (11.10). This miniaturized Creation story echoes the first chapter of Genesis, in which "God saw all the things that he had made, and they were very good" (viditque Deus cuncta quae fecit et erant valde bona) (1:31). At the same time, it reinscribes the Platonic distinction between forms such as the Good, which in their simplicity can be predicated only of themselves, and their material instantiations, which can be predicated of many different things. As soon as Augustine produces this synthesis, however, he starts to introduce qualifications. To begin with, the distinction between form and instantiation does not apply to the relationship between the Father and the Son, who is "begotten" (genita) rather than "created" (creata), and so joins his Father as "the immutable and co-eternal Good" (incommutabile bonum . . . et coaeternum) (11.10). But, as we have seen, Augustine also identifies both God and Christ with the form of Wisdom. To complicate matters further, Augustine goes on to associate Wisdom with two distinct sets of forms. He first places Wisdom among those things which "are fundamentally and truly divine . . . because in them quality and substance are one and the same, and because they are divine, or wise, or blessed without participation in anything which is not themselves" (principaliter vereque divina sunt, quod non aliud est in eis qualitas, aliud substantia, nec aliorum participatione vel divina vel sapientia vel beata sunt) (11.10). That is to say, he places the form of Wisdom within a restricted class of divine virtues, which also contains the forms of Divinity and Blessedness. Later, he describes Wisdom in particular as containing "all the invisible and immutable forms of . . . visible and mutable things" (omnes invisibiles atque incommutabiles rationes rerum etiam visibilium et mutabilium) (11.10). Wisdom, then, also serves as a repository for the forms of material things, the paradigms according to which God creates the world in Genesis. Both of these types of forms complicate

Augustine's initial statement of divine simplicity. If God is not only the Good but also Wisdom, Divinity, and Blessedness, then he would seem to be many things rather than just one. And since God contains the forms of all created things, his nature also seems to be complex rather than simple. Because the Platonic forms are simultaneously like God in their immutability and unlike God in their multiplicity, they fit uneasily into Augustine's metaphysics.

These complications notwithstanding, Augustine's account of the forms, like Cicero's before him, had a profound impact on medieval personification allegory. In the most general terms, Plato's distinction between form and instantiation corresponds to the distinction between personification and authorial persona that structures many medieval allegorical narratives. In a text like Christine de Pizan's *Livre de la Cité des Dames* (*Book of the City of Ladies*), the personifications of Reason and Justice represents Reason and Justice themselves, or Reason and Justice absolutely, understood as Platonic forms. In contrast, Christine's authorial persona represents a different kind of being, self-consciously flawed and unstable. As a particular she longs to participate in Reason and Justice but cannot do so completely or permanently. This difference in status between instantiation and form corresponds to a difference in knowledge. Although Reason is always already well acquainted with Christine's authorial persona, Christine does not initially recognize Reason as a personification because she does not initially know Reason as a form. This motif of delayed recognition is a common feature of medieval allegories in part because, for Plato, humans must struggle to achieve knowledge of the forms. In the Platonic tradition, individuals come to know the forms through philosophical dialectic or visionary experience, and we should expect to see both of these processes represented in formal personification allegory.

The Augustinian tradition of visionary allegory includes works such as Mechthild of Magdeburg's *Fliessende Licht der Gottheit* (*Flowing Light of the Godhead*).[20] The encounter Mechthild describes between a numinous Lady Love and a yearning but fallible soul mirrors the process by which, for Augustine, particulars come to know universals. Lady Love is Love itself, or Love as a Platonic form, revealed to the soul that clings to God through the "flowing light" of divine illumination. As Mechthild puts it, "I do not know how to write, nor can I, unless I see with the eyes of my soul and hear with the ears of my eternal spirit and feel in all the parts of my body the power of the Holy Spirit."[21] Like Augustine, Mechthild attributes knowledge of the forms entirely to God, renouncing any claim to human authorship. In "On Ideas," this emphasis on divine authorship allows Augustine to detach the forms from their pagan origin. Here, it allows Mechthild to write despite her imputed feminine weakness. The contrast with Cicero's model of formal personification is instructive. Because Cicero's inner vision of Eloquence is grounded in his philosophical and rhetorical training, it mirrors that training in being gendered masculine. Cicero accordingly personifies the form of Eloquence as the masculine Orator rather than a feminine Eloquentia. Mechthild, in contrast, insists that she cannot write except to record her visionary experience, sidestepping the "contradiction" of feminine authorship by attributing authorship to God. In the process, she claims a very different kind of truth for her Lady Love than Cicero does for his Orator. Where Cicero subjects his inner vision of Eloquence to an ongoing philosophical dialectic, addressing himself to Brutus and (at least theoretically) standing ready to hear his rebuttal, Mechthild's God tells her that her book "flows continuously / Into your soul from my divine mouth. / The sound of the words is a sign of my living spirit / And through it achieves genuine truth."[22] Although both personifications are based on the forms, Cicero's Orator is susceptible to dialectical revision in order to "approximat[e] more nearly to a semblance of the truth," while Mechthild's Lady Love is always already perfect, like the form of Love itself.

Mechthild's Love plausibly belongs to the restricted class of forms Augustine identifies as "fundamentally and truly divine"—as do other visionary personifications such as Christine de Pizan's Justice and Hildegard of Bingen's Justice, Wisdom, and Charity. Indeed, it would be surprising to find an Augustinian personification who does not belong to this restricted class of divine virtues. As we have seen, Augustine equates the forms of these virtues with God in a way that troubles his claim of divine simplicity. Wisdom, Blessedness, and the others are intrinsically and substantially divine, rather than merely divine by participation. Thus, for Mechthild, Love struggles with and eventually dominates God, "forc[ing] the exalted Trinity to pour itself utterly into the humble virginal womb of Mary."[23] Newman acknowledges this dynamic by characterizing these Virtues as goddesses, existing alongside the Christian God in a system of inclusive rather than exclusive monotheism. They are not, however, independent entities so much as aspects of a God who, for Augustine, is simultaneously simply and substantially all of the divine virtues. Despite Hildegard's and Mechthild's claims of inerrancy, then, their personifications are not realist as Huizinga and Barfield understand the term. For Newman, Hildegard's Charity is "God *as* a goddess," a feminine representation of the Holy Spirit rather than a separate being.[24] She is ultimately a way of understanding God, indeed an interpretation of scripture—and so, like Gregory the Great's Bride and Bridegroom, an allegorical machine for lifting the soul toward God.

Although many medieval debate poems are similarly concerned with knowledge of the Platonic forms, they tend to take their cues from the Ciceronian rather than the Augustinian tradition of Platonism. While a poem like the *Debate between Winter and Spring* (*Conflictus Veris et Hiemis*), traditionally attributed to Alcuin, seeks to understand Winter itself and Spring itself, or what we might call the essence of Winter and Spring, its titular personifications are natural instead of numinous. The reader is expected to come to know them by working his way through the poem's alternating stanzas, testing the debaters' claims against each other and perhaps against his own experience of the changing seasons. When Spring wins the debate, he does so not only by outreasoning Winter but also by redefining him. Rather than a lord who forces the other seasons to work for him as bondsmen, Winter becomes a beggar who lives from their largesse:

> You are not their lord, but an arrogant and needy pauper.
> You're not even capable of feeding yourself without help,
> unless you are provided with food by the cuckoo who is about to come.
>
> Non illis dominus, sed pauper inopsque superbus,
> Nec te iam poteris per te tu pascere tantum,
> Ni tibi qui veniet cuculus alimonia praestet. (40–42)[25]

Spring succeeds insofar as his audience, inside and outside the poem, recognizes this characterization of Winter. This dialectical approach to personification extends to poems on theological topics, with dialogues between Christian and Jew and between Body and Soul forming their own subgenres with roots in Ciceronian rhetoric.[26] Many later allegorical poems contain important elements of disputation, including *Piers Plowman*, where the most curricular section of the poem seeks to define the strengths and weakness of, and relationships among, Wit, Study, Clergy, and Scripture. Later, Langland's version of the debate of the Four Daughters of God revises Robert Grosseteste's original in a decidedly Ciceronian direction. The beginning of the vision is impeccably Augustinian, pairing an otherworldly setting with the Dreamer's unusually strong truth claim, "I sauȝ sooþly, *secundum scripturas* [according to scripture]" (B.18.112). But as soon as the Dreamer's experience becomes primarily auditory rather than visual, the Virtues become less numinous and the conventions of debate poetry begin to predominate, as when Truth derides Mercy's argument as "a tale of waltrot" (B.18.142, cf. C.20.144). Ultimately, the debate is Ciceronian because it aims to demonstrate rather than reveal Christian truth.

Although I have here touched on only a few Platonic accounts of the forms, privileging those influential during the Middle Ages, even this narrow sampling offers a sense of their diversity and the diversity of formal personifications. In the *Flowing Light of the Godhead*, Mechthild of Magdeburg comes to know Lady Love in the same way that, for Augustine, human beings come to know all the forms: through divine illumination. Mechthild represents God himself as authenticating her book, holding it in his right hand as he proclaims that it contains "my personal secrets" and "portrays me alone."[27] Love's authority is absolute because, as one of Augustine's paradigmatically divine virtues, she *is* God, or at least an aspect or interpretation of God. Ciceronian formal personifications likewise refer to forms in the divine mind, but these forms are not paradigmatically divine in the manner of Wisdom, Justice, and Blessedness. They tend instead to represent the forms of human virtues, such as Eloquence, or natural phenomena, such as Winter and Spring. They come to be known primarily through reason rather than divine illumination and often specifically through a process of Socratic hypothesis and correction. For this very reason, not only their claims but also their very identities are subject to debate and potentially to revision. Although they point toward Platonic forms existing eternally in the mind of God, they represent them provisionally, on the basis of philosophical dialectic, rather than absolutely, on the basis of revelation. In Cicero's terms, although both Love and Eloquence "shine forth at some times and in some places," they rarely do so at the same time or in the same place.

DAEMONIC PERSONIFICATION

Although many critics assume, as Mann does, that all Platonic personifications are based on the forms, an important subset of studies instead links them with Plato's daemons. In the twentieth century, Angus Fletcher's account of personification allegory as a sort of daemonic agency was arguably the most influential. Fletcher's daemons are the minor deities of Greek and Roman religion, intermediate and intermediary between human beings and the higher gods. Presiding over specific domains of human life such as love and sleep, they are simultaneously external and internal to their human adherents, so that one can speak of either "obeying" or being "possessed by" a daemon. In both cases, the human adherent's actions are channeled within very narrow bounds. When an adherent obeys Sleep, he can do nothing but sleep; when possessed by Love, she can do nothing but love. For Fletcher, this characteristically limited sphere of action likewise defines personifications:

> If we were to meet an allegorical character in real life, we would say of him that he was obsessed with only one idea, or that he had an absolutely one-track mind, or that his life was patterned according to absolutely rigid habits from which he never allowed himself to vary. It would seem that he was driven by some hidden, private force; or, viewing him from another angle, it would appear that he did not control his own destiny, but appeared to be controlled by some foreign force, something outside the sphere of his own ego.

Simultaneously energizing the daemoniac and stripping him of an independent will, the daemon transforms its adherent into a personification—or worse, "a robot, a Talus"—as he repeats the same actions over and over again.[28] More recently, Andrew Escobedo has sought to recuperate Fletcher's daemonic model of personification by reversing its emphases. Where Fletcher sees personification as a diminished form of personhood or literary characterization, Escobedo sees it as a means of energizing or animating otherwise static abstractions. The daemoniac is not stripped of his free will because he continues to do what he wants to do. Instead, his daemon represents or embodies his will, understood as a semi-independent agent in some respects internal and in some respects external to the self. For Escobedo, this conception of the will, which he sees as specific to medieval and early-modern Christianity, combines with the legacy of classical daemonology to explain the efflorescence of personification during the European Middle Ages and Renaissance.[29]

Fletcher traces daemonic personifications to Plato's *Apology* and *Symposium*, while Escobedo expressly "leaves open the question . . . of whether to understand literary personification as philosophical realism or nominalism."[30] Both, however, treat daemonic agency as a characteristic of personification itself rather than a means of distinguishing one variety of personification from another.[31] In doing so, they lose access to the particularity of daemonology, first as a strand within pagan Neoplatonism and then as a site of ambivalence—and, at times, controversy—within medieval Christianity. While personifications based on the forms are authoritative and relatively inaccessible, as befits the Neoplatonic understanding of the forms as ideas in the divine mind, those associated with daemons are ontologically "closer" to humans. As guardian spirits who accompany people through life and lead them to judgment after death, daemons bequeath to "daemonic" personifications their mediating and often specifically tutelary role. Since daemons are subject to human passions, daemonic personifications also experience emotions—including negative emotions such as anger, impatience, and jealousy—that more exalted personifications do not. As a result, they are both less mechanical and less authoritative than Fletcher and Escobedo acknowledge.[32] As low-level divinities, daemons are also immersed in the polytheism of classical religion in ways that the Platonic forms are not, rubbing shoulders with Olympian gods and deified heroes. While Augustine condemns all daemons as demons, the familiar minions of the devil, other Christian writers allegorize them, attributing to daemons a mythic status akin to that of Jove and Venus. In contrast to the perfection of formal Neoplatonic personifications, daemonic Neoplatonic personifications are often morally ambiguous and ontologically limited.

The discrepancy between formal and daemonic Neoplatonic personifications can be traced, at least in part, to disagreements within the Platonic tradition about the range or extent of the forms. Does everything in the created world, no matter how debased, correspond to a transcendent form? Or do forms correspond only to the higher things in life? We have already seen a reflection of this disagreement in Augustine's treatments of the forms. In "On Ideas," Augustine mentions only two forms—Horse and Man—both corresponding to concrete nouns, and more specifically to natural phenomena. It is difficult, however, to imagine a holy, pure, and rational soul, cleaving to God in love, beatified by divine illumination of the form of Horse. The *City of God* addresses this problem by imagining two distinct classes of forms. One corresponds to objects in the material world, and so includes Horse and other natural forms, while the other is composed of the divine virtues, paradigmatically Divinity, Wisdom, and Blessedness. The *City of God* does not, however, explain how these two classes of forms relate to each other, or even how both can be understood as forms given their apparent differences. Nor is it clear that these different kinds of forms can be known in the same way. Augustine asserts that the soul must be "like those things which it endeavors to see" and offers a compelling vision of the soul making itself "sound, pure, serene" in order to perceive the forms of Soundness, Purity, and Serenity. Surely, however, the soul does not prepare to cognize the form of Horse by making itself as horselike as possible. To do so, the soul would need to descend rather than ascend the Neoplatonic hierarchy of being, making itself more bestial rather than more divine—certainly not Augustine's intention.[33]

This tangle does not originate with Augustine but rather with Plato's own ambiguity about what kinds of things correspond to forms. Plato's frequent references to the forms of mathematical qualities and moral virtues suggest that he regards them as paradigmatic. In the *Republic*, guardians-in-training progress from the former to the latter, with the forms of numbers and shapes serving as a gateway to the more difficult but ultimately more consequential forms of Justice and the Good. Plato refers much less frequently to forms that correspond to material objects, mentioning Bed and Table in the *Republic* (596b), Bee in the *Meno* (72b–c), and Shuttle and other hand tools in the *Cratylus* (389a–d). In the *Parmenides*, he translates these different degrees of frequency into different degrees of certainty. The Socrates of the *Parmenides* expresses complete confidence in the existence of forms of moral virtues, admits to doubt about the existence of forms of fire, water, and man, and all but dismisses the possibility of forms of "hair and mud and dirt, or anything else totally undignified and worthless" (130c). Given the forms' transcendent, otherworldly status, it is evidently easier to associate them with virtuous qualities than with material objects, while within the category of material objects, it is easier to associate them with human beings and the four elements than with base or degraded inanimate objects.

Plato never mentions forms corresponding to negative qualities such as hate, pride, and avarice. Indeed, in the light-filled otherworldly realm of the *Phaedrus*, there seems to be no place for them. Everything in that realm, the forms very much included, is beautiful and exalted. Augustine, the former Manichean, theorizes negative qualities more explicitly as the diminishment, corruption, or privation of good ones. Since they are not entities in their own right, they do not correspond to forms. People become evil not by participating in a form of Evil but by participating in a diminished or corrupted way in the form of Good (*Enchiridion* ch. 4). While this argument may be theologically sound, it is epistemologically problematic. If knowledge is defined as knowledge of the forms, how are we able to cognize evil and its various subcategories, including hate, pride, and avarice? How were medieval Christians able to grasp or "handle" them, as advocated by penitential treatises such as Robert Mannyng's *Handlyng Synne*? At the very least, Augustine would need to posit a distinct mode of knowing evil. He would also need to demonstrate that we grasp the concepts of the sins differently than we grasp the concepts of the virtues, or even the concepts of man and horse. Negative qualities represent one of the most important areas of discontinuity, or mismatch, between the Platonic forms and the material world said to partake of or participate in them. Whether the forms are located in a transcendent otherworld or the mind of the Christian God, they fall short of explaining our understanding of evil—and even our ability to recognize dirt when we see it.

Platonists respond to these uncertainties about the nature and extent of the forms in a variety of ways, each claiming to represent Plato's true intentions. Plotinus emphasizes transcendent moral forms such as Beauty, which he describes as "the Choragus of all Existence, the Self-Intent that ever gives forth and never takes," while Xenocrates offers a much more prosaic definition of the forms in general as "the paradigmatic cause of regular natural phenomena."[34] Xenocrates's view predominates in the doxographical tradition, as in the *Didaskalikos* or *Handbook of Platonism* written, perhaps by Alcinous, early in the current era:

> Form is defined as an eternal model of things that are in accordance with nature. For most Platonists do not accept that there are forms of artificial objects, such as a shield or a lyre, nor of things that are contrary to nature, like fever or cholera, nor of individuals, like Socrates and Plato, not yet of any trivial thing, such as dirt or chaff, nor of relations, such as the greater or the superior. For the forms are eternal and perfect thoughts of God.[35]

In the *Handbook*, the forms correspond to orderly natural phenomena, as contrasted not only with man-made objects such as shields and lyres but also with aberrations such as fever and cholera, which the author sees as corruptions or perversions of nature. As thoughts of God, the forms explicitly exclude things that are not worth thinking about, such as dirt and chaff. They also implicitly exclude abstractions such as the moral virtues, an omission that Gersh suggests may result from privileging the *Timaeus*, which mentions only natural forms, over the rest of Plato's works.[36] Whatever its cause, this omission has the effect of opening up space within the Platonic universe for an elaborate daemonology. Intermediate between gods and men, Platonic daemons embody the ethical abstractions that Cicero, Plotinus, and Augustine understand primarily as forms. In doing so, they furnish the Middle Ages with an alternative paradigm for Platonic personification allegory, one that associates personified abstractions with other kinds of "in-between" beings, including the Olympian gods.

The Neoplatonic category of the daemon develops from brief discussions in Plato's *Apology*, *Symposium*, *Phaedo*, and *Republic*. In the first of these, Socrates refers to a *daimonion* that has been with him throughout his life, and whose voice warns him against wrong conduct (31c–d, 40a). While modern readers often psychologize this voice as Socrates's conscience, most Neoplatonists understood the daemon to be a real being, ontologically intermediate between gods and humans.[37] This conception owes much to the *Symposium*, where Socrates recalls his youthful instruction in love by the wise Diotima. In a dialogue set within the larger dialogue, Diotima leads Socrates to understand that the abstraction Love (Eros) is not a full-fledged Olympian deity but rather a daemon, something "in between mortal and immortal" (202d). In Diotima's account, Love is not Aphrodite's son but her servant, the child of a drunken liaison between Plenty and Poverty. Although never explicitly identified as such, Plenty and Poverty are presumably daemons as well, for Diotima asserts that such spirits "are many and various" (203a). This less-than-exalted origin allows Love to mediate between gods and men by carrying prayers and sacrifices to heaven and conveying responses and commands back to earth. Because Love does not himself possess beauty and wisdom, he seeks them avidly, offering humans a model of right conduct that the higher gods, in their eternal beauty and wisdom, cannot provide. Diotima claims that, as a lover of beauty and wisdom, Love is the paradigmatic philosopher and so should serve as an example to the participants in the symposium, who must come to understand wisdom as the true beauty and the love of wisdom as true love. In *Phaedo* and the *Republic*, Plato offers a narrower depiction of daemons as guardian spirits who accompany individuals through life and lead them to judgment after death (107d–108c; 617d–e, 620d–e). Here, too, they mediate between mortals and the higher gods, bridging the gap between individual human actions and abstract ideals of right and wrong.

Judging from elaborations of Plato's daemons by Plutarch, Apuleius, and Maximus of Tyre, daemonology was very much "in the air" in the first and second centuries of the common era.[38] Of these, Apuleius's *On the God of Socrates* offers the most systematic account, transmitted to the Middle Ages directly through a sizable manuscript tradition as well as indirectly through Apuleius's influence on Calcidius.[39] A self-described Platonic philosopher, Apuleius seeks to resolve the problem of the relationship between particulars and universals by multiplying ontological categories, developing a series of nested three-part schemas to fill the void between the Supreme God and the material world.[40] First dividing all beings into gods, daemons, and mortals, he then subdivides daemons into three additional categories: never embodied daemons such as Love and

Sleep (Hypnos); previously embodied daemons such as ancestral *lares* and the souls of heroes; and embodied daemons, or the souls of the living. As intermediate beings, all three kinds of daemons share eternal life with the gods, susceptibility to emotion with humans, and animateness and rationality with both. Generally invisible to humans, for "the strands of their bodies are so loose-knit, lustrous, and fine-spun that all the rays of our gaze are let through by their loose texture, thrown back by their lustre, and baffled by their fineness" (fila corporum possident rara et splendida et tenuia usque adeo ut radios omnis nostri tuoris et raritate transmittant, splendore reverberent ut subtilitate frustrentur), they can nonetheless reveal themselves when they so choose (11.144–45).[41] For Apuleius as for Plato, daemons serve "individual humans as witnesses and guardians in the conduct of their lives" (singulis hominibus in vita agenda testes et custodes), advising them while they are still living and testifying on their behalves after death (16.155). In this latter capacity, the daemon is not an advocate, as in adversarial judicial systems, but rather an omniscient observer "not only of all our actions but even of all our thoughts" (omnium non modo actorum verum etiam cogitatorum) (16.155). Daemons are simultaneously "low" enough to offer detailed reports of human doings without loss of dignity and "high" enough to testify unimpeachably to what they have seen.

As the foregoing begins to suggest, Apuleius's daemons are deeply enmeshed in Roman religious practice, to the extent that they might be regarded as a theorization of that practice. In contrast to the heavenly gods, who for Apuleius are so exalted that they "enjoy a constant state of mind in eternal calm" (semper eodem statu mentis aeterna aequabilitate potiuntur), daemons resemble humans in their experience of pity, indignation, anguish, and joy (12.146). Consequently, they can be propitiated by offerings and offended by neglect as the higher gods cannot. In a section of *On the God of Socrates* that shows careful attention to Roman divinatory practices, daemons are also charged with communicating with humans via portentous dreams, prophetic entrails, bird flights and bird cries, lightning bolts, seers, oracles, and other traditional forms of divination. Xenocrates excludes negative powers such as Fever from the realm of the forms but acknowledges them as daemons specifically in order to account for their cults, while Apuleius, through a careful deployment of terminology, seeks to group various empirical cult practices within the umbrella category of daemon worship. He interprets cults of *genii*—the elements of divinity present in individuals, families, and localities—as the worship of embodied daemons, and cults of ancestors and heroes as the worship of previously embodied daemons. At the top of Apuleius's hierarchy, never-embodied daemons correspond to the cults of personified virtues and perhaps also to the cults of negative powers such as Fever and Death.[42] Apuleius's demonology thus seeks simultaneously to ratify and to rationalize the highly variable practice of Roman religion, showing awareness and acceptance of local cult practices in Greece, Egypt, and his own native Numidia. The category of daemon unifies a potentially infinite variety of local gods and even gives them a kind of universal standing. At the same time, it defines them as permanently subordinate to the three echelons of "higher" gods, culminating in the One "who is the master and source of all things, freed from all bonds of being acted upon or acting" (qui omnium rerum dominator atque auctor est, solutum ab omnibus nexibus patiendi aliquid gerendive) (3.124).

Calcidius draws heavily on Apuleius for an extended discussion of daemons in his translation of and commentary on Plato's *Timaeus*. The *Timaeus* itself mentions daemons only in passing for, as the narrator Timaeus explains in Calcidius's translation, "to give an account of the invisible divine powers known as daemons is a task greater than our human ability is capable of sustaining" (invisibilium divinarum potestatum quae daemones nuncupantur praestare rationem maius est opus quam ferre valeat hominis ingenium) (40d). Timaeus thus places daemons outside of the realm of philosophy, including Socrates's rigorous dialectic as well as his own looser form of philosophical speculation. Rather than inquiring into the nature of daemons, he urges,

> Let us then trust those who in their books long ago, when they themselves revealed their relationship and propinquity to the divine race, left to posterity perennial records of the nature of the gods, their ancestors and forebears, and of the progeny of each.

> Credamus ergo his qui apud saeculum prius, cum ipsi cognationem propinquitatemque divini generis praeferrent, de natura deorum maiorum atque avorum deque genituris singulorum aeterna monumenta in libris posteritati reliquerunt. (40d)

That is to say, the existence of daemons should be accepted as a matter of faith or trust, subject to the authority of the earliest writers. Even this disclaimer, however, has the effect of positioning daemons as mediating figures, since the writers' authority—in his commentary, Calcidius identifies them as the mythological poets Orpheus, Linus, and Musaeus—

depends on their status as the sons and grandsons of deities (127). It accordingly defines daemons as gods who intervene in the human world, indeed as gods whose sexual relationships with humans have produced a race of poet-heroes. In the *Timaeus*, it is not clear to what extent this category of daemons overlaps with that of the Olympian gods, whose traditional histories are likewise to be accepted on faith and likewise recount sexual adventures with mortals. Although Orpheus's mother is generally identified as the muse Calliope, in some stories his father is the god Apollo, while in others he is Oeagrus, the mortal king of Thrace. Nor is it clear how Timaeus-the-narrator's respect for traditional stories fits with his claim to offer a companion piece to the *Republic*, in which Socrates bans stories that falsify the nature of the gods by representing them in a negative light (377a–383c). The *Timaeus*'s brief, oblique treatment of daemons locates them at the intersection of philosophy, religion, and poetry without addressing the conflicts among these disciplines.

Calcidius discusses daemons at much greater length in his commentary. Although there is no scholarly consensus about whether Calcidius was himself a Christian, he seems to have written for a Christian patron, and his insistence that daemons are not gods but created beings has the effect of reducing, though not eliminating, potential conflicts with Christian doctrine. In Calcidius's account, the Demiurge creates daemons to fill the ontological as well as physical space between the stars—represented in the *Timaeus* as perfectly spherical and eternally constant living beings—and mortal humans. Their existence is thus an expression of the perfection of the Craftsman's work, as well as a necessary component of the harmony of microcosm and macrocosm:

> Given, then, that the divine and immortal race of living beings is celestial, associated with the stars, while the temporary, perishable one subject to passion is associated with earth, it is necessary that there should be between these two some intermediate to connect the extreme limits, just as we see in the cases of musical harmony and the world itself.

> Quare cum sit divinum quidem et immortale genus animalium caeleste sidereum, temporarium vero et occiduum passionique obnoxium terrenum, necesse est esse inter haec duo medietatem aliquam conectentem extimos limites, sicut in harmonia videmus et in ipso mundo. (131)

Whereas Calcidius's stars resemble Apuleian gods in being "immortal, impassible, and rational" (immortale . . . et impatibile idemque rationabile) and humans are "mortal and subject to passions" (mortali passionibusque obnoxio)," daemons are simultaneously immortal and passionate (131). Indeed, they are prompted by their feelings of empathy to look after the human race, delighting in the virtuous while recoiling in pain from the wicked. As a result, Calcidius's daemons resemble Platonic and Apuleian daemons in serving as guardians of individual human beings, mediating on their behalf by "interpreting and reporting our prayers to god and likewise . . . interpreting and reporting god's will to humans, revealing to him our needs and bringing divine aid down to us" (nobis sint interpretantes et nuntiantes deo nostras preces et item hominibus dci voluntatcm intimantes, illi nostram indigentiam, porro ad nos divinam opem deferentes) (132). This mediating function prompts Calcidius to derive the Greek *daimones* from *daêmones*, or knowers. But he also associates daemons with "those the Hebrews call holy angels" (quos Hebraei vocant sanctos angelos), evoking the literal Greek and Latin sense of *angelus* as messenger (132). Calcidius thereby justifies daemons' existence not only as a matter of natural philosophy but also through the testimony of multiple witnesses. He argues—much as Augustine did for the forms—that daemons must be real because they are so widely accepted.

Calcidius also follows Apuleius in recognizing distinct subtypes of daemons. Evidently concerned that Christians will understand all daemons to be demons, in the sense of "minions of the adverse power" (adversae potestatis satellites), he begins by emphasizing that the term *daemon*, like the term *angelus*, is "imposed indifferently upon good and evil beings" (promisce bonis et improbis positum) (133). Dividing the heavens into regions of ether and air, he goes on to assign ethereal daemons to the former and aerial daemons to the latter. Both are invisible and intangible, looking upward in obedient service to God and downward to care for mortals. The aerial daemon, however, is progressively "more disposed to experiencing passion the closer it comes to Earth" (quanto est terrae propinquior, eo passioni affectus accommodatior), suggesting a metaphysical continuum in which a daemon's ontological and moral status is directly proportional to its dwelling place's distance from earth (135). Calcidius contrasts both of these classes of virtuous daemons with those who "don the shadowy form of bloodless images, taking on the filth of corporeal density, often serving even as avengers of crime and impiety by sanction of divine justice" (exsanguium quoque simulacrorum umbraticas formas induuntur obesi corporis illuviem trahentes, saepe etaim scelerum et impietatis ultores iuxta iustitiae divinae sanctionem) (135). Dwelling closest to earth, the daemons in this last category are affected by earthly lust, making them "the cause of gratuitous and frequent suffering" (ultro etiam plerumque laedunt), implicitly by raping mortal women (135). Calling these daemons "deserter angels" (desertores angelos), Calcidius associates them with the fallen angels Augustine describes in his commentary on Genesis 6:11, where he wonders whether "some spirits with bodies of air" (aliqui spiritus elemento aerio corporati) can have intercourse with human women (Calcidius 135, *City of God* 15.23). Calcidius accordingly seeks to harmonize Platonic and Christian accounts of daemons by incorporating the second as a kind of subdiscipline within the first. His daemons include but are not limited to Christian demons. Even though he describes the lowest echelon of daemons in both classical and Christian terms, he tends to attribute their misbehavior to their inherent ontological inferiority rather than to a fall from virtue into vice.

Although Calcidius does not specifically equate his daemons with personifications, they are similar kinds of intermediate beings.[43] At the very least, Calcidius's daemonology seems to color his interpretation of the *Timaeus*, pushing him to understand Plato's World-Soul, Providence, Matter, and Nature as continuous personifications who, like daemons, occupy the ontological space between the numinous Craftsman God and his phenomenal creations. The *Timaeus* lays the groundwork for this kind of interpretation through repeated local moments of personification. As we have already seen, Plato describes the Receptacle as feminine and compares the relationship of Demiurge, Receptacle, and created being to that of a human father, mother, and child. He imagines a similar relationship between Necessity and Intellect: "For this ordered world is of mixed birth: it is the offspring of a union of Necessity and Intellect. Intellect prevailed over Necessity by persuading it to direct most of the things that come to be toward what is best, and the result of this subjugation of Necessity to wise persuasion was the initial formation of this universe" (48a). These lines briefly animate Intelligence and Necessity, transforming them from abstractions into nonce personifications as they engage in the distinctively human acts of "persuading" and being "subjugate[d] . . . to wise persuasion." Necessity and Intelligence disappear almost as soon as they come into being, however, as the narrator turns to his audience to discuss the order of presentation of his text. In fact, Plato's Timaeus takes this occasion to remind his audience that his explanations are imagistic and probabilistic rather than authoritatively truthful, before pausing his narrative for prayer: "Let us therefore . . . call upon the god to be our savior this time, too, to give use safe passage through a strange and unusual exposition, and lead us to a view of what is likely" (48d). Nonce personification seems to be as far as Timaeus is willing to go in his speculative philosophy, defining a boundary past which it becomes too "strange and unusual."

In his commentary, Calcidius transforms Plato's isolated moments of personification into a semicontinuous narrative, with the personifications World-Soul (Anima Mundi), Providence (Providentia), and Matter (Silva) as its protagonists. Commenting on the passage just cited, Calcidius identifies Necessity with Matter and Intelligence with Providence, creating continuous characters in place of Timaeus's nonce personifications. As he puts it, "*Necessity* . . . is what [Plato] uses here to designate *hylê*, which we can call *silva* in Latin" (necessitatem porro nunc appellat hylen, quam, nos Latine silvam possumus nominare) (268). He emphasizes that the sensible world is not produced by mixing Providence/Intelligence and Matter/Necessity as if they were inert substances but rather through their reasoned deliberations as sentient beings (269). Echoing the comparison of the Demiurge and the Receptacle to husband and wife in Plato's *Timaeus*, Calcidius represents Matter as "offer[ing] herself completely without resistance for adornment, since the divine mind penetrates and informs her completely" (perpetiente exornationique se facilem praebente, penetratam siquidem eam usque quaque divina mens format plene) and as "not resisting the adornment she received but being overcome in such a way as to yield willingly to the majesty of the craftsman and submit to his wisdom" (nec adversum exornationem suam resistentem sed ita victam ut maiestati opificis libens cedat pareatque eius sapientiae) (269, 270).[44] These and subsequent comments in the same vein have the cumulative effect of transforming Matter from an abstraction *compared* to a wife and mother in Plato's *Timaeus* into a personification who *is* a wife and mother in Calcidius's commentary (273–74, 287, 298–99). Calcidius even stages a little drama of feminine domestication, representing Matter as exchanging autonomy for ornamentation as she yields to the penetration and the wisdom of the Craftsman God. In other words, Calcidius attributes to the *Timaeus* not only continuous characters but also the rudiments of a romance plot.

The romance plot thickens when Calcidius suggests that there are multiple claimants to Matter's affections. The Demiurge's rivals are none other than the lowest daemons, who in Calcidius's account "are affected by earthly lust and have an excessively high level of communion with matter [silva], which the ancients referred to as the malign soul" (tanguntur . . .

terrena libidine habentque nimiam cum silva communionem, quam malignam animam veteres vocabant) (135). It is certainly possible to interpret "silva" in this passage as an inert substance, translating "quam" as the inanimate "which." Given Calcidius's broader practice of personifying Matter, however, and his characterization of her here as a "malign soul," it is equally possible to interpret "silva" as a woman who directs her attentions and her body either to the Demiurge or to wicked daemons. Calcidius's understanding of the Receptacle as in some ways sinister, responsible for the discrepancies between the perfection of the forms and decidedly imperfect material beings, comes directly from Plato's *Timaeus*. Calcidius alone, however, is responsible for the suggestion that a personified Matter finds herself caught up in an ongoing love triangle, directing her affections sometimes to the Craftsman God, sometimes to wicked daemons. While character and plot never become the primary structural elements of Calcidius's commentary, his work begins to define a Neoplatonic universe in which personifications are understood as ontologically intermediate beings similar to, if not precisely identical with, classical daemons.

Apuleius and Calcidius together help to lay the groundwork for classical daemons' complicated afterlife during the Middle Ages. While some medieval writers understood daemons as real beings, others understood them as allegories, or *integumenta*. In general, writers in the first group followed Calcidius in identifying daemons as angels or devils. The enormously influential *On the Celestial Hierarchy* assimilates daemons to angels but does not associate them with prosopopoeia.[45] Augustine equates daemons specifically with fallen angels, arguing that they cannot be beneficent because humans require no mediation beyond that of Christ. Although good angels are ontologically intermediate between gods and men, they cannot mediate between them as daemons are said to do because they lack Christ's mortality. As a result, angels are neither suitable objects of worship nor transmitters of prayers but instead wish humans to join them in worshipping God. Similarly, although Christian martyrs are in some ways equivalent to pagan heroes such as Hercules, Augustine cautions that they should not be confused with, or worshipped as, the previously embodied daemons described by Apuleius. Augustine accordingly accepts daemons as real beings, but defines them as exclusively evil:

> they are spirits whose sole desire is to harm us: who are entirely alien to justice, swollen with pride, livid with envy, and subtle in deceit. They do indeed dwell in the air; but they do so only because they were

> cast out from the sublimity of the higher heaven, and justly condemned for their irreparable transgression.
>
> spiritus nocendi cupidissimos, a iustitia penitus alienos, superbia tumidos, invidentia libidos, fallacia callidos, qui in hoc quidem aere habitant, quia de caeli superioris sublimitate deiecti merito inregressibilis transgressionis. (*City of God*, 8.22)

For medieval writers in the Augustinian tradition, daemons thus become the familiar demons of Christianity: minions of the devil who roam the earth tempting saints, making bargains, and wreaking minor forms of havoc.

A second group of writers incorporate important aspects of daemonology into personification allegory. In general terms, daemonic personifications take the daemons' place as intermediate, tutelary figures who engage one on one with individual mortals in order to lead them to truth. More specifically, daemons' predilection for suddenly manifesting themselves to their human charges corresponds to the typical allegorical scene in which the authorial persona is caught off guard by the abrupt appearance of a personification who claims to have known him or her since infancy. Daemonology likewise accounts for medieval personifications' tendency to rub shoulders with departed souls and various orders of pagan gods, in this respect doing a better job of anticipating medieval allegorical practice than modern criticism often does of describing it. We have seen that Apuleius defines daemons primarily by their function, suggesting that they can be drawn from any stratum of the Roman pantheon that lies between the embodied soul and the transcendent One. He describes Socrates's daemon alternately as a god, an always disembodied spirit, and a formerly embodied *lar*, while characterizing Minerva, Juturna, and Venus, who would ordinarily be classified as invisible gods, as daemons when they act as guardians to Achilles, Turnus, and Aeneas.[46] Medievalists, in contrast, commonly define personifications in opposition to the pagan gods. Although James Paxson excludes the Venus of Chaucer's *House of Fame* from his study of personification except "in structural relation to genuine personification characters," Venus in fact features so prominently in so many different personification allegories that she is difficult to set aside.[47] Rather than separating abstract personifications from the rest of the Greco-Roman pantheon, many medieval authors follow Apuleius in admitting different varieties and degrees of divinity. For Chaucer and others, previously embodied daemons, disembodied daemons, and invisible gods coexist within literary works just as they coexist within Neoplatonic daemonology.

These writers did not understand daemons to be "real" in the same way that Augustine did. Instead, they situated them within the medieval tradition of integumental interpretation, itself a Platonic inheritance. This tradition has its roots in the fictional and dream narratives within Plato's writings, especially the richly imagined, nonfactual account of the creation of the universe in the *Timaeus*. It gained force from Stoic allegorical interpretations of Homeric epic and other early writings, such as those Cicero attributes to Balbus in *On the Nature of the Gods*.[48] Although integumental interpretation was largely confined to the margins of schoolbooks during the early Middle Ages, it gained momentum in the twelfth century from the Neoplatonic commentaries of William of Conches and Bernardus Silvestris and continued to flourish through the *aetas Ovidiana* of the fourteenth and fifteenth centuries.[49] Winthrop Wetherbee describes its logic as follows:

> The assimilation of secular writings to Christian contexts . . . was justified by the conviction that Plato and other ancient philosophers and poets had expressed their deepest wisdom mysteriously, shrouding it in veils of imaginative detail which might consist of mere invented personifications and cryptic etymologies, or involve the use of an extended myth or *fabula*. The relation of such fictions to their underlying truths was like that of the visible world to the divinely ordained cosmic order, and could be discerned by the same rational means, once the presence of such *involucra* was recognized.[50]

In contrast to scriptural allegoresis, which seeks deeper meaning in a sacred history itself understood to be literally true, classical *involucra* or *integumenta* invite readers to discover the truth behind a fictional narrative. For medieval readers, therefore, daemons and other pagan deities simultaneously occlude and point toward a hidden truth, while for medieval writers they become an important means of marking a work as truthful but not factual. For Christian readers and writers alike, daemons can only point toward the truth, or be in some way truthful, once they have been stripped of their status as divinities, indeed of their status as substantial beings.

The twelfth-century Platonist commentator William of Conches exemplifies this mode of reading and writing. Although I will provide an extended reading of William's commentary on Boethius's *Consolation of Philosophy* in chapter 4, for now it suffices to point out that William did not understand Philosophy as a substantial being but rather as a representation of Boethius's "own better wisdom, speaking for the spirit against the flesh."[51] While William does not for a moment doubt the truth of the consolation that Philosophy offers, he considers Philosophy herself to be allegorical or mythical rather than directly real. When Philosophy is understood in this way, her sumptuously described garments—like those of Alan of Lille's Nature, some six hundred years later—become veils that simultaneously conceal and make known a deeper wisdom. So, too, does her femininity, which—in contrast to the masculinity of formal Platonic personifications such as Cicero's Orator—plausibly functions as a marker of her status as an *integumentum*. For the normatively masculine writers and readers of daemonic allegories, the feminine body is at once the beautiful truth behind the veil and itself a beautiful veil, figuring the even more beautiful truth of the masculine divine order.[52] At the same time, the feminine beauty of figures like Philosophy and Nature contributes to the overall harmony of the works in which they appear, in part by cuing masculine readers to appreciate them and the texts in which they figure as aesthetic objects. This seemingly limited, rhetorical appreciation ultimately leads in turn, via the Platonic logic of microcosm and macrocosm, to an appreciation of the harmony of the *musica mundana*. Precisely because of her integumental attributes, Philosophy can lead Boethius to philosophical truth more effectively than an unpersonified philosophy would be able to do.

Medieval daemonic personifications, then, are fully Platonic without being fully, or at least uncomplicatedly, realist. They exist within an implicitly or explicitly Platonic universe in which material beings are understood as imperfect instantiations of eternal forms and where microcosm is linked to macrocosm within an ordered hierarchy of being. Within that universe, their purpose is to help their interlocutors, and by extension, their readers, to grasp eternal truths. Philosophy guides the Boethian prisoner toward understanding himself not just as an individual human being but also as an instantiation of the eternal form of Man, to which he should conform himself to the best of his ability. As the prisoner begins to recognize himself as an instantiation of Man, he also begins to recognize his place within the universe, first seeing his emotional turbulence as a temporary phenomenon analogous to a cloudy sky, then understanding his hard-earned inner harmony as a reflection of the harmonious movements of the stars. Philosophy, however, leads the way to the real without herself being real. She "embodies" philosophy in the same way that Venus "embodies" sexual desire: neither as pure fiction nor as a direct representation of truth. For both Boethius and William of Conches, daemons stand in an affirmative relation to the Christian real that falls short of both divine revelation and philosophical truth but cannot be reduced to mere rhetoric. For high- and late-medieval authors including Bernardus Silvestris and Alan of Lille, Jean de Meun and Chaucer, this ambiguous status allows daemons to serve as important markers of the emergent category of the literary.

In sum, classical Platonism bequeathed to the Middle Ages two distinguishable paradigms of personification allegory. Formal personifications are based on the Platonic forms, as transmitted to the Middle Ages by Augustine and others. These Platonists understood the forms to exist eternally in the mind of God as well as temporarily in the minds of the relatively small number of humans morally and intellectually qualified to understand them. The genres most closely associated with formal personification are debate and mystical vision. The first of these genres descends, via Cicero, from Plato's Socratic dialogues, with the author often figured as a student who grows in knowledge through hypothesis and correction. The second genre develops from Augustine's emphasis on divine illumination as a means of knowing universals in the divine mind and so tends to represent the author as a largely passive recipient of divine revelation. The paradigm of daemonic personification, in contrast, is derived from Plato's daemons, who are intermediate between gods and mortals in the Neoplatonic hierarchy of being. Daemons tend to be tutelary rather than numinous and frequently appear alongside other superhuman beings of Roman antiquity, from deified heroes to Olympian gods. Given daemonic personifications' close association with the allegorical interpretation of pagan texts—first through glosses in early medieval schoolbooks, then through the commentary tradition of the high and late Middle Ages—they are frequently bookish in a way that formal personifications are not. The authors of daemonic allegories, in turn, tend to present themselves as scholars rather than visionaries, and their texts are much more likely to cite classical sources. In addition, while the authors of daemonic allegories consistently represent themselves as ontologically inferior to the personifications with whom they converse, the gap between authorial persona and personification is less pronounced than in formal personification allegories. While formal personifications tend to be changeless and serene, daemonic personifications can be changeable, emotional—and sometimes even funny.

All of the Platonic personifications I have discussed function as engines of thought, designed to perform different kinds of cognitive and affective work. Understood in this way, formal personifications become tools for coming to know the forms they represent. Cicero's Orator, of course, serves as the organizing principle for his final treatise on rhetoric. Even as he represents the Platonic form of Eloquence, then, the Orator also becomes a site for Cicero and his audience to refine, and ideally synthesize, their understanding of what Eloquence is or means or is able to do. Similarly, while Mechthild of Magdeburg's personification of Love represents the form of Love—one of the small subset of forms that, for Augustine, represent aspects of divinity—she is also a brilliantly original tool for interpreting and internalizing scripture. Rather than claiming to represent a new or independent truth, she presents scriptural truth to cognition in new ways. As befits their origins in the *Timaeus*, daemonic personifications tend to represent hypotheses about the created world. They are tools for imaginative world building and philosophical speculation rather than scriptural interpretation or dialectical reasoning. Both of the varieties of Neoplatonic personification I have described differ from Prudentian personifications in that they descend from on high, emanating from the One rather than being shown as formed through human craftsmanship. They accordingly tend to be teachers rather than sites of identification.

CHAPTER FOUR

Hello, Nurse! The Boethian Daemon

For medievalists, Boethius's Philosophy has long served as a convenient point of origin for Neoplatonic personification allegory, even though she is not wholly original. The main elements of the *Consolation of Philosophy* are already present in Plato's *Crito* and *Phaedo*, where an unjustly imprisoned philosopher who is awaiting execution composes poetry, dreams that he is approached by "a beautiful and comely woman," and recounts a personified Philosophy's efforts to prepare her charges for death (*Crito* 44a; *Phaedo* 82e–84b).[1] Pierre Courcelle and Joachim Gruber have traced the development of Philosophy in the intervening literary tradition.[2] For Cicero, Philosophy is mother, medic, and schoolmaster, dispelling the fog that clouds her followers' vision and teaching them to know themselves. Seneca's Philosophy remains a healer, especially a restorer of vision, but is characterized above all as a goddess and queen. Majestic and radiant, she holds court among the deified moral virtues and is worshipped by her human followers. In Augustine's writings, Philosophy retains her traditional role as nurse of human philosophers and mother of the seven liberal arts but is also associated with the biblical personification of Wisdom described in Proverbs and Ecclesiasticus and thus with Christ as the Word of God. She appears to Augustine with a luminous visage after he reads, in tandem, Neoplatonic treatises and the Pauline Epistles.[3] Philosophy, therefore, played an important role in pagan and Christian Platonism long before Boethius wrote his *Consolation* in the sixth century, with many of her attributes demonstrating a remarkable stability.

Boethius's Philosophy differs from her predecessors by serving as the protagonist of the work in which she appears rather than as a local rhetorical ornament or the subject of a story within a story. Although the dialogic structure of the *Consolation* recalls the *Crito* and *Phaedo*, Boethius breaks from Plato by reassigning Socrates's role as the dialogue's primary teacher to the personified Philosophy. The sheer number of words Philosophy speaks and sings over the five books of the *Consolation* renders her dynamic rather than static, a literary character rather than a local verbal or visual image. Her relationship to the Boethian narrator is also new—and it is precisely this gendered relationship between *magistra* and *discipulus* that exerted such an outsized impact on medieval personification allegory. This chapter accordingly focuses on Philosophy as a character, especially in relation to the Boethian prisoner. What kind of a being is she, and how does she fit within the Neoplatonic universe that she herself describes? Is she best understood as a formal personification, a daemonic personification, or something else entirely? The answers to these questions, in turn, have important consequences for the relationship between Philosophy and Boethius's authorial persona. Is their relationship that of a form and its material instantiation? Or is it personal, like the relationship between Socrates and the daemon who warns him away from ill conduct? Does Philosophy address her interlocutor generically, as a philosopher or an everyman, or does she hail him individually, as Boethius? Just as important, how does the prisoner respond? Does he seek to participate in the form of Philosophy? If so, is such participation an end in itself or a step toward participating in the higher form of the Good? If not, how does the narrator resist participation—and how are we to understand such resistance? In the absence of participation, does the *Consolation* offer its narrator, or its readers, any other relationship with the Good?

I will seek to answer these questions first by considering Boethius's text within its original historical milieu, then by considering its afterlife during the high and late Middle Ages. I will argue that although Philosophy is undoubtedly a Neoplatonic personification, she does not represent the form of philosophy, understood as an idea in the divine mind. She is insufficiently awe-inspiring and—as she herself readily admits—does not speak with the requisite authority. Instead, she is best understood within the framework of Neoplatonic daemonology. Philosophy herself intimates that she is the daemon who counseled Socrates in life and stood by his side when he was martyred, and promises to do the same for the Boethian prisoner. Boethius, however, recalibrates her role for his own Christian era. While Philosophy continues to teach the young the basics of rationality and consult with the wise about moral and political philosophy, by the end of the *Consolation* she no longer promises transcendence or offers herself as an intermediary between mortals and the highest divinity. The prisoner instead approaches God through humble prayer, while Philosophy redefines her domain as worldly philosophy.

The rest of the chapter examines Philosophy's legacy as a daemonic personification. While I contend that Boethius originally produced Philosophy within the context of classical daemonology, later medieval writers did not understand her in those terms. Indeed, all three major medieval commentators on the *Consolation*, echoing Augustine's position that all daemons are minions of the devil, specifically exclude the possibility that Philosophy is an actual daemon, a real being. Instead, they read her integumentally, as a rhetorical trope who is not mere rhetoric because she points toward a hidden truth. This mode of reading allows the commentators to assign Philosophy the formal characteristics of a daemon, stripped of their troubling pagan content. As careful readers of the *Consolation*, the commentators notice her variable height and the narrator's less-than-flattering attention to the insubstantiality of her clothes. Above all, they notice her femininity, including her uncomfortable resemblance to the dangerously seductive figures of Fortune and the Muses. Collectively, these observations lead the commentators to assign Philosophy an intermediate degree of authority, higher than that of the prisoner, especially in the early reaches of the work, but far from transcendent—and thus far from a divine revelation of a form. Philosophy's perspective is valuable but limited, providing an important corrective to the prisoner's despair but failing to grasp the whole picture. If anything, the commentators assign less authority to Philosophy than Boethius does, in part because they are less tolerant of her potentially indecorous conduct and in part because they wish to treat the *Consolation* as a work of practical morality, concerned with ethical behavior in this world rather than spiritual transcendence. In doing so, I will suggest, they help to define a subtype of personification that plays an important role in the mythographical tradition of medieval allegorical writing that stretches from the *Complaint of Nature* and the *Roman de la Rose* to *Piers Plowman* and the *Parliament of Fowls*.

PHILOSOPHY THE DAEMON

What kind of a being is Philosophy? While this question has received relatively little attention from medievalists, it has been a subject of lively debate among classicists. Although a consensus remains elusive, John Marenbon identifies three chief lines of argumentation.[4] The group of critics he calls "Christianizers" emphasize the *Consolation*'s scriptural echoes and intermittent religious imagery in order to characterize the work as a sacred dialogue that leads the narrator back to God. For Friedrich Klingner in the early twentieth century, Philosophy is an angel who descends to the prisoner's bedside in a holy vision, while in Wendy Elgersma Helleman's 2009 study she serves, via association with the biblical personification of Wisdom, as a type of Christ.[5] Marenbon's "Augustinists" assimilate the *Consolation* to Augustine's *Confessions* and early philosophical dialogues, comparing Boethius's Philosophy to Augustine's personifications of Continence and Reason. Interpreted in this way, Philosophy becomes a human discipline or faculty rather than a divine messenger, representing the continuity of pagan and Christian Neoplatonism rather than their rupture. Like the human faculty of Reason in the *Soliloquies*, however, she points the way to a specifically Christian truth. Marenbon's "Hellenist" critics, including Gruber and Courcelle, emphasize the *Consolation*'s relationship to the pagan classical tradition. For these writers, Philosophy represents a version of reason strictly limited to the natural realm and available to pagans and Christians in equal measure. Although Courcelle does not deny that Boethius was a Christian, he sees him as anticipating Aquinas's distinction between reason and faith—and situating Philosophy exclusively within the former domain.[6] Finally, Joel Relihan has courted controversy in part by combining Marenbon's Hellenist and Christianizing tendencies.[7] While Relihan finds that Boethius characterizes Philosophy in pagan terms, he argues that Boethius also presents her as severely limited, if not deeply flawed, in order to prompt readers to seek the stronger medicine of Christian theology. According to Relihan, Boethius uses the genre of Menippean satire to mock Philosophy's divine pretensions and undermine her arguments, thus suggesting that prayer to the Christian God offers the only true consolation.

This lack of critical consensus reflects genuine ambiguities in Philosophy's characterization. On the one hand, Philosophy appears to the Boethian prisoner as a specifically pagan goddess, either in a dream vision (since she visits the prisoner in bed) or as an epiphany. We have seen that Prudentius's transcendent personification of Wisdom, at once a Christian goddess and a figure of Christ, derives her numinous aura from scriptural citation. Her temple is built, almost line by line and stone by stone, from chapter 21 of the book of Revelation, while she herself is presented as the Christian fulfillment of the priest Aaron, as described in Numbers 17:6–8. Boethius likewise renders Philosophy godlike through citation, but his description insistently recalls the divinities of pagan antiquity rather than Christian scripture. Philosophy's position standing above the prisoner's head, together with her combination of youthful vigor and great age, evokes a tradition of divine manifestations that dates back to Homer and Hesiod.[8] Her variable height, which rises from "the ordinary measure of man" (communem . . . hominum mensuram) until it "penetrate[s] the heavens themselves and [i]s lost to the sight of men" (ipsum etiam caelum penetr[atur] respicientiumque hominum frustr[atur] intuitum), mimics the ascent of Neoplatonic philosophy from the material realm to the transcendent One (1.1.2). It also evokes the goddess Pheme of Hesiod's *Works and Days* and her Roman counterpart, Virgil's Fama, who grows until she "walks on the ground with her head hidden in the clouds" (ingrediturque solo et caput inter nubila condit) (*Aeneid* 4.177). The *Iliad* furnishes an additional counterpart in the goddess Discord (Eris), "who is only a little thing at the first, but thereafter / grows until she strides on the earth with her head striking heaven."[9] Philosophy's burning eyes and the garment she weaves with her own hands recall Athena's appearances to Achilles and Diomedes. Relihan connects the robes' torn and dirtied state to the meager clothing of Love, the paradigmatic philosopher in Plato's *Symposium*.[10] Together these allusions establish such a close relationship between Philosophy and the pagan gods, especially as represented in classical epic, that Ann Astell places Boethius's prosimetrum "firmly in the epic tradition as a rich series of Stoic and Neoplatonic writings had contextualized it."[11]

On the other hand, Philosophy's actions in the rest of the *Consolation* fall short of this early promise. In the *Iliad*, we catch our only glimpse of Athena's "elaborate / dress, which she herself had wrought with her hands' patience," as she casts it aside to don her war gear. The ensuing battle leaves both Greeks and Trojans shivering in fear at the sheer power of her divinity, their differences temporarily forgotten in the face of their shared mortality (5.734, 5.862–63). In contrast, Boethius's Philosophy has only one garment—and thus, only one guise—and her actions are much more mundane. Her closest approximation of a superhuman act is "gathering the cloth of her robe into a twist" (contracta in rugam veste) in order to wipe the prisoner's eyes, which have become clouded through attention to the human world (1.2.7).[12] Although this restoration of the prisoner's mental vision echoes yet another moment in the *Iliad*, in which Athena clears the mist from Diomedes's eyes so that he can distinguish between gods and mortals, the Boethian context is strikingly homely.[13] Where Athena outfights the best of the Achaeans by an enormous margin, Philosophy combines a more traditional femininity with low social status, as her gesture recalls that of a nursemaid wiping the eyes of a crying child. The supernatural dimension of this act, which occurs at the end of the second prose section, is further attenuated by the naturalism of the *metrum* that immediately follows, which compares the clearing of the prisoner's vision to the wind driving clouds from the face of the sun. After Philosophy restores the prisoner's sight, she addresses him through what Courcelle calls "schoolroom arguments, syllogisms, *exempla*, that is to say the usual toolkit of anyone who engages in reasoning or demonstration."[14] Although I do not follow the Hellenists who bracket the opening description of Philosophy to define her as simply a personification of "the tradition of philosophical thinking in which Boethius was educated," they are right in stressing that she engages with the prisoner as a philosopher, in the tradition of the Socratic dialogue.[15] After going to considerable lengths to describe Philosophy as a goddess, Boethius presents her conversation with the prisoner in a familiar, very human, form.

I argue that this contradiction—and, more broadly, the contradictions among the three schools of Boethius criticism described by Marenbon—can be mitigated if not reconciled by thinking of Philosophy not as full-fledged goddess but as an ontologically intermediate figure akin to a Neoplatonic daemon. That is to say, she is undeniably "higher" than the Boethian prisoner, especially when he is blind and bedridden at the beginning of the *Consolation*. Descending from above, she serves as his personal tutor or adviser, tailoring her counsel to his particular circumstances and emotional state. She does not, however, claim to be all-knowing, and makes a point of associating herself with the middling power of Fate, which translates divine power into earthy terms, rather than with all-seeing Providence. This intermediate status is simultaneously denoted by, and expressed through, Philosophy's femininity, which renders her susceptible to *raptus* by the Stoics and Epicureans and entangles her in a sexual rivalry with the Muses and Fortune. Instead of representing a departure or contradiction, this oscillation between the divine and the faintly ridiculous is consistent with the tradition of classical daemonology, as discussed in chapter 3. Boethius also takes steps to adapt the classical daemon for his Christian milieu. Taking a middle line between Calcidius and Augustine, he accepts the existence of beneficent spirits who help to execute the divine will but specifies that they do not concern themselves with spiritual matters or seek to mediate divine mercy. Indeed, by the end of the *Consolation*, Philosophy's domain has been reduced to moral and political philosophy. Rather than leading the prisoner toward transcendence, she instructs him to pray humbly, and directly, to God.

Although Philosophy is less numinous than Athena, the two figures do resemble each other in important respects. Athena appears to Achilles with "terrible eyes shining" near the beginning of the *Iliad* much as Philosophy appears to the prisoner with "burning eyes" (oculis ardentibus) near the beginning of the *Consolation* (*Iliad* 1.200; *Consolation* 1.1.1). In doing so, she presumably wears the robes of peace she has woven with her own hands, manifesting as the goddess of wisdom rather than the goddess of just war. In this capacity, Athena offers Achilles advice and even bribes him to forget his quarrel with Agamemnon, promising "shining gifts" to replace, threefold, those he has lost (*Iliad* 1.213). She does not, however, seek to compel him, or otherwise exercise her divine powers. Her advice to moderate his anger could just as easily come from a human counselor, or even from Achilles's own capacity for reason. Athena's conversation with Achilles, moreover, is not monologic. Achilles not only makes the final decision, but also has the last word:

> Then in answer again spoke Achilleus of the swift feet:
> 'Goddess, it is necessary that I obey the word of you two,
> angry though I am in my heart. So it will be better.
> If any man obeys the gods, they listen to him also. (*Iliad* 1.215–18)

Achilles here obeys both Athena (and her companion Hera) and his own rational self-interest. Anticipating the Roman formula "do ut des," he listens to the gods so that they, in turn, will listen to him.

Writing in the sixth century, Boethius would have known these lines not only directly from Homer—he was reputedly the last philosopher in the Western tradition to be fully literate in Greek—but also as interpreted again and again by Neoplatonists. Robert Lamberton identifies Athena's appearance to Achilles as a traditional site of allegorical interpretation, with Athena "represent[ing] the restraining force of wisdom, reason, or mind, calming the impulsive emotions."[16] Building on that tradition, Plotinus uses the *Iliad*'s striking image of Athena catching Achilles by his hair, so that he spins around to face her, to figure the Neoplatonic philosopher's turn inward to perceive the unity of self, God, and One (*Enneads* 6.5.7). Apuleius argues that for the duration of this same encounter Athena serves as Achilles's daemon, making herself visible to him alone and offering him wise counsel (*On the God of Socrates* 145, 166). All of these versions of Athena offer plausible models for Philosophy, as wisdom restraining impetuous emotions. All are also located simultaneously within and outside the self. In the allegorical tradition, mind takes the form of a goddess, the better to command attention. For Plotinus, Achilles's turn toward his divine interlocutor is at the same time an inward turn, leading to the dissolution of the distinction between self and other. And, as we saw earlier, Apuleius understands the Socratic daemon as simultaneously a semidivinity, intermediate between mortals and the higher gods in the Neoplatonic hierarchy of being, and an inner voice or private vision that helps individuals to identify the right course of conduct. In each case, Philosophy is both a goddess *and* a representation or embodiment of human wisdom.

Among these models, the one developed in the greatest detail, and the one that maps most closely onto Boethius's personification of Philosophy, is the daemon. Philosophy's daemonic associations begin in the *Phaedo*. Seeing the souls of her followers "imprisoned in and clinging to the body" and "wallow[ing] in every kind of ignorance," she diagnoses them as victims of misdirected desire (82e). Finding that "the prisoner himself is contributing to his own incarceration most of all," she offers him a treatment that interweaves gentle encouragement with logical demonstration (82e–83a). She counsels a withdrawal from sense perception and emotion that ultimately leads to a radical separation from the material world, with the result that the philosopher is already "close to death" during his lifetime, eagerly awaiting an end that he has "wanted and practiced for a long time" (65a, 64a). The *Phaedo* juxtaposes this portrait of Philosophy with a discussion of daemons who, if they do not quite belong to quite the same discourse, nonetheless fulfill a very similar function. As Socrates puts it,

> We are told that when each person dies, the guardian spirit [*daimon*] who was allotted to him in life proceeds to lead him to a certain place, whence those who have been gathered together there must, after being judged, proceed to the underworld with the guide who has been appointed to lead them thither from here. . . . The well-ordered and wise soul follows the guide and is not without familiarity with its surroundings, but the soul that is passionately attached to the body . . . hovers around it and the visible world for a long time, struggling and suffering much until it is led away by force and with difficulty by its appointed spirit. (107d–108b)

Whereas earlier in the *Phaedo* Socrates engages in logical demonstration, here he simply recounts what "we are told," locating his discussion in the domain of myth or religion rather than philosophy. And yet Socrates's daemons resemble his personified Philosophy in serving as guides and guardians, and especially in helping their followers to prepare for death by separating themselves from bodily passions. After death, the daemon leads the "well-ordered and wise soul"—in context, the soul of the philosopher—to the stability of divine truth. The *Phaedo*'s daemons, then, serve as a kind of double for Philosophy, doing the same work of nurturing individual souls and preparing them for death.

Later Platonists take this juxtaposition a step further, combining Plato's daemons and tutelary personifications into a single class of being. Apuleius takes Socrates's daemon as his starting point, elaborating on its multiple roles and reciprocal, mutually beneficial relationship with its human charge. Such a daemon is

> a personal guardian, an individual governor, an inspector in the household, a personal supervisor, an inner attorney, a continuous overseer, the one and only judge, an inseparable witness, a critic of the bad and commender of the good. If it is rightly acknowledged, recognized with attention, and served with reverence, just as it was served in justice and innocence by Socrates, it can provide a clear view forward when things are doubtful, warning in times of uncertainty, protection in peril, and aid in need; it is a being which can, by means of dreams, signs, or even perhaps by face-to-face encounter when the occasion demands, help you by sweeping away evil, promoting good, raising up lowliness, supporting weakness, elucidating obscurity, guiding success, and rectifying adversity.

> privus custos, singularis praefectus, domesticus speculator, proprius curator, intimus cognitor, adsiduus observator, individuus arbiter, inseparabilis testis, malorum improbator, bonorum probator, si rite animadvertatur, sedulo cognoscatur, religiose colatur, ita ut a Socrate iustitia et innocentia cultus est, in rebus incertis prospector, dubiis praemonitor, periculosis tutator, egenis opitulator, qui tibi queat tum insomniis, tum signis, tum etiam fortasse coram, cum usus postulat, mala averruncare, bona prosperare, humilia sublimare, nuntantia fulcire, obscura clarare, secunda regere, adversa corrigere. (*On the God of Socrates* 16.156)

This long list of roles includes functions we now think of as distinct, including judge, attorney, and witness. Evidently the daemon is simultaneously close enough to its charge to serve as an advocate while distant enough to remain an impartial observer. It acts as an interior guide to right and wrong, in the manner of a conscience, while at the same time keeping track of good and bad deeds in anticipation of a final judgment.

It is at once higher than and subject to, even defined by, the human being it attends.

Although this definition would seem to correspond to the kind of undifferentiated or multipurpose daemon described in the *Phaedo*, Apuleius's examples are in fact two personified abstractions: Love and Sleep. Evidently, they relate to their charges in much the same way that Athena, in her guise as the goddess of wisdom, relates first to Achilles in the *Iliad*, then to Odysseus in the *Odyssey*. Apuleius interprets this latter text in the final lines of *On the God of Socrates*, referring to Athena by her Latin name, Minerva:

> Homer . . . presented Wisdom (which he in the manner of the poets named Minerva) as that hero's constant companion. It was with this comrade that Odysseus underwent all his terrible dangers, and conquered all adversity.

> Homerus . . . semper ei comitem voluit esse prudentiam, quam poetico ritu Minervam nuncupavit. igitur hac eadem comite omnia horrenda subiit, omnia adversa superavit. (24.177-78)

Apuleius here treats Homer's references to Athena as a personal goddess, with a proper name, as poetic fictions. Odysseus's daemon is actually the personified abstraction Wisdom. Simultaneously internal and external to Odysseus, she is both cause and effect of his circumspection. That is to say, Wisdom attends upon Odysseus because he acts wisely, and Odysseus acts wisely because he listens to the counsel of his "constant companion." At the same time, the goddess's abstract name suggests that, rather than being exclusive to Odysseus, she stands willing to offer the same kind of counsel to anyone who obeys her precepts. Wisdom is Odysseus's daemon because he listens to her so closely rather than because she speaks only to him.

Should we understand Philosophy, then, as the daemon of Boethius's prisoner? Certainly, she is simultaneously divine and mundane, internal and external, inclusive and exclusive in the manner of a Neoplatonic daemon. In addition, the evidence critics adduce both in favor of and against her divinity seems to support this intermediate hypothesis. As we have seen, the dense network of classical allusions in the *Consolation*'s first prose section compares Philosophy not only to Athena/Wisdom but also to Homer's Discord and Virgil's Fame, as well as to the Love of Plato's *Symposium*. Discord and Fame are not only abstractions—and thus, in Apuleius's terms, daemons—but also mediate between the human world and that of the higher divinities, as implied by their variable height. And Love, as we saw in chapter 3, is not only the *Symposium*'s first philosopher but also its paradigmatic daemon. As an intermediate figure, he is tasked with carrying prayers and sacrifices to heaven and conveying commands and responses back to earth. Just as important, the evidence Marenbon and others cite against Philosophy's divinity is equally consistent with her status as a daemon. Both her famous hymn of prayer to the Creator in the third book and her later reference to "someone who is even superior to me" (quidam me quoque excellentior) are consistent with a daemon's position near the midpoint of the Neoplatonic hierarchy of being (3.m9, 4.6.38).[17] Philosophy positions herself as simultaneously higher than the mortal prisoner and lower than the "superior" power.

In the course of this same discussion in book 4, prose 6, Philosophy associates herself with the broad category of intermediate beings. She begins by characterizing Fate as an intermediate power, contrasting it with both the ordinary doings of mortals and the unmoving simplicity of divine Providence. Fate, in turn, is driven by some or all members of a class of semidivinities that includes angels, daemons, stars, Nature, the World Soul, and unspecified "divine spirits":

> Now whether Fate is driven by certain divine spirits that are servants of Providence; whether the sequence of fated events is woven together [*texitur*] by the World Soul or by all of nature in service to it, or by the heavenly motion of the stars, the power of angels, the multiform resourcefulness of daemons, or by some of them or all of them together; this is at any rate perfectly clear, that Providence is the unmoving and simple form of the things that are to be carried out, and Fate is the interweaving in motion and the ordering in time of those things that divine simplicity arranged so that they could be carried out.[18]

> Sive igitur famulantibus quibusdam providentiae divinis spiritibus fatum exercetur seu anima seu tota inserviente natura seu caelestibus siderum motibus seu angelica virtute seu daemonum varia sollertia seu aliquibus horum seu omnibus fatalis series texitur, illud certe manifestum est immobilem simplicemque gerendarum formam rerum esse providentiam, fatum vero eorum quae divina simplicitas gerenda disposuit mobile nexum atque ordinem temporalem. (4.6.13)

Listing a wide array of intermediate beings, Philosophy carefully refrains from detailing their operations or privileging one kind of being over another. She does, however, accept the existence of the general category of intermediate beings and associates all of them with her own signature activity of weaving. The *Consolation* repeatedly characterizes Philosophy as a weaver, not only associating her with Athena/Wisdom as the weaver of her own robes but also linking the robes' "cunning manufacture" (subtili artificio) and "indecomposable material" (indissolubili materia) to Philosophy's deftly constructed arguments (1.1.3).[19] By emphasizing the interweaving of Fate, as contrasted with the "unmoving and simple form" of Providence, this passage further associates Philosophy with angels, daemons, and the World Soul. Indeed, weaving seems to be the characteristic activity of lower forms of divinity, their intricate enactment of the divine will in time and space contrasting with the stable perfection of the unmoved mover. In this context, the *Consolation*'s fuzziness about the exact natures, roles, and relationships of these intermediate beings allows Philosophy to acknowledge the limits of her own knowledge, in contrast to God's omniscience. In a period in which the status of the lesser deities of pagan Neoplatonism was actively contested, especially among Christians, it also allows Boethius to posit a general class of intermediate beings without staking out a clearly defined, and thus controversial, position. As described here, his Philosophy becomes a subordinate deity within a system of inclusive rather than exclusive monotheism, akin to, though not explicitly identified with, Platonic daemons.

We have seen that Newman considers inclusive monotheism to be a condition of possibility for Neoplatonic personification.[20] She sees such personifications, however, as representations of the forms, which Neoplatonists locate within the divine mind as part of a single divine reality. Although this paradigm accounts for personifications like Prudentius's Wisdom, who is at once a transcendent form and a figure of Christ, it fits less easily with Boethius's Philosophy, who explicitly places the Platonic forms beyond her ken. In Philosophy's model of cognition, which draws on both Plato and Aristotle, there are four modes or stages of knowing: through the senses, through the imagination, through reason, and through "the one simple form itself in the pure vision of the mind" (ipsam illam simplicem formam pura mentis acie) (5.4.30).[21] The first three types of knowledge are characteristically human and ultimately depend on sense perceptions: Boethius follows Aristotle in holding that reason abstracts universals such as *man* from observations of empirical men. Formal knowledge, in contrast, is the prerogative of the highest divinity. It perceives "by a characteristic single stroke of mind . . . seeing all things in advance" (illo uno ictu mentis . . . cuncta prospiciens), in terms very similar to those Boethius uses to define Providence, which "looks out at all things as if from some lofty head of things" (ab excelso rerum cacumine cuncta prospiciat) (5.4.33-34, 5.6.17–18). For Boethius, the forms are located in the divine mind, as in Newman's model, but they are so exalted that they can tell us little about his personification of Philosophy. As is typical of daemons, her modes of knowing and feeling are closer to humans than to the highest divinity.

Where earlier critics tended to treat Philosophy as thoroughly numinous and awe-inspiring, more recent work increasingly identifies mock-heroic elements in her characterization. Boethius's debt to the multigenre, prosimetric form of Menippean satire has long been acknowledged, and even Peter Dronke, who describes Philosophy as "the ideal love of [Boethius's] mind, the embodiment of all he could hope to know of truth on earth," recognizes that she can also be arrogant, temperamental, and possessive.[22] Winthrop Wetherbee sees the *Consolation* as "more profoundly dialogic than its Neoplatonic models, whose idealism it both invokes and challenges," and accordingly considers Philosophy's authority to be more partial and tenuous than that of her predecessors.[23] Mark Miller explores the ways the *Consolation*'s dialectical form complicates philosophical positions long held to be self-evident, including the "Boethian" imperative to renounce earthly attachments, while Jessica Rosenfeld examines the ways in which Aristotelian commentators on the *Consolation* sought to rehabilitate sensible experience and human connections.[24] Relihan goes furthest in emphasizing Philosophy's shortcomings, arguing that the "cunning manufacture" and "most microscopic threads" (tenuissimis filis) of her robes suggest that they are made "of gossamer, of nothing," thus drawing negative attention to the subtlety and artificiality of philosophical argumentation (1.1.3). At the same time, he finds that Philosophy's dirty and tattered garments, manifestly divisible at the hands of the Stoics and Epicureans, disqualify her from being the source of indivisible truth.[25]

I would add that Philosophy's ill treatment at the hands of the Stoics and Epicureans connects her limitations specifically to her femininity. Philosophy describes herself as the victim of an attempted *raptus*:

> Surely in the court of the ancients as well, even before the era of our beloved Plato, we often fought the great fight against the insolence of stupidity; and though he himself survived, his teacher Socrates won the victory of an unjust death while I stood at his side. And afterward, when the herds of the Epicureans and Stoics and the others, each after its own fashion, were attempting to go and seize [*raptum*] his legacy and were dragging me off kicking and screaming as if I were to be a

> part of their ill-gotten gains [*praedae*], they ripped apart [*abreptis*] the robe that I had woven with my own hands; they tore scraps from it and went away, each of them believing that I had gone off with them in my entirety.

> Nonne apud veteres quoque ante nostri Platonis aetatem magnum saepe certamen cum stultitiae temeritate certavimus eodemque superstite praeceptor eius Socrates iniustae victoriam mortis me adstante promeruit? Cuius hereditatem cum deinceps Epicureum vulgus ac Stoicum ceterique pro sua quisque parte raptum ire molirentur meque reclamantem renitentemque velut in partem praedae traherent, vestem quam meis texueram manibus, disciderunt abreptisque ab ea panniculis totam me sibi cessisse credentes abiere. (1.3.6–7)

Whether or not this account of attempted rape was originally intended to be funny, the self-described philosophers, who believe they have convinced Philosophy to run away with them when they hold only scraps of her garment in their hands, are surely meant to be ridiculous. In addition to failing as abductors, they are so sexually incompetent that they cannot tell the difference between holding a woman and holding a piece of cloth. But is Philosophy likewise an object of derision? At the very least, her encounter with the Stoics and Epicureans emphasizes her limited power. Where Athena terrifies Greeks and Trojans alike with her prowess on the battlefield, Philosophy is quickly captured by her enemies and reduced to the status of war booty. Although she kicks and screams to get away, her efforts are ineffectual, and she owes her escape not to her own power but to her captors' stupidity. Whether or not Philosophy accrues blame for making herself susceptible to attack, via the misogynist trope of the woman who "asks for" sexual assault, the attempted *raptus* robs her of dignity and authority.

Nor is this the only occasion when Philosophy's femininity undermines her authority. She also stoops to sexual rivalry, banishing the Muses from the prisoner's bedside as "Sirens" (Sirenes) and "little stage whores" (scenicas meretriculas) and showing a similarly competitive interest in the prisoner's relationship with his "mistress" (dominam) Fortune (1.1.11, 8; 2.1.17). All of these figures are linked not only by their femininity and their interest in the prisoner but also by their association with the comic stage. As "scenicas meretriculas," the Muses play the part of the meretrix, or courtesan, a stock character in Roman comedy, and Fortune arguably occupies this role as well. The primary love interest of the young male protagonist, the courtesan can be either young and genuinely in love with the *adulescens* or—as is implicitly the case here—older and deceptive. When Philosophy insults the prisoner and engages in tirades against the Muses, she herself slips into the comic role of the *matrona*, or outraged wife and mother. Although loving toward her children and often devoted and loyal, the *matrona* is funny in part because she is temperamental, shifting from endearments to invective in the blink of an eye. At various moments all three figures even wear masks, in the manner of the comic stage.[26] These comic associations, specifically linked to Philosophy's femininity, prevent her from being taken entirely seriously.

Rather than being contradictory, this oscillation is consistent with Philosophy's daemonic nature. Love, the paradigmatic daemon of the *Symposium* with whom Philosophy shares her tattered garment, is simultaneously admirable and comic. We have seen that, in Plato's version of his genealogy, Love is not Aphrodite's son but her servant, the child of an extramarital affair between the allegorical opposites Poverty and Plenty. In a reversal of patriarchal gender norms, Poverty "schemed up a plan to relieve her lack of resources" by conceiving a child with the drunken Plenty (203c). As befits his parents, Love is ragged, shoeless, and homeless as well as a lover of the beautiful and the good. He is also a consummate schemer, expert in enchantments, potions, and special pleadings, with little respect for the social order. This less-than-exalted origin not only allows Love to mediate between mortals and the Olympian gods but also makes him the first and paradigmatic philosopher. His very imperfection, his desire for beauty and wisdom that he does not himself possess, makes him a model of right conduct as the higher gods, in their eternal perfection, cannot be.[27] For Apuleius, daemons are awe-inspiring when they manifest themselves to humans but act as glorified household servants to the higher gods, carrying messages between heaven and earth. They also immerse themselves in the messy materiality of Roman divinatory practices, "marking prophetic entrails" (extis fissiculandis) and "directing divinatory bird flight" (praepetibus gubernandis) (*On the God of Socrates* 6.134). In other words, they do the work that is beneath the dignity of the heavenly gods, who—at least as described in the Platonic philosophical tradition—remain on high, unmoved and unmoving, in an eternal state of calm.

If we accept that Philosophy represents something like a Neoplatonic daemon, what does that mean for the *Consolation* as a whole, and especially for her relationship with the Boethian prisoner? The prisoner tells us that when he studied philosophy, Philosophy accompanied him in the same way that, in Apuleius's account, Athena/Wisdom accompanies Odysseus. As he puts it, "You were yourself constantly at my side, steering me whenever I was going to say something or do something" (Me dicturum quid facturumve praesens semper ipsa dirigebas) (1.4.32). She nursed him as an infant and fed him as a child, until he emerged "into the strength and vigor of a mature mind" (in virilis animi robur) (1.2.2). During this entire period, the prisoner dwelled in Philosophy's house and presence while she, in turn, was implanted within him, driving the desire for mortal things from his mind (1.3.2, 1.4.38). This symbiotic relationship is similar to Philosophy's relationships with earlier philosophers. She tells us that she stood beside Socrates as he "won the victory of an unjust death," an evocation of the *Phaedo* that equates Philosophy with Socrates's *daimonion*. Later, she speaks "through the mouth of Plato" (Platonis ore) in a reversal of the usual direction of prosopopoeia (1.4.5). By the time we meet the prisoner at the beginning of the *Consolation*, however, he has become estranged from Philosophy, having ceased to recognize her or listen to her counsel. This loss of intimacy is marked by the fact that Philosophy now speaks to the prisoner in a pedagogical dialogue rather than within or through him, as with Socrates and Plato. And yet Philosophy still promises to "share with you in collaborative effort the burden that you have come under because of the hatred of my name" (sarcinam quam mei nominis invidia sustulisti, communicato tecum labore partirer) (1.3.4–5). This labor of companionship seems to define Philosophy's place in the cosmic order, as she shifts into the third person to articulate what sounds like a divine decree: "It was forbidden that Philosophy leave unaccompanied any innocent's path" (Philosophiae fas non erat incomitatum relinquere iter innocentis) (1.3.5). In this capacity, Philosophy witnesses not only the prisoner's actions but also the motives behind them, from his initial, laudable decision to seek political office out of "enthusiasm for the community of all good people" (commune bonorum omnium studium) to his later, more dubious efforts to blame others for his fallen condition (1.4.9). Like an Apuleian daemon, Philosophy is simultaneously a solicitous nurse and an impossibly intimate, sometimes implacable judge.

Philosophy also resembles a Platonic daemon in seeing her primary role as preparing the prisoner for death.[28] As befits a psychopomp who has escorted generation after generation of philosophers to the afterlife, her robes are "obscured by a sort of gloom of untended antiquity, such as is found on the smoke-covered death masks of one's ancestors" (veluti fumosas imagines solet, caligo quaedam neglectae vetustatis obduxerat) (1.1.3–4). In classical Roman religion, these masks represent the presence of the deified dead in the world of the living, playing an important role in funeral rites and domestic worship. The "gloom" on Philosophy's garment suggests that she, too, passes back and forth between the realms of the living and the dead. More broadly, the *Consolation* reenacts the prison drama of the *Phaedo*, with Philosophy urging the prisoner to model himself on Socrates and those who followed in his footsteps. She describes these philosophers as pursuing rather than accepting martyrdom, actively seeking "the enjoyment of true happiness not only through death but even through pain and torture" (beatitudinis fructum non morte solum verum etiam doloribus suppliciisque) (2.4.29). Although Philosophy initially offers the prisoner gentle remedies, the cup of bitter medicine she promises him as a final cure recalls Socrates's hemlock. She represents its poison, which destroys the body, as inverting the soul-killing venom of the strumpet Muses. The fatherland to which Philosophy seeks to lead the prisoner, after a long and arduous ascent, is clearly located beyond the earthly realm. She imagines him retiring to an impregnable citadel while his enemies "occupy themselves with the plundering of useless baggage" (circa diripiendas inutiles sarcinulas occupantur) (1.3.13). As the opposing army ravages philosophers' bodies and material possessions—the verb Philosophy uses again derives from *rapere*, encompassing both plunder and rape—she pictures her charges laughing from on high, "protected by a wall that marauding stupidity is forbidden to assault" (vallo muniti quo grassanti stultitiae adspirare fas non sit) (1.3.14).

The most glaring problem with Philosophy's imagined scenario is that—as befits a work with important mock-heroic elements—the Boethian prisoner is no Socrates. As a result, Philosophy is forced repeatedly to rewrite the *Phaedo* to accommodate her interlocutor's comparative weakness. In theory, the relationship between the prisoner and Philosophy should mirror the relationship between Socrates and his daemon. In practice, the prisoner's lethargy, which initially manifests itself as an inability to speak, pushes Philosophy to take over Socrates's role as the teaching voice of the dialogue. Even after the prisoner regains his voice, Philosophy must find a way to remind him of Socrates's central proposition: that man is not merely, as the prisoner puts it in Aristotelian terms, a "rational and mortal animal" (rationale animal atque mortale) but also an immortal soul (1.6.15). For his part, the prisoner not only occupies Socrates's position as an imprisoned philosopher awaiting death but also takes on the role of Socrates's companions, who initially resist but eventually accede to his arguments for the immortality of the soul. Weeping copiously at his own misfortune, the prisoner even plays the part of the grief-stricken female relatives Socrates banishes from his jail cell (1.m1.1–4). Although

Philosophy performs a version of this office on the prisoner's behalf when she casts out the tragic Muses, she cannot reproduce Socrates's normatively rational and masculine philosophical community. Instead, she offers her tear-stained charge a tempered femininity, replacing the tragic Muses with her own philosophical Muses and offering maternal care as a replacement for Fortune's blandishments. Like the songs inserted among the *Consolation*'s prose arguments, which liken the prisoner's tears to violent, wind-tossed waves, these concessions mark the prisoner's distance from Socrates. They also highlight the individuality of the relationship between the daemon and each soul in its charge. While the daemonic message of emotional restraint and separation from the world remains largely consistent, the best mode of delivering that message depends on character and circumstance. Philosophy thus enacts, in microcosm, the will of God, who, "when he has looked down from the high watchtower of Providence, sees what is appropriate for each person, and supplies to each what he knows to be appropriate" (cum ex alta providentiae specula respexit, quid unicuique conveniat agnoscit et quod convenire novit accommodat) (4.6.30–31). Playing the role of Fate in carrying out divine Providence, she tailors her approach to the prisoner's weakened condition.

Perhaps the most important consequence of these limitations is that Philosophy never succeeds in bringing the prisoner to his fatherland. As Relihan points out, the prisoner does not die within the confines of the *Consolation*. Even more fundamentally, beginning in the fourth book the *Consolation*'s logic is no longer one of ascent. The prisoner turns away from the upward path when, as he puts it, "I had not yet forgotten the sorrow that was planted within me, and so I interrupted [Philosophy's] train of thought just as she was getting ready to say something else" (Ego nondum penitus insiti maeroris oblitus intentionem dicere adhuc aliquid parantis abrupi) (4.1.1). He insists that before Philosophy leads him to the "true light" (veri . . . luminis), he needs to learn more about darkness, to understand the existence of evil (4.1.2). The prisoner, then, turns back toward darkness in the manner of Orpheus, whose story Philosophy has just retold in the final meter of book 3. His interruption mirrors the backward glance that Philosophy warns against in moralizing the fabula of Orpheus and Eurydice:

> Mortal men! This tale points at you,
> You who seek to conduct your minds
> To the light of the day above:
> Let no man give a backward glance

In defeat, to the caves of Hell—
What he takes with himself as his
He will lose when he sees the dead

Vos haec fabula respicit
Quicumque in superum diem
Mentem ducere quaeritis.
Nam qui Tartareum in specus
Victus lumina flexerit,
Quidquid praecipuum trahit
Perdit, dum videt inferos. (3.m12.52–58)

Despite this warning, the turn to darkness is treated with surprising sympathy, both in the lyric itself and at the beginning of the ensuing prose section. In the *metrum,* Philosophy registers the magnitude of Orpheus's loss and anticipates his backward glance by dignifying his love with its own law: "Who can give to such love a law? / Love is law to itself alone" (Quis legem det amantibus? / Maior lex amor est sibi) (3.m12.47–48). In the *prosa,* she shows herself willing to answer the prisoner's question because it is framed in appropriately philosophical terms rather than as a tear-stained elegy. Perhaps, as a personification of Philosophy, she has no choice, since the prisoner's question undeniably falls within her remit. As the prisoner earlier pointed out, she is responsible for the worldly disciplines of moral and political philosophy, having decreed through the mouth of Plato that "states would be happy and prosperous if either those devoted to wisdom should rule them, or if it were to happen that those who did rule them devoted themselves to wisdom" (beatas fore res publicas, si eas vel studiosi sapientiae regerent vel earum rectores studere sapientiae contigisset) (1.4.5). But she also tends sympathetically to the prisoner's emotions, to his sorrow at "the fact that evil things can exist at all, or that they can pass unpunished, when the helmsman of all things is good" (cum rerum bonus rector exsistat, vel esse omnino mala possint vel impunita praetereant) (4.1.3). To be sure, from a human perspective evil is a cause for sorrow, and the prisoner's desire for justice is not easy to dismiss, especially when expressed, as here, as concern for others rather than self-pity. Even as Philosophy seeks to lead the prisoner upward to individual salvation, he looks back out of love for "the dead" who will be left behind.

Philosophy initially envisions her discussion of evil as a momentary diversion, promising that "after we've run through all the things that I think I must first set before it . . . I will equip your mind with wings, so that it can raise itself on high" (decursis omnibus quae praemittere necessarium puto . . . pennas etiam tuae menti quibus se in altum tollere possit adfigam) (4.1.8–9). The prisoner's persistent questions, however, seem to defer his upward journey indefinitely, or at least beyond the frame of the *Consolation*. The last mention of the path to the fatherland occurs at the beginning of book 5, where Philosophy warns the prisoner that if he continues to interrupt her, he may never reach his destination:

> I'm hurrying to make good the debt of my promise and to open up for you the path by which you may be carried back to your fatherland. But these questions—even though they are quite useful to know, they are all the same a little off to one side of the path of what I had proposed. And it's reasonable for me to be afraid that you'll be exhausted on the sidetracks and won't be able to bear up for traveling the straight path through to its end.
>
> "Festino," inquit, "debitum promissionis absolvere viamque tibi qua patriam reveharis aperire. Haec autem etsi perutilia cognitu tamen a propositi nostri tramite paulisper aversa sunt, verendumque est ne deviis fatigatus ad emetiendum rectum iter sufficere non possis." (5.1.4–5)

Relihan sees the prisoner's deferral of ascent as an effort to defer death: if he manages to keep Philosophy talking long enough, he will be able to escape execution.[29] But the *Consolation* is not *One Thousand and One Nights*. As in Plato's *Crito* and *Phaedo*, the prisoner has already been sentenced to death by the state in which he lives, in accordance with its laws. And while Philosophy prepares the prisoner to undergo his sentence, she is not his executioner. Nor does she advocate suicide, a possibility Socrates likewise rejects in the *Phaedo* (61c–62d). At issue, then, is not the timing of the prisoner's death but the state of mind in which he will die. In keeping with Socrates's claim in the *Phaedo* that "no one may join the company of the gods who . . . is not completely pure when he departs from life," Philosophy wants the prisoner to separate himself from all human concerns before he dies (82b–c). Worrying that the prisoner's persistent questions about the nature of evil and the relationships among Providence, Fate, and free will distract him from that imperative, she hurries for his sake rather than her own, because she understands transcendence to be a prerequisite for salvation.

The prisoner's willingness to tarry is more difficult to parse—especially since, having found his voice in the middle reaches of the *Con-*

solation, he barely speaks in its final book. This silence may simply be a sign of failure: the *Consolation* makes it clear that, even with Philosophy's help, the prisoner will never be Socrates's equal. And yet, as many of Marenbon's "Christianizing" critics point out, at the end of the *Consolation* the privileged mode of connection with the divine shifts from Neoplatonic participation to prayer. In the middle of the third book, as Philosophy and the prisoner near their point of highest ascent, Philosophy suggests that the prisoner's goal should be a participatory union with God:

> Since people become happy by securing happiness for themselves, yet true happiness is divinity itself, it is obvious that they become happy by securing divinity for themselves. . . . Therefore, every truly happy person is God. But, to be sure, God is one by nature; however, nothing prevents there being as many gods as you please by participation.
>
> Nam quoniam beatitudinis adeptione fiunt homines beati, beatitudo vero est ipsa divinitas, divinitatis adeptione beatos fieri manifestum est. . . . Omnis igitur beatus deus, sed natura quidem unus; participatione vero nihil prohibit esse quam plurimos. (3.10.23–25)

Although Socrates's definition of participation in the *Phaedo* is self-consciously vague, it emphasizes commonality, as small things share in Smallness and good ones share in the Good (100d–101b).[30] In the final book of the *Consolation*, in contrast, the prisoner identifies prayer as the "one and only avenue of exchange between human beings and God" (unicum illud inter homines deumque commercium) (5.3.34). The basis for this sacred "commercium" is not commonality but difference, as the supplicant's prayerful recognition of his own inadequacy elicits, but cannot earn, the gift of divine grace. While the participation described by Socrates and Philosophy is available only to a philosophical elite, prayer is open to all who humble themselves—that is to say, to those who recognize their own lowliness rather than to those who endeavor to ascend. The goal of union with God remains the same, but the means of attaining that union changes dramatically. The prisoner also distinguishes much more strongly than Philosophy does between the kinds of union that can be attained in this life and the kinds of union that can be attained in the next. For Philosophy, death barely matters because the true philosopher has already cut all ties to the material world. For the prisoner it matters enormously because it will finally allow him to join the "inapproachable light" (inaccessae luci) of divinity (5.3.35). Seth Lerer aptly suggests that we understand the "missing" *metrum* at the end of the *Consolation*—the *metrum* the prosimetrum's pattern of alternation has led us to expect—as the prisoner's silent prayer.[31]

Does Philosophy, then, talk herself out of a job? If the path to salvation requires prayer rather than philosophical ascent and depends on humble sincerity rather than dialectic, what remains for Philosophy to do? Relihan argues that the *Consolation* documents Philosophy's failure. And yet the text of the *Consolation* ends not with Philosophy's banishment but with a speech in which she combines a call to prayer with a rededication to philosophy as a worldly discipline:

> Therefore, all of you: Avoid vices, cherish virtues; raise up your minds to blameless hopes; extend your humble prayers into the lofty heights. Unless you want to hide the truth, there *is* a great necessity imposed upon you—the necessity of righteousness, since you act before the eyes of a judge who beholds all things.
>
> Aversamini igitur vitia, colite virtutes, ad rectas spes animum sublevate, humiles preces in excelsa porrigite. Magna vobis est, si dissimulare non vultis, necessitas indicta probitatis, cum ante oculos agitis iudicis cuncta cernentis. (5.6.47–48)

In these lines, Philosophy seems finally to accept the prisoner's change of direction. Using second-person plural forms to speak to all readers of the *Consolation* rather than exclusively to the prisoner, she advises them to seek righteousness in this world rather than transcendence. In a sense, we have returned to the version of Philosophy who governed the prisoner's career in public service and who spoke through "the mouth of Plato" in the *Republic* rather than in the *Crito* and *Phaedo*. If the Greek letters pi and theta woven into Philosophy's garment indicate the practical and theoretical branches of philosophy, as has long been assumed, she here returns with the prisoner to her starting point, to moral and political philosophy. She still accompanies the prisoner as he approaches death, as befits his daemon, and she still equips him for salvation—but now his path is defined by ethical conduct rather than Neoplatonic ascent. In some respects, this new role diminishes Philosophy. In comparison to a Christian God who sees and judges every action and responds to every prayer, she necessarily becomes smaller and more worldly. Prayer and grace have taken over her traditional daemonic role as intermediary between human beings and the highest divinity. And yet in another sense, Philosophy's work remains as important as ever. By the end of the prosimetrum, she and the prisoner have rewritten the *Phaedo* by defining a new way to prepare for death—and making it available to readers of the *Consolation*. Where the *Phaedo* invites its readers to marvel at Socrates's exceptionality, at his preternatural calm in the face of death, the Boethian prisoner walks a path that readers of the *Consolation* can realistically follow.[32] They need journey with Philosophy only part of the way, before humbly placing themselves in God's hands.

Thus conceived, Philosophy remains daemon-like, but with carefully delimited capacities. She retains her role as a nurse and a teacher, charged with imparting the discipline of wisdom to upper-class adolescents. Planted by God in the minds of the wise, she continues to accompany them through their lives, teaching them to understand their individual fates in the universal terms of Platonic philosophy. But she does not have access to the transcendent vision of Providence, nor does she play a significant role in the prayerful encounter between the suppliant Christian and divine grace. As a daemon within a specifically Christian universe, her status is somewhat less than granted by Calcidius, who in his Christianizing commentary on the *Timaeus* imagines daemons "interpreting and reporting god's will to humans, revealing to him our needs and bringing divine aid down to us" (132). Yet it remains greater than is allowed by Augustine, who sees daemons as inherently evil because he accepts no mediator except Christ. In the *Consolation*, Philosophy teaches her charges to live with justice in this world so that they can approach their divine judge in a state of righteousness.

PHILOSOPHY IN THE MIDDLE AGES

While many classicists have recently complicated their understanding of Philosophy and the journey she proposes to the Boethian prisoner, many medievalists still see the *Consolation* as tracing a straightforward narrative of Neoplatonic ascent. In Dronke's account, a numinous Philosophy helps the Boethian prisoner "to win *for himself* that insight into the divine principle present in the world, which he has been taught to accept since youth in the Neoplatonic schools."[33] Some medievalists transfer this numinous conception of Philosophy to her medieval descendants, as when Andrew Galloway links Boethius's *Consolation of Philosophy*, Alan of Lille's *Complaint of Nature*, Jean de Meun's continuation of the *Roman de la Rose*, Guillaume de Deguileville's *Pèlerinage* trilogy, and Langland's *Piers Plowman* in a tradition of "debate between a transcendentally authoritative feminine figure . . . and a human being (who is almost always . . . male) seeking or needing assistance."[34] Newman goes a step further, categorizing the protagonists of many of these same works as allegorical goddesses, "substantive beings" as opposed to "mere rhetorical tropes."[35] Other medievalists see these same personifications as complicated, or even compromised, but treat this complication as a departure from rather than an elaboration of their Boethian source.[36] Only a handful of medievalist critics draw a direct line between the limitations of Boethius's Philosophy and those of her descendants. Among them, Wetherbee finds that "the major poets who appropriate the *Consolation* to their own purposes tend to respond to its existential quality, its psychological complexity, and the difficulties Boethius's Prisoner encounters in his attempts to assimilate Philosophy's teaching."[37] William Heise argues more specifically that even though medieval writers were not familiar with the classical genre of Menippean satire, as close readers of Boethius they nonetheless perceived the *Consolation*'s ironic potential, using it as a springboard for their own literary endeavors.[38] For this small group of medievalists, Philosophy's limitations are central to her legacy.

The remainder of this chapter takes up where this last group of critics leaves off, arguing that—like her Boethian predecessor—the medieval Philosophy is best characterized as a daemonic personification. To be clear, I do not wish to suggest that medieval writers understood Philosophy *to be* a classical daemon. Almost by definition, the medieval Philosophy is cut off from the classical tradition that manifests itself in the *Consolation*'s dense network of citations. Although she still has eyes that glow like fire and a garment woven with her own hands, these details no longer recall the Athena of the *Iliad*, just as her garment's tattered hem no longer recalls the Love of the *Symposium*. To the extent that medieval commentaries on the *Consolation* discuss classical daemonology, they follow Augustine in equating daemons with demons.[39] The commentators instead approach Philosophy in much the same way they approach the classical gods, treating her as an *integumentum* that simultaneously obscures and points toward philosophical truth. This mode of reading allows them to attribute to Philosophy the formal characteristics of classical daemons without any accompanying pagan content. For the most important medieval commentators, Philosophy remains an intermediate figure who oscillates between the divine and the ridiculous, even as she serves the Boethian prisoner as a personal guide. If anything, Philosophy's femininity features even more prominently in the commentaries than it does in Boethius's text, becoming a device for exaggerating Philosophy's daemonic characteristics. She is demoted from physician to sickroom attendant, and readers are instructed to leave her behind as they approach the higher reaches of her namesake discipline. For the Platonist William of Conches as for the Aristotelians Nicholas Trevet and William of Aragon, Philosophy becomes an aide to beginning philosophers rather than a mentor to giants of the field such as Socrates and Plato.

The commentaries I examine resolve a number of misconceptions about the medieval reception of Boethius's Philosophy. First, they counter Johan Huizinga's claim that medieval readers naïvely understood Philosophy to be a real, concrete being. As we will see, all three commentators explicitly identify Philosophy as a rhetorical trope and thus as the self-conscious verbal creation of the author Boethius. Second, they make it clear that they do not understand Philosophy to be either a Platonic form or the direct representation of a Platonic form, whether that form is divinely revealed in the manner of Mechthild of Magdeburg's Love or approximated dialectically in the manner of Cicero's Eloquence. Like Boethius, they treat the forms as so far "above" Philosophy that they are beyond her ken. Third, the commentators do not present Philosophy as a site for identificatory self-formation in the manner of the Prudentian personifications discussed in chapters 1 and 2 but as a tool to be deployed insofar as she is useful, then set aside when she is not. William of Conches, in particular, encourages readers to depersonify Philosophy whenever her femininity becomes a hindrance. Far from treating Philosophy as awe-inspiring or numinous, then, the commentators amplify her daemonic characteristics, diminishing her stature and authority compared to Boethius's original personification. To the extent that Philosophy refers to an underlying truth, she does so indirectly, via the framework of integumental allegory—and in William of Aragon's terms "obscurely" and "imperfectly." The Philosophy of the medieval commentary tradition has less in common with Mechthild of Magdeburg's exalted Love than with the pagan gods in Virgil's *Aeneid* and Ovid's *Metamorphoses*.

The Platonist William of Conches, author of a commentary named *Glosae super Boetium* (Glosses on Boethius) by its modern editor, was a prominent member of the school of Chartres.[40] Although his commentary was composed in the early twelfth century, it builds on an earlier tradition of marginal glosses often associated with Remigius of Auxerre. Incorporating but also superseding those glosses, it survives in its original form in at least seventeen manuscripts, in a thirteenth-century revision in at least eleven more manuscripts, and as marginal glosses and compiled with other commentaries in many additional codices. Although William was a committed Platonist, to the point of attracting censure for describing Plato's World Soul as an integumental representation of the Holy Spirit, his commentary does not treat Philosophy as a fully authoritative figure, much less as numinous or transcendent in the manner of an Augustinian formal personification. Instead, she is first and foremost an *integumentum*: a prosopopoeia crafted by Boethius both to indicate and to occlude a deeper philosophical truth. As such she is not mere rhetoric, since she points beyond herself to an underlying reality. At the same time, she is not uncomplicatedly real, having instead the same mythic or allegorical status that William assigns to the pagan gods. In this capacity, his version of Philosophy represents, in quick succession, the biblical personification of Wisdom, the academic discipline of Philosophy, and the human faculty of reason. At key moments, she also ceases to represent anything at all, with William instructing his readers to reduce her from a personification to a series of philosophical precepts. In important respects this mutability reflects that of classical daemons, as Philosophy transforms herself in order to become what her students need her to be. In William's commentary, however, these accommodations become so extreme that Philosophy ceases to lead her charges and begins to follow them, a shift in status that is expressed, in part, through his increased emphasis on her femininity.

Criticism of the *Glosae super Boetium* has had relatively little to say about Philosophy or her relationship with the Boethian prisoner. Instead, it has concentrated primarily on William's use of allegorical interpretation to find truth behind the veil of fable. As Alastair Minnis and A. B. Scott put it, "In the hands of scholars like William . . . the literary theory of *fabula* derived from Cicero, Macrobius, and Isidore was integrated and vastly extended to become an all-embracing system of 'secular allegory' which comprised historical, philosophical, physical/astrological, and moral interpretations of pagan myth and metaphor."[41] Where Macrobius had licensed allegorical reading of "fabulous narrative" (narratio fabulosa), which "rests on a solid foundation of truth" (fundatur veri soliditate) even though it is "treated in a fictitious style" (per quaedam composita et ficta profertur), William finds philosophical value in a much wider range of texts.[42] Lodi Nauta sees these integumental readings as performing a number of distinct functions: bringing Platonic ideas into harmony with Christian orthodoxy; moralizing elements of pagan myths deemed base or immoral; and challenging established readings, often by offering naturalistic interpretations of biblical passages or Christian doctrines.[43] Critical attention to William's commentary has focused overwhelmingly on his treatment of a relatively small group of Boethian *metra* that espouse Neoplatonic doctrine and allegorize classical myth: the Timaean hymn of 3.m9; the journey of Orpheus in 3.m13; the encounter between Ulysses and Circe in 4.m3; and the stories of Agamemnon and Iphigenia, Ulysses and Polyphemus, and the labors of Hercules in 4.m7. Although Wetherbee claims, almost in passing, that "Philosophy comes to [the prisoner] as his own better wisdom, speaking for the spirit against the flesh," he turns almost immediately to William's gloss on the grief-torn Muses, the "lacerae Camenae" who both mirror and intensify the prisoner's miserable state.[44] My reading of the *Glosae super Boetium* seeks to redress this imbalance. Wetherbee notes that William pays disproportionate attention—twenty-three pages in the modern edition—to the *metrum* on Orpheus and Eurydice.[45] The description of Philosophy in the first prose section of the *Consolation* occupies William's attention for some twenty-nine pages, however, and he continues to comment regularly on her characterization throughout the first book. These discussions support Wetherbee's claim only in part. They likewise complicate James Paxson's assumption, shared to an important extent by Newman, that rhetorical personification and Neoplatonic personification are somehow incompatible. Where Paxson asserts that Neoplatonic personification is blind to its own rhetorical underpinnings and that self-consciously rhetorical personification is necessarily terminist or nominalist, William of Conches characterizes Philosophy as both a guide to a higher reality *and* an instance of prosopopoeia. Indeed, she is simultaneously and sequentially a rhetorical trope, the biblical Wisdom, the human virtue of wisdom, and the academic discipline of philosophy.

As befits Boethius's place in the Christian canon, but in marked contrast to the opening of the original *Consolation*, William's commentary begins with an encomium of Boethius as author. William's preface rewrites the prisoner's self-pitying complaint in book 1, prose 4 as a combination of epic and hagiography, supplementing it with details from Boethius's other works to cast the author as an exemplary soldier of Christ. First battling on behalf of the faith with words, Boethius disputes with the heretics Nestorius and Eutyches, confounding them in a public council. Then, "armed with the strength of faith" (uirtute fidei armatus), he uses his authority to shield innocents from the "tyrannical rage" (tyrannica rabies) of the Arian Theodoric, king of the Goths and conqueror of the Romans (*accessus* 14–16). This opposition prompts Theodoric to arrange for Boethius's arrest on trumped-up charges and his conviction using manufactured evidence. Under sentence of death, Boethius composes the *Consolation* not for his own sake but as a form of pastoral care, lest "in a similar case someone less perfect or experienced might be cast down to the point of desperation" (aliquem minus perfectum uel peritum simili casu usque ad desperationem posse deprimi) (*accessus* 28–30). As described in William's *accessus*, then, Boethius fits the profile of a Christian martyr, always already perfect and fighting fearlessly for the faith. Yet he also qualifies as one of the philosophical martyrs Philosophy describes in *Consolation* 1.3, joining Socrates in winning "the victory of an unjust death" at the hands of a tyrannical state. In the case of Boethius, who fought as a Christian but wrote a work of ethical rather than theological consolation, the two categories overlap, and even threaten to collapse into each other. Although most of the information in the *accessus* is derived from the prisoner's speech of self-defense, William transforms it from an extended lament, "barked out" (delatravi) in the first person by a narrator who barely qualifies as human, into an impersonal and authoritative account of Boethius's achievements (1.5.1).

With a preface like this, the *Glosae super Boetium* cannot treat the *Consolation* as a work of autobiography. Rather, William represents Boethius-the-author as something like a puppet master, staging a drama in which Boethius-the-prisoner requires consolation and a personified Philosophy is brought on stage to console him. As William explains at the beginning of his gloss on the first prose section,

> Earlier Boethius shows himself to be someone who needs a consoler. Having done so, he brings in the consoler—that is to say, Philosophy, in the aspect of a woman. And this is prosopopoeia, or the fashioning [*conformatio*] of a new person. And he brings in a new person in order to avert boredom; and therefore [he brings in] that person, that is to say Philosophy, in order to commend his work, which is nothing other than, when the flesh grieves for the loss of worldly things, Philosophy teaches not to grieve for them. He introduces her in the aspect of a woman because she softens the ferocity of souls, or because she nourishes infants with her milk, that is the less wise with easier teachings, or because Philosophy, that is to say wisdom, is referred to by a feminine noun, both by us and by the Greeks, or because women are more accustomed to care for the sick than men, and Boethius was like a sick person.
>
> Hucusque ostendit Boetius se talem qui indigeat consolatore. Hoc facto introducit consolatorem, scilicet Philosophiam sum specie mulieris. Et est prosopopeia, id est conformatio nouae personae. Et idcirco introducit nouam personam ut uitet fastidium; idcirco talem, scilicet

> Philosophiam, ad commendationem sui operis quod non est aliud nisi, cum caro doloret de temporalium amissione, Philosophia docebat non esse dolendum. Introducit autem eam sub specie mulieris, quia mollit ferocitates animorum, uel quia nutrit lacte suo infantes, id est leuioribus sententiis minus sapientes, uel quia feminino nomine uocatur et apud Graecos et apud nos Philosophia, scilicet sapientia, uel quia mulieres melius solent assidere aegris quam uiri; Boetius uero quasi aeger erat. (1.1.1–15)

Philosophy is here treated explicitly as a rhetorical trope, fashioned by Boethius-the-author in order to convey his lesson of philosophical consolation as effectively as possible.[46] William's reference to *conformatio* suggests that Boethius forms or shapes Philosophy as if he were a sculptor, but it is also a technical rhetorical term, the standard Latin translation of *prosopopoeia*. His Philosophy chases away readerly *fastidium*—nausea, distaste, or disgust, especially in the face of overabundance—in much the same way that, within the text, she chases away the tragic Muses. In its place, she offers readers a wholesome pleasure, recommending the *Consolation* in ways that the author cannot do in propria persona. In important respects, Philosophy's role is similar to that of the metrical sections of the *Consolation*, of which William says, "In his prose Boethius uses reason for consolation; in his verse he interposes pleasure, so that grief is driven away" (prosa igitur Boetius utitur ratione ad consolationem, in metro interponit delectationem, ut dolor remoueatur) (*accessus* 61–63). As a rhetorical rather than strictly philosophical element of the *Consolation*, Philosophy prevents the reader from surfeiting on rational discourse, lest he turn away in disgust.

William also pays special attention to Philosophy's femininity. He initially suggests that Philosophy's gender, like the rest of her persona, is the product of Boethius's rhetorical fashioning. If Boethius had been so inclined, he presumably could have introduced a personification *sub specie viri* rather than *sub specie mulieris*. And yet, even as William characteristically offers a series of possible interpretations, with the implication that the reader should choose among them as he sees fit, cumulatively they suggest that Philosophy's femininity is overdetermined. Philosophy must be feminine not only to reflect the grammatical gender of the relevant Greek and Latin nouns but also so that she can offer the reader a respite from the relentlessly masculine rationality of the *Consolation*'s propositional content. Her work as a feminine personification is thus emotional rather than argumentative. She soothes troubled souls and cares for the sick not as the highly trained physician of the original *Consolation* but as a sickroom attendant who offers unskilled nursing and emotional support. She also nurses the reader in another sense, as a mother or wet nurse. This relationship, which is simultaneously biological and emotional, makes it clear that Philosophy's gender is anything but arbitrary even as it brings a new degree of detail to her embodiment. Philosophy is not abstractly feminine in the manner of a feminine noun; nor is she a veiled figure with nothing underneath. Instead she has a concretely imagined female body, with breasts full of milk. This level of bodily detail renders Philosophy an embodiment of philosophy rather than a mere mouthpiece for philosophical propositions. As a personification, she elicits an emotional reaction from the character Boethius—and thus from the *Consolation*'s imagined readers—that her teachings alone cannot produce.

This initial characterization of Philosophy as a prosopopoeia establishes the framework for the rest of the *Glosae super Boetium*. In the remainder of the commentary, William interprets Philosophy integumentally in much the same way that he later interprets Ulysses's encounter with Circe and the twelve labors of Hercules. Recognizing the divine elements in Boethius's initial description of Philosophy, he first associates her with the biblical personification of Wisdom, glossing the lemma "She was so full of eternity that it was impossible to believe she was of our own age" (aevi plena foret ut nullo modo nostrae crederetur aetatis) as follows (1.1.1):

> That is, of the age of men, which is when man was made or from the time man appeared. But Wisdom is not of the age of men, because Wisdom exists before all creatures. Whence Salomon: *I, Wisdom, came forth from the mouth of the Most High, first-begotten before all creatures.*

> Id est aetatis hominum, quod est cum homine factum uel ab homine inuentum. Sed sapientia non est aetatis hominum, quia ante omnem creaturam sapientia extat. Vnde Salomon: *Ego sapientia ex ore altissimi prodiui primogenita ante omnem creaturam.* (1.1.137–42)

The scripture William cites, from the Vulgate version of Ecclesiasticus, marks the beginning of Wisdom's extended first-person assertion of divinity. Readers of the commentary would have been expected to supply the rest:

> I came out of the mouth of the most High, the firstborn before all creatures: / I made that in the heavens there should rise light that never

> faileth, and as a cloud I covered all the earth: / I dwelt in the highest places, and my throne is in a pillar of a cloud. / I alone have compassed the circuit of heaven, and have penetrated into the bottom of the deep, and have walked in the waves of the sea, / And have stood in all the earth: and in every people, / And in every nation I have had the chief rule: / And by my power I have trodden under my feet the hearts of all the high and low: and in all these I sought rest, and I shall abide in the inheritance of the Lord.
>
> Ego ex ore Altissimi prodivi / primogenita ante omnem creaturam / ego in caelis feci ut oriretur lumen indeficiens / et sicut nebula texi omnem terram / ego in altis habitavi / et thronus meus in columna nubis / gyrum caeli circuivi sola / et in profundum abyssi pentravi / et in fluctibus maris ambulavi / et in omni terra steti / et in omni populo et in omni gente primatum habui / et omnium excellentium et humilium corda virtute calcavi / et in his omnibus requiem quaesivi / et in hereditate eius morabor. (24:5–11)

In interpreting Philosophy as Wisdom, William associates her with God's chief lieutenant, creatrix of the material world, ruler of all nations, and governor of all hearts. Wisdom's most notable attribute is the sheer power through which she dominates land, sky, and seas, although she can also make herself small enough to seek shelter within individual hearts. A few lines later she compares herself simultaneously to brook, river, and sea. At once accessible and overwhelming, life-giving and potentially destructive, and yet still fundamentally unified, she flows out of paradise and penetrates to the lowest parts of the earth (24:40–46). This divine language contrasts sharply with William's characterization of Philosophy as a prosopopoeia just one hundred lines earlier and seems to contradict William's earlier restriction of femininity to the domestic sphere. Where Philosophy the personification breastfeeds infants and tends to the sick, Philosophy the goddess compasses the circuit of heaven and walks in the waves of the sea.

Taken together, these two identities as goddess and prosopopoeia represent the limit cases of Philosophy's ontological range in the *Glosae super Boetium*. On the one hand she is a rhetorical trope, the product of the author's expert craftsmanship and manipulation of gendered images. On the other hand, she points toward something wholly real, to Wisdom as either a divine power or an aspect of divinity. In between, Philosophy becomes, as needed, the academic discipline of philosophy and the human quality of wisdom. These readings are more traditionally integumental, as when William turns Philosophy's handwoven clothing into the quadrivium. The man who wishes to pull her clothes aside, revealing her naked body underneath, becomes a seeker of academic knowledge:

> It should be noted that Philosophy's garments are said, by a certain similitude, to be the quadrivium and other philosophical works. For just as the body is contained and hidden beneath garments, so wisdom is contained in these aforesaid things and hidden from the less learned.
>
> Notandum quod uestes Philosophiae quadam similitudine quadruuium dicuntur et cetera philosophica opera. Quia quemadmodum corpus infra uestes continetur et occultatur, sic sapientia in praedictis continetur et minus eruditis occultatur. (1.1.203–8)

In this description of Philosophy, William renders an integumental reading in something close to paradigmatic form. The garment that alternately veils and reveals Philosophy's body is a literal as well as figurative involucrum, while her body stands, almost as literally, for the corpus of philosophical knowledge. Personification thereby becomes a figure for, as well as a guide to, the procedure of integumental reading. William further emphasizes this point when he specifies that "the gathering of Philosophy's robe in folds is nothing other than collecting the lessons of different philosophical works in one volume, as in this book" (contractio uestium Philosophiae in rugam non est aliud quam collectio diuersarum sententiarum de philosophicis operibus in unum uolumen ut est liber iste) (1.2.90–92). The pleats in Philosophy's robe become the folded pages on which the *Consolation* is written, while her body, as the truth behind the veil, represents the work's moral lessons. William thus allegorizes not only reading in general but also the specific act of reading that he engages in as he writes his commentary and that his reader engages in as he toggles back and forth between the *Consolation* and the *Glosae*. Boethius's personification of Philosophy becomes the paradigmatic *integumentum*, to which all others implicitly refer.

Like William's accounts of Philosophy as goddess and prosopopoeia, this model of integumental reading depends on Philosophy's femininity. It departs from them, however, in treating her as a wholly passive object of sexual conquest. In likening the surface meaning of the text to Philosophy's garments, William encourages his readers to disrobe her as they progress toward a deeper, more desirable truth. The acquisition of wisdom thus becomes, intrinsically rather than accidentally, a sexualized act of penetration. Philosophy herself neither encourages nor resists these advances. To the extent that the reader encounters resistance, it is located in Philosophy's clothes, which—as the surface level of the text—turn away the unlearned with their dense argumentation. Both the tightly woven textile and the tightly woven text, in other words, serve as barriers to entry. The nakedness of Philosophy's body under her clothes must likewise constitute its own encouragement, since Philosophy does nothing to speed things along. In the original *Consolation*, the scene in which Philosophy wipes the worldly blindness from the prisoner's eyes arguably represents the pinnacle of her superhuman powers. In the *Glosae*, the moment becomes curiously agentless, with William explaining that "through this work collected from various philosophical works all pain is removed from Boethius' rational faculty" (hoc opere de diuersis philosophicis operibus collecto a ratione Boetii remotus est omnis dolor) (1.2.93–95). The Boethian prisoner is here consoled by philosophy rather than Philosophy. As soon as the reader penetrates to the meaning of the text, both the prosopopoeia and the goddess disappear. Philosophy exists in order to be unmade, reduced to pure doctrine or *sententia*.

As in William's interpretation of pagan myths, this kind of integumental reading becomes a favorite means of neutralizing perceived improprieties. When William construes the myth of Jupiter and Semele, he sidesteps their adultery by allegorizing him as ether and her as earth to produce a scientific-sounding account of the fertilization of plants.[47] When he reads the scene in the *Consolation* in which Philosophy, "stirred up for a moment" (commota paulisper), derides the Muses as "little stage whores," he comments (1.1.7–8):

> It should be noted that [Boethius] says that Philosophy was disturbed, but only for a short time, because it is natural for men to become angry—that is why irascibility is said to be a natural power of the soul—but the wise temper their anger and bring it to an end. Whence it is said in the Psalm: *Be ye angry, and sin not.*

> Notandum quod dicit Philosophiam commotam sed paulisper, quia est naturale homini irasci—unde irascilitas dicitur naturalis uis animae—sed sapientis est iram temperare et finire. Vnde in Psalmo dicitur: *Irascimini et nolite peccare.* (1.1.424–28, Psalms 4:5)

Relihan argues that at this point in the *Consolation* Boethius's Menippean satire is directed against Philosophy, and I have pointed to the Boethian

Philosophy's emotional and sometimes comic behavior as evidence of her status as a Neoplatonic daemon. Whereas the heavenly gods are unchanging and immovable, daemons share human emotions both for good and for ill. William of Conches responds to this same crux by minimizing Philosophy's anger, describing it as natural, temperate, and short-lived. He also shifts its locus from Philosophy as a feminine being, potentially jealous of the Muses' intimate relationship with the prisoner, to Philosophy as a representation of wise men. Such men become angry because, as the Psalmist recognizes, anger is part of the human condition; it is both inevitable and acceptable as long as it is not allowed to grow into the sin of wrath. This emphasis on wise men effectively unmakes Philosophy yet again in order to avoid the impropriety of an outraged *matrona*. Instead, she represents a group of normatively masculine human beings, both in their experience of anger and in their ability to control it. In the process, she momentarily ceases to be a personification, since instead of signifying *through* her feminine embodiment, she signifies despite it.

William, then, posits a much closer relationship between personification and integumental reading than is usually recognized. The feminine personification of Philosophy, with her body hidden beneath an elaborate garment, embodies William's characteristic mode of reading. Indeed, her very existence invites readers to draw back the veil of surface meaning to reveal the allegorical significance underneath. In this context, the veiled meaning is alluring in large part because it is hidden, even as it helps to solve the problem of a pagan or otherwise unseemly literal sense. Integumental reading plays peekaboo with the body of the text, which is also the feminine body of the personification. Even as it is sexually charged, however, this mode of reading includes its own escape valve. When Philosophy's body threatens to become unseemly, as when she approaches the misogynist stereotype of the jealous woman, it can be circumvented via the same integumental procedure William uses on pagan texts. In such cases, William invites his clerkly audience to read past Philosophy's feminine body to the collectivity of wise men she represents. Personification, then, becomes a specialized machine for clerks much as a hoist is a specialized machine for builders. Rather than lifting its users toward transcendence, as imagined by Gregory the Great, it facilitates "deeper" reading—a change in metaphorical direction that corresponds to William's interest in this world as well as the next. As a machine, however, it can, and indeed must, be set aside when it no longer serves its user's larger purpose.

In the *Glosae*, then, Philosophy is even more variable than she is in the *Consolation*, both more human and more divine, more fictional and more real. To the extent that William theorizes this fluctuation, rather than simply offering a series of disconnected and potentially incompatible alternatives, he does so via Boethius's description of Philosophy's "height of a measure hard to fix" (statura discretionis ambiguae) (1.1.2). For William, this changeable height is the key to Philosophy's overall changeable nature:

> That stature is difficult to determine in that it does not have a fixed limit, because now it appears to be greater, now less. Philosophy's stature is therefore difficult to determine, because at one time it seems small as she discusses small matters, such as the inculcation of morals in ethics, household management in economics, and the governance of the commonwealth in politics. It seems greater, however, when she discusses heavenly matters, and greatest when she discusses the creator. . . . And this is *effexegesis*, that is an explanation of what comes before.

> Statura illa est discretionis ambiguae in qua non est certus terminus, quia modo maior apparet, modo minor. Philosophiae ergo statura discretionis ambiguae est, quia modo parua uidetur cum de paruis tractat ut de institutione morum in ethica, de dispensatione familiae in economica, de gubernatione reipublicae in politica. Maior uero uidetur cum de caelestibus tractat, maxime de creatore. . . . Et est effexegesis, id est expositio praecedentum. (1.1.143–52)

Philosophy's variable height allows her to lead her students up the ladder of philosophical knowledge, from the basics of individual self-government to the contemplation of the universe and its creator. But it also suggests that what Philosophy says at any given moment determines who and what she is. As Philosophy spans the philosophical curriculum from ethics to theology, she also spans the ontological range from human to divine. In this, Philosophy resembles Platonic daemons, who likewise change in height and mediate between humanity and divinity. William explains Philosophy's shape-shifting, however, as an example of the rhetorical trope of *effexegesis*, or explanation of preceding material. He accordingly suggests that here and throughout the *Consolation*, it is Philosophy's nature to change her nature, the better to accommodate her pupils' varying needs. The normative direction of change is from low to high, as Philosophy supervises her charges' literal and figurative growth from infancy to adulthood. William stipulates, however, that it can also make sense to reverse course, acknowledging that Philosophy's students must sometimes descend from higher to lower knowledge "for the sake of the common good" (causa communis utilitatis) (1.1.347). William's Philosophy, then, is a tutelary figure who accompanies her charges wherever they need to go. In doing so she parts ways with the Philosophy of the *Consolation*, who, until the very end of the work, consistently seeks to lead the prisoner toward transcendence, sometimes despite his protestations to the contrary.

This variable characterization risks conflating Philosophy with Fortune, who is constant only in her changeability. As depicted in the *Glosae*, the two have much in common. Both are exemplary instances of prosopopoeia, introduced for the sake of rhetorical variation (2.2.1–6). Where Boethius describes Fortune's "multiformes . . . fucos," her many tricks, her ever-changing use of paints, rouges, and dyes, William glosses *fucus* as "a color superimposed on natural color, but often applied for the sake of deception, when something is added to hide the truth" (color superpositus naturali colori, sed saepe ponitur pro deceptione cum ueritati celandae aliquid adiungitur), associating it with rhetorical ornamentation in general, or what he calls "rhetorical color" (rhetorici coloris) (2.1.3; 2.1.23–25, 36). Fortune, then, joins Philosophy as a paradigmatic example of prosopopoeia, from *prosopon* (face, mask) + *poiein* (to make), making up her own face for the dual purposes of adornment and disguise. She implicitly represents the dark side of personification, as well as the broader use of rhetoric to mislead rather than to educate. William seeks to distance Fortune from Boethius's personification of Philosophy by distinguishing between *eloquentia sine sapientia* (eloquence without wisdom) and *eloquentia cum sapientia* (eloquence with wisdom) (2.1.31–45). He cannot carry this distinction to its logical conclusion, however, because he cannot bring himself to imagine Philosophy adorning herself with the cosmetics and rhetoric he has just associated with eloquence. Instead, he insists that what Boethius calls Philosophy's "vivid color" (colore vivido) is "the beauty of philosophy and the delight of wisdom, and this color is vivid, that is natural, because philosophical propositions are beautiful and delightful without the adornment of rhetorical color" ([p]hilosophiae pulchritudo et delectatio sapientiae, et est color ille uiuidus, id est naturalis, quia sine omni ornatu rhetorici coloris pulchrae sunt et delectabiles philosophicae rationes) (1.1.5, 1.1.127–30).[48] Ultimately, William can only protect Philosophy from impropriety by once again reducing her to a series of philosophical propositions, which can be beautiful and delightful without the complications of a female body. This undoing of Philosophy suggests a fundamental discomfort with personification—and rhetorical ornamentation more generally—as an inherently deceptive and feminizing process that can only partly be contained by distinguishing between Philosophy's *eloquentia cum sapientia* and Fortune's *eloquentia sine sapientia*.

Philosophy, as I have tried to show, occupies an ambiguous if not ambivalent position in William of Conches's *Glosae super Boetium*. Rather than conforming to a single paradigm of personification, she is by turns a rhetorical trope, a goddess, an academic discipline, and a human faculty. This variability makes Philosophy extremely useful. As a tutelary figure, she can become whatever the situation demands, whatever her students need her to be. But this same variability limits her authority, not least because, in the Neoplatonic paradigm, worldly changeability is contrasted with the divine stability of the forms. In the best-case scenario, Philosophy becomes a follower rather than a leader, remaking herself rather than the situation in order to achieve harmony between the two. We have seen that in the *Consolation*, Philosophy is almost relentless in her desire to lead the prisoner to his otherworldly fatherland, warning him sternly against even so much as a backward glance. In contrast, in the *Glosae* she is content to accompany her charges down as well as up the hierarchy of disciplines, provided that their actions remain consistent with the public good. Rather than discoursing on the meaninglessness of political honors, in the manner of her Boethian predecessor, she stands ready to advise officeholders on the best course of action. This shift not only transforms the *Consolation* into a prototype for medieval mirrors for princes but also casts Philosophy as Aristotle to the reader's Alexander, wiser than but still subordinate to the reader she counsels. In the worst-case scenario, Philosophy's variability associates her with Fortune's initially seductive but ultimately deceptive femininity. By comporting herself according to the situation and needs of her students, she comes dangerously close to the changeability of Fortune, who initially shows everyone the face they want to see. William responds to this danger by instructing his readers to depersonify Philosophy, turning her into a collection of philosophical precepts when she risks becoming unruly. Implicitly, William can turn Philosophy into the biblical Wisdom because he can also reduce her to a series of "philosophicae rationes" whenever the occasion demands. Some of this variability can perhaps be attributed to the discontinuous genre of commentary, which allows for alternative and sometimes mutually contradictory interpretations. But it also bespeaks a desire to limit Philosophy's authority, to associate her with elementary pedagogy rather than higher education. In important respects, Philosophy's status is lower than that of Neoplatonic daemons, who guide their charges from above and stand ready to represent them at the seat of judgment.

William of Conches exerted such a powerful influence on later commentators and translators that for much of the twentieth century Nicholas Trevet was derided as a plagiarist.[49] The accusation, of course, is wildly anachronistic, misunderstanding not only medieval commentaries in general, but also the relationship between William's and Trevet's commentaries in particular. A better comparison would be to successive versions of a textbook or scholarly edition. The first defines the field in its day but eventually comes to be seen as out of date. The second, recognizing the enduring usefulness of the original, revises it to account for the contemporary critical conversation. Trevet's revisions, composed around 1300, draw heavily on rediscovered Aristotelian texts. Nonetheless, he treats William "with a lot more respect and awareness of common ground than often was expressed by a new generation of scholars for the old."[50] Trevet's commentary, which survives in more than one hundred manuscripts and a wide variety of adaptations—and seems to have stood open on Chaucer's desk as he composed the *Boece*—mediates William's understanding of Philosophy to new generations of medieval readers.[51] Trevet follows William in treating Philosophy as a daemonic personification, while continuing to reduce her stature and undermine her authority. He contrasts Philosophy with the biblical Wisdom, treating her as the goddess's worldly double, a rhetorical personification who prepares readers to be illuminated by the goddess herself.

Trevet begins his commentary with a discussion of an Augustinian formal personification, but the personification is the biblical Wisdom rather than the Boethian Philosophy. His prologue echoes William of Conches by citing Ecclesiasticus, while combining a Platonic epistemology with an Aristotelian vocabulary of causation:

> Every effect whose starting point is an intellectual operation is attributed to an individual soul as the efficient cause. This book is just such an effect: its starting point and efficient cause was Boethius' soul, to the extent that divine, illuminated Wisdom made herself visible, through which [the soul] gleamed with doctrine, most usefully for itself and for others. Whence it can be said of his soul, from Ecclesiasticus 51, *My soul shone in her wisdom.*
>
> Omnis enim effectus cuius principium est operacio intellectualis attribuitur proprie anime tamquam cause efficienti. Talis effectus est liber iste cuius principium efficiens fuit anima Boecii in quantum diuina sapiencia illustrata extitit per quam sibi et aliis utiliter luxit

> in doctrina. Unde de anima sua dicere potuit istud Ecclesiastici 51: *In sapiencia illius luxit anima mea.* (prologue 9)[52]

Boethius's soul is here the efficient cause of the *Consolation of Philosophy,* but only insofar as it is illuminated by the numinous Wisdom, traditionally associated with Christ. Where William's quotation from Ecclesiasticus emphasizes Wisdom's sheer power, Trevet's emphasizes her intimate, even symbiotic relationship with the wise man. The verse he cites describes the culmination of a process of coming to know that begins a few lines earlier:

> She flourished as a grape soon ripe. / My heart delighted in her, my foot walked in the right way, from my youth up I sought after her. / I bowed down my ear a little, and received her. / I found much wisdom in myself, and I profited much therein.

> Defloriet tamquam praecox uva / laetatum est cor meum in ea / ambulavit pes meus iter rectum / a iuventute mea investigabam eam / inclinavi modice aurem meam et excepi illam / multam inveni in me ipso sapientiam multum profeci in ea. (51:19)

In these lines, the speaker alternately pursues Wisdom as a desirable if otherworldly young woman and internalizes wisdom as a moral and intellectual discipline. As the passage continues, he begins to use his wisdom to teach, inviting the "unlearned" (indocti) to draw close so that they, too, can take in "divine . . . Wisdom" (51:31). The speaker even describes this meeting as consolatory, urging his listener to "let your soul rejoice" (laetetur anima vestra) in receiving Wisdom (51:37). Trevet thus places Boethius-the-author in the role of the speaker of Ecclesiasticus 51:18–38. He first becomes wise by encountering Wisdom, in this case through the medium of light rather than sound in keeping with the widespread Augustinian understanding of knowledge as divine illumination. Then, glowing with reflected light, he seeks to share his wisdom with others by composing the *Consolation*. Readers of the *Consolation* in turn occupy the position of the unlearned in Ecclesiasticus, invited to draw close to Boethius—in part by reading Trevet's commentary—so that they too can be illuminated by Wisdom.

Trevet's initial discussion of Philosophy, which depends heavily on William, feels worldly, even commonplace, in comparison:

> This is the first prose section in which Boethius brings in the person who consoles—that is, Philosophy—and practices prosopopoeia. According to the second book of Isidore's *Etymologies*, chapter 13, prosopopoeia is when personhood is imposed on a thing that does not have personhood, as with Philosophy. And note that Boethius suffering and Philosophy consoling are nothing other than the mind suffering from the oppression of sensuality and reason consoling through the vigor of wisdom. . . . It should be known that Philosophy is here introduced in the person of a woman, for a three-fold reason: first, that in both Greek and Latin *philosophy* is a feminine noun; second, that just as a women nourishes her baby with milk, so philosophy nourishes those who are less wise with gentle teachings; third, because a woman is naturally more compassionate and so a more suitable person for consoling the miserable and caring for the sick. For Boethius was like a sick person.
>
> Hec est prosa prima in qua inducit Boecius personam consolantem scilicet Philosophiam et facit prosopeiam. Est enim prosopopeia secundum Isidorum Ethimologiarum libro secundo, capitulo 13, quando persona imponitur rei que personam non habet, cuiusmodi est Philosophia. Et nota quod Boecius dolens et Philos[o]phia consolans non sunt aliud nisi animus dolens ex aggrauacione sensualitatis et racio consolans ex uigore sapiencie. . . . sciendum est quod Philosophia hic introducitur sub persona mulieris, cuius triplex est racio: quarum una est quod tam apud Grecos quam apud Latinos philosophia feminini generis est; secunda quia sicut mulier lacte suo infantem nutrit, sic philosophia lenibus sentenciis minus sapientes; tercia quia mulier naturaliter est magis compassiua et ideo aptior persona ad consolandum miseros et assidendum egris. Boetius autem quasi eger erat. (1.1, pp. 24–25)

Trevet follows William in presenting Philosophy as an instance of prosopopoeia, adducing the same three reasons for her femininity.[53] He also follows William in interpreting Philosophy via an integumental gloss. In this case, Boethius-the-prisoner is the mind buffeted by sensuality, while Philosophy is "reason" consoling with "the strength of wisdom." Trevet stops short, however, of his predecessor's direct equation of Philosophy with the biblical Wisdom. Instead, Trevet's Philosophy draws on or mediates the vigor of a more earthly wisdom, delivering it to the prisoner in a way that will restore him to health without overwhelming his diminished forces. For Trevet, Wisdom is a heavenly power, either a goddess in her own right or a figure for Christ, while Philosophy is a carefully crafted prosopopoeia whose primary domains are the nursery and the sickroom. Wisdom is all but omnipotent, while Philosophy's authority depends on her charges' infantile or disabled state. When the infants she nurses grow up and the sick men to whom she tends become well, they will no longer need her.

Despite these differences, Wisdom and Philosophy perform similar roles within their respective spheres. As Wisdom illuminates Boethius-the-author, filling him with the divine light, so Philosophy heals Boethius-the-prisoner, restoring him with her sound advice. Both roles are intimate, and both are paradigmatically rather than accidentally feminine, inspiring or enabling men to reach their full potential. They even help different versions of the same man, with Philosophy tending to the abject and sinful Boethius within the text while Wisdom tends to the powerful and saint-like Boethius outside it. Trevet thus suggests that, in his wisdom, Boethius structures the *Consolation* in a way that mirrors his own experience as author, which itself mirrors the interaction between the wise man and Wisdom in Ecclesiasticus. Trevet's Philosophy is accordingly a reduced, domesticated version of the biblical goddess. Instead of embodying truth directly via divine illumination, she points toward it integumentally via prose and verse. Trevet defines Philosophy as a daemonic personification by characterizing her as a more elementary, more worldly, more speculative version of the biblical Wisdom. She heals men's souls and teaches them to be rational, preparing them to be illuminated by her divine counterpart.

Although once thought to have been composed in 1335, the Boethius commentary by the "arch-Aristotelian" William of Aragon almost certainly predates Trevet's.[54] The mistaken dating can be attributed in part to William of Aragon's relatively confrontational attitude toward earlier commentaries, including that of William of Conches. A more committed Aristotelian than Trevet, he warns his readers, "We should not impute to Boethius, who knew Aristotle very well, the crimes of the Platonists" (Nec imponemus Boecio platonicorum crimina, qui ualde bene Aristotelem intellexit) (3.m9, p. 190). While William of Aragon's commentary survives in just five manuscripts, its prologue achieved a separate afterlife in medieval French translations of the *Consolation*, including the prefaces to Jean de Meun's *Li Livres de Comfort de Philosophy* (The Book of Comfort of Philosophy) and the anonymous *Le Livre de Boece de Consolacion* (Boethius's Book of Consolation).[55] As part of Jean de Meun's translation, William's preface was another of the texts on Chaucer's desk as he composed the *Boece*. William of Aragon joins William of Conches and Nicholas Trevet in treating Philosophy as a daemon despite his otherwise strongly Aristotelian metaphysics. He goes further than either, however, in limiting her authority. Although he acknowledges that personification can help to lay the foundations for higher knowledge, he defines it as an inherently feminine and material trope that cannot approach the transcendent immateriality of the First Cause. Indeed, his Philosophy is so "low" that she sometimes inspires laughter rather than reverence from her followers, even within her restricted domain.

Of the three Boethius commentators, William of Aragon grants Philosophy the least authority, accentuating and sometimes even exaggerating her daemonic traits. He is also the only commentator who does not explicitly identify Philosophy with prosopopoeia, although he does subject her to rhetorical analysis:

> It should be known that, in one way, Philosophy is understood via antonomasia to stand in for the science of the most universal first causes which is called metaphysics, and first Philosophy and second Al-Farabi [are understood as] the art of arts and the discipline of disciplines in this way. In another way, Philosophy is understood to stand for the real sciences, that is metaphysics, physics, and morality, and is understood in this way by Boethius, as will become clear. In a third way Philosophy is understood more broadly according to that which is comprehensive and regulative in every scientific habit, and in this way the name of Philosophy is widely accepted and Boethius, too, considers her in this way, substituting her clothes for herself, as will become clear when he speaks of this.
>
> Intelligendum est quod Philosophia uno modo accipitur anthonomasice pro sciencia causarum uniuersalissimarum primarum que Methaphisica dicitur et prima Philosophia et secundum Alpharabium ars arcium et disciplina disciplinarum hoc modo; alio modo accipitur Philosophia pro scienciis realibus, scilicet Metaphisica, Phisica et Moralis, et hoc modo accipit eam Boecius, ut patebit; tercio modo accipitur Philosophia large secundum quod est comprehensiua et regulatiua omnis habitus scientifici et hoc modo communiter accipitur nomen Philosophie et sic eciam considerat eam Boecius hic subdens sibi uestes, ut patebit sentenciando de ipsis. (1.1, pp. 13–14)

William of Aragon here specifies that there are three ways to understand philosophy: as the highest form of metaphysics, the exalted science of First Causes; as the "real sciences," which include physics, ethics, and the lower metaphysics; and as the *habitus* of science, the disciplinary practice of scientific thought. While each of these forms of philosophy is distinct, the first is nonetheless set against the other two. William associates the higher metaphysics with Aristotle and Al-Farabi, often referred to as respectively the "First Master" and "Second Master" of later medieval philosophy. Al-Farabi is famous for identifying the First Cause of Aristotelian metaphysics with God, to be approached through negative theology since it cannot be known by intellectual means. As a result, the First Cause is not susceptible to the kinds of analysis Philosophy carries out in dialogue with the Boethian prisoner. Indeed, William suggests that it may not be approachable via personification at all. He claims that with regard to the higher metaphysics, Philosophy signifies via the rhetorical trope of antonomasia, which substitutes epithets such as "First Master" and "Second Master" for proper names such as Aristotle and Al-Farabi. In this context, "Philosophy" simply becomes another name for Aristotle, akin to the more common epithet "Philosopher." Implicitly, antonomasia replaces prosopopoeia because bodies are not suitable vehicles—either materially or conceptually—for approaching the transcendent and immaterial First Cause.

William of Aragon associates the second two aspects of philosophy with personification. He promises that Philosophy's *habitus*, in the sense of characteristic garment, will become a site for considering the *habitus* of philosophy, in the sense of disciplinary practice. He goes on to attribute this work of habituation to Philosophy as a specifically feminine personification:

> It should be known that Philosophy, in these second and third aspects, is described by all philosophers in the form of a woman, and for good reason. For woman is naturally ordained to give birth to and nourish men. That is her proper and perfect work, and because only Philosophy makes men perfect by nourishing them and gently forming them, we read in *The Lives of Philosophers* that Demosthenes and Plato each said that he had two mothers, namely Nature and Philosophy, and that Nature made them first, as rough, material beings, before Philosophy, cleansing them from vices, formed them in divine goodness, nourishing them with virtues and sciences.

> Sciendum quod Philosophia secundo uel tercio modo accepta ab omnibus philosophis est sub forma mulieris descripta, et hoc racionabiliter. Mulier enim ad hoc naturaliter est ordinata ut uirum pariat et nutriat.

> Istud est opus suum proprium et perfectum, et quia sola Philosophia uirum facit perfectum munde nutriendo et suauiter informando, secundum quod legitur libello *De uita philosophorum* Demoscenen et Platonem dixisse, quilibet enim eorum dixit se duas habuisse matres, scilicet Naturam et Philosophiam, et quod Natura primo fecerat quasi materiales et rudes eos, Philosophia uero a uiciis eos mundans uirtutibus et scienciis nutriens diuinis bonitatibus informauit. (1.1, p. 14)

The second two aspects of philosophy can be represented by Philosophy as a personification rather than an instance of antonomasia because they are "lower" moral and intellectual pursuits. In contrast to his predecessors, however, William of Aragon treats Philosophy not as a specifically Boethian invention but rather as the common intellectual heritage of all right-thinking men. Too widespread to be an extemporaneous rhetorical performance, she instead embodies a timeless truth elaborated by, and constitutive of, generation after generation of philosophers. Philosophy's femininity is a central part of this shared heritage. As the "mother" of each philosopher's virtuous second nature, she plays a role similar to that of the personified Grammar of medieval educational discourse, teaching her charges to replace their disordered first nature with a disciplinary *habitus*. Where each man's first birth is literal and material, and so tainted by original sin, his rebirth to Philosophy is figurative and virtuous.[56] For William of Aragon, the personification of Philosophy therefore occupies an important middle ground. As an embodied female figure, she can meet men where they are and provide them with the sustenance they need, with their earliest lessons in science and virtue figured as mother's milk. But because her body is rhetorical rather than real, she can also take them where they need to go, leading them to the brink of the higher metaphysics that William identifies as a wholly intellectual—and thus entirely masculine—realm.

Despite William of Aragon's resolutely scientific vocabulary and emphasis on Philosophy as a figure of speech, he does not sever all connections between Philosophy and the biblical Wisdom. In keeping with his commitment to the personified Philosophy as a truth universally acknowledged, at least among wise men, he surveys the iconography with which she has traditionally been represented: lying in bed, because the quiet soul is made prudent and acquires philosophy; standing in the doorway of a temple, with a caption above her head describing her origin and utility; and as a queen seated on a throne, displaying the breasts with which she nourishes her followers (1.1, pp. 22–23). To these he adds the same passage from Ecclesiasticus cited by William of Conches (24:7–10). Where William of Conches's explication of this passage focuses primarily on Wisdom herself, William of Aragon's focuses primarily on Solomon, both as a wise man and as the traditional author of the biblical wisdom books. He argues that Solomon understood Philosophy in the same way Boethius did, "even though he did not say so expressly in his book of Wisdom about that very same person" (quamuis non ita dixisset expresse libro Sapiencie in persona ipsius) (1.1, pp. 22–23). Solomon's Wisdom and Boethius's Philosophy accordingly become alternate means of representing a single truth about the nature of knowledge. Boethius uses the details of Philosophy's appearance to represent the different domains of knowledge (divine, natural, moral, etc.), while Solomon uses the details of an allegorical landscape. Boethius depicts the seven liberal arts via the ladder on Philosophy's robe, while Solomon does the same with the seven columns of Wisdom's temple (1.1, p. 23; cf. Proverbs 9:1). In short, Philosophy and Wisdom remain associated, but their resemblance depends on the shared wisdom of their respective authors. Because wise men understand the world in similar ways, they choose to represent it in similar terms.

For William of Aragon, however, this human wisdom is not infallible. In the *Consolation*, Philosophy's garments, woven with her own hands, are "perfectly finished of the most microscopic threads, of cunning manufacture and of indecomposable material" (tenuissimis filis subtili artificio, indissolubili materia perfectae) (1.1.3). As glossed in William's commentary, these details signify not only that Philosophy alone illuminates difficulties and shows forth the order of things but also that classical philosophy was often transmitted through excessively subtle poetic metaphors:

> Ancient philosophizers transmitted much of this science obscurely and imperfectly on account of the negligence of ignorance or on account of the metaphors of poets, since many of them were poetasters.
>
> Antiqui philosophantes multa de huius scienciis tradiderunt obscura et imperfecta propter negligenciam ruditatis aut propter methaphoras poetarum, plurimi enim poetizantes fuerunt. (1.1, p. 18)

When viewed as an instance of personification rather than antonomasia, William of Aragon's Philosophy is "low" enough that he can gently poke fun at her—and the pagan philosophers who collectively created her. We can hear an echo of William of Conches's ambivalence about mixing philosophy and rhetoric, despite his attempt to distinguish Philosophy's *elo-*

quentia cum sapientia from Fortune's *eloquentia sine sapientia.* We can also hear an echo of Relihan's reading of the *Consolation* as Menippean satire, which cites this same detail as evidence that Philosophy is not always to be taken entirely seriously: "To draw attention to the subtlety of philosophical argument is rarely complimentary."[57] For William of Aragon, the personified Philosophy is thus emphatically a partial figure. Her domain encompasses the two lower fields of philosophy rather than the discipline as a whole. Even within her domain, the details of her presentation sometimes inspire ridicule rather than reverence. Although she is generally a useful guide, she can also embody obscurity and imperfection.

In William of Aragon's commentary, this understanding of Philosophy's limitations serves as the basis for a broader theory of personification or character making. In his prologue, William distinguishes Philosophy and the Boethian prisoner on the one hand from the Boethian author on the other. Drawing on Plato's distinction between sensible goods, which can be perceived by the senses, and intelligible goods, which must be grasped by the intellect, William argues,

> Boethius sets himself up in the part of a person disturbed and agitated by passions rooted in the senses, and brings forward Philosophy in the part of a person who seeks intelligible goods. So in his own part he displays his afflictions and their motivating causes, and in the part of Philosophy he brings forward arguments which eliminate these afflictions and show their consolation. And for this reason, this book is called *The Consolation of Philosophy.*
>
> Boecius in parte hominis turbati et passionibus sensibilibus agitati se statuit, et in parte hominis bona intellectus sequentis Philosophiam inducit; et ita ipse ex parte sui ipsius dolores et causas motiuas ostendit, et ex parte Philosophie causas annullantes huius dolores et consolacionem ostendentes adducit. Et ideo *De consolacione Philosophie* dicitur iste liber. (prologue, p. 6)[58]

Like William of Conches, William of Aragon here values personification for its emotional force, its ability to offer comfort in troubled times. If anything, he emphasizes this element of the *Consolation* even more strongly than his predecessor. But he also more clearly extends personification into a general principle of person-making, treating Philosophy and the Boethian prisoner as products of the same rhetorical process. Although Philosophy's perspective, freed from the sway of the senses, is obviously "higher" than that of the prisoner, each one still represents a limited point of view. The only unified or universalizing perspective is that of the author—and perhaps, ultimately, the virtuous reader—who both suffers from worldly misfortune in the manner of the prisoner and rises above it in the manner of Philosophy. As William makes clear earlier in his prologue, the Boethian author is a hero "not because of insensibility to pain" (non propter doloris insensibilitatem) but because "he shows that he bears his misfortune very well and wisely, and endures his pain as befits one who is manly and great-hearted" (optime et prudenter ostendit se suam ferre fortunam et uirilis et magnanimus existens sensum sui doloris habere) (prologue, p. 6). This emphasis on persevering through pain obviously owes much to William of Conches's representation of Boethius as a martyr.[59] As described by William of Aragon, however, it also underscores the *Consolation*'s dialogic form, whose value inheres in the interaction of opposing sides. Personification here becomes a tool for articulating a limited point of view. As such, it allows the Boethian author to define the two sides of a debate without giving either one absolute priority. It also helps to produce the literary critical distinction between author and narrator.

The limitations William of Aragon places on Philosophy are part of his larger reframing of the *Consolation* as a work of advice to princes.[60] We have already seen hints of such reframing in William of Conches's commentary, which emphasizes Boethius's noble birth and political leadership while defending "low" uses of philosophy as long as they serve the public good. William of Aragon's depiction of the Boethian author as not only nobly born but also "manly and great-hearted" in his opposition to tyranny builds upon this precedent while aligning Boethius with chivalric ideals. So, too, does his explicit association of the *Consolation* with Aristotle's *Politics* and *Nicomachean Ethics*—which strongly influenced the later medieval tradition of advice to princes—and decidedly moderate stance on the value of worldly goods. In contrast to both the Boethian prisoner, who despairs at the loss of his wealth and status, and Philosophy, who insists that these goods have no value whatsoever, William of Aragon argues that the *Consolation* as a whole instructs its readers in the proper use of earthly power:

> Although Boethius made [this work] for his consolation, those things which are disputed in it clearly teach each person to distinguish among different goods and to which good men ought to direct their hearts and minds, and if men receive an abundance of other goods, it shows what their use should be.

> Licet Boecius ad sui consolacionem fecisset, tamen que in eo disputantur euidenter edocent quemlibet inter bona discernere et ad quod bonum debent homines dirigere cor et mentem et, si alia bona hominibus affluant, ostendunt qualis debeat usus esse. (prologue, p. 4)

Philosophy here provides a counterweight to the prisoner's original position rather than authoritative instruction on the disposition of worldly goods. William implies that the position of the Boethian author is closer to that of the prisoner in the final two books, when he has stopped feeling sorry for himself but refuses to let go of the more general problem of injustice, whereby "punishments for crimes overwhelm good people, and evil people snatch away the rewards of the virtuous" (scelerumque supplicia bonos premant, praemia virtutum mali rapiant) (*Consolation* 4.5.4). The prisoner wants wise men to wield worldly power so that they can govern the polis with justice, rewarding the virtuous and punishing the wicked. In his prologue, William of Aragon uses this position to frame the *Consolation* as a whole, treating it as a work of practical moral instruction—with particular attention to the needs of ruling elites—rather than as a treatise on renouncing worldly attachments.

This approach to the *Consolation* evidently appealed to Jean de Meun, since he appropriated it in the prologue to his own *Livres de Comfort*. William of Aragon's framing of the *Consolation* as a treatise on ethics and politics parallels de Meun's dedication of his translation to King Philippe le Bel of France, as does his treatment of the Boethian author as an exemplary servant of the public good. In placing limits on Philosophy, William also places limits on her claim that wise men must be indifferent to worldly success. This shift in emphasis allows de Meun to position the *Consolation* as a guide to the responsible use of power in this world rather than as a guide to renunciation and transcendence. Philosophy is recast as a helper in this endeavor, an adviser who offers a valuable initial perspective but does not get the last word. She points toward truth rather than representing it directly, but this gesture has become less precise and must be read in conjunction with the contrasting position of the Boethian prisoner in order to grasp the *Consolation*'s overall message. William's and Jean's shared conception of Philosophy, then, is the least authoritative of the three medieval versions I have examined. Banned entirely from the highest reaches of philosophy, she risks transmitting even the lower reaches of the discipline "obscurely and imperfectly," and is soon surpassed by the Boethian prisoner, her own student. The overly intricate weaving of her garments holds her up to derision specifically as a badly dressed woman, a fashion victim whose elaborate and expensive clothing does not show her to advantage in the way she had hoped. Although she nourishes men during their intellectual childhood, she later becomes an object of mingled affection, condescension, and humor, in the manner of an old nurse.

CONCLUSION

My aim in this chapter has been to analyze Philosophy as a personification, to figure out what kind of a being she is. I have tried to show that both in the *Consolation* itself and in its medieval commentaries, Philosophy is a limited figure rather than a transcendent or fully authoritative one. Boethius's Philosophy is undeniably a Platonic personification in the sense of being located within an explicitly Platonic universe, as described in the Timaean hymn of book 3, meter 9 of the *Consolation*. She teaches the prisoner to understand himself not only in Aristotelian terms as a rational animal but also in Platonic terms as a being with a soul, and does everything she can to guide him toward Platonic transcendence. Philosophy does not, however, embody a Platonic form, as those critics who examine Platonic personification generally suggest. For Boethius the forms are perceptible only to God, and perhaps—Boethius makes a point of speaking conditionally—to a select group of men insofar as they participate in divinity. The forms are emphatically not visible to a figure like the Boethian prisoner as he lies in bed at the beginning of the *Consolation*, overcome by lethargy and blinded by grief. Nor are they accessible, or even representable, via prosopopoeia, as indicated by Boethius's decision to personify the faculties of Sense, Imagination, and Reason that allow the soul to derive universals from sense perception, while refraining from personifying the divine intelligence that perceives the forms.[61]

Instead, Philosophy has much more in common with Platonic daemons, as elaborated by Plato, Apuleius, and others. Often identified with abstractions such as Love and Sleep, daemons occupy a position in the Neoplatonic hierarchy between ordinary mortals and the transcendent One. Although they serve as tutelary figures, advising their mortal charges and representing them before the seat of judgment, they are also distinctly limited. The details of Boethius's description of Philosophy, including her flashing eyes and handwoven but tattered garment, consistently link her with classical daemons. So, too, do the satirical elements of her characterization emphasized by Relihan and others, including her displays of sexual jealousy when confronted by Fortune and the Muses. Perhaps the ultimate measure of Philosophy's limitation is that she does not succeed in bringing the prisoner to his otherworldly fatherland. Instead, having redirected Philosophy's attention to the problem of righteous conduct in this world, the prisoner decides to seek salvation through prayer rather than transcendence. Much as Virgil, Dante's indispensable guide through Hell and Purgatory, cannot accompany him through Paradise, Philosophy plays a crucial but limited role in guiding the prisoner through Boethius's Neoplatonic universe.

Medieval commentators on the *Consolation* followed Augustine in condemning classical daemons as agents of the devil. And yet, because they were careful readers of the *Consolation*, closely attuned to Boethius's characterization of Philosophy, they noticed that she has many of the formal characteristics of a daemon. She is an intermediate rather than transcendent figure; she is variable, concerning herself sometimes with earthly matters and sometimes with heavenly; she serves as a guide or counselor to individual human beings, tailoring her teaching to their emotional as well as intellectual needs; she is less than fully authoritative, sometimes even ridiculous. They also noticed that all of these traits are gendered feminine. In the *Consolation*, Philosophy's femininity already undermines her authority as her sexual jealousy threatens to place her on the same ontological plane as Fortune and the Muses. In the commentaries, her gender becomes even more destabilizing. Although Philosophy retains her role as a nursemaid and tutor to beginning philosophers, for mature philosophers she becomes less a guide than—at best—a helpmeet Where in the final books of the *Consolation* Philosophy shifts her attention, quite subtly, from the contemplation of the heavens to earthly justice, the medieval tradition emphasizes her role as an adviser to princes, concerned primarily with ethics and politics. William of Aragon bars her from the highest reaches of philosophy entirely, on the grounds that she is too "low" to offer insight into the exclusively masculine realm of first causes. In accentuating Philosophy's limitations, he subordinates her to the Boethian author, whom he treats as responsible for the *Consolation*'s overall dialectic. Philosophy thus becomes the embodiment of a particular point of view, to be placed in dialogue with other, competing points of view, rather than an embodiment of divine authority.

As a daemonic personification, Philosophy also occupies an intermediate space between rhetoric and reality. While a pagan like Apuleius may well have understood daemons such as Love and Sleep to be real, semidivine beings, Christian writers instead understood them as *integumenta*. Instead of embodying the truth of the forms, in the manner of formal personifications, they point—indirectly, and often "imperfectly and obscurely"—toward a truth that remains hidden. As a result, they do not serve as sites of identification in the manner of Prudentian personifications but rather as tools to be taken up and set down as the situation demands. Embodying a limited perspective and often occupying a limited domain, they generally represent one point of view among many, appearing alongside other figures who approach the same issues from a different angle. It follows that daemonic personifications are speculative in ways that other kinds of personifications are not. Rather than revealing patent truths, they furnish their readers with tools for conducting thought experiments.

This understanding of Philosophy as a daemonic personification in turn enables a revised understanding of an important tradition of medieval allegorical writing. With their indirect and provisional truth claims, daemonic personifications lend themselves to philosophical and even literary elaboration in ways that other kinds of personification do not. It should therefore be unsurprising that we encounter Philosophy's descendants in texts ranging from the *Complaint of Nature* and *Roman de la Rose* to *Piers Plowman* and the *Parliament of Fowls*. In these poems, Philosophy's daughters serve as important tools for speculation precisely because they are intermediately rather than transcendentally authoritative. Their integumental status is often marked by the fact that they rub shoulders with pagan gods, while their shortcomings are marked by—and often explicitly linked to—their femininity. As a result, they serve as suitable guides for the young, the ignorant, and the backward—including narrators who are, as in the commentators' view of the *Consolation*, rather buffoonishly constructed as such. In contrast, they invite higher-ranking members of their audience to exercise their own judgment, adopting a given personification's point of view only insofar as, and for as long as, they find it convincing and useful. Philosophy thus inaugurates a poetic tradition based on speculation rather than truth claims, populated by limited characters, and subject to the critical judgment of elite readers. In doing so, she helps to propagate a number of textual characteristics that we now think of as literary.

PART III

Aristotelian Personification

CHAPTER FIVE

E Pluribus Unum: Abstracting Universals from Particulars

For most of the last century, literary critics thought of personification as, in Jill Mann's terms, "quasi-inevitably embod[ying] a 'Platonizing' tendency," which "assumes or implies that abstractions such as Truth, Justice, Love, Hate, Pride, Avarice and the like are not mere words, but reflections of Ideas that have a real, albeit supra-sensible, existence."[1] In doing so, they ignored not only the variety within Platonic personification, as discussed in chapter 3, but also the possibility of Aristotelian personification, despite Aristotle's enormous influence on medieval thought from the thirteenth century onward. The present chapter seeks to remedy this deficiency by surveying some of the interpretations of Aristotle's metaphysics and epistemology that gained traction during the later Middle Ages and investigating their consequences for personification allegory. In what ways can personifications be said to embody a characteristically Aristotelian metaphysics? How can Aristotelian personifications, as a class, be distinguished from their Platonic counterparts? Do they look, speak, and act differently? Just as important, are there meaningful distinctions to be made *within* the category of Aristotelian personification? How might a moderately realist personification differ from a nominalist one?

To the extent that critics have considered Aristotelian personification, they have primarily focused their attention on nominalism. In doing so, they have tended to conflate the work of the medieval philosophers known as *nominales* or *nominalistae* with the nominalism of twentieth-century post-structuralists such as Paul de Man. Like de Man, Ockham posits a material realm consisting entirely of particulars. Universals such as *horse* and *man* exist only within the human mind. In contrast to de Man, however, Ockham argues that *horse* and *man* refer naturally rather than conventionally or arbitrarily to a given set of particulars. That is to say, Ockham posits a single concept of *horse* and a single concept of *man* to which all right-thinking people subscribe. James Paxson's influential *Poetics of Personification* disregards this distinction, however, when it claims that medieval writers such as Langland anticipate de Man's understanding that "terms are terms," conventional signs with no signified beyond the individual human mind.[2] This conflation of medieval and modern nominalism prompts Paxson to cast his net too widely, arguing that all self-consciously rhetorical medieval allegories are necessarily nominalist. It prompts other critics, from Borges to Mann, to cast their nets too narrowly, assuming that medieval nominalism is incompatible with personification, or at best produces personifications that are "just a game."[3] One need not share Mann's low opinion of post-structuralism to recognize that it does not furnish an adequate account of medieval Aristotelianism or its consequences for medieval personification allegory.

Barbara Newman is part of a much smaller group of critics who give serious consideration to both Platonic and Aristotelian varieties of personification—in part because she recognizes that, far from being the mutually exclusive products of different time periods or metaphysical paradigms, they regularly rub shoulders within the same works. Acknowledging that "it would be foolish to pretend that all personifications should be granted the same ontological status or the same degree of authorial conviction," she cautions,

> One of the most delicate tasks facing the interpreter of visionary and allegorical texts is to decide how seriously to take the goddesses and other personifications that appear in them—or, in other words, to distinguish between substantive beings and mere rhetorical tropes. . . . We might account for our perception of different ontological planes by distinguishing Platonic personifications from Aristotelian ones, reading the former as epiphanies or emanations of a superior reality, the latter as "accidents existing in a substance," personified only for the sake of analytical clarity.[4]

Newman first defines Neoplatonic personifications: they are described using scriptural or liturgical language; they elicit expressions of awe from their interlocutors; they are serious rather than ironic or parodic; and they are intimately linked to God. Aristotelian personifications lack these qualities: they are explanatory devices rather than substantive beings; they are described using ordinary language; they are worldly rather than awe-inspiring or numinous; they are ironic rather than serious; and they lack Platonic personifications' association with divinity. Since Newman's *God and the Goddesses* focuses on the feminine divine, she primarily considers the "highest" subgroup of Platonic personifications: the transcendent formal personifications associated with divine emanation or illumination. In contrast, she defines Aristotelian personifications in the "lowest" possible terms. In describing them as "mere rhetorical tropes," with no connection to universals, she follows Paxson in linking them to twentieth-century nominalism rather than to medieval nominalism or moderate realism. Nonetheless, Newman identifies important attributes of medieval Aristotelian personifications. They do indeed have a reduced ontological status, in the double sense of being both "lower" and less "real" than their Platonic counterparts. They are often associated with irony and social critique—although, as we have seen, "lower" varieties of Neoplatonic personification, including Boethius's Philosophy, can be associated with satire as well. And they tend to be concerned with the present world rather than the kingdom of heaven.

Like Newman, Suzanne Conklin Akbari defines what she calls "horizontal" allegory primarily through contrast with Neoplatonism. In her account, "vertical" allegory derives its structure from the correspondence between microcosm and macrocosm in the Neoplatonic hierarchy of being. As its name suggest, it uses lower truths to point toward higher truths, located outside the text—and indeed outside the material world—in a transcendent realm. In contrast, the chief characteristic of horizontal allegory is seemingly its propensity to deconstruct itself:

> In horizontal allegory, personifications lose their fixed identity as embodied abstraction and behave in ways that suggest they are less personifications than personae, fictional characters with motivations and emotions. Vertical allegory points toward a hidden meaning that the reader must construct within his own mind, a transcendent truth that cannot be conveyed through literal language; horizontal allegory satisfies the reader here and now, exposing the double (or triple) meaning of language explicitly within the text as pun or euphemism. Vertical allegory aims to convey a transcendent truth that cannot be expressed through literal language, whether it concern God, creation, or the nature of identity; horizontal allegory celebrates the play of words and the unfixed nature of linguistic meaning.[5]

Akbari here follows Paxson and Newman in opposing a historically specific medieval Neoplatonism to a version of nominalism that has more in common with post-structuralism than with Ockham and his contemporaries. As a result, she treats horizontal personification less as a literary form in its own right than as a step toward our contemporary understanding of fiction and literary character. Governed fitfully, if at all, by the concepts they claim to represent, horizontal personifications are well on their way to the mimetic representation of individual human beings. As defined by Akbari, horizontal allegory represents the penultimate stage in a teleological process of disenchantment that culminates in the *Canterbury Tales*, where Chaucer finally "uses up the genre of allegory," inaugurating the era of mimetic characterization.[6]

Although Mann, like Akbari, stops short of identifying Aristotelian allegory by name, she invests it with a greater degree of historical specificity. We have seen that, in her 2014 essay on allegory in *Piers Plowman*, Mann insists that all personification is "Platonizing." To my mind, she comes closer to the truth in her 1991 Morton Bloomfield lecture on the same topic, where she suggests that Langland's personifications are in effect Aristotelian: "Whereas other allegorists work on 'Platonizing' principles, penetrating the veil of physical experience to reach the transcendental reality behind it, Langland shows us abstractions as inextricably embedded in concrete individuals. So his Seven Deadly Sins are not represented as the timeless 'essence' of Gluttony, Avarice, Sloth, and so on, but are the sum of a myriad of individual instances of gluttonous or avaricious behavior. Avarice has no existence apart from the avaricious." Although Mann never gives a name to Langland's non-Platonic allegory, she later describes it using a characteristically Aristotelian vocabulary of "substances" and "accidents." Her description of non-Platonic personification also hews much more closely to a specifically Aristotelian metaphysics than either Newman's or Akbari's. As we will see in more detail below, Aristotle understands forms, or universals, as existing within material beings, which he in turn understands as form-matter, or hylomorphic, compounds. The human mind comes to know universals such as *gluttony* and *avarice* by abstracting them from sense perceptions of gluttonous and avaricious individuals. It follows that the universal *avarice* cannot exist in the absence of avaricious individuals—and neither can its personification. For the Mann of 1991, Aristotle's metaphysics accounts for the fact that "Langland's allegorical fiction never leaves the world of concrete reality behind but subsumes it."[7] We should expect Aristotelian personifications, then, to be not only more worldly than their Platonic counterparts, both morally and thematically, but also immersed in the kinds of mimetic detail often associated with literary rather than philosophical realism.

In her study of high- and late-medieval personifications of Nature, Kellie Robertson takes this historical and philosophical specificity a step further. Examining the advantages and disadvantages of different systems of nomenclature, she warns against an oversimplified understanding of the binaries Neoplatonic versus Aristotelian, Augustinian versus Thomistic, and cosmographical versus encyclopedic. The Middle Ages inherited neither a pure Platonism nor a pure Aristotelianism, and these systems were further hybridized by medieval philosophers. As a result, these terms should be understood as defining "'poles' or nodes rather than . . . a strict binary, since writers who employed them, whether academic or popular, occupied many graduated positions along the continuum running between them." Nonetheless, Robertson identifies two distinguishable approaches to representing the natural world, underwritten by fundamentally different understandings of nature itself:

> On one side was the transcendent model associated with an Augustinian tradition that held nature could only be discussed by metaphoric means because nature, as an extension of the divine plan, remains inscrutable to the human intellect. What cannot be observed directly must be discussed indirectly. From this insight arose the mythographic mode of imagining nature, one that asserts correspondences between allegorical figures and natural forces. . . . On the other side we find a model of immanent analogy associated with an Aristotelian view that posited a shared causation between the human and the nonhuman worlds. The same series of causes that explains the production of a bronze statue—material, formal, efficient, and final—could explain equally well how the acorn becomes the oak. . . . On this view, analogy functions as an ontological binding agent that guarantees the unity of very different processes of sublunary growth and change.[8]

In Robertson's reading, a Neoplatonic personification of Nature signifies through her clothing and attributes. Her discourse, stern but serene, unfolds God's transcendent plan for humanity. An Aristotelian personification of Nature, in contrast, tends to be much more person-like: garrulous, disorganized, even in some cases vicious. Rooted in the material world, and so unable to escape her feminine embodiment, she also risks becoming the expression of an antifeminist stereotype, whether the female *magister* of the *Roman de la Rose* or the *vieille* of the *Pèlerinage de la Vie Humaine*. While many critics identify a single, decisive shift between these two kinds of allegorical practice, Robertson traces a dialectical process that begins with the Neoplatonic allegories of the twelfth century, transitions in the thirteenth century to the more immanent personifications associated with moderate realism, and then shifts again in the fourteenth century to account for John Duns Scotus's and Ockham's critiques, not so much of Aristotle himself, but of his interpretation by moderate realists. She cautions that these fourteenth-century allegorists must be understood as distinct from both sets of predecessors.

Although each of these critics seeks to define a counterpart to Platonic personification, none of them focuses on Aristotelian personification as such. Newman and Akbari oppose medieval Platonism to twentieth-century nominalism, while Robertson focuses on shifting representations of Nature rather than on personification per se. Mann's 1991 position is complicated by her later insistence that all allegory is inherently Platonic. Even taken on its own terms, however, her 1991 description of Langland's allegory is implicitly rather than explicitly Aristotelian and so necessarily lacks a certain specificity. The remainder of this chapter accordingly will consider the ways in which Aristotelian metaphysics and epistemology, as articulated in the Middle Ages by both moderate realists and nominalists, speak to personification allegory as a literary form. In doing so, it seeks to counter the assumption, common through much of the twentieth century, that Platonic but not Aristotelian thought "trickled down" from academic circles to more general literate discourse. I thus join not only Robertson, but also James Simpson, Mark Miller, Jessica Rosenfeld, and others who have argued for the broadly cultural and specifically literary impact of Aristotelian philosophy, as well as for the mutual influence of lay and clerical interpretations of Aristotle's thought.[9] Aristotle's accounts of the relationship between particulars and universals, of cognition as a process of abstraction from sense perception, and of the kinds of mental beings later called *entia rationis* all contributed to new versions of personification allegory.

The first half of the chapter examines the medieval tradition of interpreting Aristotle usually called "moderate realism." Moderate realists such as Aquinas hold that human beings can attain knowledge by abstracting it from sense perceptions of empirical objects. They argue that wrathful individuals, for instance, contain within themselves the universal *wrath* and that humans can understand *wrath* by observing, reflecting on, and reasoning about wrathful individuals. A moderately realist personification of Wrath would likewise be abstracted from sense perceptions of the material world. In contrast to personifications based on the Platonic forms, which are timeless and virtuous almost by definition, moderately realist personifications can be positive, neutral, or negative, depending on the sensory data they seek to organize. Because they are derived from sense perceptions, they can also be strikingly historically specific and are often characterized by a wealth of empirical detail.

The second half of the chapter focuses on the medieval *nominales*, now conventionally referred to as nominalists. Although the *nominales* are likewise Aristotelians, they interpret Aristotle as positing a material realm consisting entirely of individuals. Thus understood, wrathful men do not contain within themselves either the universal *wrath* or the universal *man*. Instead, they are simply this wrathful man, and that wrathful man, and that other wrathful man—with as many different kinds of wrath and as many different kinds of man as there are angry individuals. The mature Ockham did continue to posit universals such as *wrath* in the human mind, but instead of understanding them as mental entities, he understood them as cognitive acts. It follows that nominalist personifications do not represent universals to the mind's eye as much as they prompt readers to cognize or conceptualize them. They tend to be puzzles or enigmas, engaging readers through their incongruity rather than through transcendent imagery or verisimilar detail. Although both subtypes of Aristotelian personification are regularly dismissed as failed attempts at Platonism, they are among the most important varieties of personification of the later Middle Ages.

MODERATE REALISM

The early Middle Ages knew Aristotle's theory of universals primarily through Boethius's translations of, and commentaries on, Porphyry's *Isagoge* (*Introduction*) and Aristotle's *Categories*. The *Isagoge* arguably achieved its greatest influence not through its propositional content but through a series of questions that it refuses to answer:

> I shall beg off saying anything about (a) whether genera and species are real or are situated in bare thoughts alone, (b) whether as real they are bodies or incorporeals, and (c) whether they are separated or in sensibles and have their reality in connection with them (2).

> De generibus et speciebus illud quidem sive subsistunt sive in solis nudis purisque intellectibus posita sunt sive subsistentia corporalia sunt an incorporalia, et utrum separata an in sensibilibus et circa ea constantia, dicere recusabo. (10–14)[10]

This short passage encompasses virtually the entire medieval debate over universals, here represented by both species-level universals such as *horse* and genus-level universals such as *animal.* At one extreme, it invokes Plato's understanding of the forms as "incorporeal" and "separated"—that is, located within a separate, immaterial realm. At the other, it anticipates Ockham by locating universals in "bare thoughts alone," existing exclusively within the human mind. Between these extremes, it accounts for Aristotle's understanding of universals as located "in sensibles" and "hav[ing] their reality in connection with them"—that is, existing within the material world, as part of material entities. It even leaves space for, though it does not specifically invoke, Neoplatonists' reinterpretation of the forms as ideas in the divine mind rather than "separated" entities in an otherworldly realm.[11] Even early medieval readers, then, were anything but naïve in their approach to universals. They located each understanding of universals relative to the others within a single, carefully delineated conceptual field.

In his second commentary on the *Isagoge*, Boethius uses Porphyry's questions as the backdrop for an Aristotelian rebuttal of Plato's theory of forms. Speaking as an Aristotelian, he concludes that universals

> subsist in one way, but are understood in another. They are incorporeal, but subsist in sensibles, joined to sensibles. They are understood, however, as subsisting by themselves, and as not having their being in others.

> subsistunt quidem alio modo, intelleguntur uero alio, et sunt incorporalia, sed sensibilibus iuncta subsistunt in sensibilibus. intelleguntur uero ut per semet ipsa subsistentia ac non in aliis esse suum habentia.[12]

Boethius distinguishes two types of universals. The first really exist but have being only within material objects, as an element in hylomorphic compounds. The second exist independently but only within the human mind. Although neither has the same degree of reality as Plato's forms, together they forge a somewhat stronger link between mental concepts and external reality than is furnished by Plato's epistemology. Having claimed to "solve" the problem of universals in this way, however, Boethius offers an unusual disclaimer: "We have carefully followed out Aristotle's view here, not because we would recommend it the most, but because this book is written about the *Categories*, of which Aristotle is the author" (Idcirco uero studiosius Aristotelis sententiam executi sumus, non quod eam maxime probaremus, sed quod hic liber ad Praedicamenta conscriptus est, quorum Aristoteles est auctor) (1.11.18–20, 37). At the last moment, Boethius declares his allegiance neither to Plato nor to Aristotle but to a third way, implicitly the Neoplatonic understanding of forms as ideas in the divine mind. He represents this third way not as a direct descendant of Platonism but rather as a synthesis of Platonism and Aristotelianism that preserves Platonism's promise of transcendence while responding to Aristotle's critique of substantial universals.

By endorsing Aristotle's critique of substantial universals, Boethius ensured that few if any medieval theologians followed Plato in arguing for the "separated" existence of universals in a transcendent, otherworldly realm. At the same time, the unusual structure of his *quaestio* ensured that Aristotle's broader "solution" to the problem of universals was widely known without being especially authoritative. It was not until the rediscovery of Aristotle's *Metaphysics* that Boethius's Neoplatonic account of the forms began to be considered untenable.[13] Thirteenth-century theologians continued to follow Boethius in locating the forms in the divine mind, where they served as paradigms for the creation of the world recounted in Genesis. But they also followed Aristotle in locating the forms "in sensibles," arguing that humans could gain knowledge of the forms through sense perception as well as through divine illumination. Even "Augustinian" theologians like Bonaventure, Matthew of Aquasparta, and Henry of Ghent held that humans gained knowledge of "low" objects by abstracting universals from the sense perception of hylomorphic compounds. "Aristotelians" like Aquinas restricted divine illumination to special kinds of knowledge such as prophecy, arguing that otherwise the human intellect gains knowledge of universals through Aristotelian abstraction. This moderately realist metaphysics and epistemology correspond to a moderately realist variety of Aristotelian personification, rooted in sense perception and corresponding to abstracted universals in the human mind.

In his *Metaphysics*, Aristotle does not object to the Platonic forms or ideas themselves but rather to the contention that they exist separately from the things they inform: "It would seem impossible that the substance and that of which it is the substance should exist apart; how, therefore, could the Ideas, being the substances of things, exist apart?" (uidebitur utique impossibile esse separatim substantiam et cuius est substantia. quaere quomodo ydee substantie rerum existentes separatim erunt?) (*Metaphysics* 991b1).[14] Some of the problems Aristotle identifies echo questions about the relationship between forms and their material instantiations raised in Plato's *Parmenides*. Like the eponymous Parmenides, Aristotle is not satisfied with the explanation, repeated in various ways throughout the Platonic corpus, that particulars "participate in" or "partake of" the forms, which in turn serve as their "models" or "paradigms." Indeed, he explicitly dismisses these accounts as "empty words and poetical metaphors" (uaniloquium . . . et metaphoras dicere poeticas) (*Metaphysics* 991a22). Aristotle likewise either rederives or borrows from the *Parmenides* the famous "third man" argument, whose validity was widely accepted during the Middle Ages. According to this argument, we recognize that Socrates and Callias share a common man-ness by reference to the form Man. But how can we recognize that Socrates, Callias, and the form Man share a common man-ness? Only by positing the form of the form Man, of which they all partake, and then the form of the form of the form of Man, and so on *ad infinitum* (*Parmenides* 132ab, *Metaphysics* 990b). Others of Aristotle's objections, however, reveal a philosophical orientation, fundamentally different from that of Plato, that considers sensible things to be worthy of investigation in their own right: how do Platonic forms, which exist in a separate, changeless realm, explain how sensible things come into being, change, and finally cease to exist? How do the forms allow us to know these sensible things, given that they exist apart from them? Together these questions led Aristotle to develop an ontology that locates forms within sensible things, which he understood as compounds of form and matter.

Aristotle's *Metaphysics* depends upon his *Categories*, which divides all being into ten broad classes, or qualities in a general sense: substance, quantity, quality (in a narrow sense), relation, where, when, being in a position, having, acting, and being acted upon. Of these, only substances can exist independently, with quantity, quality, relation, and so on existing "in" substances, a relationship that Aristotle explains somewhat ambiguously: "By being 'present in a subject' I do not mean present as parts are present in a whole, but being incapable of existence apart from the said subject" (In subiecto autem esse dico quod, cum in aliquo sit non sicut quaedam pars, impossibile est esse sine eo in quo est) (*Categories* 1a24–26). In a proposition such as *Socrates is pale*, *pale* is a quality that exists "in" and is ontologically dependent on the substance *Socrates*. *Socrates* can exist without being *pale* but *pale* cannot exist except "in" *Socrates* or some other substance. The *Categories* applies a similar logic within the category of substance. In the proposition *Socrates is a man*, *man* is a "secondary substance" predicated of the "primary substance" *Socrates*. Here, *man* cannot exist except as predicated of *Socrates* or some other primary substance, but the reverse is also true: *Socrates* cannot exist if he ceases to be a *man*. Aristotle maintains these distinctions, if not this nomenclature, throughout his corpus. We have seen that in *On Interpretation* primary substances are called particulars, while secondary substances and insubstantial qualities are called universals because they are predicated of many particulars. Elsewhere, Aristotle characterizes *man* as "essentially" predicated of *Socrates*, while *pale* is "accidentally" predicated of Socrates. In all of these cases, Aristotle departs sharply from Plato by treating individual substances, rather than transcendent forms, as the fundamental entities in his ontology. All other beings—in the philosophical sense of things that exist—have a reduced or derived status.

Aristotle does not abandon Plato's forms entirely, however, for in his *Physics* and *Metaphysics* he subdivides the primary substances of the *Categories* into form and matter. He argues, moreover, that the most important element within the primary substance is its form, since we generally speak of a *statue*, a *man*, or a *house* rather than of *gold*, *flesh*, or *bricks*. Even when we speak of a *golden statue*, we mark the subordination of matter to form through the subordination of adjective to noun, with the adjective's gender, case, and number dependent on those of the noun. Aristotle goes on to claim that a father imparts form to his offspring in much the same way that an artist imparts form to a work of art, with both giving shape and meaning to what is initially disorganized matter (*Metaphysics* 1033b23). He sees no need to posit a "separated" form, as Plato does, because "the begetter is adequate to the making of the product and to the causing of the form in the matter" (sufficiens est generans facere et speciei causam esse in materia) (*Metaphysics* 1034a4–5). As described in this passage, and as understood by the moderate realists, each human father imparts the universal form of *man* to his offspring, so that all humans share the same form, while each human mother contributes a different mass of matter. As Aristotle puts it, Callias and Socrates "are different in virtue of their matter (for that is different), but the same in form" (diuersa quidem propter materiam [diuersa namque], idem uero specie) (*Metaphysics* 1034a6–7). The father's form universalizes, while the mother's matter particularizes or individuates. For Aristotle, then, forms are immanent rather than transcendent, and compounded with matter rather than self-subsistent.

This new metaphysics demands a new epistemology. For Plato, humans acquire knowledge of the forms either through philosophical dialectic or through the soul's recollection of the forms from the time before it entered "this thing . . . which we call a body." Augustine, building on Plotinus and others, developed Plato's doctrine of recollection into a doctrine of divine illumination, whereby especially rational and virtuous souls receive knowledge of the forms directly from the divine mind. The senses "admonish" the mind but, as Gerard O'Daly explains, "do not fulfill the requirements of knowledge or, in themselves, lead to the intellection of truths."[15] For Aristotle, in contrast, the human intellect actively abstracts knowledge from sense perceptions.[16] When a given sense organ perceives an object, it is changed by that object such that "the one acted upon is assimilated to the other and is identical in quality with it" (passum autem assimilatum est et quale illud) (*On the Soul* 418a6).[17] First the individual sense organ, then the common sense, and finally the imagination strip away the material specificity of the initial sense impression to produce an image that can be grasped by the intellect and stored in the memory. Although this act of intellection mirrors the act of sense perception, it differs in that "what actual sensation apprehends is individuals, while what knowledge apprehends is universals" (quoniam singularium qui secundum actum sensus, sciencia autem uniuersalium) (*On the Soul* 417b22). Cognition is thus a process of abstraction, beginning with the perception of particulars and ending with knowledge of universals. It is also fundamentally imagistic, for even after the mind grasps universals, "the faculty of thinking them thinks the forms in the images" (species quidem igitur intellectivum in fantasmatibus intelligit) supplied by the imagination (*On the Soul* 431b2). The endpoint of each act of cognition is judgment, whereby the intellect decides either to pursue or to avoid the universal it has abstracted (*On the Soul* 431b5).

In Aristotle's system, this process accounts for the cognition of both essential or substantial forms such as *man* and *stone* and accidental forms such as *pale* and *heavy*, which likewise can be abstracted from sense perception. Aristotle also extends image-based cognition to abstract objects, although they clearly represent a limit case in his thinking. His clearest explanation of this process occurs in *On Memory*:

> The subject of "images" has already been considered in our work *de Anima*. Without an image intellectual activity is impossible. For there is in such activity an incidental affection identical with one also incidental in geometrical demonstrations. For in the latter case, though we do not for the purpose of the proof make any use of the fact that the quantity in the triangle . . . is determinate, we nevertheless draw it determinate in quantity. So likewise when one exerts the intellect . . . although the object may not be quantitative, one envisages it as quan-

titative, though he thinks it in abstraction from quantity; while, on the other hand, if the object of the intellect is essentially of the class of things that are quantitative, but indeterminate, one envisages it as if it had determinate quantity, though subsequently, in thinking it, he abstracts from its determinateness.[18]

Quoniam autem de fantasia prius in hiis que sunt de anima dictum est, et intelligere non est sine fantasmate. Accidit enim eadem passio intellectui que quidem et in describendo: ibi enim nulla utentes quantitate trigoni determinata, tamen finitam secundum quantitatem describimus; et intelligens similiter, etsi non intelligat quantum, ponitur ante oculos quantum, intelligit autem non secundum quod quantum est. Si autem natura sit quantorum, infinitorum autem, ponitur tamen quantum determinatum, intelligit autem secundum quod quantum solum. (449b30–450a6; cf. *On the Soul* 431b)

Aristotle compares the cognition of an abstraction to a geometric demonstration in which a mathematician draws a triangle with sides and angles of determinate dimensions in order to represent the more abstract idea of an indeterminate triangle, or a triangle in general. This drawing is, in an important sense, a misrepresentation, since it necessarily depicts a particular triangle, while the geometric proof applies to all triangles, whatever the measurements of their sides and angles. Nonetheless, both the mathematician and his audience find the image of the determinate triangle useful in thinking about the indeterminate triangle as they proceed, step by step, through the demonstration. In this case, the image of the determinate triangle, like a personification, is a tool for thinking, while the indeterminate triangle is the object of thought. This process can be generalized to all acts of cognition. The intellect uses images as tools for thought, even though it thinks at a higher level of abstraction than the images themselves can accommodate. For Aristotle, images are thus starting points for thought, valuable as long as the thinker recognizes the ways in which they do and do not correspond to the objects of thought they help to generate.

Medieval Aristotelians sought to systematize this epistemology while reconciling it with their Christian faith. Aquinas followed Augustine in assigning divine illumination an essential role in human cognition. But where for Augustine the divine light intervenes continuously to produce human knowledge, for Aquinas it often intervenes just once in a lifetime, endowing the agent intellect with the capacity to think independently.

Thereafter, "humans do not need a new illumination, added onto their natural illumination" (non . . . indiget ad cognoscendam veritatem in omnibus nova illustratione superaddita naturali illustrationi) in order to attain knowledge.[19] Distinguishing among Augustine's originally synonymous names for the Platonic forms, Aquinas asserts that ordinary cognition does not refer to divine *rationes* except as mediated by intelligible species (*species intelligibilis*), which he defines as mental representations of universals abstracted from the imagination's phantasms. Each intelligible species in turn actualizes the potential intellect, which forms as its own mental representation a universal concept (*conceptus*) or mental word (*verbum*), with the latter term evidently resonating with the biblical characterization of Christ as the Word of God.[20] Like Aristotle's images, Aquinas's intelligible species and universal concepts are tools for thought rather than objects of thought, except in the unusual case of thinking about cognition itself. As the end point of this process of abstraction, universal concepts such as *man*, *pale*, and *justice* become what Aquinas and other moderately realist Aristotelians call "beings of reason" (*entia rationis*).[21] These entities come into being through thought and exist in the mind yet have their foundation in the material world, as predicates of Aristotelian primary substances. Initially imprecise, they are refined through reasoning and reflection to produce an increasingly complete understanding of *man*, *pale*, *horse*, and the like, approximating or corresponding to the *rationes* that Aquinas—like all medieval moderate realists—continues to locate in the divine mind.[22]

Aristotle's theory of universals, like Plato's theory of forms, offers a general paradigm for personification allegory. Moderately realist Aristotelian personifications are based on universals first observed "in sensibles," then abstracted into *entia rationis*. Just as, for Aristotle, universals such as *justice* and *evil* are abstracted from sense perceptions of just and evil men, and indeed cannot exist without them, so moderately realist personifications figuratively emerge from—and sometimes even revert to—the qualities of particular persons. We have seen that Newman associates Aristotelian personifications with satire, and they are certainly not far to seek in that tradition. In the morality play *Mankind*, the personified vices New Guise, Nowadays, and Nought owe their existence to their prevalence as accidents in earthly substances rather than to a preexisting schema such as the Seven Deadly Sins. The names *New Guise* and *Nowadays* suggest that these characters dress in the latest fashions, and they reinforce this impression by reshaping Mankind's traditional plowman's coat into "a fresch jakett after the new gyse," shortening it so much that it becomes both feminizing and ridiculous.[23] The joke works only insofar as the jacket reflects and exaggerates actual clothing practices, and it works only as long as those practices remain current. When I teach *Mankind,* I sometimes ask students to rewrite this scene for their own social milieu, substituting contemporary fashion choices that will make their friends laugh. This classroom exercise highlights the timeliness of the Vices' joke as well as its basis in actors' and audience members' observations of the material world. As "beings of reason," New Guise, Nowadays, and Nought are tools of thought abstracted from sense perceptions. Within the broader context of the play, their purpose is to help the audience to judge whether fashionable clothing—and by extension the ever-changing world itself—should be pursued or avoided. They also exist as accidents in the substance of the fashionable. New Guise, Nowadays, and Nought tell the audience that they dwell offstage among empirical individuals, listing William Fyde, Master Huntyngton of Sauston, Wylliam Thurlay of Hauston, Pycharde of Trumpyngton, Wyllyham Baker of Waltom, Rycherde Bollman of Gayton, and Wyllyam Patryke of Massyngham as notorious fashion victims.[24] Modern editors note that all of these people and places are local to *Mankind*'s performance area and suggest that the players may have used the names of audience members to create customized lists for each performance.[25] This close connection to empirical individuals, accentuated by the Vices' repeated trips through the audience, is characteristically Aristotelian rather than Platonic. Indeed, the Vices demonstrate their dependence on particulars in a very concrete sense when they halt the play to take up a collection. By making the audience's support a condition of their continued presence, they represent themselves as embodiments of the audience members' own vicious qualities.

We see a similarly Aristotelian dynamic in the second passus of *Piers Plowman,* in which the personified Liar leads a contingent of individual persons—all at least implicitly liars—in Lady Meed's wedding procession. Although Langland is too scrupulous to follow the *Mankind* author in naming names, he emphasizes Liar's status as a being of reason abstracted from particulars rather than a material body subject to corporal punishment. When Langland's king orders his constables, "if y lacche Lyere, lat hym noȝt ascapen / Er he be put on þe pillory," he uses *lacchen* in a physical sense, instructing his agents to grasp Liar and deliver him to punishment (B.2.204–5).[26] Liar, however, takes advantage of his pursuers' failure to grasp his nature as an Aristotelian universal, evading capture by dressing as and dwelling among a series of pardoners, physicians, spice merchants, minstrels, messengers, and friars—all professional groups satirized for their mendacity. In other words, Liar hides from the king's men by rejoining the particulars from which he has been abstracted—as Langland's readers, at least, should recognize. Liar cannot be pilloried, as the king intends, because he has no material existence except as an accident in the substance of individual pardoners, physicians, and spice merchants. He can, however, be grasped conceptually, and so made to serve out his sentence—as well as his Middle English *sentence*, his meaning—in a different way. In effect, Langland's criticisms of late-fourteenth-century social mores seize and pillory Liar in the only way possible, by exposing his machinations to public view in an idiomatic and accessible literary vernacular.

These examples should not be taken to suggest, however, that moderately realist Aristotelian personifications are inherently satirical. Instead, moderately realist personification lends itself to satire, among other literary forms, because it takes as its starting point the things of this world. Although Plato does not explicitly deny the existence of negative forms such as those corresponding to *Mankind*'s Vices and Langland's Liar, he never discusses them, and later Platonists consistently exclude them from the tradition. Negatively valued formal personifications are accordingly scarce or nonexistent. Daemonic personifications, likewise, are generally positive if limited tutelary figures, carefully distinguished from demons and other malign spirits. In contrast, Aristotle's position that universals exist in and can be abstracted from all instantiated substances and qualities underwrites a much wider range of personifications. These personifications function as tools for thinking about the universals with which they are associated in many of the same ways as Aristotle's images and Aquinas's beings of reason. They are frequently generated ad hoc in response to pressing empirical problems rather than as elements of a preexisting text or schema. We see this dynamic with Langland's Hunger, whom I will discuss in more detail in chapter 7. Invoked by Piers Plowman in a high-stakes, deadly serious thought experiment, Hunger is imagined as a solution to a pressing social problem: the presence of freeloaders in a subsistence agricultural economy. He fulfills his mission in a dual manner that is characteristically Aristotelian. In the material world, hunger makes itself felt by wringing men's bellies until they cry and sinking deep hollows into their cheeks. Thus manifested, it is inescapably a quality of material beings, whose suffering Langland describes in arresting terms. As an *ens rationis*, however, Hunger also engages Piers in an earnest discussion of social and agricultural policy in the aftermath of the Black Death. In doing so, he helps Piers—and through him, Langland's readers—to think about hunger in Aristotle's sense of actively grasping and manipulating a universal in order to decide whether it should be pursued or avoided. In this case, the judgment is emphatically negative: although hunger might briefly create the appearance of a disciplined and well-organized community, it cannot generate a virtuous social order. Crucially, however, Hunger cannot be discharged as a being of reason until the quality of hunger ceases to exist as an accident in the substance of the folk. Langland's embodiment of Hunger is thus derived from and depends on the bodily condition of hunger even as it helps readers to gain conceptual purchase on the way hunger operates as a social phenomenon, indeed as a tool of public policy.

Other moderately realist Aristotelian personifications share some or all of Hunger's salient characteristics: they are morally neutral or negative, they respond to an immediate problem, and they are abstracted from experience rather than revealed from on high. As such, they tend to be historically specific in ways that their Platonic cousins are not and are often described with considerable verisimilar detail. Moderate realism thus lends itself to the representation of sin, especially when a personified Sin is an aggregate of the behavior of many individual sinners. Langland's Covetise describes his corrupt business practices as a tradesman, a draper, a usurer, a rural laborer, and an overseas merchant with what Derek Pearsall calls "minute circumstantiality" and even incorporates the traditionally feminine roles of weaver and brewer by confessing on behalf of his wife.[27] Gathering into himself a seemingly uncountable number of shady business deals from all sectors of the economy, he organizes them and presents them to cognition as instances of the universal *covetousness*. As analyzed by Claire Waters, the Sluggard in William of Waddington's *Manuel des Pechiez* is similarly put together from particular acts of laziness or, more precisely, from particular failures to act, which collectively produce a personification.[28] These examples make it difficult to treat mimetic detail as the antithesis of allegory. Instead, mimetic detail marks a specific kind of personification, understood as abstracted from empirical beings rather than existing prior to them. The distinction between moderately realist personifications and novelistic characters depends on their *use* of concrete detail. Covetise's cheeks, lolling "as a leþeren purs," and his twelve-year-old tabard, so threadbare that even lice avoid it, are representative rather than idiosyncratic details (B.5.189).

Aristotelian personification also overlaps, but is not coextensive with, the category of personification allegory sometimes called typification. Paxson defines these figures, variously denominated isotypes, exempla, or exemplary property characters, as "individual representatives of *classes* of human beings who are hopeful, faithful, friendly, etc." He adduces as examples Jean de Meun's Friend (Ami) and John Bunyan's Hopeful and Faithful, to whom we could add figures such as Langland's Glutton and *Everyman*'s Cousin. In Paxson's analysis, which builds upon that of C. S. Lewis, these isotypes are only marginally personifications because their names are typically neither abstract nouns nor mass nouns but rather count nouns and adjectives.[29] For Aristotle, however, universals are defined by their relationship to particulars rather than by grammatical rules. This same logic appears to govern medieval allegorical practice. Far from asserting an ontological distinction between Kindred and Cousin, *Everyman* treats them as virtually interchangeable. Both are abstracted from the qualities of empirical individuals, and they react to the prospect of death as frightened relatives often do rather than as they ideally should (as we would expect in the case of Neoplatonic formal personifications). Given that *Everyman* presents itself as "a treatyse . . . in maner of a morall playe," intended to help the members of its audience prepare for death, they also resemble beings of reason, enjoying a real if limited existence within the mind as tools for thought.[30] At least in this instance, both isotype and abstraction function as moderately realist Aristotelian personifications, at once derived from and providing purchase on empirical phenomena.

MEDIEVAL NOMINALISM

Up to this point, I have sought to distinguish among the types of personification allegory supported by different varieties of medieval realism. If none of these varieties corresponds to the naïve realism described by Huizinga, they do posit the existence of universals outside the human mind, in the mind of God and in material objects. The remainder of this chapter considers a category that many critics consider to be either a contradiction in terms or "just a game." Even for de Man and other twentieth-century post-structuralists, nominalist personification is "hallucinatory" and "uncanny" because it calls attention to its own lack of reference.[31] Medieval nominalism, however, operates somewhat differently. Like de Man, Ockham denies the extramental existence of universals. He departs from him, however, in understanding universals as concepts that refer naturally rather than conventionally to groups of empirical individuals. I argue that medieval nominalist personifications correspond to these conceptual universals. Instead of seeking to represent universals with images visible to the mind's eye, they prompt readers to cognize universals, often via riddles or puzzles.[32]

We have seen that the Neoplatonic Augustinian tradition assigns both ontological and epistemological priority to universals in the divine mind, citing the inherent instability of the temporal realm. For Aristotelians, the issue is more complicated. Aristotle himself grants ontological priority to particulars but epistemological priority to universals, characterizing the latter as the fundamental objects of knowledge.[33] Thirteenth- and early-fourteenth-century moderate realists generally accepted a modified version of Aristotle's first position, agreeing that universals do not exist substantially except in particulars while reserving ultimate but often distant ontological priority to universals in the divine mind. They differed, however, in their reception of Aristotle's second position, which they increasingly saw as unable to explain the cognition of particular individuals *as* particular individuals.[34] As we saw above, Aristotle argues in *Metaphysics* 7.8 that individuals such as Callias and Socrates are "the same in form" but "different by virtue of their matter." How, then, can the mind know Callias and Socrates as individuals, given that in Aristotle's epistemology it grasps forms rather than matter? This problem led scholastic theologians to posit various "higher" principles of individuation, located in the soul rather than the body. It also led them to define a process whereby the mind can know individuals as well as universals—that is, to define a process whereby the mind can know Socrates both as a distinct individual and as an instance of the universal *man*.

Many writers struggled with this problem of individuation before Ockham provided a nominalist solution. In the thirteenth century, individuation fueled debates over the nature of Aristotle's agent intellect. On one side, Averroists posited a single, separate, and divine entity containing all universals within itself, while on the other Aquinas insisted that the agent intellect is an individual faculty of the human soul. In the *Summa Theologiae*, he argues that a single intellect, common to all knowers, is theologically incompatible with the soul's individuality before God, even as it makes philosophical nonsense of a proposition such as *Socrates thinks*.[35] Where the Averroist Siger of Brabant doubts that the intellect can know individuals, since by its nature it cognizes only universals, Aquinas suggests that the intellect can know individuals indirectly by reflecting on the imagination's particularized phantasms.[36] He hypothesizes that beings can be individuated by considering the quantity of their prime matter or by distinguishing common from "signate" matter.[37] By the fourteenth century, however, Aristotelians had begun to treat Aquinas's account as itself insufficient, instead seeking a nonmaterial principle of individuation. Scotus defines each empirical substance as simultaneously a *quid*, or "what," and a *haec*, or "this," with the substance's *quidditas*, or whatness, determined by the familiar Aristotelian universal "in sensibles," and its *haecceitas*, or this-ness, determined by "some positive entity that by itself determines the nature to singularity" (per aliquam entitatem positivam, per se determinantem naturam ad singularitatem) (*Ordinatio* 2, d. 3, p. 1, q. 6, 142).[38] To use our familiar example, Socrates's *quidditas* identifies him as a man, while his *haecceitas* identifies him as the individual Socrates. Scotus distinguishes both *quidditas* and *haecceitas* from qualities such as *paleness*, which are present in individuals accidentally, and from matter, which he characterizes as "altogether indistinct and indeterminate" (omnino indistinctum et indeterminatum) (*Ordinatio* 2, d. 3, p. 1, q. 5, 131). *Quidditas* and *haecceitas* together comprise a given individual's form, which is in turn united with matter to produce the individual. Scotus accordingly assigns to *haecceitas* a diminished ontological status similar to that of Aristotelian universals: it exists substantially only "in sensibles," while existing independently only in the mind. This metaphysical system allows for the direct cognition of individuals while denying as "nonsense" (inconveniens) the nominalist position that a given material substance is "individual or singular from itself—that is, from its nature" (ex se sive ex natura sua sit individua vel singularis) (*Ordinatio* 2, d. 3, p. 1., q. 1, 3, 1). Willard Quine, the mid-twentieth-century philosopher, memorably dismissed this kind of multiplication of entities as an ontological "slum" and a "breeding ground for disorderly elements."[39]

Writing a generation after Scotus, Ockham takes his predecessor's "nonsense" argument seriously, all but eliminating the ontological and epistemological problems associated with individuation. For Ockham, material substances simply *are* individuals and can be directly cognized as such. He achieves this redefinition by returning to the roots of the medieval problem of universals in Aristotle's *Categories* and its commentary tradition. Wielding his famous razor, Ockham argues that it is not necessary "to multiply entities according to the multiplicity of terms, so that for every term there is a thing" (multiplicare entia secundum multitudinem terminorum, et quod quilibet terminus habet quid rei)—an error he attributes not to Aristotle but to his own contemporaries' misreading of the Aristotelian tradition (*Summa Logicae* 1.51.240–41).[40] Instead, Ockham reinterprets eight of the ten Aristotelian categories as linguistic rather than substantial, attributing being only to substance and quality.[41]

For moderately realist Aristotelians, similarity, as a subcategory of relation, is a real entity, albeit one existing only within and by virtue of individual substances. From this point of view, substances are similar when similarity exists "in" both of them. For Ockham, in contrast, substances are similar when the qualities "in" them are themselves similar:

> For the truth of "Socrates is similar to Plato," it is required that Socrates have some quality and that Plato have a quality of the same species. Thus, from the very fact that Socrates is pale and Plato is pale, Socrates is similar to Plato and conversely. Likewise, if both are dark or hot, they are similar without anything else added.
>
> Ad veritatem istius "Sortes est similis Platoni" requiritur quod Sortes habeat aliquam qualitatem et quod qualitatem eiusdem speciei habeat Plato. Unde ex hoc ipso quod Sortes est albus et Plato est albus, Sortes est similis Platoni et e converso. Similiter, si uterque sit niger vel calidus, sine omni alio addito ipsi sunt similes. (*Summa Logicae* 2.11.57–64)

Ockham accordingly has no need to posit entities such as similarity, quantity, and cause, much less entities such as "when-ness" (quandalitas) and "where-ness" (ubitas), whose very names allow him to mock his rivals for their ponderously overpopulated ontologies (*Summa Logicae* 1.41.8–11). Rejecting such awkward nominalizations, Ockham understands *quando* (when) and *ubi* (where) as instead describing relationships among substances and qualities. He treats their role in logical propositions as analogous to their role in Latin grammar, where they are adverbs rather than nouns.

This streamlined ontology requires a relatively complex account of meaning. To begin with, Ockham distinguishes spoken and written words on the one hand from concepts—which he calls mental words—on the other. The former are human conventions, signifying "willfully" (ad placitum) and "according to voluntary imposition" (secundum voluntariam institutionem) and differing from one language to the next. In contrast, the latter "naturally signify what they signify" (naturaliter significat quidquid significat) and are at least ideally common to all humans (*Summa Logicae* 1.1.46–52).[42] Within the class of concepts or mental words, Ockham distinguishes absolute terms, which represent substances and qualities, from connotative terms, which represent the remaining Aristotelian categories. Where absolute terms can be defined only as the sum of the things to which they refer, connotative terms can be restated as a combination of absolute terms and relational or noncategoric terms such as *under* and *of*. For Ockham, the Aristotelian category of *cause* is thus redefined as "'something upon the existence of which another thing follows' or 'something capable of producing something else,' or something of that sort" ("aliquid ad cuius esse sequitur aliud" vel "aliquid potens producere aliud," vel aliquid huiusmodi) (*Summa Logicae* 1.10.49–51). Ockham deploys a similar semantic analysis to dispense with many of the abstractions that feature so prominently in accounts of personification allegory, reducing *horseness* (equinitas) to *horse* (equus) and *humanity* (humanitas) to "man as man" (homo secundum quod homo) or "man insofar as he is man" (homo in quantum homo) (*Summa Logicae* 1.8.20ff). For Ockham, these abstractions signify even more indirectly than connotative mental words, since they are features of spoken and written, rather than mental, language. Overall, this model has the effect of greatly decreasing the proportion of words that refer to things, while increasing the proportion of words that refer to other words.

Turning to the remaining Aristotelian categories of substance and quality, Ockham extends his principle of parsimony by recognizing only primary substances and their qualities as truly existing. For Ockham there is no such "thing" as man, only individual men such as Plato and Socrates. Likewise, there exists no general quality of paleness, only the individual paleness of Socrates, the individual paleness of Plato, and so on—as many palenesses as there are pale things. Ockham articulates this position by revisiting Porphyry's questions about universals at the beginning of the *Isagoge*:

> Now it must be maintained as indubitable that any existing thing imaginable is in itself and without any addition a singular thing and one in number (numerically one). . . . Secondly, it must be maintained that no universal is outside of the mind, really existing in individual substances . . . [and] it must be maintained that genera and species, and generally all such universals, are incorporeal because they exist only in the mind, in which there is nothing corporeal.

> Est autem tenendum indubitanter quod quaelibet res imaginabilis exsistens est de se, sine omni addito, res singularis et una numero. . . . Secundo tenendum quod nullum universale est extra animam exsistens realiter in substantiis individuis . . . tenendum est quod genera et species, et universaliter omnia talia universalia, non sunt corporalia; quia non sunt nisi in mente, in qua non est aliquid corporale.[43]

Where the moderate realists privilege Aristotle's claim in *Metaphysics* 7.8 that universals exist in substances, Ockham instead invokes *Metaphysics* 7.13, which he paraphrases as saying, "It is impossible that a substance should be anything that is said universally" (Videtur impossibile substantiam esse quodcumque universaliter dictorum).[44] The upshot is that for Ockham universals exist in the mind but not "in sensibles," a position that allows him to account for individuality while dispensing with quasi entities such as Scotus's *haecceitas*. In short, universals are nothing other than concepts.

Ockham does not, however, eliminate all connection between concepts on the one hand and things on the other. As we have seen, he specifies that concepts are not imposed willfully or arbitrarily, in the manner of spoken and written words, but instead signify "naturally" and universally. Even though Ockham's concepts do not refer to universals "in sensibles," they do designate natural categories. The individuals signified by the concept *man* share similarities with each other that they do not share with individuals signified by the concept *donkey* or the concept *bird*. At the same time, individuals signified by the concepts *man*, *donkey*, and *bird* share similarities with each other that allow them to be distinguished, as *animals*, from the individuals signified by *stone* and *book* and *house*. Ockham cites approvingly Augustine's claim in *On the Trinity* that "we think about man according to species. For we have, as if it were by a rule, an imprinted knowledge of human nature, in accordance with which whatever we see like that, we know right away it is a man" (secundum speciem de homine cogitamus. Habemus enim quasi regulariter infixam naturae humanae notitiam, secundum quam quidquid tale aspicimus, statim hominem esse cognoscimus) (*Ordinatio* 1.2.8.42; cf. *On the Trinity* 8.4.7).[45] Ockham also follows Augustine and the moderate realists in positing, albeit in a modified form, "ideas" in the mind of God (*Ordinatio* 1.35.5).[46] Together these elements of Ockham's theory of universals point toward an objective rather than subjective relationship between concepts—that is to say, mental words—and the material world. As Mikko Yrjönsuuri puts it, for Ockham "the language in which we think is universal because in the final analysis both its glossary and its grammar are defined by the world itself, not by our own minds."[47]

Given this context, what *are* Ockham's concepts? The answer to this question changes over the course of his career. For the early Ockham, the mental word is a being of reason, really existing within the mind. He calls this mental being a *fictum*, from *fingere*, meaning "to represent in thought," "to imagine," "to think," but also "to form or fashion by art," explicitly equating it with Augustine's "image" (imago), "likeness" (similitudo), "phantasm" (phantasma), and "species" (*Ordinatio* 1.2.8.54). A *fictum* refers equally to all of the individuals within a given class because it resembles all of them equally:

> And that [*fictum*] can be called a universal, because it is an exemplar and indifferently related to all external singulars. On account of this likeness . . . it is able to supposit for external things that have a similar being outside the intellect. In this way, the universal is not the result of generation but of abstraction—which is nothing but a kind of picturing [*fictio*]
>
> Et illud [fictum] potest vocari universale, quia est exemplar et indifferenter respiciens omnia singularia extra, et propter istam similutudinem . . . potest supponere pro rebus extra quae habent consimile esse extra intellectum. Et ita isto modo universale non est per generationem sed per abstractionem, quae non est nisi fictio quaedam. (*Ordinatio* 1.2.8.24)

Ockham goes on to compare the mind's work of *fictum* making to God's work of creation, with the important caveat that where God possesses a genuine "productive power" (virtutem productivam) capable of generating empirical beings, the human mind possesses only a "fictive power" (virtutem fictivam) capable of generating beings of reason (*Ordinatio* 1.2.8.22). Although *fictum* has a broader semantic range than its modern cognate *fiction*, it nonetheless carries some of the same connotations, especially in Ockham's contrast between God's power of mental creation and the mind's parallel, but diminished, power of mental representation. *Ficta* in the human mind are analogous to creatures as they "were truly cognized by God" (vere fuerunt cognitae a Deo) before the creation, except that instead of generating individuals, they are abstracted from them (*Ordinatio* 1.2.8.65).

The later Ockham uses his razor to dispose of ontologically diminished beings within the mind just as he had earlier disposed of ontologically diminished beings outside of the mind.[48] He defines universals or concepts as qualities "in" the mind just as paleness is a quality "in" Socrates. He equates these qualities with mental acts:[49]

> The concept is really the act of intellection itself, so that then a universal would be nothing but a general intellection of a thing. This

> intellection—since one singular is not more understood by it than another one is—would be indifferent and common to all singulars. So insofar as it would be more general or less general, it would be more universal or less universal.

> Conceptus est realiter ipsa intellectio, ita quod tunc universale non esset nisi intellectio confusa rei, quae intellectio, quia ipsa non plus intelligitur unum singulare quam reliquum, ipsa esset indifferens et communis ad omnia singularia; et ita, secundum quod esset magis confusa et minus confusa, esset magis universale vel minus universale. (*Ordinatio* 1.2.8.7)

In other words, the mind can think of Socrates and Plato either distinctly as individuals or generally as examples of the species *man* and the genus *animal*. While distinct cognition considers the features that particularize Socrates as Socrates and Plato as Plato, general cognition refers equally to Socrates, Plato, and all other men or animals the thinker has previously cognized. The difference between the species-level universal *man* and the genus-level universal *animal* arises from the degree to which a particular act of cognition is generalized: a greater degree of generalization produces a greater degree of universality. This model of cognition not only does away with beings of reason as tools for thought but also, as Robert Pasnau points out, eliminates the ghostly "mind's eye" that observes them.[50] For the later Ockham, cognition is no longer primarily a form of vision, as it had been since Augustine, but rather a form of action. Universals are thought; they are not beings the mind sees.

This nominalist "revolution," as it is sometimes called, has repeatedly been associated with the eclipse of personification allegory as a literary form. At least at first, this claim seems plausible. For a nominalist, only individuals objectively exist. Shouldn't a nominalist literature, then, concern itself with individuals rather than personifications? Ockham, however, continues to understand universals as concepts; as Marilyn McCord Adams puts it, his metaphysics is "less misleadingly classified as a form of conceptualism."[51] And these concepts furnish a plausible subject matter for personification allegory, especially given that many or even most personification allegories are set within the human mind. As models for a specific kind of personification allegory, the *ficta* posited by the early Ockham have much in common with the mental representations described by the moderate realists. They differ in that the realists' beings of reason are abstracted from universals "in sensibles," while the early Ockham's *ficta* refer to groups of individuals. In both systems, however, universals exist as independent mental entities, visible to the mind's eye—and thus as something suggestively similar to personifications. While the later Ockham distances himself more thoroughly from the moderate realists, he still posits a connection between human cognition and external reality by insisting that concepts signify "naturally" rather than conventionally. Stopping short of a "ruthless" nominalism in which terms ultimately signify only their failure to signify, he represents the limit case of a medieval metaphysics that, whatever its other commitments, assigns a meaningful degree of reality to universals in the human mind. Personifications conceived in terms of this very general paradigm represent universally accessible mental phenomena and help their readers to conceptualize the material world.

What, then, might medieval nominalist personification allegory look like? Most obviously, we should not expect to encounter personified universals outside of the human mind—that is to say, outside of dream visions and related explorations of an inner landscape.[52] Within the human mind, we should expect nominalism to influence the relationship between persons and personifications, assigning greater ontological weight to the former. Where in the *Flowing Light of the Godhead* Mechthild of Magdeburg assigns a higher degree of reality to Lady Love than to her own authorial persona, we would expect a nominalist allegory to reverse this dynamic. Indeed, a nominalist personification should represent or engage with the authorial persona's thinking process, either implicitly or explicitly. We might therefore look to personifications such as Langland's Thought and Wit, whom the protagonist generates by thinking at length about what he does and does not know. Neither of these personifications receive much visual description because, like the late Ockham's concepts, they are not independent beings visible to the "mind's eye" but simply what the mind does. To the extent that Langland does describe the appearance of Thought and Wit, they are merely duplicates of his authorial persona, as befits their status as *his* thought and *his* wit. They are grasped conceptually rather than seen, making an identifying description misleading or superfluous.

This emphasis on action rather than appearance suggests that Ockham's metaphysics lends itself to the kinds of personification that Morton Bloomfield identifies as dynamic rather than static, developed primarily through narrative rather than static verbal or visual images. Bloomfield notes that in a sentence such as "Truth always treads down error," it is actually the verb that personifies, "driv[ing] us back to the subject so that we may reinterpret it as a personification."[53] The late Ockham similarly understands universals as thoughts that drive the mind back to empirical substances and qualities, reinterpreting them as members of a class. They allow us to understand the justice of a particular man as an instance of a universal concept of justice, to be thought about, debated, and finally acted upon as such. On this reading, we should not look primarily for nominalist personifications but rather for nominalist personifiers, mostly verbs, that retrospectively transform common nouns into personifications. Given that medieval scribes did not routinely capitalize the names of personifications in the manner of modern editors, for medieval readers this retrospective process of personification would have been a more prominent part of reading allegorical texts than it is today. In *Piers Plowman* manuscripts, for instance, most instances of personification have to be identified after the fact through a cognitive process similar to the one described in general terms by Ockham and more specifically by Bloomfield.

Langland demonstrates an acute awareness of this process and indeed employs it to achieve narrative effects. When the members of Meed's wedding party set out for Westminster in passus two, it falls to Guile to arrange for their transport:

> Thenne gan [g]yle borwen hors at many gret maystres
> And shop þat a shereue sholde bere [m]ede
> Softliche in sambure fram syse to syse. (C.2.176–77)[54]

Reading this passage without editorial capitalization, it does not become clear that the sheriff carries a personified Meed on his back rather than gold in his purse until one reaches the phrase "in sambure [in a saddle]." Personification, here, is emphatically a retrospective process, marked by a degree of surprise and pleasure as the reader realizes that the sheriff and meed have exchanged roles. Meed *should* be an inanimate object, prized only for its use value. But the sheriff irrationally treats Meed as something to be desired and served, giving her the status of an alluring young lady on horseback. In doing so, he effectively depersonifies himself, forfeiting both his masculinity and his humanity as he allows Meed to ride him like a hired hack.[55] Langland, then, satirically invites his readers to exclude the sheriff from the category of *man* in both the specific sense of adult male and the general sense of human being. In order to do so, they must redefine *man* as a moral category, while recategorizing the sheriff as an *animal*, and perhaps more specifically as a beast of burden. In philosophical terms, Langland asks his readers to rederive the widely accepted Aristotelian definition of man as a rational animal, excluding the sheriff from the category of *man* because he behaves irrationally. He does so, however, via an entirely allegorical rather than philosophical vocabulary and in a way that is fully immersed in—indeed, generated by—the social realities of late-fourteenth-century England. For a lay reader, the difference between these two approaches may well be the difference between memorizing a Latin definition such as "homo animal rationale est" and knowing it "as kyndely as clerk doth his bokes" (C.7.182).

The well-known illustration of these lines in Oxford, Bodleian Library MS Douce 104 suggests that at least one medieval reader understood them in broadly congruent, though by no means identical, terms. The image of Lady Meed riding atop the sheriff both isolates this passage as especially worthy of readers' attention and focuses that attention on the intimate and philosophically complex relationship between the sheriff and Meed (fol. 10r). Kathleen Scott points out that the sheriff in this manuscript is much better dressed than sheriffs in other fifteenth-century manuscripts.[56] Arguably, then, he bears *meed* upon his back in two distinct senses: as an alluring young woman and as a sumptuous, fur-lined garment. Indeed, some of the richness of Meed's clothing in an earlier Douce illustration, including its deep red color and fur lining, seems here to have been transferred to the sheriff, as if they are aspects of a single being (fol. 8r). This impression is reinforced by the matching colors of the sheriff's hose and Meed's dress as well as by the way she sits vertically on his shoulder rather than riding him horseback as in Langland's text. In the Aristotelian vocabulary shared by Ockham and the moderate realists, *meed* here seems to be an accidental quality of the sheriff: it exists "in" his substance rather than independently and is contingent in the sense of being a quality that he could, at least in theory, cease to possess. At the same time, the sheriff elevates Meed to a position of authority by dressing in her garment and carrying her on his shoulder. In the image as in the text, personification is a moral and cognitive act rather than the expression of a metaphysical given, in ways that coincide with Ockham's understanding of universals as acts of thought rather than beings of reason. We may see a more consequential example of this phenomenon in the triad of Do-well, Do-bet, and Do-best. While the dreamer's interpretation of "do well" as a personified noun rather than an imperative verb may be a misconstrual akin to the sheriff's mistaken cognition of *meed*, it also subjects Do-well to the intellectual scrutiny that structures the remainder of the poem.

As enigmatic occasions for thought, figures such as Meed and Do-well can be grouped with the riddling or puzzling personifications of Deguileville's *Pèlerinage de la Vie Humaine*. When Deguileville's pilgrim encounters a woman who is flawlessly beautiful and elegantly arrayed, we initially expect her to be an Augustinian formal personification. The pilgrim's primary reaction to seeing her, however, is not awe but astonishment, for in addition to holding a mallet and a bundle of switches in her hands, she carries a broom in her mouth. After acknowledging that carrying a broom in one's mouth would ordinarily be a mark of insanity, the pilgrim explains that this particular broom neither impairs the woman's aura of wisdom nor interferes with her ability to speak. Eventually, we learn that she is a personification of Penance and that the broom is her tongue; she uses it to sweep the house of Conscience, casting out the filth of sin through the sacrament of confession. Rosemund Tuve argues that the enjoyment of allegory consists in thinking through precisely this kind of riddle: in her account, "Guillaume is counting somewhat on the pleasure felt in recognition of identity, but more on the pleasure we take in recognizing the truth of something experience confirms."[57] I would add that the moment in which the reader figures out the riddle is also the moment in which the woman becomes a personification, a representation of the concept of *penance* rather than an as-yet-unrecognized individual. Or we might say, more precisely, that the woman becomes a personification at the moment when she prompts the reader to generate a coherent concept of *penance*. The pleasure of Deguileville's allegory comes from cognizing this universal.

It is important to note that, although Deguileville's Penance is described in visual terms, she does not look like either a Neoplatonic or a moderately realist personification. In Neoplatonic allegories, the high moral value of formal personifications is conventionally depicted via physical beauty, expensive clothing and jewelry, and elevated social status. As Emily Steiner puts it, this strand of personification "reveals the hermeneutic or spiritual worth of something by representing it materially."[58] In keeping with the Neoplatonic logic of microcosm and macrocosm, a formal personification characterized as the daughter of God usually looks like an idealized version of the daughter of an earthly king. In contrast, since moderately realist personifications are abstracted from sense perceptions of empirical individuals, they are characterized by verisimilar rather than idealized detail. Because these details are often drawn from otherwise disparate individuals who share a quality such as acquisitiveness or self-indulgence, a single moderately realist personification can speak first as a merchant, then as a craftsman, then as an aristocrat—or first as a man, then as a woman—in a way that can feel inconsistent to modern readers. Each of the personification's many "faces," however, reflects humanity as it is rather than as it should be. Deguileville's Penance departs from both of these paradigms because she does not look like a person at all, whether real or ideal. With a broom in place of a tongue, she is easier to conceptualize than to visualize. The purpose of her description is not to produce an image that can be used as an ongoing tool for thought but rather, as Robertson says of Deguileville's use of personification more generally, "to leave the physical referent of allegory behind."[59] Once the broom-tongued woman has prompted a reader of the *Pèlerinage* to conceptualize *penance*, she becomes largely superfluous. She is less a representation of a universal than an occasion for cognizing one.

This is not to claim that Deguileville—or, for that matter, Langland—is an Ockhamite, much less a nominalist in the modern sense. I subscribe to the critical consensus that Deguileville's metaphysics and epistemology are basically Augustinian.[60] The most prominent personification in the *Pèlerinage*, the crowned and bejeweled Divine Grace (Grace Dieu), is unmistakably an Augustinian formal personification. Nonetheless, Deguileville followed academic debates closely and shares with Ockham emphases on God's absolute power and the unconstrained agency of the human will.[61] Under these circumstances, there is nothing to preclude, and much to support, Deguileville's experimentation with what I have been calling nominalist personification, even as he subordinates it to Neoplatonic personification within the structure of his poem. Indeed, as we will see, it is extremely common for multiple kinds of personification to rub shoulders within a single literary work. This propinquity can reflect the structure of scholastic argumentation. Poets at times embody positions with which they disagree in order to refute or even ridicule them and at times use multiple kinds of personification to explore unresolved problems. It can also reflect a genuinely hybrid metaphysics or epistemology, in which (for instance) Augustinian principles govern a "higher" realm while Ockhamite principles govern a "lower" one. Here the broom that so astonishes Deguileville's pilgrim, turning its wielder into an embodied puzzle rather than an object of reverence, also marks her as Divine Grace's servant, the "chaumberere" whose job is to "sweepe alle filthes, and remeeve and clense."[62] Penance's subordinate position seems to make her an appropriate site for exploring new modes of personification. So, too, does the complexity of the concept she represents. Penance is ill-suited for formal personification because it is not itself transcendent—even as, for Deguileville, it enables the transcendent experience of divine grace.

The medieval "rediscovery" of Aristotle, then, has important implications for personification allegory. It does not mean that every subsequent personification must be understood as Aristotelian—or that a particular writer's personified creations necessarily correspond to his metaphysics. In the *Vita Nova,* Dante defends Neoplatonic personification on literary grounds even as he uses an Aristotelian vocabulary of substance and accident and seemingly subscribes to an Aristotelian metaphysics. He values Neoplatonic personification as a literary convention that connects his vernacular poetry with classical precedents rather than as a representation of metaphysical reality.[63] Other high- and late-medieval writers, however, break with tradition to produce allegories that reflect their self-consciously "modern" worldviews. For the moderate realists in this group, allegory takes as its starting point the things of this world. Its personifications can be neutral or negative as well as positive, and are abstracted from experience rather than produced through dialectic or revealed from on high. Often generated in response to pressing empirical problems rather than as elements of a preexisting schema, they tend to be much more historically specific than Platonic personifications and are often presented with a striking degree of verisimilar detail. For medieval writers interested in experimenting with nominalism, personification looks quite different. In keeping with Ockham's understanding of universals as cognitive acts, nominalist personification is primarily a mental process. Deguileville's Penance, whose tongue is a broom, does not represent *penance* in any kind of straightforward way. Instead, she prompts readers to cognize *penance* as they figure out the puzzle she represents. Langland showcases a much more local version of this process, in which readers must decide, retrospectively, whether to interpret a given term universally or particularly. For both sets of writers, personification no longer points primarily to a "higher" reality but rather back to the empirical world.

CHAPTER SIX

Dreaming of Aristotle in the *Songe d'Enfer* and *Winner and Waster*

Aristotelians began to challenge traditional Platonic accounts of personification as early as the first half of the twelfth century. Perhaps the first sign of this disruption occurs in Conrad of Hirsau's *Dialogue on the Authors* (*Dialogus Super Auctores*), a structured conversation between a schoolteacher and his adult student that works its way systematically through the grammar curriculum. The Master (Magister) initially instructs the Student (Discipulus) to read Prudentius integumentally, in the manner of a traditional Neoplatonic allegory: "This author should be read and studied for the spiritual senses of his works, in which senses are scattered, as it were, flowers of moral discipline" (Auctorem istum misticis sensibus legendum et discendum, in quibus sensibus interdum quasi flores disciplinae moralis apparent).[1] The Student breaks the pattern of the dialogue, however, by raising a more pressing concern:

> I do not wonder as much about that subtlety of meaning as about Faith or Chastity and the other Virtues waging war against a troop of Vices, when such things are rather qualities or accidents of a faithful and a chaste or a patient person, qualities which cannot be seen or be thought capable of fighting. Places and persons can be seen, as can the substances of all kinds of corporeal and tangible things, but their qualities, as I have told you, cannot be seen.
>
> Non tam mirror ipsam significativae literae subtilitatem quam fidem vel pudiciciam et ceteras virtutes vitiorum choro rebellantes, cum magis hoc fideli et pudico vel patienti accidat quam eorum qualitatibus, quae nec videntur nec pugnare posse probantur: videri possunt loca vel

> personae vel quarumcumque corporalium vel contrectabilium rerum substantiae, qualitates earum, sicut a te didici, videri non possunt.[2]

The Student here objects that faith and chastity cannot be represented as corporeal beings because, in Aristotelian terms, they are qualities or accidents, existing only "in" substances rather than as substances in their own right. As such, he jokes, they cannot possibly be judged fit for military service. The Student implies that Prudentius's personifications—at least as explained by the Master—rest upon a misunderstanding of Aristotle's categories and more broadly upon a Platonic metaphysics that accords too much substance to faith, chastity, and patience. That is to say, he identifies a mismatch between the traditional Platonic paradigm for interpreting personification allegory and his own Aristotelian understanding of substances and accidents.

We see a similar attempt to square Platonic personification with Aristotelian metaphysics in Dante's late-thirteenth-century *Vita Nova*. Commenting on his own poetry, Dante seeks to justify his traditional use of personification despite an Aristotelian worldview that he evidently shares with his imagined readers:

> Here, a person worthy of having every doubt clarified might be doubtful and might doubt my speaking of Love as if he were a thing-in-itself, and not only as an intelligent substance, but as if he were a corporeal substance—which, according to truth, is false, because Love is not a substance in itself but is an accident in a substance.

> Potrebbe qui dubitare persona degna da dichiararle ogne dubitazione, e dubitare potrebbe di ciò ch'io dico d'Amore come se fosse una cosa per sé: e non solamente sustanzia intelligente, ma sì come fosse sustanzia corporale. La qual cosa, secondo la verità, è falsa, ché Amore non è sì come sustanzia, ma è uno accidente in sustanzia.[3]

In these lines, Dante demonstrates that he is thoroughly versed in Aristotelian philosophy, deploying the technical vocabulary of accident and substance and translating the Aristotelian formula "ens per se ipsum, per se subsistens" (a thing-in-itself, a corporeal substance). Later in the same commentary, he refers to Aristotle as "the Philosopher" and alludes to his *On the Parts of Animals* by defining man as a laughing animal.[4] Dante explains that he uses an older style of personification not because he attributes a real and separate existence to universals but for the sake of literary tradition. He follows the Greek and Latin poets who, since antiquity, "have addressed inanimate things as if they had sense and reason, and also have made them talk" (ànno parlato a le cose inanimate sì come se avessero senso o ragione e fattele parlare insieme).[5] Implicitly, the key issue is not the transition from a predominantly Platonic to a predominantly Aristotelian worldview but the transfer of poetic authority from past to present and from Latin to vernacular. Indeed, commenting on the tension between the status of Love as a Platonic personification and the status of *love* as an Aristotelian accident was itself a commonplace in Italian literary circles.[6] Dante joins not only Conrad of Hirsau but also fellow poets such as Guido Cavalcanti in demonstrating a growing critical awareness of the divergence between a largely Platonic tradition of literary personification and the spread of an Aristotelian metaphysics and epistemology. Despite Huizinga's and his followers' claims to the contrary, Aristotelianism is not a modern imposition on medieval literary texts.

Whereas Conrad and Dante approach the relationship between Aristotelianism and personification primarily as critics, emphasizing the discontinuity between the literary tradition of Platonic personification and their own era's predominantly Aristotelian worldview, other medieval writers seek to develop a specifically Aristotelian variety of personification. In the two literary texts I focus on in this chapter—Raoul de Houdenc's early-thirteenth-century *Songe d'Enfer* (Dream of Hell) and the anonymous mid-fourteenth-century *Winner and Waster*—Aristotelian personification emerges from a crisis of representation, from a sense that traditional devices and modes of expression cannot adequately account for the contemporary world. The *Songe d'Enfer* rewrites the *Psychomachia* in a way that would probably make sense to Conrad of Hirsau's Student. Raoul's Vices defeat his Virtues, reflecting his experience of the corruption of feudalism rather than the idealism of the Platonic order. The most dynamic of these Vices are specifically Aristotelian, gaining their vigor from the prevalence of qualities such as avarice, graspingness, and drunkenness among Raoul's contemporaries. Instead of being derived from an existing moral schema, such as the Seven Deadly Sins, they are abstracted from the qualities of particular individuals and social groups. Like Raoul de Houdenc, the author of *Winner and Waster* associates Aristotelian personification with the decline of the aristocratic household as a social, moral, and economic institution. Having been cast out of the great hall, the poem's narrator struggles to represent the world beyond its walls. After experimenting with vernacular heraldry, which proves unable to account for the emergence of merchants and guildsmen as important social and economic actors, the poem "finds" the Aristotelian personifications Winner and Waster as the best way to represent the dizzying volume and variety of people and practices in mid-fourteenth-century England. As representations of Aristotelian universals "in sensibles," Winner and Waster are abstracted from sense perceptions of empirical individuals. As machines of the mind, they allow vernacular readers to gain conceptual purchase on economic phenomena and their social, moral, and even emotional repercussions long before the development of a specialized economic vocabulary.

This chapter focuses on the *Songe d'Enfer* and *Winner and Waster* in part because they represent points of origin for Aristotelian personification allegory within their respective literary milieux. As described by its modern editor, the *Songe d'Enfer* is "the first fictional narrative, in the first person, to be presented as the report of a dream" as well as "the first known otherworld voyage in which the stages of the journey are represented by personified vices."[7] Raoul de Houdenc, then, can be said to pioneer the literary genre of allegorical dream vision, in which personifications are explicitly presented as mental phenomena rather than direct representations of reality. This dream framework is conducive to Aristotelian personification allegory because it makes no claims about the existence of personifications, or the universals they embody, outside the human mind. As arguably the "earliest instance of [dream vision] in post-Conquest English," *Winner and Waster* is much more likely to have borrowed its framework from the *Songe* and its French successors than from the Old English *Vision of Drycthelm* or *Dream of the Rood*.[8] Thomas Bestul names the two poems' shared genre "allegorical romance," while A. C. Spearing assigns them to the "supergenre" he calls *dit* in French and *autography* in English, which he sees as originating in thirteenth-century France before crossing the Channel as part of the cultural exchange brought about by the Hundred Years War.[9] Within this same context of exchange, Judith Davidoff identifies *Winner and Waster* as the first poem to translate the framework of the *chanson d'aventure* from a lyric to a narrative setting, inaugurating a long-lived literary category that coincides to an important extent with Spearing's autography.[10] As self-consciously "modern" vernacular poems, the *Songe d'Enfer* and *Winner and Waster* break with earlier traditions of allegorical representation to help define the paradigm of Aristotelian personification allegory for their substantial body of medieval imitators. In doing so, they use Aristotle's metaphysics to attempt to make sense of a social world that Neoplatonism had twisted itself into knots trying to explain.

Both Raoul de Houdenc and the *Winner* author experiment with moderately realist rather than nominalist Aristotelian personification. That is to say, their personifications are not mental puzzles designed to elicit acts of cognition but instead correspond to "beings of reason" abstracted from sense perceptions of empirical individuals. Both poems dramatize the relationship between their personifications and the persons from whom they are abstracted, whether courtiers in the case of Raoul's Grasping or vintners, woolmen, and merchants in the case of the eponymous Winner. Where Winner seems to be generated by the narrator's efforts to come to terms with, to present to cognition, a group of tradesmen too large to be cognized individually, Grasping actually grows in size and strength to reflect the growing number of grasping individuals in his society. As one would expect from an Aristotelian metaphysics, both sets of personifications are secondary to the persons from whom they are derived. They emerge belatedly in response to, rather than anticipating, their earthly instantiations, and they have a reduced ontological status relative to Platonic forms. Both sets of personifications are also linked to their corresponding persons by an abundance of verisimilar detail, not all of it wholly consistent. Since Winner represents the quality of acquisitiveness in countless empirical individuals, he speaks now as a merchant, now as a craftsman, now as a landowner, now as a member of the royal household. This proliferation of worldly detail contrasts with the otherworldly descriptions of Prudentian and Neoplatonic personifications as well as with the lack of description—or, in the case of Deguileville, deliberately incongruous descriptions—associated with nominalist personifications. Instead of sitting on jeweled thrones or carrying brooms in their mouths, the moderately realist Aristotelian personifications of the *Songe d'Enfer* and *Winner and Waster* engage in the ordinary human activities of eating and drinking, working and sleeping—activities that, in the latter work in particular, are often described in precise, verisimilar detail. They are also predominantly masculine, perhaps as a means of marking their dependence on the male-dominated social world.

ARISTOTELIAN VICES ON THE PATH TO HELL

The *Songe d'Enfer*—sometimes also called the *Voie d'Enfer* (Way of Hell)—enjoyed considerable influence in the thirteenth and fourteenth centuries, surviving into the modern era in ten manuscripts.[11] Huon de Méry, author of *Li Tournoiemenz Antecrit* (The Tournament of Antichrist), a later-thirteenth-century recasting of the *Psychomachia*, praises Raoul in the same breath as Chrétien de Troyes.[12] The conclusion of the *Songe d'Enfer*, in which devils feast upon the fried tongues of sweet-talking lawyers and heretics roasted à la Parisienne, spawned a minor trope in medieval French poetry, with such banquets appearing in the *Tournoiemenz Antecrit*, the anonymous thirteenth-century *Salut d'Enfer* (whose punning title can be read as either Hell's Greeting or Hell's Salvation) and the fabliau *Saint Piere et le Jougleor* (*Saint Peter and the Jongleur*).[13] More broadly, the soul's pilgrimage through an otherworld of personified abstractions would go on to become an important narrative device. Beginning with two different versions of a *Songe de Paradis* or *Voie de Paradis* (Dream of Paradise or Way of Paradise), positioned as sequels to the *Songe d'Enfer* in surviving manuscripts, it would go on to structure the works of Deguileville, Langland, and Bunyan.[14] Even more broadly, Raoul's genre of first-person dream vision would become one of the most important markers of imaginative writing in the later Middle Ages, from Guillaume de Lorris and Dante to Langland (again) and Chaucer. Although much of this wider influence was mediated by the *Roman de la Rose* and the *Pèlerinage de la Vie Humaine*, Raoul de Houdenc represents himself as speaking to a worldwide francophone audience: "I come from Saxony / And from Champagne and from Burgundy, / From Lombardy and from England / I've been all around the world" (je vieng de Saissoingne / Et de Champaingne et de Borgoingne, / De Lombardie et d'Engleterre: / Bien ai cerchie toute terre) (413–16).[15] His hopes for an insular audience seem to have been borne out, albeit modestly, by an Anglo-Norman version of the poem surviving in Oxford, Bodleian Library MS Digby 86, a miscellany of Middle English, Anglo-French, and Latin works copied between 1271 and 1283.[16] The *Songe d'Enfer* thus played a role in English as well as continental literary history and could plausibly have exerted a direct as well as an indirect influence on the later Middle English tradition of allegorical dream visions.

Despite its originality and influence, the *Songe d'Enfer* has received relatively little critical attention. The dominant approach remains that of Hans Robert Jauss, who associates the poem with contemporary vernacular religious allegory but must immediately introduce important caveats: it exhibits neither that genre's characteristic "aversion for the world in general" nor its "hostile attitude towards courtly ideals."[17] Instead, the poem situates itself within the tradition of the *Psychomachia*, as interpreted by the proliferation of manuscript illustrations, archivolt and capitular sculptural programs, and decorative objects depicting Prudentius's characteristic battles between personified Vices and Virtues. It seems to be in this broad sense that Raoul treats the *Psychomachia* as a commonplace that he expects his audience in great households—and perhaps also in wayside taverns—to recognize. Implicitly, he asks his readers and listeners to entertain two intertextual thought experiments. What would happen if Prudentius's contests between Virtue and Vice occurred in "modern" times? And how should we understand the relationship between personifications and empirical phenomena? Although some of Raoul's personifications seem to belong to, or at least recall, the Neoplatonic tradition of formal personification, these figures are quickly upstaged by their Aristotelian successors. As the dreamer approaches hell, the personifications he encounters become increasingly variable, masculine, and worldly, deriving their being from the qualities of empirical persons rather than eternal principles.

The first personification the dreamer encounters in the *Songe d'Enfer* combines elements of Prudentian and Neoplatonic personification. The dreamer's initial meeting with Greed (Envie), the doyenne of Covetousness (Covoitise) in the land of Disloyalty (Desleauté), seems calculated to evoke the timeless truth of 1 Timothy 6:10: "Greed is the root of all evil" (Radix enim omnium malorum est cupiditas). As the hostess of the first way station along the road to hell, Greed partakes of this verity much as Prudentius's Pride partakes of the proverb "Pride goeth before destruction: and the spirit is lifted up before a fall" (Proverbs 16:18). Indeed, in a gesture reminiscent of Prudentius's Indulgence, Greed "attacks" by welcoming her victim into her lavishly appointed home, described as a "pleasant dwelling and beautiful way of life" (plesant ostel et bele vie) (24). As in Tree of Vices diagrams, where *cupiditas* is represented as the first step along the "way of death" (via mortis), covetousness here serves as the gateway to the rest of the deadly sins. While Greed's femininity conforms to both the Prudentian and Neoplatonic traditions of personification, her high social status and relative lack of activity link her more strongly to the latter. As befits her role as lady of the castle, her only action is to lodge the dreamer well ("Envie bien me herbega") as he begins his journey into sin (27).

Greed is soon upstaged, however, by a pair of much more vigorous personifications: Trickery (Tricherie) and Avarice. The two are introduced as Greed's ladies-in-waiting, with their status as subsidiary sins expressed by their status as dependents in Greed's household. But instead of standing silently in their mistress's shadow, in the manner of the subsidiary sins in the *Psychomachia*, they interact with the dreamer directly, pressing him for news of their followers in the country from which he has just come. In doing so, they establish a characteristically Aristotelian connection between the dream world of personified abstractions and the empirical world of ordinary human beings:

> They came to see me, both together, and rejoiced greatly to see me in their country. Shortly, without any hesitation, Avarice came to me demanding news of the avaricious, asking that I tell her what they were doing and how they were keeping. She asked how each one of her relations was prospering.

> Por moi veoir toutes ensamble
> I vindrent et grant joie firent
> De ce qu'en lor païs me virent.
> Tantost, sanz plus contremander,
> Vint Avarisce demander
> Que je noveles li deïsee
> Des avers, et li apreïsse
> Lor fez et lor contenemenz.
> Si com chascuns de ses parenz
> Se demaine m'a demandé. (32–41)

Avarice, in particular, is very insistent with her guest, demanding that he update her on every single one of the avaricious. This interest fits with Avarice's allegorical nature, suggesting that she counts the avaricious in the same way that the avaricious count their coins. As befits an Aristotelian metaphysics, however, it also begins to establish the priority of the material world as the place where the contest between the Virtues and Vices will ultimately be decided. Trickery and Avarice become dynamic and narratively interesting figures, eclipsing their mistress Greed, insofar as they connect themselves to this empirical reality.

The dreamer's response to Avarice reverses the familiar dynamic of the *Psychomachia*, in which the Virtues triumph over the Vices in an almost ritualistic sequence. He reports that the avaricious have all but destroyed a personified Generosity (Larguece):

> And I immediately told her a tale which she received well, in which I told her that her people had chased Generosity from the country, and had pursued Generosity so thoroughly that she had neither tower nor stronghold, nor did she know where she could hang on. Nor can Generosity endure much longer, for she/it is in such dire straits that not even the rich have any of it. I told her this tale, and she had great joy of it.

Et je li ai tantost conté
Un conte qu'ele tint a buen,
Quar je li contai que li suen
Avoient du païs chacie
Larguece, et tant s'est porchacie
Sa gent que Larguece n'avoit
Tor ne recet, ne ne savoit
Quel part ele peüst durer;
Ne le pot mes plus endurer
Larguece, ainz est en si mal point
Que chiés les riches n'en a point.
Ce li contai; grant joie en ot. (42–53)

Raoul here reimagines a battle not from the *Psychomachia* itself but from its iconographic tradition, which generally depicts Generosity (Largitas), rather than Prudentius's enigmatic Works, as the opponent of Avarice. Where Conrad of Hirsau attributes the Prudentian Virtues' victory over the Vices to the moral strength of early Christians, Raoul suggests that the lax morals of his own contemporaries have produced the opposite result. He initially characterizes Generosity's defeat in military terms, as the loss of castles and walled towns. The avaricious have chased her from one stronghold after another, reducing her to penury and powerlessness and bringing her to the verge of extinction. The loss of towns and castles, however, implies the defeat or desertion of the vassals who hold them, allowing Raoul to connect Generosity's fate to the empirical behavior of French-speakers. In the last line of the passage, Raoul takes the further step of depersonifying generosity entirely, treating it as a quality of empirical persons rather than an independent being. Implicitly, Generosity can endure as a personification only as long as there exist generous human beings. She becomes less and less powerful as the numbers of the generous dwindle. When they cease to exist entirely—even among the rich, who can easily afford to give—she will pass away.

The poem's break with Neoplatonism gains momentum in the next episode when the dreamer encounters the masculine personification Grasping (Tolirs), the lord of Broken Faith (Foimentie). Like Avarice, Grasping presses the dreamer for news, this time not about grasping human beings but about "Grasping on this earth, / One of his godsons" (Tolirs en ceste terre, / Uns siens filleus) (112–13). In response, the narrator recounts a battle between the earthly Grasping and a personified Giving (Doners), evidently modeled on the *Psychomachia* in a general sense even though it does not correspond to any particular battle:

> I responded truthfully when I told him that Giving was wretched and destitute, poor and naked and in distress. He who used to enjoy the right of primogeniture is now a younger son, now insignificant. Giving does not dare to show his hands, Giving languishes, that's how it stands. Giving will never have two good moments in succession in any noble household. When Giving holds court, he seems to have an unhealthy heart, he is always pressing his hand against his chest. He is miserable, despised, hated, and blamed, while Grasping is handsome and has a good reputation. He is not despised or downtrodden, but is tall and well developed, with a strong heart, body, arms, and hands, while Giving is a dwarf.
>
> Respondi voir, quar je li dis
> Que Doners ert las et mendis,
> Povres et nus et en destrece;
> Qui soloit avoir l'ainsneece
> Or est mainsnez, or est du mains;
> Doners n'ose moustrer ses mains,
> Doners languist; ce est la somme.
> Jamés Doners chiés nul haut homme
> Ne fera deus biaus cops ensamble.
> A hautes cors de Doner samble
> Que il n'ait mie le cuer sain,
> Qu'en son sain tient adés sa main,
> Lais, chetis, haïs, et blasmez.
> Tolirs est biaus et renommez;
> N'est pas chetis ne recreüs,
> Ainz est et granz et parcreüs.
> De cuer, de cors, de braz, de mains,
> Est granz assez; Doners est nains. (117–34)

Where the avaricious defeat Generosity through a military campaign, Grasping overcomes Giving less violently, but no less viciously, by damaging his reputation. Giving is poor and naked because he no longer has any standing in noble households, where gifts of clothes simultaneously reward service and confirm the recipient's insider status. Once treated as the lord's son and heir, he has now become a nonentity whose word carries no weight. Giving has become quite literally insignificant, both as a person and as a word. This diminished reputation corresponds to, or even produces, a physical diminishment, as manifested first by an illness that compromises the personification's vital force and then by a literal loss of stature. Giving seems to become a dwarf over the course of the narrator's speech, even assuming the dwarf's marginal position in the noble household, as Grasping becomes correspondingly taller and stronger. It is almost as though the dreamer contributes to Giving's downfall, as his tale further damages the virtue's reputation. As the dreamer proceeds toward hell, he seems to be drawn further and further into sin, contributing news and artful stories to the Vices' households in the manner of an itinerant jongleur.

The doubling of personifications in this episode (and more briefly in the preceding one, where the otherworldly Trickery also has an earthly counterpart) recalls the doubling of universals in Aristotle's metaphysics. The otherworldly Vices correspond to beings of reason—that is, to universals in the mind—by existing only within the dream world. Although they are directly available to cognition, as evidenced by their often extended conversations with the dreamer, they do not exist within the material world and so must depend on their doubles to fight on their behalves. The earthly Vices, in turn, correspond to universals "in sensibles," which exist in the material world as the formal element in hylomorphic compounds. In the same way that universals "in sensibles" are not directly available to cognition, the earthly Vices are not present in the dream world, and their deeds must always be recounted secondhand. They seem, however, to derive their power not from their otherworldly namesakes but from their existence as qualities or accidents in empirical persons. In an Aristotelian metaphysics, universals are usually considered to exist only as long as they are instantiated in at least one empirical substance, and this same logic seems to govern the *Songe d'Enfer*.[18] The earthly Generosity and Giving will cease to exist when there are no more generous and giving human beings, while the earthly Grasping's continued existence is assured because there are so many takers. Indeed, Raoul imaginatively elaborates Aristotle's system by suggesting that universals exist to different degrees, depending on the number of substances in which they are instantiated. Giving dwindles away as humans cease to give, while Grasping becomes more robust as more of them begin to take. We are here a long way from the serene realm of the immutable Platonic forms, which are by definition immune to earthly change. We are quite close, however, to the Master's response to the Student's objections in Conrad of Hirsau's *Dialogue*, which encourages him to understand personified universals in terms of the empirical persons from whom they are abstracted: "Faith for the faithful person, Idolatry for the idolater, and so on for the others" (Fides pro fideli, ydolatria pro ydolatra et sic de ceteris, ut virtuosus per virtutem, per vicia viciosus ostendatur).[19] Seen in this way, the collective attack of the avaricious on Generosity is all but indistinguishable from Grasping's attack on Giving. Virtually the only difference is that the former gain in strength by becoming more numerous, while the latter gains in strength by becoming larger. The earthly Grasping, in other words, anticipates Hobbes's Leviathan by gathering all graspers into a single, monstrous corporate self.[20]

As the dream proceeds, the world through which the dreamer travels continues to degrade, becoming increasingly Aristotelian. Leaving Broken Faith, the narrator crosses the foul river Gluttony (Gloutonie) to reach not another great hall but a Base Tavern (Vile Taverne), where he sits down to gamble with the masculine personifications Dirty Trick (Mestret), Cheat (Mesconte), and Chance (Hasart).[21] Instead of inquiring after safely anonymous classes of sinners, these personifications identify their followers by name, calling out Charles and Mainsens who lodge with Hypocrisy (Papelardie) in Chartres, Hermers and Guiars, the hunchback artisan Jehan, Gautiers Moriaus, Michiel de Treilles, Girart de Troies, and dant Sauvage; a little later the dreamer also names Gautier l'Enfant and Guilliaume de Salerne (167–201, 223–30, 290–92). This stretch of the poem seems to have been received in some quarters as a breach of decorum, with a number of copyists either substituting general references for Raoul's personal names or omitting these lines altogether.[22] At least one scribe, in contrast, took advantage of the opportunity to name names. The early copy of the poem in Paris, Bibliothèque Nationale, MS français 25433 replaces Guilliaume de Salerne with Robert de Corçon, an unpopular papal legate active in France in 1213–14—evidently in order to score points against a political enemy. The list of names likewise delights Chance and his associates:

> Chance . . . was happy and enlivened the whole affair. And every man and woman there was full of joy; it was the greatest occasion I have ever known, such as will never occur again.

> Hasars . . .
> Fu liez et esbaudi l'afere.
> Et tuit et tuites firent joie;
> Ne cuit que jamés si grant voie,
> Quar onques mes tele n'avint. (210–15)

The dreamer's superlatives highlight the Vices' new liveliness and vigor alongside the dreamer's own deepening involvement in sin. Rather than deriving from a preexisting schema of paired vices and virtues, as in the iconographic tradition of the *Psychomachia*, or even from a biblical principle such as "radix . . . malorum est cupiditas," Chance, Cheater, and Dirty Trick seem to owe their existence to the human institution of the tavern, which produces seemingly unlimited quantities of human beings who possess the relevant vicious qualities. In short, these human beings, in their Aristotelian particularity, become the life of the Vices' party.

The progressive debasement of Raoul's otherworld continues when Drunkenness (Yvrece) and her son Throwdown (Versez) join the revelers in the Base Tavern:

> With that great joy came Drunkenness, the mother of Throwdown, and her son with her, side by side. Throwdown is tall and well developed, and much loved and held in reverence in his country and in his land, and he says that he was born in England.

> Avoec cele grant joie vint
> Yvrece, la mere Versez,
> Et ses filz o li lez a lez.
> Versez est granz et parcreüz,
> Et molt est amez et creüz
> En son païs et en sa terre,
> Et dist qu'il est nez d'Engleterre. (216–22)

Following immediately on the heels of the Vices' great celebration, Drunkenness's entrance indicates that as the party proceeds the revelers begin to possess the Aristotelian quality or accident of drunkenness, which is in turn abstracted into a personified universal. Instead of being temporally as well as ontologically prior to empirical instances of drunkenness, as in the Platonic model of form and instantiation, Drunkenness comes into being as a personification quite literally "with that great joy." The name of Drunkenness's son links the actions of pouring a drink (*verser à boire*) and throwing something to the ground (*verser à terre*).[23] Implicitly, then, he enters the Base Tavern at his mother's side because its occupants become aggressive as they become drunk. He also seems to gain power directly from drunken aggressiveness in the material world. Raoul locates his power base specifically among the English, who are stereotyped in medieval French texts as heavy drinkers and tavern wrestlers.[24] The implication is that there are so many aggressive drunks in England that they render Throwdown "so marvelously strong, and so stout-limbed and so extraordinary, that he throws even the largest on their backs" (si fors a merveille / Et si membruz et si divers / Qu'il gete le plus granz envers) (230–32). By this point, nearly all traces of the traditional Platonic universe have disappeared: Raoul's predominantly masculine personifications are now base rather than noble, variable rather than stable, and contingent on rather than independent from the material world.

Having established their connection to the material world, Raoul's personifications stand ready to take on the dreamer directly. Up to this point, the dreamer has narrated a *Psychomachia*-like battle at each station along the route to hell. In the Base Tavern, he himself battles Vice, accepting Throwdown's challenge to a drinking contest that doubles as a mock epic version of single combat. As befits Throwdown's double name, the dreamer suffers injuries such as an unsteady gait and ringing head that could result from either drinking or fighting, culminating when Throwdown throws down the narrator with "an English wrestling move" (un des jambés d'Engleterre) that does him "great mischief" (grant meschief) (277, 283). All of this punning suggests that Throwdown prevails not because he is inherently stronger than the dreamer but because the increasing incidence of aggressive drunkenness in the thirteenth-century Anglo-French world has afforded him a temporary advantage. In a sense, the dreamer is undone by the company he keeps, which both calls Throwdown into being—or at least calls him over from England—and makes him virtually impossible to resist. The narrator succumbs to vice through peer pressure, or by participating in the corrupt institution of the tavern, as much as through individual moral weakness.

To an important extent, then, Raoul de Houdenc associates Aristotelian personification with sin. The poem begins in a recognizably Neoplatonic mode, with Greed, the doyenne of Covetousness, representing scriptural truth within the larger structure of Raoul's fable. She is not herself the Platonic form of greed or envy, because she can walk and talk and host dinner parties, but she seems to signify her namesake sin as an eternal and changeless universal, both prior to and unaffected by its earthly instantiations. Beyond the pleasure afforded by her fictional surface, her primary role within the poem is to evoke the timeless biblical truth "greed is the root of all evil." Almost immediately, however, this familiar Platonic paradigm begins to disintegrate. Rather than attacking the personified Virtues directly, as in the *Psychomachia*, Trickery and Grasping act through earthly namesakes whose behavior can only be explained in Aristotelian terms. The earthly Grasping is ontologically subsequent to, and depends upon, the instances of graspingness in particular human beings, while his opponent, Giving, similarly depends upon instances of the quality of openhandedness. The outcome of their struggle does not reflect absolute values such as truth or merit but rather the empirical incidence of graspingness and openhandedness in the early-thirteenth-century francophone world. Raoul imaginatively elaborates Aristotle's metaphysics by representing Grasping growing into a superman and Giving dwindling into a dwarf as idealized feudal practices give way to mercantile ones. Once Aristotelian personification gains a beachhead, it spreads quickly. Masculine personifications begin to outnumber feminine ones, and the scene shifts from the traditional courtly setting of Neoplatonic allegory to the Base Tavern. Instead of having an earthly double, Throwdown gains his strength directly from the all-too-numerous aggressive drunks who frequent actual taverns. As the dreamer approaches hell, in other words, both the moral universe through which he moves and the personifications who inhabit it become increasingly Aristotelian. This shift from Platonic to Aristotelian personification coincides with both the Vices' victories over the Virtues and the dreamer's own increasing sinfulness. To proceed toward hell is to align oneself more and more with the way things are—that is to say, with the fallen state of the material world—and less and less with the way they should be. Aristotelian personification becomes the characteristic literary mode of a debased modernity. It is uniquely capable of explaining how, in Raoul's experience of thirteenth-century France, Vice can defeat Virtue despite the latter's moral superiority.

Within the *Songe d'Enfer*, however, Aristotelian personification also points toward a remedy for vice. At the individual level, Raoul has already indicated that personified virtues such as Generosity and Giving gain power from empirical human beings who possess the qualities of generosity and openhandedness. At least in theory, a renewal of personal morality would thus strengthen the Virtues and weaken the Vices. Raoul places much more faith, however, in reforms to what we might call public policy. Drunkenness consoles the dreamer for his defeat by Throwdown by ushering him into Castle Brothel (Chastiau Bordel), where he degrades himself further in the company of the feminine Shame (Honte) and the masculine Theft (Larrecin). When Theft asks for tidings of his followers, however, the dreamer interrupts the pattern of the narrative thus far by transmitting unwelcome news: "The king dispenses justice so strictly . . . that thieves are in a bad way" (Li rois en fet tel justice . . . / Que larron sont en mauvés point) (328–30). Whereas the maladministration of the socioeconomic institution of the great hall has allowed vices such as Grasping and Trickery to thrive, the proper administration of the king's justice keeps Theft and his followers in check. Crucially, the king or lord of whom Raoul speaks acts not as a private individual but rather as an officeholder, as the head of what Ernst Kantorowicz calls a "*corpus morale et politicum* [moral and political body] in the Aristotelian sense."[25] Although the empirical king is responsible for devoting sufficient resources to the administration of justice and appointing trustworthy agents to act in his name, the system he oversees is greater than he is. From this point of view, only aggregates such as Aristotelian corporate persons seem to have the power to act against aggregates such as Grasping and Throwdown. In doing so, they institutionalize virtue just as the Base Tavern institutionalizes vice, creating the conditions under which an empirical person such as the dreamer either succumbs to or triumphs over sin. Raoul's understanding of virtue and vice as corporate persons accordingly leads to a call for political rather than merely ethical change as a means of reclaiming the victories of the *Psychomachia*.

In the *Songe d'Enfer*, then, Aristotelian personification is associated both positively and negatively with political and theological ideas of incorporation. In contrast to Platonic personification, it represents vice as a collective rather than a purely individual problem. To be sure, individuals still choose between personified Virtue and Vice in the long-standing tradition of decision allegory. As the dreamer's disastrous encounter with Throwdown illustrates, however, they do so within institutions that are themselves either virtuous or vicious. Throwdown's prodigious size is derived from the prodigious drunkenness of the denizens of the Base Tavern and results in a fight against the dreamer that is barely a fight at all. Although the dreamer remains morally culpable for his physical and spiritual fall, the *Songe d'Enfer* makes it clear that the tavern, as a social institution that magnifies the power of vice, plays a crucial role in his defeat. In doing so, it echoes the penitential discourse of treatises such *Somme le Roi*, which describes the tavern as "the fount of sin," "the devil's school," and the devil's "own chapel."[26] The *Songe d'Enfer* likewise condemns great halls where grasping replaces gift-giving as the primary means of social advancement. In Raoul's nostalgic vision of the feudal order, power and prestige accrue to those who give the greatest gifts, so that Giving flourishes. He is seated in the position of honor at the lord's right hand. In contrast, in the self-consciously "modern" world in which the poem is set, the lord's personal disregard for Giving discourages the entire household from giving, generating a vicious cycle. Once again, individuals remain responsible for their own actions, but their decisions are shaped by the institutions in which they find themselves. It follows that the spiritual consequences of individual acts of grasping and drunkenness are both personal and collective. Such acts damn individual sinners if they do not repent but also help to create a congregation of the unfaithful. Instead of participating in the mystical body of the church, sinners are ultimately incorporated into the collective body of the damned where—at least as imagined by Raoul's successor, Huon de Méry—they become part of the army of the Antichrist.

Raoul's understanding of sin as a collective problem also means that vice increasingly assumes a masculine form. Feminine personifications are clustered toward the beginning of the poem, where they are associated with the more or less Platonic figure of Greed. In the later, more Aristotelian reaches of the poem, feminine personifications tend to appear only in situations where a female body is allegorically necessary. The feminine Drunkenness is the mother of Throwdown and leads the way to sexual sin, while Shame consummates that sin with the dreamer in Castle Brothel. Even in these scenes, however, the dreamer's primary interlocutors are the masculine Throwdown and Theft. Raoul's Aristotelian universe is overwhelmingly a man's world, despite the fact that he writes in a Romance language in which abstract nouns are predominantly grammatically feminine. Neither this grammatical fact nor the potentially weightier literary tradition of feminine personifications seems to give Raoul a moment's pause, as he assigns masculine bodies to a seemingly endless array of verb forms (Tolirs, Doners, Versez) and grammatically masculine nouns (Mestrait, Mesconte, Hasart, Larrecin). This preference for masculine personifications seems to stem from Raoul's emphasis on the public and collective nature of vice, as well as from his decision to situate it within male-dominated social institutions. When Hercules chooses between feminine personifications of Virtue and Vice in the first known decision allegory, he implicitly chooses between sexual partners. Although Vice is more immediately alluring, Hercules wisely opts for the more modest Virtue, who promises a more fruitful long-term union. This structure represents moral choice as both normatively masculine and deeply intimate: a decision about how to orient masculine desire. In the *Songe d'Enfer*, the decision maker remains normatively masculine, but Vice now represents a version of the self rather than the Other. Grasping is masculine because he incorporates all of the masculine decision-makers who have adopted the habit of grasping. Furthermore, Grasping and Giving both dwell within the patriarchal institution of the noble household, where the latter enjoys the privileges of the first-born son before he is demoted to the status of a disfavored—and ultimately disposable—younger brother. To the extent that a grammatical rule holds sway here, it would seem to be the rule that treats a mixed-gender group as grammatically masculine. Although Raoul surely would have acknowledged giving and grasping as qualities of empirical women as well as of empirical men, the aggregates Giving and Grasping are masculine in the same way that, in French, a mixed group of givers or graspers is denoted by a masculine plural. That is to say, Raoul follows both Aristotelian theory and grammatical practice in treating the masculine as universal.

This preference for masculine, Aristotelian personifications rather than feminine, Platonic ones has wider implications. In the *Songe d'Enfer*, the best ways to battle against vice are political and economic—in the Aristotelian sense of managing an *oikos*, a household—rather than ethical. Raoul thus praises the king's strict administration of justice as a means of combatting Theft and suggests that the heads of noble households have the power to reestablish Giving in a position of honor. Importantly, these endeavors do not need to be 100 percent successful in order to be effective. Any progress the ruler makes will diminish the size of the personified Vice, allowing his subjects to fight it—both individually and collectively—on more equal terms. Implicitly, this process begins with the public performance of the *Songe d'Enfer* itself, most likely during Lent, as an alternative to more debased forms of entertainment. Listening to the poem and following its advice will begin to cut Vice down to size. To be sure, the *Songe d'Enfer*'s praise of generosity is self-interested, as Raoul, the traveling jongleur, aligns openhanded lords with Giving and stingy ones with Grasping. At the same time, he suggests that his poem can contribute to the reestablishment of the great hall as a virtuous institution, one that can sponsor a return to *Psychomachia*'s victories of Virtue over Vice.

THE CRISIS OF REPRESENTATION IN *WINNER AND WASTER*

Winner and Waster follows the *Songe d'Enfer* in rewriting Prudentius's *Psychomachia* for a self-consciously "modern" world.[27] The threatened battle between the protagonists' armies, later transmuted into a debate, recalls the blows and tirades exchanged by Avarice and Generosity and their respective followers in the medieval *Psychomachia* tradition. It also restages the *Songe d'Enfer*'s confrontations between Avarice and Generosity and between Grasping and Giving within the high- and late-medieval genre of allegorical romance. We have seen, however, that Raoul de Houdenc maintains a traditional understanding of the virtues of generosity and giving even as he represents avarice and grasping as produced by the breakdown of the social institution of the great hall. The *Winner* author, in contrast, represents both sides of the debate as corrupted by the same social breakdown. In doing so, he adopts a characteristically Aristotelian understanding of virtue as the mean between two equally vicious extremes. Bestul has pointed out that the nouns *wynnere* and *wastoure* and the verbs *winnen* and *wasten* were regularly used in Middle English penitential discourse to designate the opposing vices of avarice and prodigality.[28] In *Winner and Waster*, the vicious extremes are opposed both to each other and to the virtue of liberality, defined in Aristotle's *Nicomachean Ethics* as the mean with regard to the getting and spending of money. To an even greater extent than Raoul de Houdenc, then, the *Winner* author rewrites the *Psychomachia* in self-consciously modern and specifically Aristotelian terms. Where Raoul urges lords to come to the aid of his dwindling personifications of Generosity and Giving, *Winner and Waster* invites them to become Liberality personified, restoring the moral center to a world otherwise hopelessly out of kilter.

In issuing his invitation, the *Winner* author, like Raoul, experiments with both personification and genre, staging the (re)invention of Aristotelian personification in the midst of a larger crisis in the traditional great hall genre of romance. *Winner and Waster* begins with a prologue that narrates the author's understanding of his historical present—an understanding that is presented objectively, in the third person, but nonetheless serves as the background for the first-person poetic making that follows. In doing so, it defines the author's relationship to changing social and literary structures, especially the poet's expulsion from the lord's great hall and the concomitant bifurcating of romance. Once a fruitful synthesis of entertainment and moral seriousness, romance splits in the course of the poem's opening lines into low-minded jape on the one hand and the prologue's own genre of social complaint on the other. Faced with this fracture, the author assigns himself the task of developing a new poetic synthesis that is adequate to the moment in which he lives but not resigned to it. His first attempt, which corresponds to the poem's first fitt, seeks such a synthesis in the new genre of vernacular heraldic poetry. Although similar to romance in its claim to serve as serious entertainment centered on aristocratic feats of arms, vernacular heraldry addresses the public sphere rather than the great hall and concerns itself with politics rather than ethics. The author soon abandons this initial attempt at synthesis, however, as vernacular heraldry proves unable to account for the proliferation of important actors in the public sphere. Indeed, he thematizes his failure, transforming it into the premise that generates the personifications Winner and Waster at the beginning of the poem's second fitt. As Aristotelian personifications, Winner and Waster define an allegorical poetics that is self-consciously personal and verisimilar on the one hand and speculative and abstract on the other. As abstractions they can account for the enormous "sowme" of merchants and guildsmen who overwhelm the first fitt's heraldic poetics without needing to describe each one (192).[29] Because they are embodied, they are also immersed in a world of representative, though not completist, realistic detail—and so can be judged as if they were persons according to existing ethical criteria. The extrainstitutional readership of *Winner and Waster* is asked to use these personifications as intellectual tools to analyze contemporary English society as well as to speculate about, project, discuss, and debate what its improvement would have to account for.

To be clear, this is the poetic project that I find enacted within *Winner and Waster* itself. It is unlikely that the author's literary ambitions were realized in the actual circulation of his work, which only survives in a single manuscript. Nor can the author's understanding of his historical present be accorded the status of objective history. Among other things, he vastly underestimates the appeal of romance to late-medieval readers beyond the institutional context of the great hall. The urban elites the author evokes at the end of the first fitt would soon be reading romances, both broadly and narrowly defined, if they had not begun to do so already.[30] Nonetheless, it would be a mistake to dismiss the *Winner* author as merely idiosyncratic. The surviving exemplar of his poem, copied in the mid-fifteenth century by Robert Thornton in the North Riding of Yorkshire, apparently stands at a number of removes from the original and displays a mix of dialects that may indicate geographic mobility.[31] *Winner and Waster* also manifestly influenced *Piers Plowman*, and so stands at a single remove from a major literary and social phenomenon. Indeed, it would seem to form part of a genealogy of *Piers Plowman* as an allegorical romance: in this connection it is worth noting that that the surviving fragments of *The Conflict of Wit and Will* also depict an altercation between allegorical personifications with at least a passing resemblance to Langland's work, in this case Wit's psychomachia of Castel Caro in A.10/B.9/C.10.[32] Although the *Winner* author laments the social and literary changes he catalogs in his prologue, he does not respond by returning to or insisting desperately upon a romance tradition that he regards as superseded. Instead, he employs an openly experimental process of trial and error to define an allegorical poetics that is itself open to further experimentation, including by later generations of authors who seek to develop a poetic vocabulary adequate to the times in which they live. In other words, he was onto something.

In order to understand why the *Winner* author experimented with what I am calling moderately realist Aristotelian personification, we need to see how he first tested older genres and found them wanting—that is to say, incapable of representing his self-consciously "modern" reality. The poem begins in the same vein as *Sir Gawain and the Green Knight*, with the promise of historically engaged, morally instructive romance:

> Sythen that Bretayne was biggede and Bruyttus it aughte,
> Thurgh the takynge of Troye with tresone withinn,
> There hathe selcouthes bene sene in seere kynges tymes. (1–3)

The author here asserts the continuity of the British royal line and, with it, a continuity of great deeds and the texts that recount them. For a moment, historiography and romance appear to be compatible, with romance dilating upon, and holding up for admiration and imitation, deeds that fit within the chronology of British history. Far from coincidentally, Derek Pearsall finds the most likely common source for the opening of *Winner and Waster* and *Sir Gawain and the Green Knight* to be Geoffrey of Monmouth's *History of the Kings of Britain*.[33] This compatibility does not last, however. The next lines force us to redefine "selcouthes," which usually refer to knightly deeds or religious wonders, as acts of breathtaking hypocrisy. The origins of this double-dealing, too, can be traced to Britain's legendary founding, specifically to Aeneas's betrayal of Troy.[34] The claim that follows, however, participates in the genre of satire—or its cousin, social complaint—rather than romance: "For nowe alle es witt and wyles that we with delyn, / Wyse wordes and slee, and icheon wryeth othere" (5–6). The multiple registers of "selcouthes" allow it to function as a hinge, turning the poem from the idealized but unsustainable genre of historical romance to one that more accurately reflects a world in which the second estate, in particular, is losing the ability to reproduce itself.[35] Sons desert their fathers and their duties for the pleasures of the metropolis, while in their absence low-born men "wedde ladyes in londe and lede hem at will" (15). Hares will soon be nesting on abandoned hearthstones if they have not begun to do so already. For the *Winner* author, the chain of exemplarity that links mid-fourteenth-century landholders to their noble ancestors, both real and imagined, is being decisively severed. History is discontinuous rather than continuous, and the return to origins that so preoccupies romance is flatly impossible.

Rather than simply abandoning romance, however, the *Winner* author doubles back, in the course of his complaint, to explain how this sorry state of affairs came to pass. The collapse of the material conditions that enabled the production and consumption of romance is itself a sign of the times:

> Whylome were lordes in londe that loved in thaire hertis
> To here makers of myrthes that matirs couthe fynde,
> And now es no frenchipe in fere bot fayntnesse of hert,
> Wyse wordes withinn that wroghte were never,
> Ne redde in no romance that ever renke herde.
> Bot now a childe appon chere, withowtten chyn-wedys,
> That never wroghte thurgh witt thies wordes togedire,
> Fro he can jangle als a jaye and japes telle,
> He schall be levede and lovede and lett of a while
> Wele more than the man that made it hymselven. (19–28)

The category of "romance" against which *Winner and Waster* defines itself is itself notoriously difficult to define. The *Middle English Dictionary* recognizes three senses of the term: the French language; a poem, history, or other written work, usually in the vernacular; and a chivalric romance.[36] Paul Strohm traces the term's evolution from general to particular, while Derek Pearsall blends the *MED*'s second two senses to describe romance as "the principal secular literature of entertainment of the Middle Ages"—a characterization that has gained currency precisely for its minimalism and inclusiveness.[37] The *Winner* author's approach to romance is evidently more prescriptive than Pearsall's, placing historical engagement and moral instruction alongside entertainment as necessary elements of the genre. Given the similarities between *Winner and Waster* and French allegorical dream visions, including the *Songe d'Enfer*, the narrator's usage may also include a hint of the *MED*'s first sense of *romance*. The author's category of romance almost certainly includes francophone works. It is quite possible, however, that the literary transition the author laments is also bound up with the decline of French as the medium of great hall reading, especially insofar as equally well-crafted and morally serious English-language texts were not yet readily available. In this scenario, the performance of carefully crafted poetry in the prestige vernacular degenerates into low vernacular doggerel recited by a "childe appon chere" as part of a wider generational shift in aristocratic language preference from French to English.

Certainly, as Vance Smith has pointed out, the "right" reading of romance was considered to be the mark of a well-ordered aristocratic household, so that the failure of romance becomes both a cause and a symptom of household degeneration.[38] More specifically, aristocratic patronage enables formal poetic *inventio*, a process the author invokes using standard Middle English translations of technical Latin terms when he speaks of "makers" (*auctores*) who "fynde" (*invenire* < *inventio*) appropriate "matirs" (*materia*).[39] The collapse of this system in favor of young performers who "jangle als a jaye"—at worst producing sound without meaning, at best parroting words they do not understand—deprives true makers not only of sustenance and audience but also of the very words that were the tools of their trade. As words lose their traditional social referents and are put to new, self-serving uses, their meanings begin to change, a phenomenon the prologue highlights first with the double sense of "selcouthes," then with "witt" in lines 5 and 25, "wyse" in lines 6, 10, and 22, and "boyes of blode" in line 14, which must be either emended or understood to refer to ambitious low-born men rather than gentlemen. Consequently, the jangling "childe" speaks but makes no sense, while the old romancer knows how to make sense but can no longer be understood because of the corruption that surrounds him. Without an audience bound by "frenchipe in fere," an interpretive community based on a common commitment to appreciating and performing "selcouthes" in the original sense of the term, his words are locked "withinn," his romance never "wroghte" and never "herde."[40]

The prologue to *Winner and Waster*, then, constitutes a thinly veiled obituary for the genre of romance as well for its close cousin, the salutary "myrthes" of the aristocratic household. Although the author uses *mirthe* as though it were a synonym of romance, the term evokes a wide range of compatible pleasures: celebration, ceremony, feasting, spectacle, story, jest, musical performance—indeed spiritual joy and heavenly bliss.[41] Tellingly, all of these "myrthes" combine pleasure with order, harmony, decorum. That is to say, they are derived from order and at the same time contribute to it, producing a virtuous cycle that is equally evident in the festive arrangement of a great hall and the harmony of a choir of angels. When the earthly versions of this cycle are disrupted, however, the synthesis represented by "myrthes" cannot be sustained. "Myrthes" accordingly devolve into the "japes" of the child performer, which offer entertainment decoupled from, indeed fueled by their disruption of, feudal order and decorum. Defined alternately as a trick, deceit or fraud, a frivolous pastime or literary trifle, a joke or remark not seriously intended, and a piece of nonsense, a "jape" is characterized by its lack of a truth claim and so cannot serve, as romance did, as an adjunct to historiography.[42] It is almost by definition ephemeral, and predominantly oral rather than written, detaching the status of "myrthes" as performance from their concern for the past and the future. In this context, it is worth noting that in the prologue romance is insistently a written genre that is read aloud in a communal setting, while the performance of the "childe" leaves no written trace.[43] The "childe" is content to be "lett of a while," and for only a while, in part because his work acknowledges no time or place but the present to which he has adapted and resigned himself.

The *Winner* author implicitly assigns the ordering function of "myrthes," their claims to truth and moral seriousness, to the prologue's own genre of social complaint. Righteous, but neither joyous nor entertaining, social complaint offers the writer who "sadly will see and the sothe telle" a means of describing the disturbances he perceives around him, giving them order by situating them in the eschatological context of the "dredfull Domesdaye" (16–17). On one hand, the japer is "levede and lovede," while on the other the author of complaint is a voice in the wilderness, writing in opposition to corrupt powers-that-be rather than in support of a virtuous status quo. While he keeps faith with his understanding of history, insistently situating current events in the context of past glories and future judgment, his utterances lack present stakes because he has no place or position from which to speak. Indeed, the last lines of the prologue suggest that the author imagines no present audience for his complaint at all: "Bot, never-the-lattere, at the laste when ledys bene knawen, / Werke wittnesse will bere who wirche kane beste" (29–30).[44] Written but never read or spoken, *Winner and Waster* is imagined as a textual appendix to the Book of Life, justifying the author's craft and bearing witness to his truthfulness.

The *Winner and Waster* prologue, then, depicts a moment of interconnected social and literary turmoil as the declining genre of romance splits into "jape" on one hand and social complaint on the other. "Jape" inherits romance's status as oral performance, its ready audience, its entertainment value, its great hall institutional location, and its support of the status quo. Social complaint takes on romance's moral seriousness, its commitment to the right ordering of society, its technical mastery, its claimed relationship to history, and its status as a written object. Since both of these genres are by definition partial and incomplete, the prologue challenges the rest of the poem to create a new generic synthesis that is at once serious and entertaining, written and performative—but addressed to an extramural reading public rather than the delimited audience of the great hall. As Thorlac Turville-Petre notes, the final lines of the prologue place enormous responsibility on the audience to receive, interpret, and transmit the poem faithfully.[45] By omitting clear generic markers and other forms of authorial guidance, the prologue couples that responsibility with an unusual degree of interpretive freedom. This openness to public interpretation sharply distinguishes social complaint from the great hall genres of romance and "jape" and is a hallmark of *Winner and Waster*'s generic experimentation more generally.

Although the answer to this challenge is contained in the body of the poem, it is also hinted at in the surviving manuscript *incipit*, which uses the generic terms *tretise* and *refrete* to approximate romance's scope and social function. In characterizing the poem as a "tretys and god schorte refreyte," the *incipit* writer takes up the mantle of judgment ceded to him by the prologue, affirming that he hears and approves the author's voice crying in the wilderness. The doubled terms suggest, however, a hybrid or compound literary form. The *MED* defines *refrete* as "debate" in this instance but offers no additional citations; in all other contexts it defines *refrete* as the refrain of a song or poem.[46] While "tretys" claims a high degree of moral seriousness and a direct pedagogical purpose, "refreyte" would seem to understand the debate form's alternating speeches as analogous to a song's recurring chorus, introducing elements of harmony and lyricism reminiscent of the prologue's vanished "myrthes." Similarly, whereas a "tretys," primarily a written form, generally seeks to convey timeless scientific truth, a "refreyte" is a time-bound, and timely, performance. This seemingly ad hoc pairing of generic terms captures *Winner and Waster*'s self-consciously experimental status, its condition as a conspicuous hybrid rather than a seamless whole. The *incipit* responds to the prologue's demand that *Winner and Waster* be situated relative to romance while at the same time acknowledging that new times demand a new generic synthesis.

If the prologue to *Winner and Waster* justifies the author's decision to write ambitious extramural poetry, then the first fitt searches for a genre in which he can actually do so. That is to say, the prologue's crisis of representation becomes the premise of the first fitt, with a first-person narrator wandering quite literally outside the walls and outside human society: "Bot I schall tell yow a tale that me bytyde ones / Als I went in the weste, wandrynge myn one" (31–32). Crucially, however, *Winner and Waster* does not present this natural setting as itself "natural" or inevitable. The author has been forced out of doors, so that the *chanson d'aventure* frame becomes a means of presenting truths that have no institutional support or intramural audience. These forms of authentication are replaced by a vision so compelling that the poem's unknown but imagined audience has no choice but to take heed. To be sure, the prologue's representational crisis does not go away. The "worthiliche wodde" and "wale medewe" are described in surprisingly violent and contentious terms, while a "jay" that "janglede one heghe," echoes the boy minstrel and interferes with the narrator's efforts to sleep (34, 40).[47] The generic conventions of the *chanson d'aventure* allow the narrator to reinterpret these interruptions, however, by transforming them into annoying background noises rather than disabling obstacles. By reimagining his absence from the lord's hall in positive rather than negative terms—by concentrating on those poetic resources available to him rather than on those he lacks—the narrator can finally sleep, dream, and produce a poem.

Not surprisingly, the first thing the narrator does when he falls asleep is dream himself a space from which to speak. In fact, initially the most salient difference between the real world and the dream world is that the latter provides such a place:

> Me thoghte I was in the werlde, I ne wiste in whate ende,
> One a loveliche lande that was ylike grene,
> That laye loken by a lawe the lengthe of a myle. (47–49)

Imagined by John Speirs as the stage for a "dramatic performance or pageant play," by Maura Nolan as "the open-air auditorium for a pageant, or the lists for a tournament," and by Vance Smith as the background "lande" of a coat of arms, the dream setting is strikingly blank and carefully delimited.[48] Regardless of the symbolic language of the events performed there, which shifts repeatedly over the course of the poem, from the author's point of view the enclosed field is a site for literary composition, for "finding" and arranging, and then rearranging, poetic *materia*. Instead of using the dream to escape from reality, the narrator uses it to gain critical distance on the social world from which he was exiled. At the same time, the *Winner* author's enclosed "lande" recalls the equally blank and delimited setting of Prudentius's *Psychomachia*, making it a space for rewriting, for adapting ancient literary forms to new times. As the poet-narrator (re)writes, he begins to catalog, and so bring order to, the violence and disorder that surround him.

Once the narrator has dreamt his blank slate, he puts it to work by probing the limits of a series of different poetic vocabularies, testing each one's ability to describe, to render legible and orderly, his contemporary social world. The first distinctive voice he tries on is that of the herald, who attempts to translate the elaborate visual spectacle he "finds" on the field into narrative terms. As Smith points out, *Winner and Waster* includes the first surviving heraldic blazon in English, anticipating the first English treatise on heraldry by as much as forty years with its description of "quarters foure: / Two with flowres of Fraunce before and behynde, / And two out of Ynglonde with sex grym bestes, / Thre leberdes one lofte and thre on lowe undir" (77–80).[49] In some ways the beginning of the first fitt recapitulates the prologue, which took romance as its starting point. Heraldry provides an alternate means of recounting the same idealized behavior of the same knightly and aristocratic class that is the stuff of romance. Whereas the prologue associates romance with the aristocratic household, however, the first fitt associates heraldry with public displays that integrate the highest-ranking members of those households into an aristocratic class. Romance, one might say, regulates aristocratic ethics, while heraldry regulates aristocratic politics. Since it concerns itself with matters of national and even international importance, heraldry addresses the poem's imagined extramural audience in ways that romance does not. Perhaps more fundamentally, whereas by the 1350s romance was a long-established English genre, vernacular heraldic poetry is the *Winner* author's own invention, or at least his own adaptation. It allows him to reconcile his poem's romance beginning and attendant sense of courtly decorum with the fact of writing extramural poetry open to English speakers of all classes and dispositions.

No sooner has the narrator defined this modified vernacular heraldry, however, than he is confronted with its limitations. Now that heraldic language can address the overwhelming majority of the inhabitants of the dream world who are not entitled to bear arms, it must also find a way to describe them. At the point of transition between his blazons of the armigerous and the nonarmigerous classes, the narrator pauses to draw attention to the magnitude and difficulty of his task: "Full wyde hafe I walked amonges thies wyes one, / Bot sawe I never siche a syghte, segge, with myn eghne" (136–37). When he resumes speaking, he has found a way to group the combatants under the aegis of banners that he describes with a conspicuously heraldic vocabulary, including the technical terms "bende" and "sable" (149, 157). Each banner is a small triumph of poetic *inventio*, as the narrator finds symbols to represent lawyers, the papal curia, and the four orders of friars by profession rather than lineage. In order to do so, however, he must mix the conventions of heraldry with those of estates satire, which traditionally describes the first and third estates while heraldry describes the second. Just as important, the narrator's reliance on the signifying power of the banners is itself freighted because the poem represents riding with unfurled banners as an act of treason, a usurpation of the king's sovereign right to wage war.[50] Thus where traditional heraldry seeks to substitute display for violence, providing a site for claims of knightly prowess that are explicitly subordinate to the authority of the king, for the nontraditional combatants in *Winner and Waster* display *is* violence, and claims to power are synonymous with treason. The narrative accordingly reaches an impasse. It can only catalog the dream's nontraditional combatants while they themselves are flagrantly out of order. The inverse of this proposition is also true: the first and third estates can only make their presence known, at least in the language of heraldry, through an act of open rebellion. Implicitly, then, the narrator has stretched his heraldic poetic vocabulary as far as it can go—to a point of legal if not actual warfare—in his effort to represent the entire populace of the dream world.

A few lines later the narrator's heraldic vocabulary breaks down completely when confronted with a seemingly endless field of tradespeople:

> And othere synes I seghe sett appon lofte,
> Some wittnesse of wolle, and some of wyne tounnes,
> Some of merchandes merke, so many and so thikke
> That I ne wote in my witt for alle this werlde riche
> Whatt segge under the sonne can the sowme rekken. (188–92)

Where the clerics' and lawyers' banners are fanciful, the merchants' marks reflect a historical phenomenon. Smith demonstrates that fourteenth-century merchants adopted distinctive signs, drawing on symbols of their trade as well as the lower reaches of heraldic vocabulary (chiefly the "marks of difference" used to distinguish younger sons) in order to represent themselves and vouch for the quality of their goods. Similarly, the army's signs of wool and wine tuns seem to represent the craft guilds—in this instance, presumably the Woolmen and the Vintners—which developed their distinctive liveries during the reign of Edward III. Implicitly, the merchants and guildsmen have already acquired, on their own initiative, the power of representation and attendant social visibility conveyed by the narrator's virtuoso banners, extending the traditional language of heraldry in order to, in Smith's terms, "signify something akin to aristocratic privilege, without fully or insistently asserting it."[51] Whatever the source of this new crisis of representation, then, it does not arise from a sense that, as commoners, individual merchants and guildsmen are unsusceptible to heraldic representation.[52] Instead, the dreamer's attempt to formulate a vernacular poetics based on heraldry seems to fail when confronted with the vast sum of people in England's increasingly mercantile society who count and must be accounted for, who signify and know how to manipulate signs. Inseparably, the heraldic voice is overwhelmed by the growing number of numerates and literates who constitute the potential if not the actual audience of an English-language poem and to whom the narrator, by figuring his poem as a written document circulating to an unknown readership, holds himself responsible. Indeed, the potential audience of *Winner and Waster* seems to be defined as those who can represent themselves heraldically or paraheraldically and are thus in an important sense the narrator's peers, or even his competitors. In the narrator's account of the merchants, poetic composition threatens for the second time in the poem to collapse into counting, while the merchants, whose métier is counting, make inroads into the herald's domain. In order to continue to practice his distinctive craft, then, the narrator must move beyond heraldry, "finding" a genre that allows him to gain conceptual purchase on, rather than simply list in loving detail, the phenomena he describes.

The crisis of representation brought on by the merchants and guildsmen seems to render any further heraldic description impossible, or at least pointless. Everything up to this point has led us to expect symmetrical treatment of the dream's two armies. Such treatment would be conventional as well as consistent with the handling of the two armies thus far in the poem. It is also consistent with the narrator's apparent goal of reducing the mass of people he sees to some kind of poetic order. When the second army is described in just a few lines, then, the failure to deliver on expectations is so marked that it can be difficult to process. When I teach this poem to undergraduates, they almost invariably lose track of the poem's literal sense at this point, and Lois Roney proposes, without any support but the disruption itself, that "someone deleted a corresponding series of satiric blazons from the Waster's army description."[53] The content of the lines themselves, however, is of a piece with the narrator's abandonment of heraldry:

And sekere one that other syde are sadde men of armes,
Bolde sqwyeres of blode, bowmen many,

That if thay strike one stroke stynt thay ne thynken
Till owthir here appon hethe be hewen to dethe. (193–96)

According to Thomas Reed and Iain Higgins, these lines identify the second army with the second estate, describing it briefly because the narrator's satiric voice can find no fault with it.[54] This scenario in which the first and third estates square off against the second misleadingly restores the poem's shattered symmetry, however, and glosses over the lines' real ambiguity. Is the second army composed of armed combatants because it is an army—the first army is similarly described as "stuffede in stele, strokes to dele" (armed to the hilt, ready to strike)—or because it represents the second estate (142)? Such questions cannot be answered because we cannot see the second army until the narrator "finds" it for us, and he shows no inclination to do so—even though, if this army *did* represent the second estate, it would presumably be legible to even the most traditional of heralds. Far from being chivalric, moreover, the terms "men of armes" and "bowmen" participate in what Brantley Bryant calls "the technical vocabulary of the new contractual system of army-raising," where they function as "accounting categories for differently armed warriors who received different levels of wages."[55] The nonnoble bowmen, in particular, draw attention to the conflict between chivalric representations of warfare and the actual battlefield strategies of fourteenth-century military commanders. Lee Patterson argues that chivalric writers' ability "to accommodate the brutality of medieval warfare to the idealistic vocabulary of the chivalric lexicon" depends precisely on the invisibility of nonnoble soldiers, whose systematic pillage and slaughter was intrinsic to, rather than a deviation from, elite battle plans.[56] The narrator's treatment of the second army thus suggests, once again, that his heraldic poetics is incapable of representing the entire field full of folk and accordingly has been set aside. By discarding his failed experiment so abruptly, the narrator draws attention to the process of experimentation itself, demanding that his readers treat literary conventions as means to an end rather than as ends in their own right.

INVENTING WINNER AND WASTER

When the *Winner* author finally "finds" the personifications Winner and Waster at the beginning of the second fitt, they emerge from the ruins of genres that have been tried and found wanting. The poem thematizes the failure first of romance, then of jape and social complaint, then of vernacular heraldry. The challenge for Winner and Waster is to represent the extramural world more successfully than any of these other genres—a proposition that the author all but invites his audience to test. On the face of it, however, personification already does a better job of defining the two extramural armies precisely because it need not describe, or even list, all of their constituent parts. Instead, picking up at the exact conceptual juncture at which heraldry breaks down, the personifications Winner and Waster abstract the overwhelming, indeed literally unrepresentable welter of empirical detail into universals that can be grasped, manipulated, and evaluated. As machines of the mind, Winner and Waster do not simply stand in for the merchants and craftsmen who "break" vernacular heraldry. They are specifically derived from them, even as they also account for the armigerous classes who fall within the traditional domain of heraldry. As Winner and Waster define English society along the new axis of economic function, they also define anybody who has enough money either to win or to waste as an important social actor.

As Stephanie Trigg has pointed out, critics disagree strenuously about the earthly identities of Winner and Waster, as well as about the abstract ideas they represent. Winner is alternately a merchant, a landowner, and a representative of the lord steward's department in the royal household, while Waster is variously a disaffected laborer, a military hero, a spendthrift aristocrat, a wealthy man who cares for the poor, a thuggish retainer, a glutton, and a courtly lover. Together, Winner and Waster represent alternately the vices of avarice and prodigality, "the variable tactics of a successful ruler," the interests and power of the middle strata, Apollonian and Dionysian energy, the lord chamberlain's department and the lord steward's department in the royal household, and the "struggle within any given person between an impulse to productive expenditure on the one hand and an impulse to *dépense* on the other."[57] Much of this disagreement stems from the poem's proliferation of verisimilar detail, which Trigg calls its "rhetoric of excess." Over the course of the poem's last two fitts, Winner and Waster are defined by their shared preoccupation with, among other topics, food storage and banqueting practices; long, drooping sleeves; linnets cooked in syrup; field, forest, and fish-pond maintenance; silk sheets; memorial provisions in wills; and people who snore and raise their buttocks in the air while they sleep (411, 350, 396–400, 235, 463, 302–7, 435–36). If not for its debate structure, anchored by the personifications themselves, the poem would disintegrate into a jumble of sense impressions. Critics cannot agree on Winner's and Waster's earthly identities because their interests and activities are not limited to any one discursive domain or social role.

Trigg associates this proliferation of detail with the breakdown of allegory, claiming that Winner and Waster "have been dramatically realized as individual figures, even personalities" to such a degree that "the poet cannot collapse them back into unproblematic allegorical abstractions."[58] If we understand Winner and Waster as Aristotelian rather than Platonic personifications, however, this same proliferation of detail becomes the stuff they are made of. It becomes constitutive rather than problematic because instead of descending from on high, either as forms or as daemons, Winner and Waster represent "beings of reason" abstracted from sense perceptions of material entities—in this case, social actors. As such they are derived from, and take into account, all of the members of their respective armies, regardless of social milieu. This tie to empirical observation allows Winner, for instance, to represent all of the productive activity in England without listing each individual merchant with his paraheraldic "mark"—or risking being called to account by pedants or interested parties if he omits a particular detail. In an Aristotelian worldview, a broad range of sensory inputs is an advantage rather than a disadvantage because it helps observers to refine their understanding of the relationships between particulars and universals. A person who observes only cats and dogs is likely to form a less accurate conception of the universal *animal* than someone who observes a wider array of species, from snakes and ladybugs to squids and whales. By the same token, the proliferation of detail in *Winner and Waster* helps the poem's readers to develop more precise and comprehensive concepts of *winning* and *wasting*. It encourages them to form initial impressions of each of these universals, then to reflect on and refine them through additional reading and observation until they have developed machines of the mind that are useful to think with.

But how should these machines to be used? Given that Winner and Waster are knightly champions of their respective armies, they might initially seem to be plausible sites of identification. Romances, chronicles, and sermons invite their readers to identify with exemplary characters whose experiences can educate them by proxy. In these contexts, identifying with a positive role model is itself a positive act, while reiteration or reenactment of the role model's choices serves as a primary path to personal virtue.[59] In *Winner and Waster*, however, the author's fundamental distrust of exemplarity—at least in the debased world in which he lives—casts suspicion on identification as well. The subsequent characterization of Winner and Waster only confirms this suspicion, since the poem's debate format allows each one to define the other, inevitably in an unflattering light. In fact, that is practically all they do. Where we would expect debaters to seek a balance between advocating their own positions and dismantling those of their opponents, Winner and Waster appear to be bent on mutually assured destruction. They are unidirectional, even mechanistic, lobbing one attack after another without pausing to rebut their opponents' arguments or otherwise defend themselves. In a sense, the single-mindedness of their debate strategy echoes the single-mindedness of their economic behavior. The effect is to render both characters distasteful, as Waster informs us of the rotting bacon hanging from Winner's rafters, while Winner catalogs the undigestible surplus of Waster's dinner parties.[60] Far from continuing romance exemplarity, they seem to embody the two forms of degradation to which the traditional social context of romance is susceptible. Winner replaces hospitality in the great hall with private accumulation, while Waster transforms the feast itself, a romance set piece, from an occasion for decorous "myrthes" into a site for unharmonious gluttony as the diners, who "brynneth for bale" in their "bowells," produce farts as loud as trumpets (357).[61] Winner's hoarding recalls Prudentius's Avarice, while the Waster's overconsumption recalls his Indulgence. If they are examples, they can only be negative ones.

If both Winner and Waster are bad examples, they necessarily leave the poem's readers to extrapolate their positive counterpart. In exemplary romance, abhorrence for a negative role model generally accentuates identification with a positive one: by casting the hero into sharper relief, the villain helps to highlight his or her virtuous characteristics. In *Winner and Waster*, in contrast, the villains oppose and define each other, so that readers' primary task is to construct a hero rather than identify with one. Although the lack of critical consensus suggests that this undertaking is not straightforward, the field of possibilities is still reasonably delimited. Whether they are imagined as political, social, economic, or psychic actors, Winner and Waster argue over the disposition of a single treasury and so belong to a single system.[62] If that system is analyzed via Aristotelian ethics, then Winner and Waster invite readers to project the virtue of liberality, or perhaps magnanimity, which specifically designates the liberality of rulers. This conceptual work is similar to the work fostered by the Aristotelian Mirrors for Princes tradition, with a particularly striking analogue to be found in the program of illustrations that accompanies Nicole Oresme's *Livre de Ethiques d'Aristote* (Book of Aristotle's Ethics), a translation of the *Nicomachean Ethics* produced for Charles V of France in the early 1370s. In one presentation copy of the *Ethiques*, a complex miniature depicts a personification of Liberality (Liberalité) flanked by Avarice on one side and Prodigality / Foolish Generosity (Prodigalité / Fole Largesce) on the other, while the corresponding miniature in another presentation copy pairs a private and feminine Liberality with a royal and masculine the Magnanimous (le Magnanime). These images ask viewers to define the virtues and vices in relation to each other as well as through their characteristic activities. Avarice accumulates piles of coins while Prodigality, like Waster, operates primarily in a gift economy and seems to be stripped of a garment he has pledged. In contrast, the miniatures depict Liberality and the Magnanimous as principles of distribution rather than consumption, each at a scale that befits his or her means. The multiple copies of the *Ethiques* with ties to Charles's court, combined with the books' own staging of their appropriate reception, suggest that these images functioned as sites for public and private discussion in aristocratic circles.[63] Although *Winner and Waster* submits itself to a broader readership, its audience is similarly invited to toggle back and forth between the characteristic behaviors of many different kinds of wasters and a general definition of wasting or prodigality, and to define prodigality in contrast to both avarice and liberality or magnanimity.[64] These kinds of readerly activities undeniably have an affective component, including disgust at both personifications' misuse of food. But they emphasize understanding—specifically, the ability to define and manipulate conceptual categories—rather than character identification.

Similar conversations can occur if Winner and Waster are analyzed from the perspective of a specifically Christian Aristotelianism. Although a faithful translation, Oresme's *Ethiques* repeatedly prompts its readers to cross-reference Christian and Aristotelian conceptions of virtue—and *Winner and Waster* is if anything more insistent. The poem's eschatological framework, which first becomes evident in the prologue, reappears in the second fitt with Waster's warning, "Thou schall be hanged in helle for that thou here spareste" (260). Winner's rebuttal paraphrases Matthew 24:40: "Forthi God laughte that he lovede and levede that other, / Iche freke one felde ogh the ferdere be to wirche" (286–87). In this exchange each personification represents virtuous as well as vicious acts, so that the poem's audience is not asked to find a mean between them but rather imaginatively to disassociate and recombine them. Some portraits of misers, such as Langland's A-text description of Covetise "in a torn tabbard of twelue wynter age," emphasize their absolute inability to part with money, even for basic household management, while others, including Langland's expanded B-text treatment of Covetise as a usurer and Oresme's stereotypically Jewish Avarice, invest money only so that it can reproduce itself as finance capital (A.5.111, B.5.237–96. Winner, in contrast, champions investments that increase productivity, with a special emphasis on estate management. He first condemns Waster because "His londes liggen alle ley, his lomes aren solde, / Downn bene his dowfehowses, drye bene his poles" and later directly exhorts him, "Teche thy men for to tille and tynen thyn feldes; / Rayse up thi rent-howses, ryme up thi yerdes" (234–35, 288–89). While Winner's behavior here occupies an extreme, it is the extreme of the most virtuous servant in the Parable of the Talents.

Winner, however, conspicuously lacks Waster's faith in divine providence as well as his rival's ability to spend freely, which if redirected to the suffering poor he repeatedly invokes would make him a type of patient poverty. It seems, then, that readers are being asked to wrestle with the mixture of virtuous and vicious elements in each personification, as well as with the conflict between the Aristotelian definition of virtue as moderation and seemingly extreme Christian ideals such as poverty (opposed by Winner) and fasting (opposed by Waster)—a conflict that also preoccupied Aristotelian theologians, with Aquinas characterizing Christian virtue as extreme in degree but moderate when performed in the right manner for the right end.[65] The fact that Winner and Waster invite so many plausible interpretations suggests that such complex and potentially contentious engagement is the poem's goal. Like the *Ethiques*, but with a more open-ended, less technical vocabulary, *Winner and Waster* offers itself as a site for serious-minded vernacular exploration of the proper role of winning and wasting in religion, ethics, and politics. The author intimates that such exploration is what one *does* in an ideally ordered mid-fourteenth-century household—either mercantile or manorial—with efforts to define the appropriate uses of wealth replacing the vanishing exemplary romance.

Winner and Waster's avoidance of technical vocabulary in this undertaking is striking and no doubt accounts for much of the critical disagreement about the poem. Where the *Ethiques* supplements Oresme's highly Latinate translation with extensive annotations, a cycle of illustrations, and a glossary, *Winner and Waster* eschews learned neologisms in favor of the aggressively vernacular lexicon of alliterative poetry, with its emphasis on colloquial language and lexical breadth. Rather than develop a technical vocabulary, *Winner and Waster* uses its titular personifications to communicate quite learned and complex concepts. It is crucial in this regard that Winner and Waster are personifications rather than persons. As such, they exceed the boundaries of individual personhood and cut across social and demographic categories to embody economic concepts—modern approximations might be consumption and nonfinancial investment—that aggregate a wide variety of individual behaviors. Like the concepts of investment and consumption, Winner and Waster can be used to understand the behavior of individuals, households, and entire populations. In this context, it is no wonder that Winner has been taken to represent everything from the personal impulse toward productive expenditure to the activities of the lord steward's department in the royal household to the share of England's gross domestic product attributable to investment—except that efforts to equate Winner exclusively with any one of these roles misunderstand his function. Instead of standing in for X or Y or Z, he is a multipurpose machine of the mind, an embodiment of the economic category or concept of winning that can be deployed at different scales and in different contexts. His characterization reflects the fact that, for Aristotelians, the universal *winning* depends upon particular human acts of winning but is also abstracted from these individual acts and can be manipulated as a category of thought independently of them. Winner's inhuman unidirectionality, or mechanism, might make him a poor debater and a poor site for ethical identification, but it renders him a valuable tool for thinking about an increasingly urban and mercantile economy. By deploying Winner and Waster as Aristotelian personifications, the poem invites its readers to move among levels of abstraction, evaluating their actions as if they were persons even as it considers those actions at the scale of the economy or the realm.

As Winner and Waster join the particular with the abstract, they also join ethics with politics, linking the moral state of the individual to the political and economic state of the realm. As we have seen, the poem represents disordered winning and wasting as a problem of sin and salvation that can be addressed through personal penance. But, as in the *Songe d'Enfer*, this disorder can also be addressed through royal and parliamentary initiatives, beginning with Chief Justice Sir William Shareshull's January 1352 speech to Parliament condemning "disturbers of the peace and maintainers of quarrels and riots" (les destourbours de la Pees et meintenours des quereles et des riotes). Waster's outraged response, which cites the speech in English translation and criticizes Shareshull by name, underscores the poem's broader interpretation of Winner's and Waster's misdeeds as simultaneously sins and disturbances of public order (317–18).[66] At the same time, *Winner and Waster*'s insistent topical references, which include the

1351 Statute of Labourers, the 1352 Statute of Treasons, and Edward III's controversial fundraising for foreign wars, define a national scope for the poem and point to a readership engaged with—and quite possibly participating in—royal, aristocratic, or parliamentary politics.[67] As Aristotelian personifications, Winner and Waster accordingly invite the judgment of readers who are imagined not only as private individuals but also as public actors who can relate individual misdeeds to larger social and political concerns. This target demographic of officeholders—actual and potential, large and small—correlates strongly with the segment of the English population that commands sufficient resources to win or to waste, effectively defining *Winner and Waster*'s readers as economic actors as well. Instead of turning away from literary craftsmanship and its long-standing association with personal ethics, the *Winner* author yokes ethics to politics and economics via a form of personification that connects the particular to the universal and demands both a public and a private response.[68]

Although *Winner and Waster*'s target audience coincides to a significant extent with that of romance, it seeks to engage that audience in strikingly different ways. Whereas a reader of romance identifies with an exemplary hero as a means of himself becoming an example to those around him, the imagined reader of *Winner and Waster* is asked to use the poem's personifications as intellectual tools to analyze problems and imagine solutions to them. As the problems have ethical, spiritual, social, economic, and political dimensions, so too do the solutions. While personal penance and upright behavior in private life represent necessary first steps toward resolving the crisis of winning and wasting defined by the poem, they are not in themselves adequate responses to it. Readers are also asked to analyze events of national significance, associating them critically with either Winner or Waster or more positively with an extrapolated alternative to both. While the poem's own topical allusions simultaneously invite such analysis and provide important loci for it, they do not delimit it. As intellectual tools Winner and Waster can be applied to virtually any economic phenomenon. Even though the poem's narrator defines himself as an outsider, an extrainstitutional wanderer who has been exiled from the great hall, he addresses—through the impersonal medium of his "werke"—a distinctly insider audience. Or, perhaps more precisely, he invites his audience to consider themselves insiders who have a stake in the realm and its fate and the authority to intervene in it, whether nationally or locally. Although *Winner and Waster* does not seem to be, as Bestul has argued, straightforwardly "a satire directed at the extravagance and greed of Edward III," it does offer its audience a set of analytically powerful but vernacular and nontechnical tools for reaching a judgment about, say, the problems of war finance—as well as for conceiving of the scope necessary to act on that judgment.[69] Indeed, this transfer of authority to the reader, at the expense of both the author outside the poem and the king within it, characterizes the poem from its beginning to its enigmatic ending.[70] In some respects, the king would seem to occupy, or would seem to want to occupy, the position of the virtuous mean of liberality, otherwise conspicuously absent from the poem. On the poem's blank and artificially delimited performance space, he stands between Winner and Waster much as Liberality stands between Prodigality and Avarice in Charles V's presentation copy of Oresme's *Ethiques*. Claire Richter Sherman notes the tight connection between liberality and the ideal ruler, especially within the Aristotelian tradition of advice to princes of the later Middle Ages.[71] At the end of the poem, however, the king explicitly abdicates this position when he defers judgment indefinitely in favor of political expediency. By this point, the poem's imagined audience of "beryns one the bynches" has already been primed to take the king's place as the official arbiter of Winner and Waster's "flyttynge" (314, 154).[72] Crucially, it is precisely this projected audience, at once relatively broad and exceptionally active and authoritative, that precipitated the crisis of representation at the end of the poem's first fitt. The genre of vernacular heraldry simply could not contain the proliferation of wealthy merchants and guildsmen capable of quasi-heraldic, and quasi-authorial, self-assertion and self-representation. Such an audience, however, both defines and enables the Aristotelian personification allegory of the poem's final two fitts.

In addition to recasting *Winner and Waster* as an origin story for Aristotelian personification, at least in Middle English, my reading of the poem reconfigures its relationship with *Piers Plowman* within a tradition of moral and political allegory. It connects the *Winner* author to Langland not, as Ralph Hanna has suggested, as the tradition-minded father of a brilliantly rebellious son, but through a shared experimental poetics.[73] *Winner and Waster* thus anticipates *Piers Plowman*'s generic structure, which Steven Justice has influentially described as "progress[ing] by literary ascesis, testing and rejecting generic formulations" until it settles into one that is sustainable.[74] More specifically, each genre is tested for its ability to account for and impose some kind of conceptual order on the "fair feeld ful of folk" (B.Pro.17). Justice emphasizes, however, that the generic experimentation of the Visio gives way to extended biblical exegesis in the Vita, whereas I see Langland's poem as an ongoing experiment with different varieties of personification, from the Neoplatonic Holy Church to the Aristotelian Hunger to the all-but-unclassifiable Anima of the later reaches of the B text. Although the *Winner* author almost certainly did not anticipate this degree of hybridity, he facilitates it by deploying personification allegory not only as an ongoing experiment, with each personification judged according to its affective power and conceptual utility, but also as the most promising literary form for representing the rapid social change of post-plague England. Like the *Songe d'Enfer* and *Winner and Waster*, moreover, *Piers Plowman* uses personification to examine both individual failings and political or institutional ones. In the later poem as in the earlier ones, personal penance is a necessary but not sufficient condition for reforming a rapidly changing society, and politics is a necessary adjunct to ethics. The tradition of satirical moral and political allegory thus bequeaths to *Piers Plowman* not only a recognizable form of personification allegory but also a characteristic mode of inviting readers to engage with it. The imagined extramural audience of *Winner and Waster*, in particular, anticipates the unusually broad and exceptionally active and authoritative readership of *Piers Plowman*.

Both *Winner and Waster* and the *Songe d'Enfer* thus treat moderately realist Aristotelian personification not only as a means of representing a new metaphysical paradigm but also as a means of gaining intellectual purchase on a new social world. It allows them to account for the growing numbers of important socioeconomic actors who congregate outside the aristocratic great hall, in taverns and guildhalls as well as on the streets of Paris and London. Both authors suggest that the new acts and actors they observe are too unheralded, and too socially disparate, to be represented by established means. They are also too numerous to name individually, although both writers use lists to convey some sense of their profusion. Aristotelian personifications resolve this representational crisis because they are abstracted from, and so responsive to, empirical observation. They are not confined to preexisting schemas or inherited categories, and so they allow authors to represent the world as it is rather than as it was or as it should be. At the same time, Aristotelian personifications offer a means of reducing the overwhelming sensorial experience of an urban street, a crowded tavern, or even a battlefield to some kind of intellectual order, to something that can be cognized. Since they are abstracted from the material world instead of descending from on high, they also become a means of incorporating or accounting for mimetic detail without becoming overwhelmed by it. In this context, it is unlikely to be coincidence that the earliest Aristotelian personifications are produced in the allegorical tradition of the *Psychomachia*. Like Aristotelian personifications,

Prudentian personifications are generated in response to human needs and human experiences. As we have seen, the *Psychomachia* makes a point of authorizing the formation of new personified Virtues in order to counter the emergence of new Vices. However, where Prudentian personifications are deified, and thus numinous, moderately realist Aristotelian personifications are abstracted, and so remain much more closely linked to the material world. In doing so, they do not simply conform to a new system of metaphysics. For both Raoul de Houdenc and the *Winner* author, they also attempt to resolve a crisis of representation by presenting emerging social phenomena to cognition with a new degree of verisimilitude.

CHAPTER SEVEN

A Good Body Is Hard to Find: Putting Personification through Its Paces in *Piers Plowman*

Thus far I have sought to isolate different varieties of personification for the sake of clarity. The chief drawback to this approach is that it treats each type of personification on its own terms and so risks giving short shrift to the relationships among personifications, whether within a single work or within a broader tradition of reception and adaptation. It also threatens to misrepresent metaphysics, where hybridity is not the exception but the rule. The tradition of hybrid personification allegory dates from at least the *Psychomachia*, where Prudentian personifications of Virtue build a temple for a Neoplatonic personification of Wisdom. For Prudentius, the differences among these figures largely come down to the fact that Faith and her sisters must fight against Vice in this world, whereas Wisdom, who is closely associated with Revelation, reigns uncontested. We see a similar hybridity in Alan of Lille's *Complaint of Nature*, even though it is often treated as a paradigmatic example of twelfth-century Neoplatonism. Precisely because all of Alan's Virtues are Neoplatonic, they are in danger of being cast out of the earthly realm and forced to "return to [their] celestial home" (ad caeleste domicilium repatriare) as humans become increasingly vicious.[1] Alan's Vices, in contrast, strongly resemble their Prudentian counterparts. In a nod to the *Psychomachia* tradition, he presents them as "daughters of ancient Idolatry" (filias Ydolatriae veteris) who are "attempting to restore their mother's dominion and raise her up from the dead" (suae matris inperium reparare conari, et . . . a mortuis excitare). Avarice, Gluttony, and Lechery are simultaneously deified and formed as personifications by their human followers. Avarice, in particular, is the one "through whom wealth is made a god in the minds of men, and the high dignity of divine veneration is offered to money" (per quam in animis hominum deificatur pecunia, nummo divinae venerationis exhibetur auctoritas).[2] Because the Vices cannot be divinely created and do not correspond to forms, Alan instead treats them as sites of Prudentian identification and self-formation (or more precisely, self-deformation). As such they mark the peril of his own times, which threaten to usher in a new era of idolatry.

The hybridity we saw in Raoul de Houdenc's thirteenth-century rewriting of the *Psychomachia,* where the personifications become less Platonic and more Aristotelian as the dreamer approaches hell, builds on this literary tradition. At the same time, it reflects a broader high- and late-medieval preference for metaphysical systems that combine Platonic and Aristotelian elements. Built in part upon Neoplatonists' and moderate realists' shared understanding of cognition as inner vision, these systems generally describe the intellection of "higher" cognitive objects in terms of divine illumination and that of "lower" objects in terms of Aristotelian abstraction. Albert the Great posits no fewer than three different kinds of intellectual light, each of which allows the "eye of the potential intellect" (intellectus possibilis oculus) to perceive a distinct class of universals. As Albert explains, "This light is natural for receiving natural objects, gratuitous for objects pertaining to belief, and glorious for objects pertaining to beatification" (Hoc lumen ad naturalia recipienda naturale est, ad credenda vero gratuitum est, ad beatificantia autem gloria est).[3] Whereas natural objects can be understood through a combination of natural light and Aristotelian abstraction, "higher" objects require gratuitous or glorious illumination. Although Albert's student, Aquinas, is often treated as an exemplary Aristotelian, he likewise assigns an ongoing role to divine illumination in the cognition of "higher" universals such as *being, unity, truth,* and *goodness,* as well as in miraculous forms of knowledge such as prophecy.[4] Conversely, the Augustinian Bonaventure, who holds that the soul's knowledge of itself and of suprasensible beings can only be produced through divine illumination, nonetheless deploys an Aristotelian vocabulary to describe the lower soul, concerned with the cognition of the material world.[5] Although each of these thinkers understands the relationship between Augustinian illumination and Aristotelian abstraction in somewhat different terms, all conceive of the latter as subordinate to the former within a hybrid epistemology. In each model, how the human mind thinks depends on what it thinks about.

These hybrid metaphysics in turn furnish a model for personification allegory. At the most basic level, their frequently shared emphasis on cognition as inner vision makes it possible to situate multiple kinds of personification within a single visual field. Whether the mind "sees" a divinely illuminated form or an abstracted intelligible species, it thinks a universal by means of an image that can, in turn, be represented as a personification. These metaphysics offer a theoretical justification for the common but otherwise perplexing allegorical practice of assigning different ontological statuses to different personifications within the same work. Barbara Newman observes that Mechthild of Magdeburg's *Flowing Light of the Godhead* assigns a higher reality to the personification Lady Love than to the personifications Lady Trust, Lady Estrangement, and Lady Pain. While Newman attributes these differences to Love's central role in Mechthild's text, they may also reflect Love's status as a "higher" cognitive object.[6] In most if not all hybrid epistemologies, the exalted Love described by Mechthild would be cognized via divine illumination and refer directly to the form of Love in the divine mind. In contrast, Lady Trust, Lady Estrangement, and Lady Pain may have a reduced ontological status because the "lower" universals *trust*, *estrangement*, and *pain* can be abstracted from sense perceptions. Since they are produced by merely human means, and must be refined via an ongoing process of reasoning and reflection, such universals are inherently less "real" than their divinely inspired counterparts. Although Mechthild was well read, she need not have based her allegory on any particular thirteenth-century metaphysical system for the general structure of these systems to have influenced her intuitions about personification. Instead, I am suggesting that the prevalence of hybrid epistemologies influenced writers' sense of the appropriateness of different kinds of personifications rubbing shoulders within a single work.

The present chapter takes *Piers Plowman* as its case study because Langland's poem is famous for the variety of its personifications. I argue that the categories of Prudentian, Neoplatonic, and Aristotelian personification allow us to see with greater precision the differences among Langland's personifications—as well as the difference these differences make. They also enable a revised understanding of what Helen Cooper calls "Langland's radical re-gendering of his personifications," which transforms traditionally feminine figures such as Raison and Luxuria into the masculine Reason and Lechery.[7] Where Prudentius's own personifications are feminine, prompting readers to divest themselves of their masculine sexuality in order to reform themselves as personifications of Virtue, Langland's Prudentian personifications are overwhelmingly if not exclusively masculine. At the beginning of the poem, the folk who "putten hem to þe plouȝ" and "putten hem to pride" do so as masculine "everyman" figures who transform themselves into masculine personifications (B.Pro.20, 23). This logic extends to Langland's normatively masculine readers, who are likewise invited to transform themselves through craft discipline, figured as walking passus by passus behind the plow. Within these passus, the first personification readers encounter is the Neoplatonic Holy Church, whom I see as a daemonic personification closely modeled on Boethius's Philosophy. If anything, Holy Church exaggerates her predecessor's daemonic characteristics of limited authority and troubling femininity. She is also an anomaly, one of the poem's very few feminine Neoplatonic personifications, and the only one who occupies the traditional daemonic role of tutor or guardian. The moderately realist Aristotelian personification Hunger is more representative of Langland's wider allegorical practice. Abstracted from Piers's observations of the effect of hunger on empirical human bodies, and at the same time an *ens rationis* or being of reason who helps Piers to decide whether hunger should be sought or avoided, Hunger's masculinity reflects the male-dominated realm of agricultural labor from which he emerges. Although women and children experience hunger in Langland's poem, they neither bring it about by refusing to plow nor alleviate it by organizing food distribution. The chapter's final case study, of the B-text Anima, in some respects recapitulates the poem's larger trajectory away from Neoplatonic personification, as the traditional feminine personification of the soul in B.9 gives way to the "sotil þyng" of B.15. The soul's ineffability means, however, that Langland turns not to moderate realism but to an experimental nominalism. The second Anima's indeterminate gender frustrates readers' desire to picture the universal *soul*, instead prompting them to cognize it—and by extension themselves—in more productive ways.

THE PRUDENTIAN PLOWMAN

Will's dream in *Piers Plowman* begins with a blank field, bounded by a "tour on a toft" on one side and a "deep dale" on the other (B.Pro.14–15). In this it resembles the dream vision of *Winner and Waster*, which likewise begins with a blank, bounded field, usually characterized as a tournament or performance space (48–49). Behind both of these fields lies the equally blank and bounded space of the *Psychomachia*, often likened to a Roman arena. Whether the connection among these works is direct or indirect, it bespeaks a shared understanding of personification as a combination of spectacle and moral performance.[8] In the *Psychomachia*, this practice occurs both within the individual psyche and in the world writ large. When Faith defeats Worship of the Old Gods, her victory represents not only an individual act of conversion but also the collective triumph of the Christian martyrs, who suddenly appear by her side to join her in celebration. In both cases, the battle against Vice is represented as an act of self-formation or self-personification. Prudentius invites his readers to reenact Faith's struggle, reforming themselves as feminine personifications of Virtue. If they do not, he warns, they will unwittingly turn themselves into personifications of Vice, passing from a virtuously militant femininity to a debased and feminized masculinity without even recognizing their own transformation. Langland likewise concerns himself with both the individual soul, poised between salvation and damnation, and the entire world. And I will argue that he, too, considers personification to be an important engine of self-formation. In the *Psychomachia*, persons become personifications as they fight against Vice, while in *Piers Plowman* persons become personifications as they subject themselves to the discipline of their crafts, whether of plowing, of praying, or of pride.

Unlike the *Winner* author, who divides his conceptual field according to the binary of production versus consumption, Langland organizes his own field according to the embodied know-how of particular disciplines. This structuring principle makes itself felt very early, as soon as the dreamer's perspective shifts from a panorama of the moral landscape to close-ups of particular groups of workers:

> Somme putten hem to þe plouȝ, pleiden ful selde,
> In settynge and sowynge swonken ful harde,
> And wonnen þat þise wastours wiþ glotonye destruyeþ.
> And somme putten hem to pride, apparailed hem þerafter,
> In contenaunce of cloþynge comen disgised.
> In preieres and penaunce putten hem manye,
> Al for loue of Oure Lord lyueden ful streyte
> In hope to haue heueneriche blisse –
> As ancres and heremites þat holden hem in hire selles,
> Coueiten noȝt in contree to cairen aboute
> For no likerous liflode hire likame to plese. (B.Pro.20–30)

These lines have long attracted critical attention for treating the plowman as the paradigm against which all other forms of life are measured.[9] In the process, they upend medieval estates theory by setting the third estate above the first. Although the morally upright hermits and anchorites are evidently related to the hardworking plowmen, not least via the rich biblical tradition of representing spiritual work as agricultural labor,

Langland's order of presentation reverses the usual hierarchy. In its place, as Andrew Galloway points out, these lines present a compressed origin story, perhaps of English life after the first devastating outbreak of plague, but also of craft knowledge itself—a story that Langland finds important enough to reprise later in the B and C prologues, when Kind Wit's foundation of "alle craftes" begins with making the people a plow, and then again in the second vision, with the crafts that proliferate outward from plowing the half acre (C.Pro.144–46; cf. B.Pro.118–20).[10] The phrase "putten hem to þe plouȝ" also resembles the Middle English idiom "putten honde to the plough," and so functions paradigmatically as well as literally. That is to say, it refers to undertaking a task in general as well as to the beginning of agricultural labor in particular.[11]

On one level, then, *Piers Plowman* begins in the postlapsarian moment when Adam, having been expelled to the subjected plain, takes up the plow for the first time. In doing so, he enacts God's punishment for disobedience, as recounted in Genesis:

> Cursed is the earth in thy work; with labour and toil shalt thou eat thereof all the days of thy life. . . . In the sweat of thy face shalt thou eat bread till thou return to the earth, out of which thou wast taken.
>
> Maledicta terra in opere tuo / in laboribus comedes eam cunctis diebus vitae tuae . . . / in sudore vultus tui vesceris pane / donec revertaris in terram de qua sumptus es. (3:17–19)

These lines' emphasis on hard physical labor, on the connection between working and eating, is reflected in Langland's insistence that his plowmen "swonken ful harde" and "pleiden ful selde." Taking up the plow for the first time, however, also marks the beginning of Adam's work of penance, a connection Langland emphasizes with the syntactical and alliterative parallelism between those who "putten hem to þe plouȝ" and those who put themselves to "preieres and penaunce." Plowing is paradigmatically penitential labor, simultaneously an acknowledgment of guilt and a new beginning, a commitment to sin no more. It is also ongoing. Putting oneself to the plow marks not only Adam's new beginning after the Fall but also each new growing season and each new workday and each new furrow. In spiritual terms, it is something that must be done again and again because the state of fallenness, like sin itself, is likewise ongoing. In the poem, this initial act of the will fittingly precedes both the first step toward redemption and the poem's first passus. Implicitly, writing—and by extension reading—the poem becomes an act of plowing, with each of its many new beginnings a new act of putting oneself to the plow.[12]

Both the Middle English idiom "putten honde to the plough" and Langland's "putten hem to þe plouȝ" recall another biblical agricultural moment: Jesus's rebuke of vacillating followers in Luke 9:62. The warning occurs at the beginning of Luke's so-called travel narrative, which recounts Jesus's final journey to Jerusalem. Soon after setting out, Jesus encounters three potential followers along the road, each of whom addresses him and receives an enigmatic reply that helps to define the nature of discipleship. The first offers to follow Jesus wherever he goes, and is told, "The foxes have holes, and the birds of the air nests; but the Son of man hath not where to lay his head" (Volpes foveas habent et volucres caeli nidos / Filius autem hominis non habet ubi caput reclinet) (9:58). The second promises to join Jesus after he buries his father, and is told, "Let the dead bury their dead: but go thou, and preach the kingdom of God" (Sine ut mortui sepeliant mortuos suos / tu autem vade adnuntia regnum Dei) (9:60). The third says he will follow Jesus after taking leave of his family, only to hear, "No man putting his hand to the plough, and looking back, is fit for the kingdom of God" (Nemo mittens manum suam in aratum et aspiciens retro aptus est regno Dei) (9:62). In this miniature parable, plowing is always already moralized, a figure for following Christ. Indeed, literal plowing initially seems to exemplify the earthly concerns with home, family, and provision for the future that Jesus here militates against. Yet the parable also equates plowing with spiritual cultivation, comparing the hard labor of following the plow to the hard labor of the journey to Jerusalem. The *Glossa Ordinaria* describes the plow of Luke 9:62 as an "instrumento compunctionis," an instrument of penance whose wood and iron resemble those of the cross, and which the disciple should use to break down his own hardened heart so that it will bear good fruit.[13] Even as it looks back to Genesis, via a typological connection to the moment when Adam first takes up the plow, this passage also looks forward to the passion that, at this moment in Luke, Jesus foresees but has not yet fulfilled.

With this biblical allusion as its starting point, Langland's poem becomes a loose reenactment of the travel narrative in Luke. Traugott Lawler has recently suggested something similar, tentatively linking B.13–17 and C.15–19 to Jesus's journey to Jerusalem in Luke 9:51–18:30. At the very least, Lawler argues, "it seems true that L[angland] responded in a special way to Luke. Luke is especially tough on the rich, and more willing than the other evangelists to speak of 'the poor' rather than 'the poor in spirit.'

He is also the only source of the story of Dives and Lazarus, and of the parable of the Good Samaritan."[14] To my mind, the parallels with Luke begin much earlier, at the moment in both texts when putting hand to plow marks the beginning of a journey from hinterland to metropolis, representing moral cultivation through the material work of plowing. In the venerable tradition of road-trip stories, both journeys are defined less by the ground they cover than by a series of morally fraught encounters along the way, encounters whose primary action turns out to be discursive. Although many of these encounters are recounted in more than one gospel, and Langland refers freely to all four, the structure of the travel narrative is unique to Luke. Jesus's journeys in Mark and Matthew are much more dispersed, and in John he visits Jerusalem four separate times. So, too, is the journey's ambiguous ending. In Luke, Jesus "steadfastly set his face to go to Jerusalem" (faciem suam firmavet ut iret Hierusalem) in order to reach its heavenly counterpart (Luke 9:51). For his followers, however, the relationship between reaching the historical metropolis and reaching the kingdom of heaven is much more vexed. Their journey explicitly continues beyond the gospel, just as for Langland's dreamer it continues beyond the Easter passus and then beyond the poem itself, amid similarly apocalyptic signs of civic and spiritual destruction. For it is in Luke that Jesus most powerfully predicts the destruction of Jerusalem, in terms evocative of the dark final passus of *Piers*. These prophecies set the stage for Jesus's followers, who in the gospel serve primarily as witnesses, to become protagonists in their own right. The ending of Luke, like the ending of *Piers*, looks beyond itself: first to Acts as the second half of the diptych, and then, projected beyond the frame of the narrative, to the broader growth of the church.

Langland's use of Luke 9:62 to structure his poem recalls the "theme" of a sermon, but it also recalls the way Prudentius uses Ephesians 6: 11–17—and, for that matter, the way Raoul de Houdenc uses Matthew 7: 13—as the silent "preamble to the preamble" of his work.[15] All three poems pay homage to their biblical pretexts while freely adapting them to their own historical moments. The *Psychomachia* honors the martyrs of the Diocletian persecution but focuses its attention on the threat of heresy, much more pressing at the turn of the fifth century, while the *Songe d'Enfer* describes the ways in which the corruption of feudal ideals and institutions leads souls to perdition. As one would expect, Langland's retelling of the journey of discipleship is similarly attuned to the particular problems of late-fourteenth-century England. For all of these authors, personification, insofar as it is simultaneously abstract and concrete, serves as a bridge between the timelessness of biblical truth and the specific historical conditions of its reception.

Like Prudentius, Langland also showcases personification as a formative process or performance. In the *Psychomachia*, the Virtues form themselves through combat. In theological terms, Prudentius holds that "it is not virtue unless it spring forth in the act of rejecting the worse and seek the right path because its nature is better" (*Hamartigenia* 695–96). In practical terms, his Virtues come into their own as they grapple with their vicious counterparts. As we have seen, the power of speech—and with it, the status of a full-fledged personification—repeatedly passes from the conquered Vice to the conquering Virtue at the moment of victory. In *Piers Plowman*, personification is likewise something one does rather than something one is. Langland's persons become personifications not through combat, however, but by engaging with allegorical machines. Langland's paradigm is, once again, the act of putting one's self to the plow. Plowman and plow are almost a single unit, engaged in intense agricultural labor. The syntactic parallelism and shared "p" alliteration linking "somme putten hem to the plouȝ" and "somme putten hem to pride" redefines plowing as an ethical as well as an economic activity. By the middle of the passage, the plow is simultaneously an agricultural tool and spiritual exercise equipment, cultivating the soil, the body, and the mind or soul via a single application of effort. It follows from this same syntactic parallelism that those who put themselves to pride subject themselves to an analogous apparatus. The poem asks us to imagine the wasters who "putten hem to pride" bent into a position similar to that of the plowmen, engaged with an invisible pride-machine that shapes their bodies and characters whether or not they realize it. Pride is implicitly a machine like the plow but opposite in its effects, unmaking both persons and agricultural produce as fast as, and as surely as, the plow makes them.

Although the plowman and the pride-man differ in the objects they engage, and potentially in the degree of intentionality with which they engage them, they are similar in other ways. While for the sake of convenience I have been referring to a man who puts himself to the plow as a plowman, it would be more accurate to say that the plow turns its user into a plowman through the work of plowing. As the user engages with his instrument, in other words, he gains expertise in operating, maintaining, and repairing it, and generally gets to be "in shape" for plowing. By analogy, the invisible pride-machine turns its users into pride-men (or, conceivably, pride-women, but the parallelism with the plowmen, combined with the more general sociolinguistic tendency to treat the masculine as the universal, suggests a default masculinity). As they engage with the pride-machine, the pride-men likewise gain a new kind of expertise, marked by their sumptuous and presumably fashionable self-presentation: "in contenaunce of cloþynge [they] comen disgised." In this context, *contenaunce* implies "pretense," while *disgisen* can refer to dressing fashionably or to disguising or malforming one's true nature.[16] When they put themselves to pride, the pride-people thus contort or deform themselves until a single trait shapes their bodies, souls, and public presentations. Their clothing marks them as pride-people in the same way that a religious habit ideally marks its wearer: as the exterior manifestation of an internal *habitus*, understood as a moral commitment and daily spiritual practice. The pride-machine, in other words, forms its users into personifications of pride, with their inner and outer selves equally oriented toward vice.

The passage's third line of syntactically parallel "p" alliteration simultaneously confirms and expands this movement from persons to personifications: "In preieres and penaunce putten hem manye." Not only are prayer and penance, like pride, imagined as machines akin to a plow, but these machines transform their users into anchorites and hermits whose geographic stability recalls that of the plowman who passes back and forth over the same plot of land. These consecrated religious possess what medieval jurists called a *dignitas* or *officium*: an eternal but place-bound figurative body that exists alongside the time-bound but mobile natural one, as a kind of avatar of religious office.[17] These exemplary anchorites and hermits are virtuous because, by remaining in their cells, they conform their natural bodies to their figurative bodies, their offices. Like the plowmen who "plei[en] ful selde," they "lyue[n] ful streyte," practicing their craft of prayer and penance instead of parading around the countryside for the sake of bodily pleasure. The inverse holds true for clergy who wander from place to place, whether unenclosed hermits and anchorites or priests who abandon their parishes. When Langland employs the term "dignites" later in the A prologue, he does so negatively, pointing to archdeacons and deans who forsake their offices, seeking material advancement in London rather than feeding the poor and preaching to the people in their home districts (A.Pro.92). These unreligious religious cut themselves in two precisely by separating their peripatetic natural bodies from their place-bound official ones. Langland departs from medieval political theory, however, in treating the office of plowman as itself a *dignitas*, indeed the original *dignitas*, produced through the mutual engagement of plowman and plow under the injunction of Genesis. According to the logic of the passage, the office of plowman, with its inherent geographic stability, becomes the paradigmatic *dignitas* from which all others are derived.

Within the universe of the poem, moreover, it is precisely those wanderers who flee their official bodies who find themselves pursued by personifications. As Cooper and others have noted, the first personifications in *Piers Plowman* appear less than fifty lines into the prologue, immediately following the catalog of those who set themselves to one apparatus or another:[18]

> Bidderes and beggeres faste aboute yede
> Til hire bely and hire bagge were bredful ycrammed;
> Faiteden for hire foode, fouȝten at þe ale.
> In glotonye, God woot, go þei to bedde,
> And risen wiþ ribaudie, þo Roberdes knaues;
> Sleep and sory sleuþe seweþ hem euere. (B.Pro.40–45)

In their gluttony, these beggars are closely related to the wasters who, a few lines earlier, undo the work of the plowmen through heedless overconsumption. Here, their begging under false pretenses, exacerbated by their misuse of the food they are given, sends them off to bed "in glotonye," in a state of deadly sin. They wake up, however, "wiþ ribaudie"—a collocation that suggests waking up alongside a personified sin. The copyist of the A text in Oxford, Bodleian Library MS Digby 145 (K) seems to have understood the phrase in exactly this way, since he characterizes the beggars in the second half of the line not as "Roberdes knaues," as in modern editions, but as "Rybaldes hewyn." Where "Roberdes knaues" seemingly refers to *roberdesmen*, "a cant term of the day for robbers," "Rybaldes hewen" suggests that the beggars wake up as the servants or dependents of a personification named Ribald.[19] Any lingering ambiguity about the presence of personification is soon put to rest with the appearance of Sleep and Sloth, who move around the world in the same way the beggars themselves do. Sleep and Sloth are not only brought into being by the beggars' rootless, gluttonous way of life but also follow them everywhere, destructive and unwanted, in a reversal of the plowman's deliberate and productive decision to follow the plow. That is to say, they shadow the beggars as a second, figurative body, an inversion or corruption of the *dignitas* of a diligent plowman or ecclesiastic. Implicitly, every member of the folk has two bodies, either the *dignitas* of a materially and/or spiritually productive office, to which the natural body conforms itself through hard work and strict discipline, or a personified sin to which wasters conform themselves without fully realizing it.

The opening lines of *Piers Plowman* establish what we might call the poem's base model of personification, the model of personification it demands of its imagined readers. As in the *Psychomachia*, each person who enters the poem is invited to transform himself into a virtuous personification by putting himself to the plow, either literally or figuratively. If he practices the discipline of his chosen craft, engaging consistently with its machinery, he conforms himself to his *officium*. If not, he instead forms himself as, or distorts himself into, a personification of sin, which leads to Sleep, Sloth, or Ribaldry taking the place of his dignity. In this context, the journey that makes up the rest of the poem can be understood in two main ways. Readers can either reenact the travel narrative of Luke, already figured within the gospel as a metaphorical act of plowing, or they can wander from one passus to the next as an unholy hermit, seeking superficial pleasure. Along the way, the poem's many conjunctions and moments of rupture offer readers who aim for the first type of journey but find themselves sliding into the second opportunities to "putten hem to þe plouȝ" anew, cultivating their own hearts with this "instrument of penance."

In keeping with the Prudentian model of personification as self-formation, this process continues over the course of the poem. It creates parallels not only among the classes of plowmen, pride-men, and penitents but also among the individual figures of Piers the Plowman, Will the dreamer, and the poem's projected or imagined reader. Our glimpses of Piers over the course of the poem are also glimpses of the idealized plowman of the prologue, as he forms himself to virtue through season after season of agricultural labor. Along the way, his plowing becomes increasingly metaphorical as he shifts from sowing grain to feed the folk to sowing the seeds of the virtues, following his "teme" (in the sense of a sermon's theme) rather than his "teme" (the main beam of a plow). Where the pride-man bows down to Pride as an idol, Piers the Plowman is increasingly deified, or at least increasingly strongly associated with the divine. For Anima in B.15, he is "Piers þe Plowman—*Petrus, id est, Christus*," leading Mary Clemente Davlin to conclude that he is "the whole Christ, the mystical Christ, the mystical body" (B.15.212).[20] In the Easter passus he lends his armor—that is to say, his body and flesh—to Christ for his joust against the devil. Needless to say, neither the dreamer nor the poem's imagined readers succeed in forming themselves to virtue to the same degree. At times, the dreamer even seems to be moving in the opposite direction, transforming himself into a personification of sin, before he takes up the plow again in penance. With every step he takes, however, he either puts himself to virtue or puts himself to vice, and *Piers Plowman* invites its readers to understand their own journeys through the poem in the same Prudentian terms. The poem's personifications make these transformations visible, holding them up to analysis so that both plowmen and pride-men can see what they have made of themselves through their labor.

THE DAEMONIC HOLY CHURCH

For Langland, each imagined reader of *Piers Plowman* is a Prudentian personification in the making, forming himself either to Vice or to Virtue. The personifications these readers encounter over the course of the poem, in contrast, conform to a variety of metaphysical paradigms and therefore have a variety of statuses. This sequence of encounters allows Langland to sample—and, eventually, to explore the limits of—the different kinds of personification available to him within the medieval allegorical tradition. In what ways do these figures help their human interlocutors to shape themselves into personifications of virtue? To what extent are their efforts successful? How do the successes and failures of individual personifications reflect, and comment upon, the metaphysical traditions from which they are derived?

After the worldly chaos of the end of the prologue, the opening lines of the first passus shift gears to establish a Neoplatonic universe reminiscent of Boethius's *Consolation*:

> A louely lady of leere in lynnen yclopђed
> Cam doun from þe castel and called me faire,
> And seide, "Sone, slepestow? Sestow þis peple–
> How bisie þey ben aboute þe maȝe?
> The mooste partie of þis peple þat passeþ on þis erþe,
> Haue þei worship in þis world, þei wilne no bettre;
> Of ooþer heuene þan here holde þei no tale."
> I was afered of hire face, þeiȝ she fair weere,
> And seide "Mercy, madame, what may þis be to meene?" (B.1.3–11)

Associated with both the light of the east and the light of heaven, the castle—identified in the prologue as the tower of Truth—evidently stands for Christian divinity. More specifically, it represents the "watchtower of the Lord" (specula Domini) of Isaiah 21:8. For many Christian writers, including Boethius, this "high watchtower of Providence" is a figure for divine omniscience, as God looks out to see "what is appropriate for each person, and he supplies to each what he knows to be appropriate" (*Consolation* 4.6.30–31). The watchtower represents the mind of God, understood as a repository of the forms that allow him, by a "characteristic single stroke of mind" to conceive "formally" everything that has been, is, and will be (*Consolation* 5.4.33).[21] Understood in these terms, Langland's Truth becomes a version of the Neoplatonic One, the form of forms from which all others emanate, usually—as here—via a metaphorics of light. At once a form and an assertion of the timeless truth of all forms, Truth is implicitly contrasted with the forms' necessarily imperfect and corruptible manifestations in the material world, as seen through the estates satire of the prologue. In the A and B texts, the establishment of a Neoplatonic universe coincides with the beginning of allegorical interpretation, through Holy Church's explanatory glosses. In these versions of the poem, allegorical interpretation seems to promise stable meaning, associated with the timelessness of the forms and contrasted with the constantly shifting signs of the field of folk.

Under these circumstances, one would certainly expect Holy Church to be a Neoplatonic personification. But what kind of a Neoplatonic personification is she? Many critics have regarded her as straightforwardly formal and numinous. For Galloway, as we have seen, she belongs to the tradition of personification allegory in which "a transcendentally authoritative feminine figure" debates "a human being (who is almost always . . . male) seeking or needing assistance." Newman goes a step further, treating Holy Church as a full-fledged allegorical goddess, even a representation of the feminine divine.[22] Others, however, see Holy Church as complicated, if not compromised. Anne Middleton compares her to Boethius's Philosophy, finding her to be significantly less patient and nurturing.[23] Steven Justice argues that, although Holy Church's discourse "contains the poem in miniature . . . that observation only exposes her quick obsolescence: if Holy Church wields such comprehensive authority, we must ask why the rest of the poem is there, why it cannot rest in the quiet plenitude of her exegesis."[24] For William E. Heise, the dialogue between Holy Church and the dreamer "explore[s] the interplay of two limited perspectives," such that "the final judgment about the truth is held at bay."[25] I see both sets of observations as correct, in the sense that Holy Church, like her ancestress, Philosophy, oscillates between the divine and the faintly ridiculous. The parallels between these two personifications have been widely recognized, beginning with Holy Church's intimate knowledge of the dreamer and rebuke of his spiritual slumber and failure of inner vision.[26] I will argue that Holy Church inherits from Philosophy a sense of the daemonic that explains some of her more puzzling features. Holy Church's descent from Truth and impeccable doctrine sit uneasily alongside her rough language, sexual jealousy, and failure to lead the dreamer to transcendence—all qualities that Langland could have derived from a careful reading of the *Consolation*.[27]

Although classicists have increasingly acknowledged the satirical elements in the *Consolation*, as shown in chapter 4, many medievalists continue to understand Boethius's prosimetrum as an uncomplicated narrative of Neoplatonic ascent.[28] It follows that they read Langland's disruptions of that trajectory, from the dreamer's penchant for digression to the poem's concern for the collective salvation of the "fair feeld ful of folk," as departures from the Boethian paradigm (B.Pro.17). In Middleton's account, "[Langland's] enterprise is the reverse of the therapeutic process Lady Philosophy offers Boethius" because it locates the dreamer within worldly history instead of alienating him from it.[29] For Eleanor Johnson, *Piers Plowman* promises a Boethian return to the fatherland via its *passus* structure, then self-consciously refuses to deliver:

> When Holy Church first appears to Will, and Will fails to recognize her, readers are urged to be aware of the *Consolation* as an intertext, and specifically as an intertext that points to the poem's investment in recuperation, recollection, and return to a lost home. . . . But, of course, the poem never quite gets to Truth in any obviously recognizable way, and the steps that the narrator Will takes to get there only rarely follow each other in a regular stepwise fashion. *Piers* is a poem, then, that invites readers to expect narrative continuity, and to expect a homeward journey, but is in fact bent on disrupting that experience at all turns.[30]

In reading Langland against Boethius, however, medievalists tend to underplay the digressions of the *Consolation* itself. The narrative structure of the *Consolation* in fact anticipates that of *Piers Plowman*. The protagonists of both works start out in a state of worldly blindness, achieve a degree of moral and spiritual ascent—marked in the *Consolation* by the famously beautiful hymn "O qui perpetua," in *Piers* by the famously beautiful Easter passus—and then, crucially, look back to the world. (A similar pattern occurs in Luke, which ends with the destruction of Jerusalem rather than the crucifixion.) We have seen that the Boethian prisoner consciously imitates Orpheus's backward glance for the wife he has left behind. Ignoring Philosophy's warning that this attachment to the world will prevent him from reaching his heavenly home, he insists that he and Philosophy "enter the realm of the conversations of the common people so that we do not seem to have withdrawn too far from the usages of humanity" (vulgi sermonibus accedamus, ne nimium velut ab humanitatis usu recessisse videamur) (4.7.7). Similarly, Langland's dreamer, awakening from his vision of transcendence, returns to his wife and daughter in an unfashionable area of London. After reengaging with the world, both works end abruptly and inconclusively, with a call for ongoing ethical action. In the *Consolation*, Philosophy herself breaks the narrative frame, addressing readers directly in the second person plural: "Therefore, all of you: Avoid vices, cherish virtues; raise up your minds to blameless hopes; extend your humble prayers into the lofty heights." In Langland's poem, Conscience sets off in search of Piers, calling for Grace until the noise awakens the dreamer. In both works, humble prayer replaces cognitive and spiritual ascent. Both texts end with a desire for justice in this world, joined to a recognition that it is unlikely to be achieved except through divine grace.

I would like to suggest that this close engagement with the ironies and digressions of the *Consolation* generates Langland's ambiguous personification of Holy Church. We have seen the ways in which Philosophy, despite her imposing appearance and tightly woven arguments, repeatedly falls short of transcendence. She abuses and insults the prisoner, describes his relationships with Fortune and the Muses in terms freighted with sexual jealousy, and fails to lead him to his otherworldly fatherland. This description can be extended, with only minor alterations, to Langland's Holy Church, who interrupts her doctrinally impeccable discourse to call the dreamer a "doted daffe," complains bitterly of social and sexual slights at the hands of Meed, and leaves her human interlocutor to his own devices at an even earlier stage of his journey than her predecessor (B.1.140). Holy Church also resembles Philosophy in her role as a mediatrix between divine providence and human fate. In the *Consolation*, Philosophy suggests that "the sequence of fated events is woven together" by intermediate beings such as angels and daemons, then associates herself with these beings through her weaving of garments and arguments, as well as through her account of the tight-knit relationships among Providence, fate, and free will. In *Piers*, Holy Church's role as mediatrix is if anything more direct, since she descends from the watchtower of Providence to the field of folk in order to instruct the dreamer. Although Holy Church does not herself address the dreamer's worries about predestination, these worries are associated with a second strongly Boethian moment in which Fortune speaks in propria persona.[31] Broadly speaking, then, Holy Church follows in Philosophy's footsteps as a daemonic personification, alternating between high and low and mediating between divine providence and human decision-making.

Holy Church also resembles Philosophy insofar as many of her lapses in decorum are tied specifically to her femininity. Both personifications' femininity mirrors and intensifies their intermediate status, rendering them at once superior and inferior to their normatively male human interlocutors. For Holy Church, these complications reach a crisis in the interpretation of a seemingly innocuous verse of scripture: "Faith without works is dead" (Fides sine operibus mortua est) (James 2:26). We have seen the same verse interpreted transcendentally in the final scene of the *Psychomachia*, where Faith takes on the attributes of her sister Works in order to build a temple from the precious stones of Revelation 21:15. In contrast, Holy Church's interpretation, framed explicitly as a warning to the rich, is strikingly worldly:

> But if ye louen leelly and lene þe pouere,
> Of swich good as God yow sent goodliche parteþ,
> Ye ne haue na moore merite in masse ne in houres
> Than Malkyn of hire maydenhede, þat no man desireþ.
> For Iames þe gentile iugged in hise bokes
> That feiþ withouten feet is feblere þan nouȝt,
> And as deed as a dorenail but if þe dede folwe:
> *Fides sine operibus mortua est.* (B.1.181–87a)

In these lines, the *Psychomachia*'s beryls, chrysolites, and sapphires become human bling rather than markers of Neoplatonic transcendence. Indeed, in the absence of works, everything is devalued, from jewels to masses to maidenheads. In the corresponding passage of the *Psychomachia*, Faith gracefully measures out the plan for the temple with a golden reed. Here, Holy Church's Faith, having lost her feet, is first a double amputee, then as "deed as a dorenail."[32] If nothing else, these descriptions seem designed to shock. Having insulted the dreamer for his stupidity and lack of education, Holy Church now seeks to address him in terms he will understand, trading high-mindedness for vulgarity. As in the *Consolation*, one of the strengths of daemonic personifications is that they can stoop to the level of sinful human beings in ways that transcendentally formal Neoplatonic personifications cannot.

We know from the *Consolation*, however, that femininity and crudity can make for an ambivalent, if not dangerous, combination. Holy Church's allusion to Malkyn and her maidenhead brings these issues to the fore even as it facilitates her engagement with the language of the folk. Malkyn plays a minor but recurring role in fourteenth- and fifteenth-century Middle English texts as a stereotypical country bumpkin, sometimes wanton and sometimes prudish but always defined by her sexuality and low socioeconomic status.[33] Even in the context of this casual misogyny, however, Holy Church's treatment of Malkyn stands out for its treatment of virginity not as state of spiritual or even bodily integrity but rather as a commodity whose price is determined by the law of supply and demand. Malkyn's maidenhead lacks value not because of anything she herself does or thinks or is but simply because no man wants it. This seemingly gratuitous market valuation of another women's sexuality makes Holy Church sound at best like a village gossip and at worst like a baud. It also anticipates the devaluation of Holy Church's own sexuality in her rivalry with "Mede þe mayde" (B.2.20):

> I ouȝte ben hyere þan heo; I kam of a bettre
> My fader þe grete God is and ground of alle graces,
> Oo God wiþouten gynnyng, and I his goode douȝter;
> And haþ yeuen me Mercy to marie wiþ myselue;
> And what man be merciful and leelly me loue
> Shal be my lord and I his leef in þe heiȝe heuene;
> And what man takeþ Mede, myn heed dar I legge
> That he shal lese for hire loue a lippe of *Caritatis*. (B.2.28–35)

From a doctrinal point of view, Holy Church's position is unimpeachable. All Christian men should love the church, and it should love them in return. As in the *Consolation*, however, it is difficult to be dignified, much less numinous, while tabulating social and sexual slights. More fundamentally, Holy Church's jealousy of Meed, like Philosophy's jealousy of Fortune, highlights her dependence on the gaze of her male interlocutors. In keeping with the tradition of sexual decision allegory stretching back to Hercules's choice between Virtue and Vice, agency lies with the male person rather than with the feminine personification. As they compete, often unsuccessfully, for male sexual attention, Philosophy and Holy Church have more in common with Malkyn than they or their fans may care to admit.

In fact, both personifications' presence within their respective texts seems to be contingent on male desire. In the *Consolation*, Philosophy suddenly appears to the prisoner in his cell after a long period of absence during which her robes have become "obscured by a sort of gloom of untended antiquity, such as is found on the smoke-covered death masks of one's ancestors." As the dialogue progresses, it becomes clear that this deathlike absence corresponds to the time the prisoner spent in the court of the Gothic king Theodoric, when he took Fortune as his mistress. Implicitly, Philosophy can remain by the prisoner's side—and more broadly within the world of the living—only as long as he continues to desire her. The same fate arguably befalls Holy Church, who disappears from *Piers Plowman* soon after the dreamer's attention is "rauysshed" by Meed (B.2.17). To be sure, Holy Church departs decorously, if hastily, with a final admonition to the dreamer to let "no conscience acombre þee for coueitise of Mede" (B.2.51). The dreamer, however, is so caught up, first in wondering about Meed's marital status, then in the preparations for her wedding, that he barely marks Holy Church's absence. He certainly does not pursue her as he later pursues Piers, or even memorialize her as he later memorializes Haukyn the Active Man. Instead, his attention merely shifts from one feminine personification to the other in the tradition of decision allegory. Holy Church disappears from the text never to return, much as first the Muses and then Fortune disappear from the *Consolation*. Although Holy Church does not necessarily cease to exist, with the poem leaving open the possibility that she returns to the tower of Truth or hurries off to receive a baptized child, she does cease to exist in any meaningful sense for the dreamer, or within the dream, as soon as he decides to pursue Meed.

Is Holy Church, then, another Malkyn? A woman whose sexuality "no man desireþ"? Quite possibly. Within the traditional gender structure of decision allegory, however, a victory can be as troubling as a defeat insofar as it violates the norm of female chastity. In the *Consolation*, Philosophy's desirability leads to doubts about her sexual purity. She is the victim of an attempted *raptus* by pseudophilosophers that violates the integrity of her supposedly imperishable robes, while her sequential relationships with genuine philosophers including Anaxagoras, Socrates, and "our beloved Plato" make her a figure akin to Chaucer's oft-married, oft-widowed Wife of Bath. Her potential promiscuity is limited primarily by philosophy's status as an elite vocation, with at most one philosopher per generation truly devoting himself to the discipline. Langland confronts the problem of Holy Church's chastity even more directly. Just as the church, as an institution, welcomes all believers, so Holy Church, as a personification, promises herself to any man who desires her. While doctrinally this offer is unexceptionable, as uttered by a feminine personification it violates both religious and cultural norms, especially given the strong romance overtones of Holy Church's vow that every such man "shal be my lord and I his leef." Seen from this angle, Holy Church's incontinent sexuality mirrors that of Meed, who likewise offers herself to any man who asks—and is accordingly condemned for being, in another strikingly vernacular appraisal of female sexuality, "as commune as þe cartwey" (B.3.132). Holy Church resembles both Philosophy and Malkyn, in other words, in escaping promiscuity only because few men desire her. She also resembles them in facing a no-win situation. If she loses out to Meed in the sexual marketplace, she becomes irrelevant, while if she outcompetes Meed, she risks similar public condemnation as a promiscuous woman, and even "an hore" (B.4.166).

This no-win situation, I suggest, provokes a crisis of personification in *Piers Plowman*. The association between daemons and unregulated, extramarital desire has deep roots in the Platonic tradition. Plato's *Symposium* treats erotic Love—the product of a drunken liaison between Poverty and Plenty—as the paradigmatic daemon. In this origin myth, daemons represent the desire to reach beyond one's self, toward a noble if unattainable good. But they are also lying, scheming, disreputable, and undignified, mixing ordinary lust with the desire for transcendence. In the *Consolation*, this association manifests itself in Philosophy's sexual jealousy, as well as in her attempted *raptus* by the Stoics and Epicureans. It is contained, however, by Boethius's decision to set the *Consolation* at the end of the prisoner's life, after Fortune has quit the field, as well as by his emphasis on philosophy as an elite discipline. During their short time together, Philosophy and the prisoner can behave *as if* their relationship is exclusive. None of these ameliorating conditions apply to Holy Church's relationship with the dreamer. To begin with, first Meed and then Fortune herself remain very much present as Holy Church's rivals, and they succeed in ravishing the dreamer not once but two or even three times.[34] Just as important, while Philosophy promises to remain with the prisoner until his execution, answering as many questions as time permits, Holy Church is unwilling or unable to accompany the dreamer from youth into old age. Even before Meed appears, Holy Church seeks to extract herself from the dreamer's persistent questioning (B.1.208–9). Implicitly, the dreamer is just one of Holy Church's many love interests and by no means the most important. As tested in the first two passus of *Piers Plowman*, then, the model of feminine daemonic personification Langland inherits from the *Consolation* simply does not work very well. Its reliance on the sexual attractiveness of a Philosophy or a Holy Church undermines her authority as a teacher and sets her up to fail. No respectable woman can compete, head to head, with the likes of Meed and Fortune. And if she does somehow compete successfully, she thereby ceases to be respectable. Although traditionally feminine daemonic personification marks the starting point of the dreamer's journey, it quickly reveals its limitations.

The remainder of *Piers Plowman*, I suggest, engages in an extended thought experiment to find a replacement for the *Consolation*'s daemonic personification allegory. Daemonic personifications do not disappear completely. They continue to be represented by figures such as Meed and her double, Fortune, described by Michael Calabrese as the "embodiment of the classical goddess Fortuna, who sets Will upon a life of pleasure and recklessness for forty years."[35] Both Meed and Fortune belong to the category of exclusively negative Neoplatonic daemons that Augustine identifies with minions of the devil. As such, they are associated with personifications such as Meed's intended husband, "oon Fals Fikel-tonge, a fendes biyete" as well as with actual denizens of hell such as Astaroth, Belial, and Gobelin (B.2.41). These negatively valued daemons passed seamlessly into Christian ontology as demons and seem to persist unproblematically in *Piers Plowman* in much the same way. Holy Church, however, is arguably the first and the last of the poem's positively valued daemonic personifications. She is also the last feminine personification whose sexual availability draws the dreamer toward salvation rather than perdition. The poem's few remaining feminine personifications can be neatly divided into good and evil based on their sexual availability. Meed, Fortune, and their ilk are diabolical temptresses. Positive feminine personifications, in contrast, are either married (like Study and Scripture) or so ontologically distant from the dreamer that he cannot interact with them (like the Four Daughters of God). Guiding the dreamer toward salvation becomes a male-dominated enterprise. It also becomes an occasion for experimenting with different kinds of personification in order to figure out which ones do which kinds of jobs most effectively.

ARISTOTELIAN HUNGER

While the opening lines of the prologue work through the allegorical tradition of the *Psychomachia* and the dreamer's encounter with Holy Church engages with the *Consolation*, Piers's conflict with wasters in A.7/B.6/C.8 elaborates the more recent allegorical history of the *Songe d'Enfer* and *Winner and Waster*. The conflict between Hunger and Waster derives not only its structure but also its moderately realist model of personification from these earlier poems. Like his Aristotelian counterparts Winner and

Grasping, the personification Hunger is abstracted from the quality of hunger in empirical persons and exists in the mind as a being of reason. As such, he helps Piers to arrive at the judgment that, according to Aristotle, is the endpoint of all cognitive acts: Should the universal in question be sought or avoided? That is to say, does hunger help or harm the postlapsarian Christian community, composed both of those who "putten hem to þe plouȝ" and those who "putten hem to pride"?

While most critical work on this section of the poem has concentrated on the interconnected themes of poverty and labor, both agricultural and authorial, a handful of critics have focused more specifically on Hunger's status as a personification.[36] The earliest of these studies subject Hunger to various forms of allegoresis in order to discover his spiritual meaning. For D. W. Robertson and Bernard Huppé, Hunger represents "the lack of spiritual food in forgetfulness of the creator"; for Katherine Trower, he is "the yearning or hungering for . . . a life of penitence and patient poverty lived out of love of Christ"; and for R. E. Kaske, he is the spiritual hunger of Matthew's version of the Sermon on the Mount (Kaske explicitly rejects an allusion to Luke's version of the Sermon, even though Luke's emphasis on bodily hunger resonates powerfully with Langland's description of famine).[37] In the 1990s, Kathleen Hewett-Smith shifted the terms of the debate when she recognized that Langland's descriptions of agricultural labor and seasonal hunger are too concrete to be readily transcended: the passage is filled with lists of very particular, materially embedded activities and objects. Defining allegory in formal, Neoplatonic terms, Hewett-Smith sees this wealth of mimetic detail as incompatible with personification. As a result, she considers Hunger to be "less successful as an abstraction" than "such successfully transcendent figures as Wit or even Envy."[38] Not until very recently has Hunger's embeddedness in the material world been seen as contributing to, rather than detracting from, his status as a personification. For William Rhodes, "The personification of Hunger creates a visible agent for a complex social process, and reveals how the personification of material forces can make bodies politically legible."[39] In this reading, Hunger becomes a mechanism for investigating the workings of this world rather than a means of overcoming it.

While my reading of Hunger is broadly compatible with Rhodes's, it seeks to locate Hunger within my broader schema of personification. I argue that Langland actively encourages such comparisons by connecting the Hunger episode to the beginning of the poem and thus to the text's early instances of Prudentian and Neoplatonic personification. Truth returns as a point of reference, this time imagined more concretely as a feudal lord who dwells in his hilltop castle while Piers labors in the fields below. This invocation of Truth renders Holy Church's absence conspicuous as, with no mediatrix to guide them in their journey, Piers and the pilgrims must do the best they can with the resources at hand. A.7/B.6/C.8 also returns the poem to the "feeld ful of folk" as a site of agricultural labor and so, all but inevitably, to the conflict between plowmen and wasters. The language of the Hunger passage likewise echoes that of the prologue, as does a dense series of allusions to the travel narrative in Luke.[40] We encounter Piers, however, some forty years after Truth first set him to plowing—or, as Piers puts it in the C text, "as for the plouh a potte me to lerne" (C.7.191). There may be a sense in which Piers has been plowing quietly in the background, unnoticed by the dreamer, throughout the poem's opening passus. The dreamer finally perceives Piers because his attention is no longer ravished by Meed and because, like the pilgrims seeking Saint Truth, he has belatedly put himself both to plowing and to penance. The Hunger episode likewise invites readers of *Piers Plowman* to begin anew, putting hand to plow again as they circle back to the "feeld ful of folk" only to encounter a new kind of personification.

Hunger is simultaneously a quality in the substance of the folk—what Porphyry calls a universal "in sensibles"—and a being of reason abstracted from sense perceptions. As a quality in the substance of the folk, Hunger comes into being, or at least makes his presence felt, in the aftermath of a poor harvest, when a significant portion of the folk begins to experience sustained hunger. More specifically, he seems to be ushered onto the field by the wasters' refusal to heed Piers's warning about the danger of shirking food production: "Worþ neuere plentee among þe peple þe while my plowȝ liggeþ" (B.6.163). The wasters' refusal to work is also a refusal to acknowledge, much less accept, God's curse in Genesis. As critics have widely acknowledged, Hunger's response to this refusal is characterized by both its brutality and its frightening mimetic detail:

> Hunger in haste þoo hente Wastour by þe mawe
> And wrong hym so by þe wombe þat al watrede hise eiȝen.
> He buffetted þe Bretoner aboute þe chekes
> That he loked lik a lanterne al his lif after.
> He bette hem so boþe, he brast ner hire guttes. (B.6.174–78)

This description of Waster's watering eyes and the Bretoner's hollow cheeks takes the place of any description of Hunger himself, whose own appearance is unimportant. Instead, Hunger is defined by what he does, by the changes he creates in Waster and the Bretoner as material beings. Hunger's haste reflects the urgency of their sensation of hunger, while his seemingly superhuman strength and appetite for fighting recall the tavern wrestler Throwdown in the *Songe d'Enfer*. Just as Throwdown derives his overwhelming power from the collective drunkenness and aggression of the merrymakers in the Base Tavern, so Hunger derives his power from the collective hunger and desperation of the folk.

Since Hunger represents a quality in the substance of the folk, it follows that he must remain on the field until they are no longer hungry. When Piers courteously asks him to leave, he either will not or cannot comply: "'I behote God,' quod Hunger, 'hennes ne wole I wende / Er I haue dyned by þis day and ydronke boþe'" (B.6.277–78). There follows yet more verisimilar detail in one of the lists that characterize this stretch of the poem, much as such lists characterize *Winner and Waster*. The folk bring Hunger curds, cream, oatcakes, green cheese, beans and bean bread, leeks, parsley, shallots, spring onions, chervil, half-ripe cherries, baked apples, pea pods, cress, and other herbs. These are the characteristic foods of the "hungry gap" in traditional agrarian societies, eaten after stores from the previous year have been exhausted and before the late-summer grain harvest. As the people feed Hunger, then, they are also desperately feeding themselves. The same logic governs Piers's offering to Hunger of a pease loaf baked for his children: in tendering this coerced "gift," Piers responds to his children's cries of hunger, to their urgent and nonnegotiable need to be fed. Their need is part of the collective and overwhelming voraciousness that causes Hunger to "eet in haste and ax[e] after moore" (B.6.295). Since Hunger does not have a material existence separate from the folk, he is hungry when they are hungry and cannot be satisfied until they have been fed.

When the summer's grain is harvested, Hunger does not depart so much as fade away, as the folk finally cease to be hungry:

> By þat it neȝed neer heruest and newe corn cam to chepyng;
> Thanne was folk fayn, and fedde Hunger wiþ þe beste—
> Wiþ good ale, as Gloton taȝte—and garte Hunger go slepe.
> And þo wolde Wastour noȝt werche, but wandren aboute,
> Ne no beggere ete breed þat benes inne were,
> But of coket or clermatyn or ellis of clene whete,
> Ne noon halfpeny ale in non wise drynke,
> But of þe beste and of þe brunneste þat brewesteres selle. (B.6.298–305)

Without editorial capitalization, the syntax of the line "Thanne was folk fayn, and fedde [h]unger wiþ þe beste" is ambiguous. The folk could be feeding either their own hunger or Hunger personified. And this ambiguity is only intensified in the ensuing lines, as it becomes clear that Hunger and the folk are both consuming the same high-quality bread and top-shelf ale. The descriptions of food and drink in the later part of the passage elaborate upon, but do not depart from, the "newe corn" and "good ale" fed to Hunger in the opening lines. Instead of quitting the field, Hunger falls asleep and so becomes imperceptible. Or is he transformed into Waster? When Hunger first appears, he takes over Waster's role as the local bully who seeks to determine food policy with his fists. When Hunger falls asleep, Waster takes up seamlessly where Hunger leaves off. They seem to represent the two faces of human appetite, one driven by lack and the other by excess.

As a moderately realist Aristotelian personification, however, Hunger exists not only as a quality in the substance of the folk but also as a being of reason abstracted from observations of the material world. That is to say, he represents Piers's conception of *hunger* as a universal, a conception that is likely to be imprecise at first and must be refined through reasoned deliberation. For Aristotle, the telos of this cognitive process is not only a right understanding of the universal in question but also a judgment about whether it should be sought or avoided. In addition to depicting hunger as a quality of material beings, then, the episode depicts Piers's thought process as he refines his understanding of *hunger* as a universal and decides whether it is desirable or undesirable. Readers are invited to do the same. That is to say, they are invited to join Piers in observing and reasoning about the effects of hunger, first by noting at close range how it wrings Waster's womb and buffets the Bretoner's cheeks, then by considering whether the curse of Genesis 3:17 should be enforced or ameliorated via social policy. In this connection, it is worth noting that neither Piers nor the reader is imagined as experiencing hunger firsthand to any significant extent. Instead, they must come to grips with *hunger* as a universal as they judge whether or not it is a social good.

Hunger's appearance on the field full of folk is overdetermined. We have seen that on one level his arrival is more or less "natural." The wasters' refusal to work leads to a poor harvest, which in turn leads to hunger as an accidental quality in the substance of the folk. For Derek Pearsall, this is enough: "Clearly Famine . . . does not come because Peres calls, but because the harvest has been bad."[41] And yet Piers does call, and his call is heeded:

"Now by Crist!" quod Peres the Plouhman, "Y shal apayre ȝow alle,"
And houped aftur Hunger, þat herde hym at the furste.
"Y preye the," quod Perus tho, "pur charite, Sire Hunger,
Awreke me of this wastors, for þe knyhte wil nat." (C.8.167–70)[42]

Instead of being contradictory or incoherent, this double causation reflects the ways in which the material problem of agricultural shortfall intersects with the intellectual problem of food policy, with the analysis of hunger as either a social good or a social evil. Even when harvests are very poor, the rich rarely experience hunger, much less starvation. Members of the nobility above the rank of knight are accordingly absent from Langland's half acre, as they are absent from Chaucer's *Canterbury Tales*. Even for Langland's knight—and for Piers himself in the C text, when Hunger compares him to the rich man of Luke 16:19–31—food ethics merely involves selecting morally suitable entertainment for feasts and distributing leftovers to the deserving poor (C.8.278–89). In his capacity as Truth's bailiff, in contrast, Piers is confronted with a much more pressing moral dilemma in the form of Waster's watering eyes, the Bretoner's lantern-like cheeks, and the widespread "bollynge of [the] wombe" characteristic of severe protein malnutrition (B.6.215). Rhodes captures this aspect of Hunger when he defines him as "the personification of the disciplinary mechanism by which Piers's interpretation and categorization of bodies as either productive or wasteful translates into physical power over those bodies."[43] More broadly, Hunger embodies a series of decisions about who should and should not receive a share of scarce food resources, as expressed, inter alia, by landholding practices, labor legislation, and institutional and individual charity. This dimension of Hunger is crucial to his nature as a being of reason, since it helps Piers—and, through Piers, Langland's readers—to come to grips with *hunger* as a universal to be sought or avoided.

When Piers initially calls upon Hunger, he treats him as a good to be sought. He seems to do so, however, more out of a desire for revenge than as the result of careful deliberation. Taking over the enforcement role abdicated by the knight, Hunger is to punish the wasters for their threats of violence against Piers's person and prevent them from taking food by force. Seen from this angle, Hunger is not just a physical sensation but also an agent of state-sanctioned violence, a "maister" who enforces "his statut" so fiercely that none dare complain (B.6.317–18). When Piers is confronted in close quarters with the consequences of his decision to enlist Hunger as an enforcer, he quickly changes course, seeking to mitigate the damage with a pease loaf. Even this brief eruption of violence, however, allows Piers to use Hunger as a threat to bring wasters into line, putting them to work threshing and thatching and whittling pegs, plastering and digging and carting dung. With the harvest already over, none of these off-season tasks are especially urgent, and none will have an immediate impact on the food supply. Instead, they resemble the make-work of some modern welfare programs, where labor functions as a moral rather than economic prerequisite for receiving food benefits. Here, too, readers are invited to trace Piers's thought process. As the administrator of the program, Piers initially finds it satisfying to see wasters work for their suppers. He soon comes to realize, however, that Hunger's presence on the half acre degrades the living conditions of "alle pore peple," regardless of their willingness to work (C.8.205). He thus acts out of a generalized "pite" when he asks that Hunger "wende / Hoom into his owene erd and holden hym þere euere" (B.6.199–200; cf. C.8.205–7). Hunger's excessive violence proves as ineffective as the knight's excessive courtesy because neither can be trusted to distinguish, as Piers seeks to do, between the deserving and undeserving poor. If Hunger's presence on the half acre puts in motion a thought experiment about the advantages and disadvantages of using hunger as an element of labor policy, that experiment seems to conclude that hunger is not a fit agent of state power.

And yet Hunger does not leave as Piers requests. In part, this is because, as we have seen, hunger persists as a quality of the folk until the harvest replenishes the food supply. And in part it is because Piers still needs Hunger, as a being of reason, to help him think through the ethics as well as the politics of food distribution. What, Piers asks, is his personal responsibility for the hungry? Hunger's advice, unsurprisingly, recalls his earlier treatment of Waster and the Bretoner. Answering first in absolute terms, he tells Piers that he must share his own food with the deserving poor but that able-bodied beggars are entitled only to "houndes breed and horse breed" to ward off starvation (B.6.214). Then, shifting into more practical terms that assume limited resources, he tells Piers first to see to his own needs, then to meet the needs of his deserving neighbors, and only then to give to strangers, who are likely to be able-bodied vagrants. Hunger stresses, however, that this hierarchy of giving is contingent on Piers's proper management of his own food consumption. In doing so, he problematizes the categories that have structured the episode thus far by comparing Piers, who has apparently missed a week of work due to overeating, to the wasters, who are hungry because they will not work. Both depart from Aristotle's virtuous mean of moderation. In advising the well-fed to "Ete noȝt, I hote þee, er Hunger þee take / And sende þee of his sauce to sauore wiþ þi lippes," Hunger suggests that they subject themselves to a gentler version of the discipline he imposes on Waster and the Bretoner (B.6.260–61). In effect, he invokes a diminutive version of himself, too weak to effect population-level changes or even enforce moderation on unwilling individuals, but strong enough to help persons of good will, including Piers himself, to avoid overeating. Where the larger Hunger is abstracted from the hunger of the poor and helps Piers to think through problems of food policy, his smaller cousin is abstracted from the physical sensations of a single individual and teaches him when and how much to eat. Implicitly, this smaller Hunger will stay behind when the larger one departs, teaching Piers self-regulation as a step toward an ethics, if not a politics, of food distribution.

To the extent that Piers reaches a judgment about Hunger, then, it is twofold. The larger, population-level Hunger should be avoided. Although Hunger motivates wasters to work, the cost he imposes, as measured in human suffering and degradation, is too high. The smaller Hunger, in contrast, is worth seeking out—at least for those, like Piers, who have more food than they need: he serves as a regulatory tool for achieving the Aristotelian virtue of moderation. In other respects, Piers's encounter with Hunger, like the debate in *Winner and Waster*, is inconclusive. Hunger's hardline position on charity for the able-bodied poor never fully answers Piers's question, "Myȝte I synnelees do as þow seist?" (B.6.229). As befits Hunger's nature as an embodiment of scarcity, he is perhaps closer to the mark in offering practical advice to those with limited resources. If Piers cannot give to all, to whom should he give first? As in *Winner and Waster*, the entire episode imagines an audience that is not poor making decisions on behalf of those who are. Such readers are encouraged to use Hunger as a tool for forming their own judgments about the role of hunger both in public policy and in Christian ethics. In important respects, Piers's exchanges with Hunger make visible this process of deliberation. As a being of reason, Hunger has a reduced ontological status compared to Piers and other Prudentian personifications. At the same time, he helps them to avoid sin by allowing them to think through potential courses of action before committing to them.

NOMINALIST ANIMA

The three personifications I have discussed thus far—the plowman, Holy Church, and Hunger—have their roots in three distinguishable, if not always empirically distinct, allegorical traditions. The formative tradition of the *Psychomachia*, the daemonic tradition of the *Consolation*, and the moderately realist tradition of the *Songe d'Enfer* and *Winner and Waster* each produce readily identifiable varieties of personification. In contrast, Langland's nominalist personification of the soul—the Anima of B.15—is idiosyncratic and experimental. To begin with, it exists only in B, being overwritten in C by the more conventional Liberum Arbitrium. Within B, it is the second of two personifications with the same name, following, and to an important extent superseding, the more conventional Neoplatonic representation of the soul in passus 9. This doubling has the effect of rendering both personifications provisional, even incomplete, but also implies a progression from the first to the second. More broadly, it suggests that Langland's continued dissatisfaction with Neoplatonic personification motivates his search for alternatives, as well as his willingness to push boundaries in order to find them. Instead of representing the soul, the second B-text Anima confronts readers with a paradox or enigma, challenging them to cognize the soul in new ways and providing them with new tools for doing so. Langland's nominalist Anima thus plays a much more important role in *Piers Plowman* than Deguileville's nominalist Penance plays in the *Pèlerinage de la Vie Humaine*. Instead of being a curiosity who occupies an explicitly subordinate position within a Neoplatonic universe, Anima becomes one of the central mysteries of the last third of the poem, pushing the dreamer—and, through him, the reader—toward a new understanding of himself as a soul.

The enigmatic Anima of B.15 is defined to a significant extent through contrast with the conventionally feminine Anima of B.9. The first B-text Anima, in turn, depends on the allegorical motif of the "castle of love," first vernacularized in Robert Grosseteste's *Chateau d'Amour* (*Castle of Love*).[44] Composed in Anglo-French in the first quarter of the thirteenth century, and so roughly contemporaneous with Raoul de Houdenc's *Songe d'Enfer*, the *Chateau d'Amour* survives in sixteen manuscripts and an English translation that itself persists in multiple versions.[45] The ultimate source for the motif, however, is the travel narrative in Luke, specifically the moment when Jesus "entered into a certain town" (intravit in quoddam castellum) along the route to Jerusalem (Luke 10:38). Grosseteste's version of the story embellishes Luke's "castellum" via the description of the New Jerusalem in Revelation 21, producing a Neoplatonic vision so otherworldly that "no tongue can describe, nor heart think, nor mouth speak" (lange ne poet descrire / quer penser, ne buche dire) its perfection (599–600).[46] God visits this castle through its closed door, leaving the lady within simultaneously a "chaste virgin, wife, and mother" (virgine chaste, espuse, e mere) (728). Although the castle sits "in the marches" (en la marche) and is besieged by personified Sins, it has such inherent integrity, and is so well defended by the Virtues, that it is never in danger of falling (581, 671). The terms of Grosseteste's allegory are not entirely stable, with the Virgin hailed sometimes as the castle itself, at other times as the lady within it. In general, however, the castle can reasonably be interpreted as the Virgin's body, while the lady who welcomes suppliants and marshals the defending Virtues personifies her will or soul. As the site where the Word is made flesh through the incarnation, the castle also represents flesh itself, or flesh as such, purified from sin so that it is overwhelmingly beautiful.[47]

Even as similarities in language and imagery suggest that this passage stands behind the portrait of Anima in B.9, Langland's changes to Grosseteste point to his dissatisfaction with traditional Neoplatonic personification. Langland's abbreviated version of the motif, recounted by Wit, features Anima rather than the Virgin Mary as the beloved of Kind, the craftsman God. She dwells in the castle Caro (Flesh), which has been "wittily enioyned"—seemingly a translation of Grosseteste's "devisa" (devised)—by Kind himself (B.9.4, 660). In Grosseteste's poem this castle sits "en la marche," which Nicholas Watson sees as representing "the border-zone between the Old and New Covenants occupied by the immaculate Virgin Mary."[48] In Langland's tropological allegory, "thise marches" instead refer primarily to the soul's contested position on the border between virtue and vice (B.9.11). Both castles are the sites of *Psychomachia*-like battle scenes, although Grosseteste's besieging army of Vices is condensed in *Piers* to a single antagonist: the "proud prikere of Fraunce, *Princeps huius mundi*" (Prince of this world) (B.9.8). Aside from its brevity, the most important innovation in Langland's version of the story is its deferral of transcendence. Anima's surroundings are resolutely mundane, and she is protected by "Sire Inwit" and the five senses rather than an otherworldly army of Virtues (B.9.18). Indeed, the constable Inwit soon upstages Anima as the scene's chief actor, for he apparently has the power to direct her "at his wille" (B.9.59). What remains in *Piers Plowman*, then, is the traditional structure of a Neoplatonic allegory, all but stripped of the allegorical goddess who should be its animating force.

Langland's rewriting of the castle motif both reflects and contributes to the often noted masculinization of personification in *Piers Plowman*. The femininity of Grosseteste's allegorical lady is overdetermined: she represents the biblical Mary, she is an object of masculine desire, and her gender situates her within a "naturally" hierarchical heterosexual relationship with God. Initially, the femininity of the B.9 Anima seems to work in much the same way. As Newman has argued, the Christian tradition of personifying *anima* rather than the closely related but less bodily *animus* has everything to do with gender, especially when the soul is characterized as God's beloved.[49] In Langland's version, the soul's femininity sets in motion a more elaborate romance plotline in which Anima is betrothed to Kind but pursued by his dashing rival, Princeps huius mundi. Where we might expect this scenario to lead to a decision allegory in which Anima chooses between two potential sexual partners, however, Langland deflects this choice to Inwit. It is thus Inwit, rather than Anima, who becomes the episode's locus of identification as well as a proxy for the similarly named Wit, the teller of this inset allegory. Wit himself, moreover, has just been established as a double for the dreamer, likewise "long and lene" (B.8.117). Inwit, then, becomes the site where the dreamer is invited to project himself into Wit's narrative, imagining himself as the faithful servant of Kind. We have come a long way from the *Psychomachia*'s invitation to cross-gender identification. In its place, Wit invites the dreamer to ally himself with Kind specifically through their shared masculinity: God "made man moost like to hymself one / And Eue of his ryb bon wiþouten any mene" (B.9.33–34). He is to do so, moreover, through his inwit, the "gretteste" element of the self, and the one most closely associated with Kind's role as "fader and formour" (B.9.59, 27). Langland thus retains the Neoplatonic connection between the divine *artifex* and human craftsman while circumventing the feminine personifications who, in texts ranging from Calcidius's commentary of the *Timaeus* to Alan of Lille's *Complaint of Nature*, traditionally mediate between them. In Langland's version of the castle of love motif, as in Wit's account of the creation, masculinity rather than femininity offers privileged access to God. Within a few dozen lines of her introduction, the feminine Anima has already been superseded.

Langland's second Anima, then, responds to what we might call a double crisis of personification. In B.9, Neoplatonic techniques for representing the soul have already proved themselves to be profoundly limited. And yet the soul cannot be adequately represented via moderately realist personification because, in contrast to phenomena such as wasting and hunger, it cannot be perceived with the senses. Instead, Langland experiments with nominalist personification, as better suited to something as mysterious and ineffable as the soul. The difficulty of understanding the universal *soul* and its central role in Christian theology means, however, that nominalist personification is more fraught for Langland than for Deguileville.[50] Before Langland can prompt his readers to cognize the soul, he must provide them with a new set of tools for thought and teach them how they should be used. As we have seen, Ockham distinguishes between spoken and written terms on the one hand and mental terms or concepts on the other. While the former are human conventions, signifying "willfully" and "according to voluntary imposition," the latter "naturally signify what they signify" and are ideally common to all humans (*Summa Logicae* 1.1.46–52). Instead of simply describing Anima in Latin or English, Langland uses the resources of both languages, and the gaps between them, to help readers to conceptualize the universal *soul*. Langland's personified Anima also prompts readers to think about the soul in new, more spiritually productive ways through their refusal to identify with any one gender—a refusal I will mark with the neutral pronouns *they, them, their*. This nonbinary gender identity pushes the dreamer, and through him Langland's readers, to come to terms with the unfamiliarity of their own souls.

Langland signals the B.15 Anima's departure from the dominant paradigms of personification by describing them primarily in negative terms. Where personification generally makes abstract nouns easier to grasp by assigning them human bodies, together with parents, spouses, children, and wardrobes that situate them within a social sphere, Anima consistently resists description. "A sotil þyng wiþalle" and "oon wiþouten tonge and teeþ," they are so unknown and unknowable that the dreamer resorts to conjuring them as though they might be a demon, one of the denizens of hell who have haunted Christian personification since Augustine (B.15.12–13). At the same time, Anima tests the limits of Langland's vernacularity, not least because they are the only acting and speaking character in the B text with a purely Latin name.[51] But neither is Anima's name proper Latin. By associating a grammatically feminine noun with a figure the dreamer refers to by the masculine pronouns "he" and "hym," Langland commits a grammatical "vice" that allegorists are usually careful to avoid (B.15.14–15).[52] Both in Latin and in English, then, Anima can only make themselves known through probing the limits of language rather than through its normal operation. Even a trope whose function is to provide bodies can barely make Anima tangible, and they threaten to slip through the cracks of English and Latin alike. The purpose of Langland's initial description is not to *show* his readers Anima, or even to tell them straightforwardly about their operations, but to encourage them to think about the nature of the soul.

This inducement to thought continues with Anima's extended act of self-naming, a passage that late-medieval scribes and readers frequently flagged for attention with colored paraph marks, rubrication, variations in script, and annotations:

> "The whiles I quykke þe cors," quod he, "called am I *Anima*;
> And whan I wilne and wolde *Animus* ich hatte;
> And for þat I kan and knowe, called am I *Mens*, 'þouȝte';
> And whan I make mone to God, *Memoria* is my name;
> And whan I deme domes and do as truþe techeþ
> Thanne is *Racio* my riȝte name, "Reson" on Englissh;
> And whan I feele þat folk telleþ, my firste name is *Sensus* --
> And þat is wit and wisdom, þe welle of alle craftes;
> And whan I chalange or chalange noȝt, chepe or refuse,
> Thanne am I Conscience ycalled, Goddes clerk and his notarie;
> And whan I loue leelly Our Lord and alle oþere,
> Thanne is "Lele Loue" my name, and in Latyn *Amor*;
> And whan I flee fro þe flessh and forsake þe careyne,
> Thanne am I spirit spechelees, and *Spiritus* þanne ich hatte." (B.15.23–36)

Italicized in modern editions, Anima's Latin names are also specifically emphasized in B-text manuscripts, with various combinations of larger lettering, red lettering, red and black underlining, and red boxes marking them alternately as keywords and as Latin interlopers in Langland's English text.[53] By highlighting the relationship between Anima's many Latin names and the alliterating English lines that surround them, the sheer density of this rubrication draws attention to the complex relationship between Latin and vernacular, demanding that readers slow down, take heed, and seek to remember. My experience teaching *Piers Plowman* to undergraduates suggests that new readers of the poem still heed these instructions. The first time I taught this passage, I made a spur-of-the-moment decision to administer a pop quiz at the end of a lively discussion. To my surprise, each of my twenty-eight students could provide a working English definition of each of Anima's Latin names, distinguishing Anima from Animus, Mens from Memoria, and so on. When I asked them to translate from English to Latin, over 80 percent of the class still achieved a perfect score, even though none of them had any formal training in Latin.

Wholly anecdotal though it is, this survey suggests that the second B-text Anima functions in part as a language-learning tool. That is to say, while Will—and through him Langland's reader—is learning what kind of a multifaceted thing the soul is, he is also mastering a Latin vocabulary that enables the necessary fine distinctions. Anima's act of self-naming is arranged roughly in the manner of a glossary, with Latin nouns equated with short definitional phrases in English and accompanied by English synonyms where these are available.[54] Even in these cases, however, the English noun does not always seem to be sufficient in and of itself. It must be rendered more specific, and usually elevated, in order to function as a reliable equivalent of the Latin. Thus "loue leelly Our Lord and alle oþere" becomes "Lele Loue" and finally Amor, while "spirit spechelees" becomes Spiritus. The English terms and definitions provide an adequate paraphrastic account of the meaning of Anima's various aspects, but the Latin transforms them into more reliable handles—and, more specifically, into tools for self-knowledge, tools for the analysis of one's own soul. For these purposes, short names are more useful than long, compound ones, and a term like *Amor* can be manipulated—subjected to a whole range of grammatical and conceptual operations—in ways that "loue leelly Our Lord and alle oþere" and even "Lele Loue" cannot.

This is not to say that Anima teaches Langland's readers to read Latin in any kind of thorough or conventional sense. If so, readers who grasped Anima's self-naming would also be able to understand the chunk of undigested Latin that follows and authorizes it, a passage based on Isidore of Seville's *Etymologies*:

> *Anima* [the soul] selects different names for different actions. As it gives life to the body it is *anima* [the soul]; as it wills, it is *animus* [intention]; as it knows, it is *mens* [mind]; as it recollects, it is *memoria* [memory]; as it judges, it is *racio* [reason]; as it senses, it is *sensus* [sense]; as it loves, it is *Amor* [love]; as it denies or consents, it is *consciencia* [conscience]; as it breathes the breath of life, it is *spiritus* [spirit].
>
> *Anima pro diuersis accionibus diuersa nomina sortitur: dum viuificat corpus, Anima est; dum vult, Animus est; dum scit, Mens est; dum recolit, Memoria est; dum iudicat, Racio est; dum sentit, Sensus est; dum amat, Amor est; dum negat vel consentit, Consciencia est; dum spirat, Spiritus est.* (B.15.39a)[55]

Instead, Anima offers a limited number of abstract nouns, all presented in the nominative case and the singular number—what amounts to a technical vocabulary having to do with the soul and the practice of introspection. In contrast to the *Etymologies* passage, these nouns are presented in a context that frees the reader from responsibility for declension and agreement, precisely the categories that most sharply distinguish Latin from English and make Langland's C.3 grammatical metaphor all but impenetrable. Anima's nouns can thus be assimilated to English in much the same way that one would assimilate any new vocabulary item. In the process, they produce genuinely hybrid or macaronic thinking—an in-between status reflected in Oxford, Corpus Christi College MS 201 (F), which presents Anima's names as a bicolored compromise between ordinary black text and the red of full-fledged Latin quotations. Readers who accept Anima's invitation to self-interrogation do so, therefore, with Latin nouns and English verbs and prepositions, achieving much of the sophistication and precision of Latin even if they do not know Latin grammar, even if—to borrow a category of economic privilege invoked in the dreamer's C.5 apologia—they did not have family or friends to support their education.

Anima, then, seems to import abstract Latin nouns in order to remedy a deficiency in English, which does not have the right nouns with the right shades of meaning to describe the human soul. The evidence for this phenomenon lies not only in the careful qualification of phrases like "Lele Loue" but in the one English term that stands alone in Anima's speech, without a Latin equivalent. *Conscience* is, of course, ultimately borrowed from Latin, probably via French, and is a close cognate of the Latin *conscientia*. By Langland's time, however, it was already well established in English: the first *Middle English Dictionary* citation in Anima's sense of "the faculty of knowing what is right" is from the *Ancrene Wisse*.[56] Anima's decision to use *conscience* rather than *conscientia*, then, is an important indicator, because it suggests that their respect for Latin is largely pragmatic. They break into Latin when no appropriate English word is available but do not seem to value Latin per se. Where many grammarians and educational theorists considered Latin to be intrinsically superior because of its sacred history or claims of privileged rationality, Anima seems mainly to be interested in what Latin can do for English speakers. Anima's position in B is all the more marked because it contrasts with the version of the speech attributed to Liberum Arbitrium in the C text, where either Langland himself or a scribal tradition substitutes "Conscientia" for "Conscience" in eight manuscripts (C.16.190). In this context, the fact that most of Anima's names are Latin seems to create an expectation that they should *all* be Latin. By resisting that expectation, Anima presents themselves as linguistically hybrid or indeterminate. They prioritize the concept of the soul over the language in which it is expressed, suggesting that the purpose of Anima's self-naming is to furnish readers with new tools for cognizing their own souls.

The second Anima's linguistic hybridity is linked to their gender hybridity. In contrast to the femininity of the earlier Anima, which corresponds to the grammatical gender of the underlying Latin noun, the Anima of B.15 is resolutely formless, presumably lacking sex characteristics in addition to teeth and tongue.[57] After this carefully neutral introduction, Anima *is* assigned a gendered personal pronoun. Like the name Anima itself, however, this gender seems to be a label that the dreamer assigns for his own convenience, in order to render the creature he encounters more familiar, and thus more understandable. Anima does not identify with either gender, instead using first-person pronouns and the universal term "creature," emphasizing their connection to the Creator very differently than Wit does in B.9 (B.15.16). Nor does Anima privilege any one of their many names—some grammatically masculine and others grammatically feminine—over the others. Despite the dreamer's pronoun use, then, Langland's second Anima never becomes masculine in the way that the first Anima is feminine, nor does their gender immediately suggest a plotline or dictate a sequence of behavior.[58] Instead, Anima's indeterminacy seems to confirm that they construct themselves according to English rather than Latin rules of grammatical gender, since the Latin requirement for agreement in gender, case, and number makes gender identification almost impossible to avoid. Anima can exist beyond or between genders precisely because they are governed by a Latin vocabulary but a relatively genderless English grammar. In doing so, they provide a powerful and nuanced vision of the human soul, one that Elizabeth Robertson argues corresponds to the genderless soul of theological discourse rather than to the gendered soul of allegory.[59]

Anima's extended act of self-naming in B.15 is thus a true Latin-English hybrid, drawing on the strengths of both languages to illustrate a concept that is not easily possible within the confines of either. English does not have an appropriate vocabulary, so Latin supplies that, along with its traditions of faculty psychology and scholastic *distinctio*. But English syntax, with its limited system of inflections, allows Langland to depict a personified Anima that participates in neither bodily sex nor grammatical gender, thus marking their distance from familiar modes of thinking and being. This personification of the soul in turn holds the whole cluster together and in fact serves its own grammatical function. That is to say, Anima's speech of self-naming makes sense only because the character Anima is saying it. In the quotation from Isidore of Seville, there is no gender ambiguity because the entire passage refers back to a single definition, like a dictionary entry. In Langland's hybrid passage, in contrast, Anima's gender ambiguity can persist because the referent is not described but speaks, using gender-neutral first-person singular pronouns. At the same time, the task of simultaneously adding eight new Latin terms to an English vocabulary is feasible only because all the terms refer back to a single, already-imagined entity. I did not assign my students to memorize Anima's names as a vocabulary list; they remembered them spontaneously as aspects of a personification that caught their attention and sustained their interest. Although Langland's description of Anima is negative in the sense that it mostly describes what Anima is not, it is undeniably striking enough to lend itself to memory work. More prosaically but more fundamentally, Langland's personification of Anima furnishes a structure around which the different aspects of the soul can be organized, and without which they cannot cohere. Anima's Latin names are relatively easy to assimilate because they refer to an allegorical figure that is itself a locus for concentrated thought. Since the names are linked to each other and to Anima, they also signify much more richly than they would if presented as a simple list.

The B.15 Anima, then, functions as a new kind of machine. Since they are irreducible to positive description, the dreamer's most basic efforts at linguistic classification reveal themselves to be arbitrary and inadequate. The dreamer uses a single name and masculine pronouns to gesture toward a personification who insists on many names and uses "I" and "creature." This cultivated ambiguity represents not just a carefully adumbrated vision of the human soul but also a self-conscious revision of the earlier Anima as a lady in a tower. Here, Langland seems to promise, we have a new and better way for thinking about the soul's workings, its capacity for judgment, and its relationship to God. This transformation is important not simply because it offers Will a new cognitive tool but because it reveals how that tool—and tools like it—are put together. In assigning a masculine pronoun to an entity he calls Anima, Will commits a solecism that must have grated on Langland's more Latinate readers. Like the annotations and rubrication that flag the passage as a whole, this dissonance alerts such readers to pay careful attention to *soul* as a concept—that is, as an Ockhamite mental term—that exceeds both Latin and English (and all other spoken and written languages). Langland's personification of Anima thus calls on both educated and relatively uneducated readers of the poem to conceptualize, and so work to improve, something as ineffable as their own souls.

In attempting to evade the binaries of masculine/feminine and Latin/vernacular, Anima also evades the dominant paradigms of personification allegory. They are neither the product of Prudentian self-formation nor a Platonic allegorical goddess nor an Aristotelian being of reason, abstracted from and still associated with a proliferation of verisimilar detail. As part of a broader effort to highlight the many varieties of medieval allegory, including *ironia*, *antiphrasis*, and *notatio*, Mary Carruthers suggests that Anima is not a personification at all but rather an instance of *pictura* whose purpose is "to summarize major subject matters, to organize these for study, and to find one's way through their complications."[60] Seen in this way, Anima responds to the dreamer's stated desire to know Do-well with a narrative map that outlines the cognitive terrain he must traverse in order to answer his question; their closest cognate is the allegorical itinerary to Truth that Piers provides to the pilgrims in A.6/B.5/C.7. For Carruthers, Anima remains a cognitive tool, but of a quite different kind than previously imagined. They belong not with Langland's other personifications but with a series of inanimate maps and diagrams made up of imagistic language, captioned images, and every conceivable combination of the two.

Although Carruthers's recognition of the range of medieval allegorical tropes is valuable, her analysis of Anima holds only in part. By passus 15, the poem's episodic structure, in which the dreamer converses with one personification after another, is strongly established. As Lavinia Griffiths puts it, "One personification tends to give rise to more personifications. They appear in branching complexes, and by a sort of metonymy confer a status similar to their own on those around them."[61] Certainly my students' emotional reaction to Anima, as a literary character, was very different from their glassy-eyed response to the B.5 allegorical map. They were interested in thinking about Anima in relation to human gender as well as in Anima's act of self-naming, which Cooper links to the naming practices in medieval romance.[62] Nonetheless, it is useful to think of Anima as at once a *pictura* and a personification, much as the destroyed Ebstorf *mappamundi*, with the head, hands, and feet of Christ marking its four compass positions, was both a representation of the deity and a map of the world. In the same way, we can recognize that Langland's Anima is a cognitive map without ceasing to see them as a personification. Like viewers manipulating the hinged belly of a *vierge ouvrante*, readers can move between one aspect of Anima and the other as best suits their reading trajectories. Such manipulation in fact classifies Anima as a subtype of *pictura* consisting of moving rather than static images, a category that includes Hugh of Saint Victor's image of Noah's ark and Clement of Llanthony's confessional cherub. Carruthers considers both of these moving images to be machines for invention rather than mere schemas, and the same holds true for Anima as they shift between personification and *pictura*.[63]

Even this is not all, however. Stephanie Batkie has complicated Carruthers's reading of Anima by analyzing them in relation to both *pictura* and its allegorical antithesis, *enigma*. She points out that despite Anima's careful efforts to distinguish the different aspects of the soul, they remain enigmatic:

> All that is known of Anima is his gender and his powerful ambiguity. From his immediate speech, issuing out of a mouth with none of the normal faculties for producing language, to the initial description of "sotil," nothing about Anima satisfies the curiosity; instead, his very lack of legibility heightens the need to categorize and identify him. He is a tantalizing blank, a void that must be classified and analyzed before the narrative can move forward. And to make matters worse, when Will is finally able to ask him for the most basic of piece of information, his name, the response is a bewildering multitude of options to select from.[64]

I have argued that Anima's gender is in fact ambiguous, along with their language and status as a particular kind of allegorical being. These multiple, interlocking levels of ambiguity are what prompted my class to pause for so long over this single figure, puzzling through Anima's description and act of self-naming in an effort to figure out who and what they are. Like the unknown knight in a romance, Anima stops their interlocutors in their tracks, challenging them to conceptualize the soul before they take another step. This challenge, I would suggest, is yet another of Langland's Boethian moments, reflecting Philosophy's insistence that the prisoner know himself not only in Aristotelian terms, as a rational and mortal animal, but also as an embodied immortal soul. As measured by the work they do, rather than by more superficial categories of resemblance, Anima can thus be seen as Philosophy's heir. In this, they supplant not only Langland's earlier formal Neoplatonic personification of the soul but also his earlier daemonic Neoplatonic personification of Holy Church, whose efforts to carry on the work of Philosophy are markedly less successful.

At the same time, Langland's negative characterization of Anima as "oon wiþouten tonge and teeþ" looks forward to another important moment of self-knowledge. In the heat of the poem's final battle for the Barn of Unity, the personified Eld runs over the dreamer's head, rendering him "balled bifore and bare on þe croune" (B.20.184). When the dreamer foolishly protests this rough treatment, telling Eld that he should have asked leave for this trespass upon private property, Eld attacks him directly, transforming him from a bystander into a participant:

> "Ye—leue, lurdeyn?" quod he, and leyde on me wiþ age,
> And hitte me vnder þe ere—vnneþe may Ich here.
> He buffeted me aboute þe mouþ and bette out my wangteeþ,
> And gyued me in goutes—I may noȝt goon at large.
> And of þe wo þat I was inne my wif hadde ruþe,
> And wisshed wel witterly þat I were in heuene.
> For þe lyme þat she loued me fore, and leef was to feele—
> On nyghtes, namely, whan we naked weere—
> I ne myghte in no manere maken it at hir wille,
> So Elde and heo it hadden forbeten. (B.20.189–98)

In another echo of the *Consolation*, Eld here continues the work of Fortune, who had earlier stripped the dreamer of his wealth and worldly position. Now his body, too, is in jeopardy. Indeed, the dreamer draws Eld's ire when he treats his hair as something he possesses by right rather than as something loaned to him by circumstance. Strikingly, however, as Eld strips away more and more of the dreamer's physical attributes—as the dreamer comes to resemble Jaques's old man in *As You Like It*, "sans teeth, sans eyes, sans taste, sans everything"—he also comes to resemble Anima as a disembodied soul (2.7.165). Like Anima, the dreamer is characterized negatively, via the attributes he does not, or does not any longer, possess. Both are explicitly toothless and implicitly genderless, with the dreamer describing at length how "þe lyme" that once distinguished him from his wife, seemingly supplying her lack, has ceased to perform its office. While the dreamer's encounter with Anima teaches him about the nature of the soul, then, his encounter with Eld teaches him that he *is* a soul—that his body is not an essential part of himself but an external object subject to the vicissitudes of Fortune.[65] As in the *Consolation*, this painful knowledge, this knowledge of the self as a soul, implicitly authorizes the dreamer's literary production. Like Boethius, "Long Will" writes in the face of death, with the self-knowledge he has attained by confronting his mortality.

From this point of view, Anima becomes one of the dreamer's most important guides, indeed a model for Langland's authorial persona. They are also an important instance of nominalist personification. Following Langland's own example, we can begin by describing what Anima is not. They are not a Prudentian personification, because they are not represented as the product of human craftsmanship with the goal of self-formation, either for good or for ill. They are not a Neoplatonic personification because they do not descend from on high, whether transcendentally, as the numinous embodiment of a Platonic form, or more intimately and ambivalently in the manner of a daemon. They are not a moderately realist Aristotelian personification because they are not abstracted from sense perceptions of the material world. Instead, they are a puzzle, a series of unintuitive propositions put into play. Like other philosophers the Middle Ages called *nominales*, Ockham denied the extramental existence of universals. In his later thought, universals persist only as cognitive acts, as the act of understanding one set of individuals as *men*, another set of individuals as *horses*, and so on. In keeping with this paradigm, I have tried to show that nominalist personifications do not seek to represent universals but to prompt their cognition. We have seen that Deguileville's Penance does not look like, or even act like, penance. Instead, the broom she carries in her mouth presents readers of the *Pèlerinage* with a visual puzzle, challenging them to use this outlandish image to understand the tongue's cleansing power in the confession of sins. Such puzzles "work" because, in contrast to most nominalists of our own era, Ockham holds that mental terms or concepts are congruent with the objective world. A properly designed personification can thus lead readers to a right conception of the universal *penance*, or of any other universal. Langland's Anima is described much less concretely than Penance and cannot be "solved" quite so neatly: they are more enigma than riddle.[66] Nonetheless, the underlying dynamic remains much the same. Anima does not look or act like the soul but instead prompts Langland's readers to puzzle over the soul, and eventually to cognize it, as a being without body or gender, without language or name. That is to say, they prompt readers to cognize *soul* as a universal, as one of Ockham's naturally signifying mental terms rather than a conventionally signifying lexical item in this or that spoken or written language.

Thus understood, Anima is not mere rhetoric or "just a game." But they do invite a measure of serious-minded playfulness, or at least elastic experimentation, as readers strive to grasp difficult and unfamiliar concepts. This same playfulness characterizes Langland's allegorical practice more broadly, which mingles formative, daemonic, moderately realist, and nominalist personification in an effort to develop a conceptual vocabulary adequate to the dreamer's journey. I have argued that the often remarked shift in the gender of Langland's personifications reflects a larger shift from characteristically feminine Neoplatonic personifications to characteristically masculine moderately realist ones. Rather than serving as a stable endpoint, however, Langland's moderately realist personifications beget even more experimental forms, such as the genderless Anima who serves as a model for the dreamer's own understanding of himself as a genderless soul (a move that echoes, though it does not duplicate, Prudentius's invitation to transgender self-personification in the *Psychomachia*). More broadly, Langland's willingness to experiment offers a fitting riposte to critics who insist that personification is either inherently realist or inherently nominalist, or inherently conservative or inherently anything, as he builds, rebuilds, and tinkers with his personifications in order to solve specific problems and answer specific questions. Understood as machines of the mind, Langland's personifications are judged as successes or failures according to their representational power rather than according to their transcendence or lack thereof. They also work collectively rather than individually. When the dreamer calls upon Kind to rescue him from Eld, Kind recalls the beginning of the poem by counseling the dreamer to learn a craft before it is too late and thus to form himself as a virtuous Prudentian personification. Now that the dreamer faces the end of his life, able neither to walk nor to hear, with the physical act of love no longer possible, this disciplinary knowledge can be boiled down to the essential work of the soul rather than the body: "Lerne to loue . . . and leef all oþere" (B.20.208). This lesson, however, seemingly can only be produced by many different kinds of personifications working together as a complex, and not entirely frictionless, machine.

NOTES

Citations of classical texts refer to the Loeb Classical Library series unless otherwise noted and are supplied parenthetically.

INTRODUCTION

1. Tamara Adlin and John Pruitt, *The Essential Persona Lifecycle: Your Guide to Building and Using Personas* (Burlington, MA: Morgan Kaufmann, 2010), 1, back cover.

2. Alan Cooper, *The Inmates Are Running the Asylum: Why High-Tech Products Drive Us Crazy and How to Restore the Sanity* (Indianapolis: Sams, 1999), 130.

3. Phil Patton, "Before Creating the Car, Ford Designs the Driver," *New York Times*, July 19, 2009, http://www.nytimes.com/2009/07/19/automobiles/19design.html.

4. See Christopher N. Chapman and Russell P. Milham, "The Personas' New Clothes: Methodological and Practical Arguments against a Popular Method," *Proceedings of the Human Factors and Ergonomics Society* 50 (2006): 634–36 (634).

5. Chapman and Milham, "The Personas' New Clothes," 635.

6. See, e.g., Roland Barthes, "The Reality Effect," in *The Rustle of Language*, trans. Richard Howard (Oxford: Blackwell, 1986), 141–48.

7. On naming practices in late-medieval poetry, see Emily Steiner, "Naming and Allegory in Late Medieval England," *Journal of English and Germanic Philology* 106 (2007): 248–75.

8. See, e.g., Gordon Teskey, *Allegory and Violence* (Ithaca, NY: Cornell University Press, 1996); James Paxson, "Gender Personified, Personification Gendered, and the Body Figuralized in *Piers Plowman*," *Yearbook of Langland Studies* 12 (1998): 65–96; Barbara Newman, *God and the Goddesses: Vision, Poetry and Belief in the Middle Ages* (Philadelphia: University of Pennsylvania Press, 2003), esp. 35–38; and Maureen Quilligan, "Allegory and Female Agency," in *Thinking Allegory Otherwise*, ed. Brenda Machosky (Stanford, CA: Stanford University Press, 2010), 163–87.

9. On personification as a literary device with a special capacity for eliciting and expressing emotions, see Mary Flannery, "Personification and Embodied Emotional Practice in Middle English Literature," *Literature Compass* 9 (2016): 166–82.

10. Chapman and Milham, "The Personas' New Clothes." Another Microsoft

persona expert, Jonathan Grudin, reports that "teams live with their personas," talking about them in off hours and even mourning their "deaths" at the hands of unsympathetic managers; see "Why Personas Work: The Psychological Evidence," in Pruitt and Adlin, *The Persona Lifecycle: Keeping People in Mind throughout Product Design* (San Francisco: Morgan Kaufmann, 2006), 642–63 (656, 662). Grudin connects personas to fictional characterization in general but not specifically to personifications.

11. Produced not long after the December 31, 2008, federal bailout of Detroit automakers, when Ford was strongly motivated to show that it was "working smarter," the Antonella advertising campaign suggests that personification enables a new kind of thinking that has led, in turn, to a new kind of car. According to this narrative, the 2011 Fiesta is not only smaller and more fuel efficient than earlier models, but also better designed and—in a hard-to-articulate way ostensibly captured by the Antonella persona itself—more *stylish.*

12. Adlin and Pruitt, *The Essential Persona Lifecycle,* 27.

13. For Gregory the Great's *Commentary on the Song of Songs,* see *Expositiones in Canticum Canticorum, in Librum Primum Regum,* ed. Patrick Verbraken, O.S.B., Corpus Christianorum Series Latina 144 (Turnhout: Brepols, 1971), and *Gregory the Great on the Song of Songs,* trans. Mark DelCogliano (Collegeville, MN: Liturgical, 2012). Throughout the book, translations are mine unless otherwise noted. When a translation is specified, as here, I occasionally make adjustments for the sake of clarity.

14. On *enigma* as a term used synonymously with allegory during antiquity, see Peter Struck, "Allegory and Ascent in Neoplatonism," in *The Cambridge Companion to Allegory,* ed. Rita Copeland and Peter Struck (Cambridge: Cambridge University Press, 2010), 57–70 (69). On enigma as a subtype of allegory, distinct from yet capable of overlapping with personification, see Mary Carruthers, "Allegory without the Teeth: Some Reflections on Figurative Language in *Piers Plowman,*" *Yearbook of Langland Studies* 19 (2005): 27–43, and Curtis Gruenler, *"Piers Plowman" and the Poetics of Enigma: Riddles, Rhetoric, and Theology* (Notre Dame, IN: University of Notre Dame Press, 2017).

15. See Augustine, *On the Trinity,* 15.9.15, in *De Trinitate libri XV,* ed. W. J. Mountain and F. Glorie, Corpus Christianorum Series Latina 50–50A (Turnhout: Brepols, 1968), 2 vols., and *On the Trinity,* trans. Stephen McKenna (Washington, DC: Catholic University of America Press, 1963). Citations of the Bible refer to *Biblia Sacra iuxta Vulgatam Versionem,* ed. Robert Weber and Roger Gryson, 4th ed. (Stuttgart: Deutsche Bibelgesellschaft, 1994), and *Holy Bible: Douay-Rheims Version* (Charlotte, NC: Saint Benedict, 2009).

16. See Augustine, *Epistolae,* 55.21.39, *Patrologia Latina* 33 (1841), 61–1094 (223), and Gregory the Great, *Moralia in Job,* ed. M. Adriaen, Corpus Christianorum Series Latina 143, 143A, 143B (Turnhout: Brepols, 1979–85), 5.31.55, 6.37.58. Augustine characterizes knowledge as a "kind of machine through which the structure of charity is built up, which will remain in eternity, even after knowledge has been destroyed" (machina quaedam, per quam structura charitatis assurgat quae maneat in aeternum, etiam cum scientia destruetur). Gregory describes "the human mind lifted on high by the machine, as it were, of its contemplation" (humanus animus quadam suae contemplationis machina subleuatus), then asserts that "the power of love is a machine of the mind which when it draws the mind out of the world, lifts it on high" (machina quippe men-

tis est uis amoris quae hanc dum a mundo extrahit in alto sustollit). For discussions of these passages, see Mary Carruthers, *The Craft of Thought: Meditation, Rhetoric, and the Making of Images, 400–1200* (Cambridge: Cambridge University Press, 1998), 22–24.

17. Carruthers, *Craft of Thought*, 81, 22–24, 5.

18. Daniel Dennett, *Intuition Pumps and Other Tools for Thinking* (New York: Norton, 2013), 2, 4, 40.

19. I here follow critics including Maureen Quilligan, *The Language of Allegory: Defining the Genre* (1979; Ithaca, NY: Cornell University Press, 1992), and Elizabeth Fowler, *Literary Character: The Human Figure in Early English Writing* (Ithaca, NY: Cornell University Press, 2003), who have sought to revive interest in personification and its uses.

20. Paul de Man, *The Resistance to Theory* (Minneapolis: University of Minnesota Press, 1986), 48.

21. For a helpful summary of critical attitudes toward medieval allegory, see Carolynn Van Dyke, *Chaucer's Agents: Cause and Representation in Chaucerian Narrative* (Madison, NJ: Fairleigh Dickinson University Press, 2005), 30, 40–44.

22. Hans Vaihinger, *The Philosophy of "As If": A System of the Theoretical, Practical, and Religion Fictions of Mankind*, trans. C. K. Ogden (1925; Middletown, DE: Random Shack, 2016), xxvi, 67.

23. Medieval writers did not share Vaihinger's underlying critical positivism, which holds that even though there is no guarantee of correspondence between ideas and things, "practical fictions" such as man, freedom, etc., can nonetheless provide a kind of scaffolding for Kantian judgment.

24. Robert Myles, *Chaucerian Realism* (Woodbridge, Suffolk: D. S. Brewer, 1994), 1–4.

25. Kathleen M. Hewett-Smith, "Allegory on the Half-Acre: The Demands of History," *Yearbook of Langland Studies* 10 (1996): 1–22 (9).

26. See Kellie Robertson, *Nature Speaks: Medieval Literature and Aristotelian Philosophy* (Philadelphia: University of Pennsylvania Press, 2017), 3, 17, 49–51; Suzanne Conklin Akbari, *Seeing through the Veil: Optical Theory and Medieval Allegory* (Toronto: University of Toronto Press, 2004), 7–20; and Newman, *God and the Goddesses*, 33–35.

27. See Jon Whitman, *Allegory: The Dynamics of an Ancient and Medieval Technique* (Cambridge, MA: Harvard University Press, 1987), 90, and C. S. Lewis, *The Allegory of Love: A Study in Medieval Traditions* (Oxford: Oxford University Press, 1936), 66–73.

28. Sarah Kay, *The Place of Thought: The Complexity of One in Late Medieval French Didactic Poetry* (Philadelphia: University of Pennsylvania Press, 2007), xi.

29. Vaihinger, *Philosophy of "As If,"* 15 (italics in original).

30. Jill Mann, "Langland and Allegory [1991]," in *The Morton W. Bloomfield Lectures, 1989–2005*, ed. Daniel Donoghue, James Simpson, and Nicholas Watson (Kalamazoo, MI: Medieval Institute, 2010), 20–41 (22) (italics in original).

31. Thomas Walsingham, *Chronicon Angliae*, ed. Edward Maunde Thompson, Rolls Series 64 (London, 1874), 322.

32. David Lawton, "The Subject of *Piers Plowman*," *Yearbook of Langland Studies* 1 (1987): 1–30 (25).

33. Eric Hoover, "Debt Protestors Denounce Colleges for Broken Promises," *Chronicle of Higher Education*, Nov. 27, 2011, http://www.chronicle.com/article/Debt-Protesters-Lament-Higher/129902.

34. The "people's microphone" is a technique used to speak to a crowd when electronic amplification is either unavailable or prohibited. Audience members near the stage echo the speaker phrase by phrase, so that those further away can hear what is said.

35. Teskey, *Allegory and Violence*, 132.

36. Vaihinger, *Philosophy of "As If,"* 73.

37. For a more detailed critique of Teskey's account of personification, see Larry Scanlon, "Personification and Penance," *Yearbook of Langland Studies* 21 (2007): 1–29 (3–10).

38. English translations of Aristotle are those of Richard McKeon, ed., *The Basic Works of Aristotle* (New York: Random House, 1941), while Latin translations are taken from the series Aristoteles Latinus. Both are hereafter cited parenthetically. Where multiple medieval Latin translations survive, I cite the one with the widest circulation unless otherwise noted.

39. This Callias, known as Callias II, seems a likelier candidate than either his wealthy grandfather, about whom relatively little is known, or his spendthrift grandson, with whom the family line apparently ended.

40. Paul Vincent Spade, ed. and trans., *Five Texts on the Mediaeval Problem of Universals: Porphyry, Boethius, Abelard, Ockham* (Indianapolis: Hackett, 1994), viii.

41. James J. Paxson, *The Poetics of Personification* (Cambridge: Cambridge University Press, 1994), 46. Paxson's taxonomy remains valuable as a sensitive analysis of subtypes within personification allegory. For a fine-grained analysis of the many varieties of personification within a single text, see Lavinia Griffiths, *Personification in "Piers Plowman"* (Cambridge: D. S. Brewer, 1985).

42. Modern counterparts to these kinds of medieval personifications are not far to seek, from Orwell's beast personifications Snowball and Napoleon to the compound name of the titular character in Joss Whedon's *Buffy the Vampire Slayer* to *Star Trek*'s Spock as a personification of logic.

43. Jill Mann, "Allegory and *Piers Plowman*," in *The Cambridge Companion to "Piers Plowman,"* ed. Andrew Cole and Andrew Galloway (Cambridge: Cambridge University Press, 2014), 65–82 (67, 81). For a similar position, see Lawrence M. Clopper, "Langland and Allegory: A Proposition," *Yearbook of Langland Studies* 15 (2001): 35–59.

44. See Erich Auerbach, *Mimesis: The Representation of Reality in Western Literature*, trans. Willard R. Trask (1946; Princeton, NJ: Princeton University Press, 1953), 261, and Angus Fletcher, *Allegory: The Theory of a Symbolic Mode* (Ithaca, NY: Cornell University Press, 1964), 368, 325.

45. Teskey, *Allegory and Violence*, 3, 17.

46. In contrast to the others, Fletcher, *Allegory*, 325, warns that "we cannot . . . condemn allegory as an instrument of universal conformity, until we have admitted that it is also the chief weapon of satire."

47. De Man, *Resistance to Theory*, 27, 45.

48. De Man, *Resistance to Theory*, 48, 45, 11, 49-50. On the "rarefied or apotheosized" character of de Man's personification, see James Paxson, "Historicizing Paul de Man's Master Trope of Prosopopeia: Belgium's Trauma of 1940, the Nazi *Volkskörper*, and Versions of the Allegorical Body Politic," in *Historicizing Theory*, ed. Peter C. Herman (Albany: State University of New York Press, 2004), 69–97 (88).

49. Influenced by de Man, an important group of studies treat allegory as a purely verbal phenomenon, including Quilligan, *Language of Allegory*, and Rita Copeland, *Rhetoric, Hermeneutics, and Translation in the Middle Ages: Academic Traditions and Vernacular Texts* (Cambridge: Cambridge University Press, 1991).

50. De Man, *Resistance to Theory*, 27.

51. Johan Huizinga, *The Waning of the Middle Ages: A Study of the Forms of Life, Thought, and Art in France and the Netherlands in the Dawn of the Renaissance*, trans. Fritz Hopman (1924; Garden City, NY: Doubleday, 1954), 204, 218, 210.

52. Huizinga, *Waning of the Middle Ages*, 219, 205, 212, 210, 205, 209, 204, 218.

53. Huizinga, *Waning of the Middle Ages*, 213, 210.

54. Owen Barfield, *Saving the Appearances: A Study in Idolatry*, 2nd ed. (1957; Middletown, CT: Wesleyan University Press, 1988), 86. For a helpful discussion of the distinction between metaphysical and Cratylic realism and further examples of medievalist critics who conflate these categories, see Myles, *Chaucerian Realism*, 1–4.

55. See Jorge Luis Borges, "From Allegories to Novels," in *Selected Non-Fictions*, ed. Eliot Weinberger, trans. Esther Allen, Suzanne Jill Levine, and Weinberger (New York: Penguin Putnam, 1999), 337–340, and Sheila Delany, *Medieval Literary Politics: Shapes of Ideology* (Manchester: Manchester University Press, 1990), 41. Akbari, *Seeing through the Veil*, 20, offers a more moderate version of the same argument, while Noah D. Guynn, *Allegory and Sexual Ethics in the High Middle Ages* (New York: Palgrave, 2007), 5–6, follows Delany in characterizing personification as foremost among a group of "essentializing tropes" even as he departs from Delany in recognizing that "medieval intellectuals do not naively believe in the transparency of verbal signifiers to sublime essences."

56. Paxson, *Poetics of Personification*, 138 (italics in original).

57. James Paxson, "Response to 'Langland and Allegory: A Proposition,'" *Yearbook of Langland Studies* 15 (2001): 47–59 (51). In this later article, Paxson deemphasizes nominalism as a framework for medieval allegory in favor of an exploration of the various forms of realism supported by recent developments in cognitive science.

58. This trend is by no means universal. A number of recent studies of personification refreshingly step away from the binary of realism versus nominalism, including the essays by Tekla Bude, Julie Orlemanski, and Claire Waters in *Yearbook of Langland Studies* 33 (2019).

59. The "naïve realist" is not exclusively the construct of literary critics. Alain de Libera identifies him in the philosopher Paul Vincent Spade's introduction to the English translation of John Wyclif's *Tractatus de Universalibus*; see de Libera, *La Querelle des Universaux: De Platon à la Fin du Moyen Age* (Paris: Editions du Seuil, 1996), 17–20. For a valuable overview of the medieval debate over universals, see Gyula Klima, "The Medieval Problem of Universals," in *The Stanford Encyclopedia of Philosophy*, ed. Edward N. Zalta, Winter 2017 ed., https://plato.stanford.edu/entries/universals-medieval/.

60. On the contested history of the term *nominalism*, see William J. Courtenay, *Ockham and Ockhamism: Studies in the Dissemination and Impact of His Thought* (Leiden: Brill, 2008), 1–19.

61. J. M. Culkin, "A Schoolman's Guide to Marshall McLuhan," *Saturday Review*, March 18, 1967, 51–53, 70–72 (70).

CHAPTER ONE

1. Hesiod, *Works and Days: A Translation and Commentary for the Social Sciences*, trans. Walter C. Neale and David W. Tandy (Berkeley: University of California Press, 1996), 760.

2. See Morton Bloomfield, "A Grammatical Approach to Personification Allegory," *Modern Philology* 60 (1963): 161–71 (163), and Priscian, *Institutiones Grammaticae*, 12.6.18–19 in Heinrich Keil, ed., *Grammatici Latini* (Leipzig: Teubner, 1857–80, 1982), vol. 2.

3. Emma Stafford, *Worshipping Virtues: Personification and the Divine in Ancient Greece* (London: Duckworth, 2000), 10–11. On the relationship between these lines and Hesiod's larger poetic project, see Philip Hardie, *Rumour and Renown: Representations of "Fama" in Western Literature* (Cambridge: Cambridge University Press, 2012), 50–57.

4. Whitman, *Allegory*, 271 (italics in original). Paxson, *Poetics of Personification*, 6, quotes this passage approvingly, while Teskey, *Allegory and Violence*, 1-31, endorses a similar distinction between literary elites who are fully aware of the workings of their allegories and more pedestrian writers who forget or suppress the act of personification in the service of religious doctrine.

5. Steven Justice, "Did the Middle Ages Believe in Their Miracles?," *Representations* 103 (2008): 1–29.

6. Paul Veyne, *Did the Greeks Believe in Their Myths? An Essay on the Constitutive Imagination*, trans. Paula Wissing (Chicago: University of Chicago Press, 1988).

7. See Dunstan M. Lowe, "Personification Allegory in the *Aeneid* and Ovid's *Metamorphoses*," *Mnemosyne* 61 (2008): 414–435 (415). Classicists, of course, have their own blind spots, including a tendency to trace the afterlives to classical personifications directly to the early modern period, omitting all mention of medieval texts; see, e.g., Stafford, *Worshipping Virtues*, 1.

8. See Harold L. Axtell, *The Deification of Abstract Ideas in Roman Literature and Inscriptions* (1907; New Rochelle, NY: Caratzas, 1987), 9–48, and Amy C. Smith, *"Polis" and Personification in Classical Athenian Art* (Leiden: Brill, 2011), 2.

9. Stafford, *Worshipping Virtues*, 12 (italics in original).

10. Lowe, "Personification Allegory."

11. See, e.g., Cicero's *On the Nature of the Gods*, 2.23.60, which cites Terence's *Eunuch*, 4.5.6: "sine Cerere et Libero friget Venus" (Venus/Love grows cold without Ceres/Bread and Liber/Wine).

12. For this critical history, see Andreas Bendlin and H. Alan Shapiro, "Personification," in *Brill's New Pauly*, ed. Helmuth Schneider, Manfred Landfester, and Hubert Cancik (Leiden: Brill 2011).

13. On the scale and religious seriousness of later personification cults, see Stafford, *Worshipping Virtues*, 177, and Gaétan Thériault, *Le culte d'*Homonoia *dans les cités grecques* (Lyon: Maison de l'Orient Méditerranéen, 1996), 182–88.

14. Walter Burkert, *Greek Religion*, trans. John Raffan (Cambridge, MA: Harvard University Press, 1985), 186. On these negative characterizations of Roman religion, often as part of a teleological narrative about the spread of Christianity, see John Scheid, *An Introduction to Roman Religion*, trans. Janet Lloyd (Bloomington: Indiana University Press, 2003), 5–8.

15. On medieval knowledge of *On the Nature of the Gods*, see Nicolette Zeeman, "Mythography and Mythographical Collections," in *The Oxford History of Classical Reception in English Literature*, vol. 1, *800–1558*, ed. Rita Copeland (Oxford: Oxford University Press, 2016), 121–50 (143n16). In the same volume, Dallas G. Denery II argues that John of Salisbury likely did not have direct access to *On the Nature of the Gods*, even though he cites it by name in his *Policraticus*; see "John of Salisbury, Academic Scepticism, and Ciceronian Rhetoric," 377–90 (380).

16. Scheid, *Roman Religion*, 28.

17. Charlton Lewis and Charles Short, *A Latin Dictionary*, s.v. "consecro."

18. On the growing practice of deifying human beings during the late Republic, see Spencer Cole, *Cicero and the Rise of Deification at Rome* (Cambridge: Cambridge University Press, 2013).

19. The italics are those of the Loeb edition. They designate the language of Cicero's ideal laws, as distinct from his commentary.

20. The phrase "consecratur manu" has been treated as something of a crux but seems to reflect Lewis and Short, *Latin Dictionary*, s.v. "manus," sense 1: "manu, *with the hand, by hand*, i.e. *artificially*, opp. to naturally, by nature" (italics in original). The dictionary cites Cicero's own *Against Verres*, 2.2.4: "urbem pulcherrimam Syracusas, quae cum manu munitissima esset tum loci natura terra ac mari clauderetur" (Syracuse, that most beautiful city, which was not only strongly fortified by art, but also protected by its natural advantages, by the sea and ground around it), as well as the collocation "manu sata," referring to cultivated grains as contrasted with those growing wild, in Caesar's *Commentary on the Civil War*, 3.44.

21. Emile Durkheim, *The Elementary Forms of Religious Life*, trans. Carol Cosman (1912; Oxford: Oxford University Press, 2001), 257.

22. James R. Harrison, *Paul's Language of Grace in Its Graeco-Roman Context* (Tübingen: Mohr Siebeck, 2003), 284.

23. *On the Laws* survives in six manuscripts, all dated before 1200. The circulation of *On the Nature of the Gods* was wider but still limited, as described above. For its ambivalent reputation, see, e.g., Augustine, *City of God*, 5.9. Alexander Neckam tellingly misstates the dialogue's name when, in the midst of a list praising other works by Cicero, he notes that "some disapprove of the book called *De multitudine deorum* [*On the Multitude of Gods*]"; see Rita Copeland and Ineke Sluiter, eds., *Medieval Grammar and Rhetoric: Language Arts and Literary Theory, AD 300–1475* (Oxford: Oxford University Press, 2009), 537.

24. On the date and authorship of *On Style*, see Doreen C. Innes's introduction to the 1995 Loeb edition, 312–21. Paxson, *Poetics of Personification*, 12, and Daisy Delogu,

Allegorical Bodies: Power and Gender in Late Medieval France (Toronto: University of Toronto Press, 2015), 20, accept an older and now generally discredited attribution of the text to the Athenian orator Demetrius of Phalerum.

25. Rosalind Thomas, *Oral Tradition and Written Record in Classical Athens* (Cambridge: Cambridge University Press, 1989), 210.

26. Plato, *Menexenus*, 234c–235c. On the puzzles posed by the *Menexenus*, in which a comic dialogue frames what would otherwise seem to be a serious oration, see Franco V. Trivingo, "The Rhetoric of Parody in Plato's *Menexenus*," *Philosophy and Rhetoric* 42 (2009): 29–58 (29–30). The *Menexenus* features Socrates as its central character but is set some thirteen years after his death, prompting one critic to conclude that Socrates himself speaks as a ghost; see Bruce Rosenstock, "Socrates as Revenant: A Reading of the *Menexenus*," *Phoenix* 48 (1994): 331–47. Citations of Plato refer to *Plato: Complete Works*, ed. John M. Cooper (Indianapolis: Hackett, 1997).

27. On archaeological evidence for cults of the dead, see Carla M. Antonaccio, *An Archaeology of Ancestors: Tomb Cult and Hero Cult in Early Greece* (London: Rowman and Littlefield, 1995), and Susan E. Alcock, "Tomb Cult and the Post-Classical Polis," *American Journal of Archaeology* 95 (1991): 447–67.

28. On cults of female ancestors, see Jennifer Larson, *Greek Heroine Cults* (Madison: University of Wisconsin Press, 1995).

29. Smith, *"Polis" and Personification*, 27–39, 91–107.

30. Paxson, "Gender Personified," 78, identifies Demetrius as the point of origin for an inherently gendered rhetorical trope in which "individual personifications are women because Personification is a woman." I argue, in contrast, that Demetrius discusses masculine ancestors and feminine countries as parallel instances of prosopopoeia and thus treats gender as a variable to be manipulated. In classical Athens, the convention of personifying the Athenian people as a mature, bearded male depends not only on the grammatical gender of the noun *demos* but also on the close association between the *demos* and Athenian democracy, which limited the franchise to adult male citizens. It contrasts with the Athenian practice of representing rival city-states through either a feminine personification of the locality or a personification of its *demos* as a beardless youth. In both cases, Athens projects its power by assigning to its personified *demos* an active, penetrative role in the Greek sex-gender system, while assigning a passive, penetrated role to the city-states it seeks to dominate. On the Athenians' general use of personification to project political power, see Smith, *"Polis" and Personification*, 38–39, and K. W. Arafat, "State of the Art—Art of the State: Sexual Violence and Politics in Late Archaic and Early Classical Vase-Painting," in *Rape in Antiquity: Sexual Violence in the Greek and Roman Worlds*, ed. Susan Deacy and Karen F. Pierce (London: Duckworth, 1997), 97–121 (110–15).

31. On this ambiguity, see Paxson, *Poetics of Personification*, 18.

32. For a general account of the *manes*, see Charles W. King, "The Roman *Manes*: The Dead as Gods," in *Rethinking Ghosts in World Religions*, ed. Mu-chou Poo (Leiden: Brill, 2009), 95–114.

33. On religious rituals honoring the *manes*, see Robert Turcan, *The Gods of Ancient Rome: Religion in Everyday Life from Archaic to Imperial Times*, trans. Antonia Nevill (Edinburgh: Edinburgh University Press, 2000), 18–37.

34. Turcan, *Gods of Ancient Rome*, 144.

35. See Ronald Mellor, "The Goddess Roma," in *Aufstieg und Niedergang der Römischen Welt*, ed. Hildegard Temporini and Wolfgang Haase (Berlin: Walter de Gruyter, 1981), vol. 2, pt. 17, no. 2, 950–1030.

36. See Michael H. Crawford, *Roman Republican Coinage*, 2 vols. (Cambridge: Cambridge University Press, 1974), and A. M. Burnett and Andrew Burnett, "The Iconography of Roman Coin Types in the Third Century BC," *Numismatic Chronicle* 146 (1986): 67–75.

37. On this formula, see Jaime Alvar, "Matériaux pour l'étude de la formule 'sive deus, sive dea,'" *Numen* 32 (1985): 236–73; Ernest J. Ament, "Aspects of Androgyny in Classical Greece," in *Women's Power, Man's Game: Essays on Classical Antiquity in Honor of Joy K. King*, ed. Mary DeForest (Wauconda, IL: Bolchazy-Carducci, 1993), 1–31 (6); and Simon Hornblower, Antony Spawforth, and Esther Eidinow, *The Oxford Companion to Classical Civilization*, 2nd ed. (Oxford: Oxford University Press, 2014), s.v. "prayer."

38. Cicero, *Response of the Haruspices*, 25. On the use of divine testimony in Roman legal proceedings, see James R. McConnell Jr., *The Topos of Divine Testimony in Luke-Acts* (Eugene, OR: Pickwick, 2014), 23–73.

39. Paxson, *Poetics of Personification*, 52, cites Paul de Man, *The Rhetoric of Romanticism* (New York: Columbia University Press, 1984), 75–76, and J. Hillis Miller, *Versions of Pygmalion* (Cambridge, MA: Harvard University Press, 1990), 238.

40. See *The Norton Shakespeare*, ed. Stephen Greenblatt (New York: Norton, 1997). Parenthetical citations of Shakespeare refer to this edition.

41. In Rome, actors were usually foreigners or slaves and always barred from full citizenship due to their profession; see Timothy Moore, *Roman Theatre* (Cambridge: Cambridge University Press, 2012).

42. On judicial uses of *sordes* and their association with mourning see A. W. Lintott, *Violence in Republican Rome*, 2nd ed. (Oxford: Oxford University Press, 1999), 16–21; Jon Hall, *Cicero's Use of Judicial Theater* (Ann Arbor: University of Michigan Press, 2014), 40–63; and Kelly Olson, *Masculinity and Dress in Roman Antiquity* (London: Routledge, 2017), 91–103. On the distinction between *sordes* and *squalor*, see Leanne Bablitz, *Actors and Audience in the Roman Courtroom* (London: Routledge, 2007), 226n85.

43. Women observed a longer mourning period, in part because they did not generally participate in public life; see Susan Treggiari, *Roman Marriage: "Iusti Coniuges" from the Time of Cicero to the Time of Ulpian* (Oxford: Clarendon, 1991), 493–98.

44. On the *sordidatus* as an exile from the world of the living, see Michel Blonski, "Les sordes dans la via politique romaine: la saleté comme tenue de travail?" *Mètis* 6 (2008): 41–56.

45. Bablitz, *Actors and Audience*, 85.

46. See, e.g., "Literary Devices," https://literarydevices.net/personification/, and Melissa Brinks, "10 Personification Examples in Poetry, Literature, and More," Prep Scholar, SAT/ACT Prep Online Guides and Tips, https://blog.prepscholar.com/personification-examples-poetry-literature.

47. Paxson, *Poetics of Personification*, 18.

48. For a particularly dense cluster of uses of *fingere* and its derived forms to discuss personification, see Quintilian, *Institutes of Oratory,* 9.2.29–37.

49. The *Parliament of the Three Ages* combines both kinds of formative personification when Eld warns his audience, "Makes your mirrours bi me, men, bi youre trouthe," as a prelude to describing the Nine Worthies. See *"Wynnere and Wastoure" and "The Parlement of the Three Ages,"* ed. Warren Ginsberg (Kalamazoo, MI: TEAMS, 1992),1.290.

50. See Fiona Somerset, *Feeling like Saints: Lollard Writings after Wyclif* (Ithaca, NY: Cornell University Press, 2014), 137–65, and "Speaking in Person," in *Medieval Literary Voices: Embodiment, Materiality and Performance,* ed. Sif Rikhardsdottir and Louise Darcens (Manchester: Manchester University Press, 2021).

CHAPTER TWO

1. S. Georgia Nugent, *Allegory and Poetics: The Structure and Imagery of Prudentius' "Psychomachia"* (Frankfurt am Main: Verlag Peter Lang, 1985), 12.

2. See Danuta Shanzer, "Allegory and Reality: *Spes, Victoria,* and the Date of Prudentius' *Psychomachia," Illinois Classical Studies* 14 (1989): 347–63. Shanzer and most other critics assume that Prudentius had ceased writing by 410 because he does not mention the sack of Rome in that year.

3. Theodulf of Orléans, *De ordine baptismi,* ch. 12, *Patrologia Latina* 105 (1831), 231a. On Prudentius's manuscript tradition and early reception, see Maurice Lavarenne, *Prudence,* rev. ed. (Paris: Societé d'édition "Les belles lettres," 1948–61), 1:xvi–xxxiv, 3:25–46, and Maurice P. Cunningham, ed., *Aurelii Prudentii Clementis Carmina,* Corpus Christianorum Series Latina 126 (Turnhout: Brepols, 1966), x–xx.

4. On the *Psychomachia* in medieval curricula, see Ernst Robert Curtius, *European Literature and the Latin Middle Ages,* trans. Willard R. Trask (1948; Princeton, NJ: Princeton University Press, 1973), 48–54. A broader group of citations is collected in Eugene Bartlett Vest, "Prudentius in the Middle Ages" (PhD diss., Harvard University, 1932).

5. See Sinéad O'Sullivan, *Early Medieval Glosses on Prudentius' "Psychomachia": The Weitz Tradition* (Leiden: Brill, 2004), and Helen Woodruff, *The Illustrated Manuscripts of Prudentius* (Cambridge, MA: Harvard University Press, 1930).

6. See Joanne S. Norman, *Metamorphoses of an Allegory: The Iconography of the "Psychomachia" in Medieval Art* (New York: Peter Lang, 1988); Jennifer O'Reilly, *Studies in the Iconography of the Virtues and Vices in the Middle Ages* (New York: Garland, 1988), esp. 39–82; and Colum Hourihane, ed., *Virtue and Vice: The Personifications in the Index of Christian Art* (Princeton, NJ: Princeton University Press, 2000), 151–442.

7. See Lewis, *Allegory of Love,* 68; Carolynn Van Dyke, *Fiction of Truth: Structures of Meaning in Narrative and Dramatic Allegory* (Ithaca, NY: Cornell University Press, 1985), 20; and Carruthers, *Craft of Thought,* 144. Although Carruthers suggests that the *Psychomachia* was written as a schoolbook, the earliest surviving responses to the *Psychomachia,* dating from the later fifth century, consider it appropriate for highly literate adults.

8. Lewis, Allegory of Love, 69.

9. A. D. Nuttall, *Two Concepts of Allegory: A Study of Shakespeare's "The Tempest" and the Logic of Allegorical Expression* (London: Routledge and Kegan Paul, 1967), 37 (italics in original).

10. Lavarenne, *Prudence*, 3.11–12. For discussions of similar positions, see Van Dyke, *Fiction of Truth*, 29–35; John P. Hermann, *Allegories of War: Language and Violence in Old English Poetry* (Ann Arbor: University of Michigan Press, 1989), 9–17, and Whitman, *Allegory*, 88–91.

11. See Lewis, *Allegories of Love*, 68, and Lavarenne, *Prudence*, 3.12.

12. Newman, *God and the Goddesses*, 34, 40.

13. The advanced literacy required to parse Prudentius's text was both disproportionately available to men and normatively masculine. Since mastering the artificial language of the grammarians was understood as the beginning of self-mastery, this "masculine" literacy was also thought to lay a foundation for virtue; see Joseph Farrell, *Latin Language and Latin Culture: From Ancient to Modern Times* (Cambridge: Cambridge University Press, 2001), 52–83, and Peter Heather, "Literacy and Power in the Migration Period," in *Literacy and Power in the Ancient World*, ed. Alan K. Bowman and Greg Woolf (Cambridge: Cambridge University Press, 1994), 177–97.

14. Lewis and Short, *Latin Dictionary*, s.v. "habitus."

15. Carruthers, *Craft of Thought*, 167. While all critics acknowledge a relationship between the *Psychomachia* and the Pauline epistles, especially Ephesians 6:11–17, they differ in their assessment of its importance. For arguments in favor of a strong influence see, in addition to Carruthers, Ralph Hanna, "The Sources and the Art of Prudentius' *Psychomachia*," *Classical Philology* 72 (1977): 108–15. For arguments for a more attenuated influence, see Pier Franco Beatrice, "L'allegoria nella *Psychomachia* di Prudenzio," *Studia Patavina* 18 (1971): 25–73, and Macklin Smith, *Prudentius' "Psychomachia": A Reexamination* (Princeton, NJ: Princeton University Press, 1976), 127–29.

16. Kenneth R. Haworth, *Deified Virtues, Demonic Vices and Descriptive Allegory in Prudentius' "Psychomachia"* (Amsterdam: Adolf M. Hakkert, 1980), 74–87, builds upon earlier discussions by Lewis, *Allegories of Love*, 48–56; and Beatrice, "L'allegoria," 27–29.

17. On these parallels, see, e.g., Stephen A. Barney, *Allegories of History, Allegories of Love* (Hamden, CT: Archon, 1979), 76; Smith, *Prudentius' "Psychomachia,"* 291–94; Martha A. Malamud, *A Poetics of Transformation: Prudentius and Classical Mythology* (Ithaca, NY: Cornell University Press, 1989), 69–75; and Marc Mastrangelo, *The Roman Self in Late Antiquity: Prudentius and the Poetics of the Soul* (Baltimore: Johns Hopkins University Press, 2008), 27–28.

18. Paxson, *Poetics of Personification*, 69.

19. Malamud, *Poetics of Transformation*, 22–24, argues that Prudentius may have adopted a moderate position on cult statues.

20. S. Georgia Nugent, "*Virtus* or Virago? The Female Personifications of Prudentius's *Psychomachia*," in *Virtue and Vice*, ed. Hourihane, 13–28 (21–24).

21. Mary F. Foskett, *A Virgin Conceived: Mary and Classical Representations of Virginity* (Bloomington: Indiana University Press, 2002), 31–33.

22. I borrow the term *contrapasso* from Dante criticism, where it describes the relationship between sin and punishment in the *Inferno*. The only exception to the

rule of double death in the *Psychomachia* seems to be Wrath, who commits suicide by impaling herself on a javelin. Nugent notes, however, that Wrath foams at the mouth, a symptom associated with asphyxiation; see "Virtus or Virago?," 27n21.

23. Cf. Psalms 56:7: "They dug a pit before my face, and they are fallen into it" (Foderunt ante faciem meam foveam et inciderunt in eam).

24. See Cyprian of Carthage, *De mortalitate*, in *Patrologia Latina* 4 (1844), 581C–602B (585B), and *De zelo et livore*, in *Patrologia Latina* 4 (1844), 637D–52A (642B). Cyprian is cited by, e.g., Augustine, *Contra duas epistolas Pelagianiorum*, 4.10.27, in *Patrologia Latina* 44 (1841), 550–638 (629), and *Contra Julianum*, 2.8.25, in *Patrologia Latina* 44 (1841), 641–874 (690).

25. M. Clement Eagan, ed., *The Poems of Prudentius* (Washington, DC: Catholic University of America Press, 1965), 2:90.

26. On the use of the term *virtus* in the *Psychomachia*, see Nugent, *Allegory and Poetics*, 88–89. While Nugent asserts that for Pride, *virtus* "clearly refers to martial valor, independent of moral judgment," to my mind the poem's dueling uses of the term represent clashing moral codes.

27. On the god Virtus, who was closely associated with Bellona, see Glenys Lloyd-Morgan, "Nemesis and Bellona: A Preliminary Study of Two Neglected Goddesses," in *The Concept of the Goddess*, ed. Sandra Billington and Miranda Green (London: Routledge, 1996), 120–28 (125–26).

28. On the construction of a specifically virile military *virtus* in the Roman army, see Sara Elise Phang, *Roman Military Service: Ideologies of Discipline in the Late Republic and Early Principate* (Cambridge: Cambridge University Press, 2008), 73–109.

29. Galen, *On the Usefulness of the Parts of the Body*, trans. Margaret Tallmadge May (Ithaca, NY: Cornell University Press, 1968), 2.630 (14.6, 2.299). The Virtues' bloodlessness is an important theme for Pride, as seen in her references to "dried-out Sobriety," "white-faced Fasting," and "Modesty with scarce a tinge of blood" in her cheeks.

30. War rape was a recognized risk for soldiers as well as civilians and for mature men as well as women and adolescents of both sexes. By virtue of his defeat, a defeated soldier temporarily assumed the status of a slave or prostitute whose bodily integrity was not legally protected. See Amy Richlin, "Not before Homosexuality: The Materiality of the Cinaedus and the Roman Law against Love between Men," *Journal of the History of Sexuality* 3 (1993): 523–73 (559–60), and Phang, *Roman Military Service*, 94.

31. Both Augustus's *Lex Julia de maritandis ordinibus* and the more relaxed *Lex Papia Poppaea* of 9 CE codify marriage as the normative adult condition and levy penalties against members of the equestrian and senatorial classes who fail to marry upon reaching adulthood. On the social status of virginity in the late antique world, see Foskett, *A Virgin Conceived*.

32. In doing so, she links herself to the most important of Paul's "spirits of wickedness," the prideful fallen angel Lucifer.

33. On these echoes, see Eagan, *Poems of Prudentius*, 2:90.

34. Henri de Lubac, *Exégèse médiévale: Les quatre sense de l'Ecriture* (Paris: Aubier, 1959–64), 2.2.214.

35. Laura Cotogni, "Sovrapposizione di visioni e di allegorie nella *Psychomachia*

de Prudenzio," *Rendiconti della R. Accademia Nazionale dei Lincei*, ser. 6, vol. 12 (1936): 441–61 (441).

36. See Cotogni, "Sovrapposizione," 441, elaborated in Ralph Hanna, "The Sources and the Art of Prudentius' *Psychomachia*," *Classical Philology* 72 (1977): 108–15.

37. See Ambrose of Milan, *De Abraham*, 1.4.22, 2.7.41, in *Patrologia Latina* 14 (1845), 419–550, and *On Abraham*, trans. Theodosia Tomkinson (Etna, CA: Center for Traditionalist Orthodox Studies, 2000).

38. On the Christian relationship to Abraham as a father at once claimed and disowned, see Janet Adelman, *Blood Relations: Christian and Jew in "The Merchant of Venice"* (Chicago: University of Chicago Press, 2008), 38–65.

39. Jean-Louis Charlet notes this connection to the visual arts; see "Signification de la préface à la *Psychomachia* de Prudence," *Revue des études latines* 81 (2003): 232–51 (242). This use of *figura* differs from Auerbach's in its insistence that the figure is incomplete and must be continually redrawn or reengraved; see Erich Auerbach, "Figura," in *Scenes from the Drama of European Literature* (Minneapolis: University of Minnesota Press, 1984), 11–76, 229–37.

40. Carruthers, *Craft of Thought*, 145–46.

41. Carruthers, *Craft of Thought*, 146.

42. See Paula James, "Prudentius' *Psychomachia*: The Christian Arena and the Politics of Display," in *Constructing Identities in Late Antiquity*, ed. Richard Miles (London: Routledge, 1999), 70–94. Although critics have traditionally interpreted the *Psychomachia* as a purely internal struggle, James and others point out that many of the battles have an important historical dimension, from Faith's crowning of the martyrs in the arena to Avarice's attempt to disguise herself as a Roman matron to Discord Heresy's attack on the unity of the church.

43. *The Acts of the Christian Martyrs*, ed. and trans. Herbert Musurillo (Oxford: Clarendon, 1972), 106–31 (118–19). An even closer analogue might be the heroine of the Acts of Thecla, who fights in a provincial Roman arena, stripped and girdled like a gladiator; see J. L. Welch, "Cross-Dressing and Cross-Purposes: Gender Possibilities in the Acts of Thecla," in *Gender Reversals and Gender Cultures: Anthropological and Historical Perspectives*, ed. Sabrina Petra Ramet (London: Routledge, 1996), 66–78.

44. For a similar association between femininity and fictionality, see Newman, *God and the Goddesses*, 39–43.

45. On the phrase "old gods," see Ad Putter, "Prudentius and the Late Classical Biblical Epics of Juvencus, Proba, Sedulius, Arator, and Avitus," in *Oxford History of Classical Reception*, vol. 1, ed. Rita Copeland, 351–76 (367).

46. Carruthers, *Craft of Thought*, 44–59.

47. Nugent, "Virtus or Virago," 20 (italics in original).

48. Sarah Salih, *Versions of Virginity in Late Medieval England* (Woodbridge, Suffolk: D. S. Brewer, 2001), 42–106.

49. On virgin martyr hagiography as pornography, see Kathryn Gravdal, *Ravishing Maidens: Writing Rape in Medieval French Literature and Law* (Philadelphia: University of Pennsylvania Press, 1991), 21–41; Simon Gaunt, *Gender and Genre in Medieval French Literature* (Cambridge: Cambridge University Press, 1995), 180–233; Catherine

Innes-Parker, "Sexual Violence and the Female Reader: Symbolic 'Rape' in the Saints' Lives of the Katherine Group," *Women's Studies* 24 (1995): 205–17; and Robert Mills, *Suspended Animation: Pain, Pleasure and Punishment in Medieval Culture* (London: Reaktion, 2005), 106–44.

50. Smith, *Prudentius' "Psychomachia,"* 157.

51. The phrase "salutiferas . . . turmas" suggests a minimum of sixty Virtues. A *turma* was a division of the Roman cavalry consisting of either thirty or thirty-two men.

52. My discussion is indebted to Carolyn Dinshaw's speculations about female-to-male transsexuality in early Christian writings in *Chaucer's Sexual Poetics* (Madison: University of Wisconsin Press, 1989), 204–5n64.

53. Marc Mastrangelo, "Typology and Agency in Prudentius' Treatment of the Judith Story," in *The Sword of Judith: Judith Studies across the Disciplines*, ed. Kevin R. Brine, Elena Ciletti, and Henrike Lähnemann (Cambridge: OpenBook, 2010), 153–68 (155).

54. See, e.g., Barney, *Allegories of History*, 67–68; Brenda Machosky, "The Face That Is Not a Face: The Phenomenology of the Soul in the Allegory of the *Psychomachia*," *Exemplaria* 15 (2003): 1–38 (21–22); Quilligan, "Allegory and Female Agency," 173; Masha Raskolnikov, *Body against Soul: Gender and "Sowlehele" in Middle English Allegory* (Columbus: Ohio State University Press, 2009), 40; and Van Dyke, *Fiction of Truth*, 61.

55. Annunciation scenes depicting Mary reading as she receives the Holy Spirit likewise play on the physical and intellectual senses of *conceive*.

56. Mastrangelo, *Roman Self*, 5, notes that Prudentius makes a strong claim for his poetry as speaking with the authority of Scripture in his *Hamartigenia*: "Examine the holy book, O reader: you will find that the Lord spoke as I say" (Sanctam, lector, percense volumen; / quod loquor, invenies dominum dixisse) (624–25).

57. Jerome, *Commentaria in Epistolam ad Ephesios*, 3.654, in *Patrologia Latina* 26 (1845), 439–554 (533b–c), translated in Vern L. Bullough, "Medieval Medical and Scientific Views of Women," *Viator* 4 (1973): 485–501 (499).

58. Barney, *Allegories of History*, 70.

59. Ambrose held a similar position on the relationship between baptism and continence, or at least was understood as doing so; see Peter Brown, *The Body and Society: Men, Women, and Sexual Renunciation in Early Christianity* (New York: Columbia University Press, 1988), 349–65.

60. Lewis, *Allegory of Love*, 70.

61. Nugent, *Allegory and Poetics*, 44.

62. Van Dyke, *Fiction of Truth*, 51.

63. Nugent, "Virtus or Virago," 17; cf. *Aeneid* 4.216–18 and 9.614–20.

64. On these different senses of *habitus* and their translation from a classical to a Christian context, see Breen, *Imagining an English Reading Public, 1150–1400* (Cambridge: Cambridge University Press, 2010), esp. 43–79.

65. On the signifying value of matronly dress in the classical world, see Jonathan Edmondson, "Public Dress and Social Control in Late Republican and Early Imperial

Rome," in *Roman Dress and the Fabrics of Roman Culture*, ed. Edmondson and Alison Keith (Toronto: University of Toronto Press, 2008), 21–46.

66. On the punning relationship between the names Ratio and Operatio, see Nugent, *Allegory and Poetics*, 55.

67. Van Dyke, *Fiction of Truth*, 56.

68. Van Dyke, *Fiction of Truth*, 61.

69. Newman, *God and the Goddesses*, 49.

CHAPTER THREE

1. See Mann, "Allegory and *Piers Plowman*," 67 (italics in original).

2. Although Plato did not have consistent terms for universals and particulars, Aristotle understood himself as offering a theory of universals to rival Plato's own, and this understanding framed later Platonic as well as Aristotelian accounts; see Gail Fine, *On Ideas: Aristotle's Criticism of Plato's Theory of Forms* (Oxford: Clarendon, 1993), 20–43.

3. I follow Stephen Gersh, *Middle Platonism and Neoplatonism: The Latin Tradition* (Notre Dame, IN: University of Notre Dame Press, 1986), 1:1–50, in treating the once controversial designations "Middle Platonism" and "Neoplatonism" as purely chronological categories.

4. Gersh, *Middle Platonism*, 1:8–11, 53–74.

5. Both of these translations had largely disappeared from circulation by the sixth century, with the *Protagoras* surviving only in fragments quoted by Priscian and Donatus. See Raymond Klibansky, *The Continuity of the Platonic Tradition during the Middle Ages, Together with Plato's "Parmenides" in the Middle Ages and the Renaissance* (Millwood, NY: Kraus International, 1982), 21–22.

6. The Demiurge is characterized as *artifex* in Cicero's translation and *opifex* in that of Calcidius. Compare Cicero's "si pulcher est hic mundus et si probus eius artifex" to Calcidius's "si est . . . pulchritudine incomparabili mundus, opifexque et fabricator eius optimus" (29a). For Cicero's translation, see *De divination; De fato; Timaeus*, ed. Remo Giomini (Leipzig: Teubner, 1975). Parenthetical citations of Calcidius refer to *On Plato's "Timaeus,"* ed. and trans. John Magee (Cambridge, MA: Harvard University Press, 2016).

7. While *Timaeus* 28a lays the groundwork for this position, it does not specifically locate the changeless model for the created world in the mind of the Demiurge. On the later conflation of the form of the Good with the Demiurge and Aristotelian Unmoved Mover, see Lloyd P. Gerson, *From Plato to Platonism* (Ithaca, NY: Cornell University Press, 2014), 196–207.

8. This so-called "mutilated" tradition of the *Orator* contains at least thirty-eight manuscripts, the earliest dating from the ninth century, while the "integral" tradition derives from a manuscript discovered near Milan in 1421; see the classification of manuscripts in Ferdinand Heerdegen, ed., *M. Tulli Ciceronis ad M. Brutum Orator* (Leipzig: Teubner, 1884).

9. This association was so strong that Valerius Maximus, in his *Memorable Doings*

and Sayings, can praise the orator Maesia of Sentium only by denying her femininity: "Because she bore a man's spirit under the form of a woman, they called her Androgyne" (Quia sub specie feminae virilem animum gerebat, Androgynen appellabant) (8.3.1).

10. For Cicero's and Plotinus's influence on Augustine, see Maurice Testard, *Saint Augustin et Cicéron*, 2 vols. (Paris: Etudes Augustiniennes, 1958); Harald Hagendahl, *Augustine and the Latin Classics* (Göteborg: Universitetet, 1967), 1:35–169, 2:479–588; and Jean Pépin, "Augustin, 'Quaestio de Ideis': Les Affinités Plotiniennes," in *From Athens to Chartres: Neoplatonism and Medieval Thought. Studies in Honour of Edouard Jeauneau*, ed. Harm-Jan Westra (Leiden: Brill, 1992), 117–34. The English term "doxography" derives from a Neo-Latin coinage by Hermann Diels; see *Doxographi Graeci* (Berlin: Weidmann, 1879), but where Diels referred only to ancient compendia of teachings about physics, the term now encompasses a broader range of philosophical summaries; see Leonid Zhmud, "Revising Doxography: Hermann Diels and His Critics," *Philologus* 145 (2001): 219–43, and, on Augustine's use of doxographies, Aimé Solignac, "Analyse et Sources de la Question 'De Ideis,'" *Augustinus Magister* 1 (1954): 307–15 (312–15), and "Doxographies et Manuels dans la Formation Philosophique de Saint Augustin," *Recherches Augustiniennes et Patristiques* 1 (1958): 113–48. On Augustine's Platonism more broadly, see Janet Coleman, "The Christian Platonism of St. Augustine," in *Platonism and the English Imagination*, ed. Anna Baldwin and Sarah Hutton (Cambridge: Cambridge University Press, 1994), 27–37.

11. On the influence of Augustine's "On Ideas" during the Middle Ages, see M. J. F. M. Hoenen, *Marsilius of Inghen: Divine Knowledge in Late Medieval Thought* (Leiden: Brill, 1993), 121–56.

12. For this and subsequent citations, see Augustine, "De Ideis" in *De Diversis Quaestionibus Octoginta Tribus, De Octo Dulcitii Quaestionibus*, ed. Almut Mutzenbecher, Corpus Christianorum Series Latina 44A (Turnhout: Brepols, 1975), 70–73, and *Eighty-Three Different Questions: A New Translation*, trans. David L. Mosher (Washington, DC: Catholic University of America Press, 1982), 79–82. Throughout this section, I draw on the source analysis in Gersh, *Middle Platonism*, 1:403–13, and Solignac, "Analyse et Sources."

13. Augustine's use of *rationes* is not entirely new. Cicero uses it in *On the Republic* 3.22 and *On the Laws* 2.4 in connection with an entity recognizable as the form of Law, although he does not name the form as such or employ a distinctively philosophical idiom.

14. For this association between Christ and the forms, see Augustine, *The Literal Interpretation of Genesis* (*De Genesi ad Litteram*), 2.8, in *Patrologia Latina* 34 (1841), 246–485 (269–70); *On Genesis: Two Books on Genesis against the Manichees and On the Literal Interpretation of Genesis: An Unfinished Book*, trans. Roland J. Teske (Washington, DC: Catholic University of America Press, 1991), 143–88; and *City of God*, 11.10.

15. Pépin, "Augustin," 128–30 (129).

16. Pépin, "Augustin," 132–33, demonstrates that Plotinus, *The Enneads*, 4th ed., trans. Stephen MacKenna, revised B. S. Page (London: Faber and Faber, 1969), 1.6.7.30–34,

cites *Phaedrus* 247b and 250bc while Paul Henry, *Plotin et l'Occident: Firmicus Maternus, Marius Victorinus, Saint Augustin et Macrobe* (Louvain: Spicilegium Sacrum Lovaniense, 1934), 105–6, demonstrates that Augustine translates an overlapping section of *Enneads* 1.6.7 in *City of God* 10.16, where he also mentioned Plotinus by name.

17. See, e.g., Plotinus, *Enneads*, 1.6.8–9.

18. Translations of the *City of God* are based on Augustine, *The City of God against the Pagans*, ed. R. W. Dyson (Cambridge: Cambridge University Press, 1998).

19. For these arguments, see Gyula Klima, "Natures: The Problem of Universals," in *The Cambridge Companion to Medieval Philosophy*, ed. A. S. McGrade (Cambridge: Cambridge University Press, 2003), 196–207 (198), and Gregory T. Doolan, *Aquinas on the Divine Ideas as Exemplar Causes* (Washington, DC: Catholic University of America Press, 2008), 83–122.

20. On the tradition of Platonism as transmitted to Middle English mystics in particular, see Andrew Louth, "Platonism in the Middle English Mystics," in *Platonism and the English Imagination*, ed. Baldwin and Hutton, 52–64.

21. Mechthild of Magdeburg, *The Flowing Light of the Godhead*, trans. Frank Tobin (New York: Paulist, 1998), 4.13.

22. Mechthild of Magdeburg, *Flowing Light of the Godhead*, 2.26.

23. Mechthild of Magdeburg, *Flowing Light of the Godhead*, 1.1.

24. Newman, *God and the Goddesses*, 139 (italics in original).

25. *Debate between Winter and Spring*, in *Poetry of the Carolingian Renaissance*, ed. Peter Goodman (Norman, OK: University of Oklahoma Press, 1985), 144–49.

26. For a general overview of the field, see Peter Binkley, "Debates and Dialogues," in *Medieval Latin: An Introduction and Bibliographical Guide*, ed. F. A. C. Mantello and A. G. Rigg (Washington, DC: Catholic University of America Press, 1996), 677–81; on body-soul debates in particular, see Raskolnikov, *Body against Soul*.

27. Mechthild of Magdeburg, *Flowing Light of the Godhead*, 2.26.

28. Fletcher, *Allegory*, 40–41, 55.

29. Andrew Escobedo, *Volition's Face: Personification and the Will in Renaissance Literature* (Notre Dame, IN: University of Notre Dame Press, 2017), 15–95. While Escobedo's association between personification and the will works well for sins such as Avarice and Envy, it is harder to square with the many medieval personifications of mental faculties. How can a personified Reason represent the will, especially in a voluntarist model in which will and reason are understood as distinct, and sometimes opposed, mental faculties?

30. See Fletcher, *Allegory*, 43–44, and Escobedo, *Volition's Face*, 35.

31. To the extent that Escobedo distinguishes among types of personification, he defines those who enact their names as "daemonic characters," while those who merely denote their names are "signs" (*Volition's Face*, 40). He strongly emphasizes the former, however.

32. Fletcher, *Allegory*, 44–45, describes the daemon as "a voice that cannot be questioned," possessing both "a perfection worthy of respect and worship" and "the power to govern man's life, down to the finest detail." As we will see, this characterization rests on a selective reading of the Platonic tradition.

33. On the dangers of just such a descent into bestial nature, see, e.g., Augustine, *Two Books on Genesis against the Manichees*, 2.8, in *De Genesi Contra Manichaeos*, in *Patrologia Latina* 34 (1841), 173–220 (201–2), and *On Genesis*, trans. Teske, 45–141.

34. See Plotinus, *Enneads*, 1.6.7, and Xenocrates, Fragment 30. For Xenocrates's account of the forms, based on the limited surviving evidence, see John Dillon, *The Middle Platonists, 80 B.C. to A.D. 220* (Ithaca, NY: Cornell University Press, 1977), 28–30.

35. Alcinous, *The Handbook of Platonism*, trans. John Dillon (Oxford: Clarendon, 1993), 9.2.

36. See Gersh, *Middle Platonism*, 1:290–91.

37. The understanding of the daemon as an interior quality of the soul, akin to conscience or self-consciousness, is not a modern invention. It can be traced to an aphorism attributed to Heraclitus, a contemporary of Parmenides: "ethos anthropos daimon," or "character is for man his daemon." See Burkert, *Greek Religion*, 179–81, 317, 331–32.

38. See Vincent Hunink, "Plutarch and Apuleius," in *The Statesman in Plutarch's Works*, ed. Jeroen Bons, Ton Kessels, Dirk M. Schenkeveld, and Lukas de Blois (Leiden: Brill, 2004), 1:251–60 (256).

39. Jean Beaujeu, ed., *Opuscules Philosophiques et Fragments*, by Apuleius (Paris: Société d'Edition "Les Belles Lettres," 1973), xxxv–xlv, identifies some twenty manuscripts of Apuleius's collected philosophical works and a dozen more containing only *On the God of Socrates*. *On the God of Socrates* is also excerpted in Augustine's *City of God*, John of Salisbury's *Polycraticum*, and Vincent of Beauvais's *Speculum Doctrinale*.

40. For Apuleius's self-description as a "Platonic philosopher" (Platonico philosopho), see *Apology* 10.6, in Apuleius, *Pro Se de Magia*, 2 vols., ed. Vincent Hunink (Amsterdam: Gieben, 1997), and *Apuleius: Rhetorical Works*, trans. Stephen Harrison, John Hilton, and Hunink (Oxford: Oxford University Press, 2001), 11–121. For modern critical accounts of Apuleius's demonology, see Beaujeu, *Opuscules*, 183–247; Dillon, *Middle Platonists*, 317–20; Gersh, *Middle Platonism*, 1:215–328; Gerald Sandy, *The Greek World of Apuleius: Apuleius and the Second Sophistic* (Leiden: Brill, 1997), 191–213; and S. J. Harrison, *Apuleius: A Latin Sophist* (Oxford: Oxford University Press, 2000), 136–73.

41. Parenthetical citations of *On the God of Socrates* refer to *Liber de Deo Socratis*, in Apuleius, *De Philosophia Libri*, ed. Claudio Moreschini (Stuttgart: Teubner, 1991), 1–38, and *Apuleius: Rhetorical Works*, trans. Harrison, Hilton, and Hunink, 185–216.

42. Apuleius acknowledges malevolent beings in the lower two orders of *daemones* but neither claims nor disclaims their presence in the highest order.

43. Peter Dronke considers Calcidius's tendency toward personification to be his most original contribution to the *Timaeus* and its tradition; see *The Spell of Calcidius: Platonic Concepts and Images in the Medieval West* (Florence: Edizioni del Galluzzo, 2008), 21–33.

44. Modern English here forces a decision about whether to refer to matter with the animate pronouns *she, her*, or the inanimate pronouns *it, its*. Latin demands no such choice.

45. On Dionysian Neoplatonism as transmitted to the Middle Ages, see M.-D. Chenu, *Nature, Man, and Society in the Twelfth Century: Essays on New Theological*

Perspectives in the Latin West, trans. Jerome Taylor and Lester K. Little (Chicago: University of Chicago Press, 1968), 79–145, and A. J. Minnis, "The Dionysian Imagination: Thomas Gallus and Robert Grosseteste," in *Medieval Literary Theory and Criticism, c. 1100–c. 1375*, ed. Minnis and A. B. Scott (Oxford: Clarendon, 1988), 165–96. On the ancient symbol and its afterlife, see Peter Struck, *Birth of the Symbol: Ancient Readers at the Limits of Their Texts* (Princeton, NJ: Princeton University Press, 2004).

46. Apuleius refers to Socrates's daemon as a god in the title of his work, as a *lar* at 17.157, and as a disembodied spirit at, e.g., 18.162. I follow Gersh, *Middle Platonism*, 1:314–15, in seeing these inconsistencies as signs of fluidity rather than authorial incompetence.

47. Paxson, *Poetics of Personification*, 7. Venus also appears in, e.g., the *Parliament of Fowls*, the *Complaint of Nature*, the *Roman de la Rose*, and the *Confessio Amantis*.

48. On this ancient tradition of allegoresis, see, e.g., Robert Lamberton, *Homer the Theologian: Neoplatonist Allegorical Reading and the Growth of the Epic Tradition* (Berkeley: University of California Press, 1989); Luc Brisson, *How Philosophers Saved Myths: Allegorical Interpretation and Classical Mythology*, trans. Catherine Tihanyi (Chicago: University of Chicago Press, 2004); and Glenn Most, "Hellenistic Allegory and Early Imperial Rhetoric," in *Cambridge Companion to Allegory*, ed. Copeland and Struck, 26–38.

49. For an overview of the scholarship on this topic, see Zeeman, "Mythography and Mythographical Collections."

50. Winthrop Wetherbee, *Platonism and Poetry in the Twelfth Century: The Literary Influence of the School of Chartres* (Princeton, NJ: Princeton University Press, 1972), 37. Beyond this mention, Wetherbee devotes little attention to personification as such.

51. Wetherbee, *Platonism and Poetry*, 93. Cf. William of Conches, *Glosae super Boetium*, ed. Lodi Nauta, Corpus Christianorum Continuatio Medievalis 158 (Turnhout: Brepols, 1999), 1.m1.

52. On heteronormative masculinity in Neoplatonic allegory, see Jan M. Ziolkowski, *Alan of Lille's Grammar of Sex: The Meaning of Grammar to a Twelfth-Century Intellectual* (Boston: Medieval Academy of America, 1985).

CHAPTER FOUR

1. On the relationship between Plato's prison dialogues and Boethius's *Consolation of Philosophy*, see Danuta Shanzer, "The Death of Boethius and the *Consolation of Philosophy*," *Hermes* 112 (1984): 352–66, and John Magee, "Boethius' Anapestic Dimiters (Acatalectic), with Regard to the Structure and Argument of the *Consolatio*," in *Boèce ou la Chaîne des Savoirs: Actes du Colloque International de la Fondation Signer-Polignac*, ed. Alain Galonnier (Louvain: Editions Peeters, 2003), 147–69 (149-50).

2. See Pierre Courcelle, "Le visage de Philosophie," *Revue des Etudes Anciennes* 70 (1968): 110–20, and "Le personnage de Philosophie dans la littérature latine," *Journal des Savants* (1970): 209–52, and Joachim Gruber, *Kommentar zu Boethius "de Consolatione Philosophiae"* (1978; Berlin: de Gruyter, 2006).

3. Augustine, *Against the Academicians*, 2.2.5–2.3.7, cf. *Confessions* 7.9.13, 7.20.26, 8.2.3.

4. John Marenbon, *Boethius* (Oxford: Oxford University Press, 2003), 154–63.

5. See Friedrich Klingner, *De Boethii consolatione Philosophiae* (Berlin: Weidmann, 1921), 117, and Wendy Elgersma Helleman, *The Feminine Personification of Wisdom: A Study of Homer's Penelope, Cappadocian Macrina, Boethius' Philosophia, and Dante's Beatrice* (Lewiston, ME: Edwin Mellen, 2009), 137–205.

6. See Pierre Courcelle, *La "Consolation de Philosophie" dans la Tradition Littéraire: Antécédents et Postérité de Boèce* (Paris: Etudes Augustiniennes, 1967), 337–44, and *Late Latin Writers and Their Greek Sources*, trans. Harry E. Wedeck (Cambridge, MA: Harvard University Press, 1969), 318–22.

7. Joel C. Relihan, *The Prisoner's Philosophy: Life and Death in Boethius' "Consolation"* (Notre Dame, IN: University of Notre Dame Press, 2006). For critical reaction to Relihan, see Marenbon, *Boethius*, 161–62, and Danuta Shanzer, "Interpreting the *Consolation*," in *The Cambridge Companion to Boethius*, ed. John Marenbon (Cambridge: Cambridge University Press, 2009), 228–54 (235–36).

8. For a comprehensive account of these parallels, see Joachim Gruber, "Die Erscheinung der Philosophie in der *Consolatio Philosophiae* des Boethius," *Rheinisches Museum für Philologie* 112 (1969): 166–86. For a helpful summary, see Marenbon, *Boethius*, 153.

9. Homer, *Iliad*, trans. Richmond Lattimore (Chicago: University of Chicago Press, 1951), 4.442–43.

10. Joel C. Relihan, "Old Comedy, Menippean Satire, and Philosophy's Tattered Robes in Boethius' *Consolation*," *Illinois Classical Studies* 15 (1990): 183–94 (188).

11. Ann W. Astell, *Job, Boethius, and Epic Truth* (Ithaca, NY: Cornell University Press, 1994), 41.

12. Translations are based on Joel Relihan, trans., *The Consolation of Philosophy* by Boethius (Indianapolis: Hackett, 2001).

13. For this parallel, see Lamberton, *Homer the Theologian*, 276, c.f. *Iliad* 5.127-28.

14. Courcelle, *Consolation de Philosophie*, 21.

15. Marenbon, *Boethius*, 154.

16. Lamberton, *Homer the Theologian*, 94.

17. Marenbon, *Boethius*, 154. More troubling for my argument is, perhaps, Philosophy's quotation of *Iliad* 4.6.53 in the original Greek. Although Relihan renders it "But it is hard to explain all these things as if I were a goddess," Boethius's use of the masculine *theos* (god) rather than the feminine *thea* (goddess) suggests a less personal interpretation.

18. I have emended Relihan's *demons* to *daemons* in order to avoid the former's negative connotations. *Sollertia*, meaning skill, quickness of mind, ingenuity, has largely positive associations.

19. See, e.g., *Consolation* 4.2.22: "I said: Weave in your other arguments; for there is no one who is in doubt that the man who has the power of his natural functioning is stronger than the man who cannot do the same" ("Contexe," inquam, "cetera; nam quin naturalis officii potens eo qui idem nequeat valentior sit, nullus ambigat").

20. Newman, *God and the Goddesses*, 320.

21. On this cognitive hierarchy and the divinity of the formal knowledge at its apex, see Elaine Scarry, "The Well-Rounded Sphere: The Metaphysical Structure of the *Consolation of Philosophy*," in *Essays in the Numerical Criticism of Medieval Literature*, ed. Caroline D. Eckhardt (Lewisburg, PA: Bucknell University Press, 1980), 91–140.

22. Peter Dronke, *Verse with Prose from Petronius to Dante: The Art and Scope of the Mixed Form* (Cambridge, MA: Harvard University Press, 1994), 41.

23. Winthrop Wetherbee, "The *Consolation* and Medieval Literature," in *Cambridge Companion to Boethius*, ed. Marenbon, 279–302 (284).

24. See Mark Miller, *Philosophical Chaucer: Love, Sex, and Agency in the "Canterbury Tales"* (Cambridge: Cambridge University Press, 2004), 111–51, and Jessica Rosenfeld, *Ethics and Enjoyment in Late Medieval Poetry: Love after Aristotle* (Cambridge: Cambridge University Press, 2011), 135–45. Miller's position contrasts with that of Seth Lerer, who in *Boethius and Dialogue: Literary Method in "The Consolation of Philosophy"* (Princeton, NJ: Princeton University Press, 1985), regards dialectic as an obstacle to be transcended.

25. Relihan, "Old Comedy," 187–90.

26. The Muses are masked in their imagined costumes as "meretriculas," Fortune initially presents a masked face to her followers, and Philosophy is masked when she speaks "through the mouth of Plato" (Platonis ore) (2.8.1–2, 1.4.5).

27. In the *Republic*, Plato objects to Homeric epic on the grounds that it misrepresents the gods as imperfect beings.

28. On Philosophy's association with death, see Shanzer, "The Death of Boethius," and Relihan, *The Prisoner's Philosophy*, 59–74.

29. Relihan, *The Prisoner's Philosophy*, 69.

30. In the *Phaedo*, Socrates describes participation as a "second best" explanation of causes, which he pursues because he has not been able to find a more definitive explanation (99c–d).

31. Lerer, *Boethius and Dialogue*, 231–36.

32. For a valuable reading of the *Consolation* as protreptic—that is, as a work that "teaches ethics by facilitating identification between its reader and its narrator who is also the protagonist of an ethical quest for truth," see Eleanor Johnson, *Practicing Literary Theory in the Middle Ages: Ethics and the Mixed Form in Chaucer, Gower, Usk, and Hoccleve* (Chicago: University of Chicago Press, 2013), 1–37 (9–10).

33. Dronke, *Verse with Prose*, 46 (italics in original).

34. Andrew Galloway, *The Penn Commentary on "Piers Plowman,"* vol. 1 (Philadelphia: University of Pennsylvania Press, 2006), 150.

35. Newman, *God and the Goddesses*, 33–35, 305.

36. See, e.g., Anne Middleton, "Narration and the Invention of Experience: Episodic Form in *Piers Plowman*," in *The Wisdom of Poetry: Essays in Early English Literature in Honor of Morton W. Bloomfield*, ed. Larry D. Benson and Siegfried Wenzel (Kalamazoo, MI: Medieval Institute, 1982), 91–122, 280–83 (98); Eleanor Johnson, "*Reddere* and Refrain: A Meditation on Poetic Procedure in *Piers Plowman*," *Yearbook of Langland Studies* 30 (2016): 3–27 (9); Maura Nolan, "The Fortunes of *Piers Plowman* and Its Readers," *Yearbook of Langland Studies* 20 (2006): 1–41 (13–14); and Frank Grady, "Chaucer's Langland's Boethius," *Yearbook of Langland Studies* 32 (2018): 271–87 (esp. 278).

37. Wetherbee, "The *Consolation* and Medieval Literature," 283; see also Wetherbee, *Platonism and Poetry*, 74–82, 158–86.

38. William E. Heise, "The Menippean Boethius in the Personification Allegories of the Middle Ages," in Relihan, *The Prisoner's Philosophy*, 111–26.

39. The primary locus for these discussions is the prisoner's statement, in *Consolation* 1.4, that Philosophy cannot be a wicked spirit because she teaches him first and foremost to follow God. The commentators caution against interpreting her as a daemon because they consider all such beings—including those regarded as benign within pagan Neoplatonism—to be demons in the Christian sense. See William of Conches, *Glosae super Boetium*, 1.4.106–112; Nicholas Trevet, *Expositio super Boetio de Consolatione*, ed. E. T. Silk, 1.4, 113–16; and María del Carmen Olmedilla Herrero, "Edición crítica de los comentarios de Guillermo de Aragón al *De Consolatione Philosophiae de Boecio*" (Ph.D. diss., Universidad Complutense de Madrid, 1997), 3.m9, 188. Subsequent citations refer to these editions, only the first of which has been published. Silk's partially revised typescript is available at http://campuspress.yale.edu/trevet/, while Dr. Herrero kindly shared with me a copy of her dissertation.

40. On William of Conches, see Nauta's introduction to his edition as well as Minnis and Scott, *Medieval Literary Theory*, 113–64, and Wetherbee, *Platonism and Poetry*, esp. 36–48, 92–104. For a general overview of the commentary tradition, see Rosalind C. Love, "The Latin Commentaries on Boethius' *De Consolatione Philosophiae* from the 9th to the 11th Centuries," in *A Companion to Boethius in the Middle Ages*, ed. Noel Harold Kaylor Jr. and Philip Edward Phillips (Leiden: Brill, 2012), 75–133, and Lodi Nauta, "The *Consolation*: The Latin Commentary Tradition, 800–1700," in *Cambridge Companion to Boethius*, ed. Marenbon, 255–78.

41. Minnis and Scott, *Medieval Literary Theory*, 120.

42. Macrobius, *Commentary on the Dream of Scipio*, 1.2.9, in *"Saturnalia": apparatu critico instruxit, "In Somnium Scipionis Commentarios" selecta varietate lectionis*, vol. 2, ed. Jacob Willis, 2nd ed. (Stuttgart: Teubner, 1994), and *Commentary on the Dream of Scipio*, trans. William Harris Stahl (New York: Columbia University Press, 1990).

43. Nauta, *Glosae super Boetium*, xxxvii–xxxviii. For more detailed discussions of William's use of *integumenta*, see Edouard Jeauneau, "L'Usage de la notion d'*integumentum* à travers les gloses de Guillaume de Conches," *Archives d'Histoire Doctrinale et Littéraire du Moyen Age* 24 (1957): 35–100; Peter Dronke, *Fabula: Explorations into the Uses of Myth in Medieval Platonism* (Leiden: Brill, 1985), 13–78; and Jane Chance, *Medieval Mythography: From Roman North Africa to the School of Chartres, AD 433–1177* (Gainesville: University of Florida Press, 1994), 1: 400–44.

44. Wetherbee, *Platonism and Poetry*, 93.

45. Wetherbee, *Platonism and Poetry*, 96.

46. William's conventional definition of prosopopoeia resembles the one in Geoffrey of Vinsauf's *Documentum de modo et arte dictandi et versificandi*, 2.2.22: "Prosopopeia est conformatio novae personae, quando scilicet res non loquens introducitur tamquam loquens"; see Edmond Faral, ed., "Les arts poetiques du xiième et xiiième siècle: Recherches et documents sur la technique littéraire du moyen âge," *Bibliothèque de l'Ecole des Hautes Etudes* 238 (1923): 263–320 (275).

47. See Dronke, *Fabula*, 27–29.

48. I here depart from Nauta's edition, which capitalizes "Philosophy" as a proper name.

49. For this critical history and its shortcomings, see A. J. Minnis and Lodi Nauta, "*More Platonico Loquitur*: What Nicholas Trevet Really Did to William of Conches," in *Chaucer's "Boece" and the Medieval Tradition of Boethius*, ed. Minnis (Woodbridge, Suffolk: D. S. Brewer, 1993), 1–33 (1–11).

50. Minnis and Nauta, "More Platonico Loquitur," 33.

51. Winthrop Wetherbee, "The *Consolation* and Medieval Literature," in the *Cambridge Companion to Boethius*, ed. Marenbon, 279–302 (282). On Trevet's commentary and its relationship to the *Boece*, see most recently Tim William Machan, ed., *Sources of the "Boece"* (Athens: University of Georgia Press, 2005), 3–23.

52. This quotation is drawn from a variant reading of Ecclesiasticus 51:26: "in sapientia ejus luxit anima mea; et ignorantias meas illuminavit" (my soul shone with her wisdom, and she illuminated my ignorance). The usual modern reading is "insapientia eius luxi" (I lamented my ignorance of her).

53. Melinda E. Nielsen notes that for Trevet these reasons comprise a unified *triplex ratio* rather than, as for William of Conches, a series of independent and potentially mutually exclusive alternatives; see "Translating Lady Philosophy: Chaucer and the Boethian Corpus of Cambridge, University Library MS Ii.3.21," *Chaucer Review* 51 (2016): 209–26 (214–16).

54. This dating, now widely accepted, was first proposed by Roberto Crespo, "Il prologo alla traduzione della *Consolatio Philosophiae* di Jean de Meun e il commento di Guglielmo d'Aragona," in Willem den Boer et al., *Romanitas et Christianitas: Studia Iano Henrico Waszink oblata* (Amsterdam: North Holland, 1973), 55–70. On William as "arch-Aristotelian," see Minnis and Nauta, "More Platonico Loquitur," 33.

55. On Jean de Meun's translation, see V. L. Dedeck-Héry, ed., "Boethius' *De Consolatione* by Jean de Meun," *Mediaeval Studies* 14 (1952): 165–275, and Glynnis M. Cropp, "Boethius in Medieval France: Translations of the *De Consolatione Philosophiae* and Literary Influence," in *Companion to Boethius in the Middle Ages*, ed. Kaylor and Phillips, 319–54 (324–25, 336–55). On the anonymous translation, see Glynnis M. Cropp, "Le Prologue de Jean de Meun et *Le Livre de Boece de Consolacion*," *Romania* 103 (1982): 278–98, and *Le Livre de Boece de Consolacion* (Geneva: Droz, 2006), 15–17.

56. On *habitus* as a virtuous second nature, inculcated by a personified Grammar, see Breen, *Imagining an English Reading Public*, 80–108.

57. Relihan, "Old Comedy," 189.

58. Crespo's edition, based on Erfurt, Wissensch. Bibl. MS Amplon. F.358, adds the following lines, which if anything strengthen my point: "Talis autem modus tractandi in genere dicitur didascalicus in quo duplex persona confingitur, scilicet docti et docentis, aut laborantis eciam et medentis. Hic autem laborantis et medentis componuntur persone quia dolor et turbacio animi ex contingentibus infortuniis ad mentis infirmitatem debenture, consolacio vero et resistencia in eisdem ad perfectionem intellectus et bonitatem ipsius, que nichil aliud sunt quam sanitas mentis nostre. Et ideo B[o]ecius in libro iste sic procedit" (59). Minnis and Scott, *Medieval Literary Theory*, 331, translate as follows: "This mode of treatment is called didactic (*didascalicus*) in terms of genre,

in which two characters are feigned, one who is taught and the other who teaches, or one who is suffering and the other who heals. In this work, the two characters of the sufferer and the healer are united in one person [i.e., Boethius], because pain and mental turmoil arising out of misfortunes are due to the weakness of the mind, while consolation and a will to resist in these misfortunes are due to the perfecting of the intellect and its goodness, in which qualities consist nothing less than the healthy state of our mind. And so, Boethius in his book proceeds as follows."

59. Rosenfeld, *Ethics and Enjoyment*, 141–43, sees this description of the author as a break with William of Conches's Platonism, deriving it instead from William of Aragon's Aristotelian commitment to sense perception as the basis of human knowledge. While I find greater common ground between the two commentaries, I concur that William of Aragon's emphasis on persevering through pain rather than overcoming or transcending it has Aristotelian overtones.

60. On the wider accommodation of the *Consolation* to the genre of advice to princes, as evidenced by patterns of dedication, citation, and juxtaposition within manuscripts, see A. J. Minnis, *Fallible Authors: Chaucer's Pardoner and Wife of Bath* (Philadelphia: University of Pennsylvania Press, 2008), 320, and Glynnis M. Cropp, "The Medieval French Tradition," in *Boethius in the Middle Ages: Latin and Vernacular Traditions of the "Consolatio Philosophiae,"* ed. Marten J. F. M. Hoenen and Lodi Nauta (Leiden: Brill, 1997), 243–65 (247, 252). On late-medieval vernacular narratives that use the *Consolation* to define an aristocratic rather than ascetic identity, see Elizabeth Elliott, *Remembering Boethius: Writing Aristocratic Identity in Late Medieval French and English Literatures* (Farnham: Ashgate, 2012), and the essays collected in Catherine E. Léglu and Stephen J. Milner, eds., *The Erotics of Consolation: Desire and Distance in the Late Middle Ages* (New York: Palgrave Macmillan, 2008).

61. See, e.g., *Consolation* 5.5.5–6: "What if sense and imagination were to speak against rational argument, and say that the universal which reason thinks it gazes upon is nothing at all?" (Quid igitur, si ratiocinationi sensus imaginatioque refragentur, nihil esse illud universale dicentes quod sese intueri ratio putet?)

CHAPTER FIVE

1. Mann, "Allegory and *Piers Plowman*," 67.

2. Paxson, *Poetics of Personification*, 138.

3. Mann, "Allegory and *Piers Plowman*," 81.

4. Newman, *God and the Goddesses*, 33–34.

5. Akbari, *Seeing through the Veil*, 14.

6. Akbari, *Seeing through the Veil*, 232. For a more detailed critique of Akbari's disenchantment model of allegory, see Scanlon, "Personification and Penance," 3–10.

7. Mann, "Langland and Allegory," 25–26, 36.

8. Robertson, *Nature Speaks*, 50–51.

9. See, inter alia, Judson Boyce Allen, *The Ethical Poetic of the Later Middle Ages* (Toronto: Toronto University Press, 1982); James Simpson, *Sciences and the Self in Medieval Poetry: Alan of Lille's "Anticlaudianus" and John Gower's "Confessio Amantis"*

(Cambridge: Cambridge University Press, 1995); Miller, *Philosophical Chaucer*; and Rosenfeld, *Ethics and Enjoyment*.

10. Parenthetical citations of Porphyry's *Isagoge* refer to *Porphyrii Isagoge Translatio Boethii et anonymi fragmentum vulgo vocatum "Liber Sex Principiorum,"* in *Aristoteles Latinus*, ed. Lorenzo Minio-Palluelo (Bruges-Paris: Desclée de Brouwer, 1966), 1.6–7:1–32 and Spade, *Five Texts*, 1–19. I adopt Spade's numbering system for ease of reference.

11. Porphyry here lays the foundation for Albert the Great's influential classification of universals as *ante rem, in re*, and *post rem*. Universals *ante rem* exist separately from and prior to particulars, whether in the Platonic realm of forms or in the mind of the Christian God, while universals *in re* exist within particulars as the formal element of hylomorphic compounds, and universals *post rem* are produced in the human mind by cognizing particulars. See Albertus Magnus, *De Praedicabilibus*, tract. 2, in *Opera Omnia*, vol. 1, ed. E. Borgnet (Paris: Vives, 1890–99).

12. Boethius, *Second Commentary on Porphyry's "Isagoge,"* 1.1.28–32. Citations refer to Boethius, *In Isagogen Porphyrii Commenta*, ed. Samuel Brandt, Corpus Scriptorum Ecclesiasticorum Latinorum 48 (Vienna: F. Tempsky, 1906), 133–348, and Spade, *Five Texts*, 20–25. I adopt Spade's numbering system for ease of reference.

13. Beginning in the eleventh century, Boethius also proved invaluable to the *magistri* who sought to piece together an Aristotelian metaphysics through the commentary tradition and a systematic search for copies of Aristotle's lost works. These resources allowed John the Sophist, Roscelin of Campiègne, Peter Abelard, and others to develop versions of nominalism in the late eleventh and early twelfth centuries, before Latin translations of the *Metaphysics* became widely available; see Irven M. Resnick, "Odo of Tournai, the Phoenix, and the Problem of Universals," *Journal of the History of Philosophy* 35 (1997): 355–74 (355–57).

14. I cite the Latin text of the *Metaphysics* from William of Moerbecke's translation, but have regularized the typeface for clarity.

15. Gerard O'Daly, *Augustine's Philosophy of Mind* (Berkeley: University of California Press, 1987), 100. For Augustine's language of "admonishment," see Joseph Owens, "Faith, Ideas, Illumination, and Experience," in *The Cambridge History of Later Medieval Philosophy: From the Rediscovery of Aristotle to the Disintegration of Scholasticism, 1100–1600*, ed. Norman Kretzmann, Anthony Kenny, and Jan Pinborg (Cambridge: Cambridge University Press, 1982), 440–59 (443).

16. On Aristotle's account of cognition and its medieval reception, with an emphasis on the faculty of imagination, see Michelle Karnes, *Imagination, Meditation, and Cognition in the Middle Ages* (Chicago: University of Chicago Press, 2011), 23–61.

17. I cite the Latin text of Aristotle's *On the Soul* and *On Memory* from Thomas Aquinas, *Opera Omnia, iussu Leonis XIII p.m.* (Rome: Commissio Leonina, 1884-), 45:1–2.

18. I have adapted this translation for the sake of clarity and consistency in the use of key terms.

19. Thomas Aquinas, *Summa Theologiae* (Oxford: Blackfriars, 1964–81), 1a2ae, q. 109., a. 1, res. Aquinas makes exceptions for transcendentals as well as for first

principles such as noncontradiction that serve as the foundation for all subsequent thought; see Robert Pasnau, *Thomas Aquinas on Human Nature: A Philosophical Study of "Summa Theologiae" 1a75–89* (Cambridge: Cambridge University Press, 2002), 296–329.

20. On the mental word in Aquinas, see Robert Pasnau, *Theories of Cognition in the Later Middle Ages* (Cambridge: Cambridge University Press, 1997), 254–71.

21. On beings of reason, see Gyula Klima, "The Changing Role of *Entia Rationis* in Mediaeval Semantics and Ontology: A Comparative Study with a Reconstruction," *Synthèse* 96 (1993): 25–58.

22. For a detailed account of Aquinas's understanding of abstraction from sense perception, see Robert Pasnau, "Abstract Truth in Thomas Aquinas," in *Representation and Objects of Thought in Medieval Philosophy*, ed. Henrik Lagerlund (Aldershot: Ashgate, 2007), 33–61 (33–36), and *Thomas Aquinas on Human Nature*, esp. 171–99, 267–329. Pasnau emphasizes that abstraction is just one part of the process of cognition. It initially produces vague concepts that must be refined through reasoning and reflection before they are useful. Nonetheless, "in the end the result of human thought is an abstract conception of the world around us" ("Abstract Truth" 46).

23. *Mankind*, ed. Kathleen M. Ashley and Gerard NeCastro (Kalamazoo, MI: Medieval Institute, 2010), 1.676.

24. *Mankind*, ed. Ashley and NeCastro, ll. 503–13.

25. *Mankind*, ed. Ashley and NeCastro, ll. 505–15n.

26. Parenthetical citations of Langland refer to *Piers Plowman: A Parallel-Text Edition of the A, B, C, and Z versions*, ed. A. V. C. Schmidt (London: Longman, 1995).

27. See Derek Pearsall, ed., *"Piers Plowman": A New Annotated Edition of the C-Text*, by William Langland (Exeter: University of Exeter Press, 2008), C.6.206n.

28. Claire Waters, "The Voice of the Sluggard: Humanizing Sloth in the *Manuel des pechiez*," *Yearbook of Langland Studies* 33 (2019): 185–204.

29. Paxson, *Poetics of Personification*, 61 (italics in original). Lewis, *Allegory of Love*, 119, condemns Ami as "hardly a personification at all" and regards his presence as "a serious, though not a fatal, defect" in the *Roman de la Rose*. For a rebuttal of his position, see Robert Worth Frank Jr. "The Art of Reading Medieval Personification-Allegory," *ELH* 20 (1953): 237–50 (246).

30. See *"Everyman" and Its Dutch Original, "Elckerlijc,"* ed. Clifford Davidson, Martin W. Walsh, and Ton J. Broos, (Kalamazoo, MI: Medieval Institute, 2007), prologue.

31. De Man, *Resistance to Theory*, 49.

32. Gruenler's *"Piers Plowman" and the Poetics of Enigma* likewise considers puzzles and riddles to be a subtype of allegory but approaches them quite differently. Where Gruenler understands enigmas to be inherently Neoplatonic, I find them to be much more metaphysically flexible and often the hallmark of an experimental nominalism.

33. See Aristotle, *Metaphysics*, 1086b, discussed in Fine, *On Ideas*, 44–65.

34. On the individual as an important category in late-medieval philosophy, see the essays in Jorge J. E. Gracia, ed., *Individuation in Scholasticism: The Later Middle Ages and the Counter-Reformation, 1150–1650* (Albany: State University of New York Press, 1994).

35. On the ancient and medieval tradition of interpreting Aristotle's agent intellect,

see Franz Brentano, "Nous Poiêtikos: Survey of Earlier Interpretations," in *Essays on Aristotle's "De Anima,"* ed. Martha Nussbaum and Amélie Oksenberg Rorty (Oxford: Clarendon, 1992), 313–41.

36. See Siger of Brabant, *In Tertium de Anima*, q. 18, in *Quaestiones in Tertium De Anima, De Anima Intellectiva, De Aeternitate Mundi: Edition Critique*, ed. Bernardo Bazén (Louvain: Publications Universitaires, 1972), 1–112 (64–69), and Aquinas, *Summa Theologiae* 1a, q. 86, a. 1. For Siger's later evolution on this point, see Camille Bérubé, *La Connaissance de l'Individuel au Moyen Age* (Montreal: Presse Universitaire de Montréal, 1964), 78–81. Aristotle himself acknowledges but does not systematically account for the cognition of particulars such as "this A"; see *De Anima* 417a29–30.

37. See Jeffrey E. Brower, "Matter, Form, and Individuation," in *The Oxford Handbook of Aquinas*, ed. Brian Davies and Eleanor Stump (Oxford: Oxford University Press, 2012), 85–103, and Pasnau, "Abstract Truth."

38. Parenthetical citations refer to John Duns Scotus, *Ordinatio*, vol. 7, in *Opera Omnia* (Vatican City: Vatican Polyglot, 1950–2011). Translations are based on Spade, *Five Texts*, 57–113. Although Scotus frequently refers to the quality of individuality as *haec*, and uses *haecceitas* itself on a few occasions, *haecceitas* did not become a standard philosophical term until after his death. For a detailed discussion of Scotus's views, see Allan B. Wolter, "John Duns Scotus (b. CA. 1265; d. 1308)," in Gracia, *Individuation in Scholasticism*, 271–98.

39. Willard Van Orman Quine, "On What There Is," in *From a Logical Point of View: 9 Logico-Philosophical Essays*, 2nd ed., rev. (Cambridge, MA: Harvard University Press, 1980), 1–19 (4). Although Quine objects to overpopulated ontologies in general, favoring what he calls "desert landscapes," he specifically argues against the "ontological jungle" associated with Alexius Meinong.

40. Although most strongly associated with Ockham, this principle of parsimony is also invoked by, inter alia, Scotus, Aquinas, and Aristotle himself. Parenthetical citations of Ockham refer to *Opera Philosophica*, 7 vols. (St. Bonaventure, NY: Franciscan Institute, 1974–88), and *Opera Theologica*, 10 vols. (St. Bonaventure, NY: Franciscan Institute, 1967–86). Translations from the *Summa Logicae* are based on *Ockham's Theory of Terms: Part I of the "Summa Logicae,"* trans. Michael J. Loux (Notre Dame, IN: University of Notre Dame Press, 1974).

41. Ockham also acknowledges the possibility of some relational entities in the special contexts of the trinity, the incarnation, and the Eucharist. On the interpretation of Aristotle's *Categories* in the later Middle Ages, see Alessandro D. Conti, "Categories and Universals in the Later Middle Ages," in *Medieval Commentaries on Aristotle's "Categories,"* ed. Lloyd Newton (Leiden: Brill, 2008), 369–409.

42. For a more detailed exploration of this topic, see Mikko Yrjönsuuri, "William Ockham and Mental Language," in *Representation and Objects of Thought*, ed. Lagerlund, 101–15.

43. William of Ockham, *Expositio in Librum Porphyrii*, 1.2.24–30, 151–55, translated in "William of Ockham's *Commentary on Porphyry*," trans. Eike-Henner W. Kluge, *Franciscan Studies* 33 (1973): 171–254 and 34 (1974): 306–82.

44. Ockham, *Expositio in Librum Porphyrii de Praedicabilibus*, proemium 1.2.108–9, cf. Aristotle, *Metaphysics*, 1038b8. S. Marc Cohen describes this discrepancy as "per-

haps the largest, and most disputed, single interpretative issue concerning Aristotle's *Metaphysics*"; see "Aristotle's Metaphysics," in *The Stanford Encyclopedia of Philosophy*, ed. Edward N. Zalta, Fall 2020 ed., http://plato.stanford.edu/archives/fall2020/entries/aristotle-metaphysics/.

45. Translations of Ockham's *Ordinatio* are based on Spade, *Five Texts*, 114–231, where these are available. In these cases, I have also added Spade's paragraph numbers to the traditional book, distinction, and question numbers for ease of reference. Cf. Augustine, *On the Trinity*, 8.4.7.

46. As Klima puts it, "Medieval Problem of Universals," n5, even "such hardheaded nominalists" as Ockham and his followers did not "directly go against the authority of St. Augustine on this issue."

47. Yrjönsuuri, "William Ockham and Mental Language," 113.

48. On this development in Ockham's thought and its relationship to the earlier work of Peter Olivi, Walter Chatton, and others, see Pasnau, *Theories of Cognition*, 271–89.

49. On Ockham's fundamental reconception of beings of reason, see Klima, "The Changing Role of *Entia Rationis*."

50. Pasnau, *Theories of Cognition*, 285.

51. Marilyn McCord Adams, "Universals in the Early Fourteenth Century," in *Cambridge History of Later Medieval Philosophy*, ed. Kretzmann, Kenny, and Pinborg, 411–39 (434).

52. We should likewise not expect to encounter personifications of any of Ockham's discarded Aristotelian categories, but this is an area where allegorical practice seems to have anticipated Ockham's razor. The medieval canon includes few if any personifications of quantity, cause, relation, time, position, or action.

53. Bloomfield, "Grammatical Approach," 65–66.

54. I suppress Schmidt's editorial capitalization in this passage in order to approximate the experience of medieval readers, who had to decide whether a noun was personified based on its context.

55. For a discussion of personification as a temporary reversal of animacy hierarchies, see Tekla Bude, "Wet Shoes, Dirty Coats, and the Agency of Things: Thinking Personification through New Materialism," *Yearbook of Langland Studies* 33 (2019): 205–29.

56. Kathleen L. Scott, "The Illustrations of *Piers Plowman* in Bodleian Library MS Douce 104," *Yearbook of Langland Studies* 4 (1990): 1–86 (21–23).

57. Rosemund Tuve, *Allegorical Imagery: Some Medieval Books and Their Posterity* (Princeton, NJ: Princeton University Press, 1966), 145–218 (162). For more recent explorations of the dynamic of Deguileville's allegory as first producing and then satisfying a "desire for exegesis," see Nicolette Zeeman, "Medieval Religious Allegory: French and English," in *Cambridge Companion to Allegory*, ed. Copeland and Struck, 148–61 (154), and Philippe Maupeu, *Pèlerins de Vie Humaine: Autobiographie et Allegorie Narrative, de Guillaume de Deguileville à Octavien de Saint-Gelais* (Paris: Champion, 2009).

58. Emily Steiner, *Reading "Piers Plowman"* (Cambridge: Cambridge University Press, 2013), 26.

59. Robertson, *Nature Speaks*, 177–222 (376n90).

60. On Deguileville as a Neoplatonist, see Kay, *Place of Thought*, 75–81, and Marco Nievergelt, "From *Disputatio* to *Predicatio* and Back Again: Dialectic, Authority and Epistemology between the *Roman de la Rose* and the *Pèlerinage de Vie Humaine*," *New Medieval Literatures* 16 (2016): 135–71. Rosenfeld, *Ethics and Enjoyment*, 122–25, and Stephanie Gibbs Kamath, "Rewriting Ancient *Auctores* in the *Pèlerinage de la vie humaine*," in *Mittelalterliche Literatur als Retextualisierung: Das "Pèlerinage"-Corpus des Guillaume de Deguileville im europäischen Mittelalter*, ed. Andreas Kablitz and Ursula Peters (Heidelberg: Winter, 2014), 321–42, see Deguileville as somewhat less critical of Aristotle.

61. Robertson, *Nature Speaks*, 190–91, argues that Deguileville followed academic debates so closely that he revised the *Pèlerinage* to distance it from Ockham's positions as these fell from favor in the middle of the fourteenth century.

62. I here cite the anonymous translation of the *Pèlerinage* into Middle English: *The Pilgrimage of the Lyfe of the Manhode*, ed. Avril Henry, EETS 288, 292 (1985, 1988), lines 1226–29.

63. Dante Alighieri, *Vita Nova*, 16.1–2. The Italian text is edited by Stefano Carrai (Milan: Rizzoli, 2009) and the English translation is by Andrew Frisardi (Evanston, IL: Northwestern University Press, 2012).

CHAPTER SIX

1. Conrad of Hirsau, *Dialogue on the Authors*, 844–46, in *"Accessus ad Auctores," Bernard d'Utrecht; Conrad d'Hirsau, "Dialogus Super Auctores,"* édition critique entièrement revue et augmentée, ed. R. B. C. Huygens (Leiden: Brill, 1970).

2. Conrad of Hirsau, *Dialogue on the Authors*, 848–54.

3. Dante, *Vita Nova*, 16.1.

4. Dante, *Vita Nova*, 16.2. On Dante's use of Aristotelian terminology, see the extensive notes to this passage in Frisardi's edition and Newman, *God and the Goddesses*, 339n86.

5. Dante, *Vita Nova*, 16.8.

6. See Guido Cavalcanti, Rime 27 ("Donna me prega"), in *Rime*, 2nd ed., ed. Marcello Ciccuto (Milan: Biblioteca Universale Rizzoli, 1987), 116–22, and Ciccuto, ed., *Vita Nuova* by Dante, 6th ed. (Milan: Biblioteca Universale Rizzoli, 1999), 16.1.

7. See Madelyn Timmel Mihm, ed., *The "Songe d'Enfer" of Raoul de Houdenc: An Edition Based on All the Extant Manuscripts* (Tübingen: Max Niemeyer Verlag, 1984), vii. Parenthetical citations refer to this edition.

8. A. C. Spearing, *Medieval Autographies: The "I" of the Text* (Notre Dame, IN: University of Notre Dame Press, 2012), 19.

9. See Thomas H. Bestul, *Satire and Allegory in "Wynnere and Wastoure"* (Lincoln: University of Nebraska Press, 1974), 36–37, and Spearing, *Medieval Autographies*, 5, 19.

10. Judith Davidoff, *Beginning Well: Framing Fictions in Late Middle English Poetry* (Rutherford, NJ: Fairleigh Dickinson University Press, 1988), esp. 63–72.

11. For descriptions of these manuscripts and the relationships among them, see Mihm, *Songe d'Enfer*, 21–51.

12. Huon de Méry, *Le Tournoi de l'Antéchrist [Li Tournoiemenz Antecrit]*, 2nd ed., ed. Georg Wimmer and Stéphanie Orgeur (Orléans: Paradigme, 1995), 3536–37.

13. Mihm, *Songe d'Enfer*, 17n61.

14. Surviving manuscripts pair the *Songe d'Enfer* with Rutebeuf's *Voie de Paradis* as well as a poem by the same name purportedly by Raoul himself. That attribution, however, has been given little credence in the last seventy years; see, e.g., Alexandre Micha, "Raoul de Houdenc est-il l'Auteur du *Songe de Paradis* et de la *Vengeance Raguidel*?" *Romania* 68 (1944–45): 316–60, and Marc-René Jung, *Etudes sur le Poème Allégorique en France au Moyen Age* (Bern: Editions Francke, 1971), 256–60. A recent exception to this trend is Jean Lacroix, whose argument that the narrative arc of the paired texts establishes a precedent for the *Commedia* is marred by his unexplained reversion to the manuscript attribution; see "Une Vision Pré-Dantesque du Bien et du Mal: L'Enfer et le Paradis de Raoul de Houdenc," *Revue des Langues Romanes* 111 (2007): 453–72.

15. Although translations of the *Songe d'Enfer* are my own, I have referred to Brian J. Levy's English version of the poem for classroom use in "Raoul de Houdenc Goes to the Movies," *Studies in Medieval and Renaissance Teaching* 12 (2005): 27–46.

16. On this manuscript, see Judith Tschann and M. B. Parkes, eds., *A Facsimile of Oxford, Bodleian Library MS Digby 86*, EETS ss 16 (1996), as well as B. D. H. Miller, "The Early History of Bodleian MS Digby 86," *Annuale Mediaevale* 4 (1963): 26–56, and Marilyn Corrie, "The Compilation of Oxford, Bodleian Library, MS Digby 86," *Medium Aevum* 66 (1997): 236–49.

17. See Hans Robert Jauss, "La Transformation de la Forme Allégorique entre 1180 et 1240: d'Alain de Lille à Guillaume de Lorris" in *L'Humanisme médiéval dans les littératures romanes du XIIème au XIVème siècle*, ed. Anthime Fourrier (Paris: Klincksieck, 1964), 107–46 (123). Jauss's arguments are cited approvingly in Jung, *Etudes*, 228; Mihm, *Songe d'Enfer*, 14–18; and Mark Burde, "Sweet Dreams: Parody, Satire, and Alimentary Allegory in Raoul de Houdenc's *Songe d'Enfer*," in *"Por le Soie Amisté": Essays in Honor of Norris J. Lacy*, ed. Keith Busby and Catherine M. Jones (Amsterdam: Rodopi, 2000), 53–74 (53–54).

18. Aristotle argues in *Categories* 14a and elsewhere that universals exist if and only if they are instantiated. Some medieval realists were more generous, arguing that universals correspond to all qualities that have been or will be instantiated, or even to qualities that are not instantiated but can be imagined. See Fine, *On Ideas*, 246–47n10, and Alessandro Conti, "Realism," in *The Cambridge History of Medieval Philosophy*, ed. Robert Pasnau (Cambridge: Cambridge University Press, 2009), 2:647–660 (660).

19. Conrad of Hirsau, *Dialogue*, 864–66.

20. On the medieval history of corporate personhood, see Ernst H. Kantorowicz, *The King's Two Bodies: A Study in Medieval Political Theology* (1957; Princeton, NJ: Princeton University Press, 1997), 193–313.

21. Levy offers a helpful explanation of these names: *hasard* refers to a popular dice game, *mestrere* means to misdeal cards or throw loaded dice, and *mesconter* means to falsely claim a winning hand or a winning throw; see "Raoul de Houdenc," 43n15.

22. On these names, see Mihm, *Songe d'Enfer*, 99n163–104n199, 106n223, 113n290–114n292 and the variants of the lines cited above.

23. For this double significance, see Mihm, *Songe d'Enfer*, 105n217.

24. See Peter Rickard, *Britain in Medieval French Literature, 1100–1500* (Cambridge: Cambridge University Press, 1956), 163–70.

25. Kantorowicz, *King's Two Bodies*, 210.

26. Scanlon, "Personification and Penance," 21.

27. See Bestul, *Satire and Allegory*, 15–16, 36–43, for *Winner and Waster*'s connection to the *Songe d'Enfer*. The two are linked, in part, by a French and Latin tradition of responding to or rewriting the *Psychomachia* that includes the *Voie de Paradis* and *Tournoiemenz Antecrit*, Henri D'Andeli's *Bataille des Sept Arts* (Battle of the Seven Arts), Vincent of Beauvais' *Speculum Historiale*, and, for critics including Jauss, the *Roman de la Rose*.

28. Bestul, *Satire and Allegory*, 17.

29. Parenthetical citations of *Winner and Waster* refer to Ginsberg's TEAMS edition.

30. On the uses of romance in late-medieval England, see Helen Cooper, "Romance after 1400," in *The Cambridge History of Medieval English Literature*, ed. David Wallace (Cambridge: Cambridge University Press, 1999), 690–719.

31. On the manuscript, scribe, and language of the poem, see Stephanie Trigg, ed., *Winner and Waster*, EETS 297 (1990), xiii–xxvii.

32. This genealogy undermines the assumption that the alliterative revival is inherently a reactionary project. On the reception history of *Winner and Waster*, with particular attention to its position within narratives of alliterative revival, see Breen, "The Need for Allegory: *Wynnere and Wastoure* as an *Ars Poetica*," *Yearbook of Langland Studies* 26 (2012): 187–229 (187–91).

33. Derek Pearsall, *Old English and Middle English Poetry* (London: Routledge, 1977), 158.

34. The story of Aeneas's betrayal of Troy, which was widely accepted during the Middle Ages, originates in *De excidio Trojae historia*, attributed to Dares Phrygius, and *Ephemeris belli Trojani*, attributed to Dictys of Crete, and is repeated in, e.g., Guido de Columnis's *Historia Destructionis Troiae* and, in English, the *Gest Hystoriale of the Destruction of Troy* and Lydgate's *Troy Book*.

35. On the historiographical claims of this opening and the bivalent use of "selcouthes" in medieval literary traditions, see Maura Nolan, "'With Tresone Withinn': *Winner and Waster*, Chivalric Self-Representation, and the Law," *Journal of Medieval and Early Modern Studies* 26 (1996): 1–28 (1, 7–8). On "selcouthes" as a hinge between genres, see Britton J. Harwood, "The Displacement of Labor in *Winner and Waster*," in *The Middle Ages at Work: Practicing Labor in Late Medieval England*, ed. Kellie Robertson and Michael Uebel (New York: Palgrave, 2004), 157–77 (158). On the prologue as an instance of "complaint on the times" or "abuses of the age," see Bestul, *Satire and Allegory*, 55–56.

36. *Middle English Dictionary*, s.v. "romaunce."

37. See Paul Strohm, "The Origin and Meaning of Middle English *Romaunce*," *Genre* 10 (1977): 1–28, and Derek Pearsall, "Middle English Romance and Its Audiences," in *Historical and Editorial Studies in Medieval and Early Modern English for Johan Gerritsen*, ed. Mary-Jo Arn and Hanneke Wirtjes (Groningen: Wolters-Noordhoff, 1985), 37–47 (42).

38. D. Vance Smith, *Arts of Possession: The Middle English Household Imaginary* (Minneapolis: University of Minnesota Press, 2003), 77–80. For Nolan, the prologue depicts the intertwined failures of poetry and of the realm, with both suffering from crises of interpretation that render truth and falsehood indistinguishable; see "'With Tresone Withinn,'" 10.

39. On the Middle English vocabulary of poetic invention and its connection to the Latin rhetorical and allegorical traditions, see Ann W. Astell, *Political Allegory in Late Medieval England* (Ithaca, NY: Cornell University Press, 1999), 23–43, esp. 35–38.

40. On "frenchipe in fere" as a patronage system, see Thorlac Turville-Petre, "The Prologue of *Wynnere and Wastoure*," *Leeds Studies in English*, new ser., 18 (1987): 19–29 (24–25).

41. *MED*, s.v. "mirth(e)."

42. *MED*, s.v. "jape."

43. In its emphasis on the written, crafted nature of serious first-person writing, the prologue to *Winner and Waster* exemplifies Spearing's supergenre of autography. Its first-person narration, however, is more specific than Spearing acknowledges: while the narrator's trajectory from great hall to wilderness is not so detailed as to be individual, neither is it wholly interchangeable. Only those who have experienced a similar loss of institutional affiliation can "speak" though the poem's "I."

44. The work's ability to bear "wittnesse" implicitly compensates for the earlier failures of "witt," to which "wittnesse" is etymologically related.

45. Turville-Petre, "Prologue," 27.

46. *MED*, s.v. "refret(e)"; the *Anglo-Norman Dictionary* similarly defines *refreit* as either a liturgical refrain or response or the refrain or burden of a discourse. Literary works described as *tretises* are notably moral, such as Chaucer's *Parson's Tale* and the romance *Ypotis*, which the Vernon manuscript associates with, e.g., *A Talkyng of þe Love of God*, Grosseteste's *Chateau d'Amour*, and treatises on the Passion and hearing Mass; see Mary S. Serjeantson, "The Index of the Vernon Manuscript," *Modern Language Review* 32 (1937): 222–61 (333–34, 338, 345, 370, 373). David Lawton points out that among alliterative works the term *tretise* is associated with *Piers Plowman* and *Mum and the Sothsegger* in addition to *Winner and Waster*; see "Gaytryge's Sermon, 'Dictamen,' and Middle English Alliterative Verse," *Modern Philology*, 76 (1979): 329–43 (331n9).

47. On these obstacles to the dreamer's sleep as a residue from the prologue, see Harwood, "Displacement of Labor," 158, and Nolan, "'With Tresone Withinn,'" 10–11.

48. See John Speirs, *Medieval English Poetry: The Non-Chaucerian Tradition* (London: Faber and Faber, 1957), 268; Nolan, "'With Tresone Withinn,'" 11; and Smith, *Arts of Possession*, 86.

49. Smith, *Arts of Possession*, 86–87.

50. "For this es the usage here and ever schall worthe: / If any beryn be so bolde with banere for to ryde / Withinn the kyngdome riche bot the kynge one, / That he schall losse the londe and his lyfe aftir" (130–133). As part of her exploration of the confusing and often contentious intersections of common-law and statutory definitions of treason in the poem, Nolan, "'With Tresone Withinn,'" 4–5, points out that this definition does not align with the one in the Statute of Treasons.

51. Smith, *Arts of Possession*, 96.

52. The same cannot be said of agricultural workers and poor city dwellers, who are conspicuously omitted as social and economic actors. In "Displacement of Labor" and "Anxious over Peasants: Textual Disorder in *Winner and Waster*," *Journal of Medieval and Early Modern Studies* 36 (2006): 291–319, Harwood attributes this omission to the author's anxious repression, but the author in fact seems quite comfortable with defining citizenship in economic terms.

53. Lois Roney, "*Winner and Waster*'s 'Wyse Wordes': Teaching Economics and Nationalism in Fourteenth-Century England," *Speculum* 69 (1994): 1070–1100 (1093). Roney also considers it possible, but less likely, that the description of Winner's army is an interpolation.

54. Thomas L. Reed Jr., *Middle English Debate Poetry and the Aesthetics of Irresolution* (Columbia: University of Missouri Press, 1990), 264, cited approvingly by Iain MacLeod Higgins, "Tit for Tat: *The Canterbury Tales* and 'The Flyting of Dunbar and Kennedy,'" *Exemplaria* 16 (2004): 165–202 (199).

55. Brantley L. Bryant, "Talking with the Taxman about Poetry: England's Economy in 'Against the King's Taxes' and *Winner and Waster*," *Studies in Medieval and Renaissance History*, 3rd ser., 5 (2008): 219–48 (240).

56. Lee Patterson, *Chaucer and the Subject of History* (Madison: University of Wisconsin Press, 1991), 177.

57. For these and similar characterizations, see Bestul, *Satire and Allegory*, 4–5; Bryant, "Talking with the Taxman," 237; Harwood, "Anxious over Peasants," 301, and "Displacement of Labor," 16; Nicolas Jacobs, "The Typology of Debate and the Interpretation of *Winner and Waster*," *Review of English Studies*, new ser., 36 (1985): 481–500 (486, 491–94); Reed, *Middle English Debate Poetry*, 261–93 (esp. 288); Roney, "'Wyse Wordes,'" 1093; John Scattergood, "*Winner and Waster* and the Mid-Fourteenth-Century Economy," in *The Writer as Witness: Literature as Historical Evidence*, ed. Tom Dunne (Cork: Cork University Press, 1987), 39–57 (50); David Starkey, "The Age of the Household: Politics, Society and the Arts, c. 1350–c. 1550," in *The Later Middle Ages*, ed. Stephen Medcalf (London: Methuen, 1981), 225–90; and Stephanie Trigg, "The Rhetoric of Excess in *Winner and Waster*," *Yearbook of Langland Studies* 3 (1989): 91–108 (93, 100), and Trigg, *Winner and Waster*, xlvi–xlvii.

58. Trigg, *Winner and Waster*, xlviii. For similar positions, see Reed, *Middle English Debate Poetry*, 289, and Roney, "'Wyse Wordes,'" 1089–90. Allan F. Westphall, "Issues of Personification and Debate in *Wynnere and Wastoure*," *English Studies* 82 (2001): 481–96, and Nolan, "'With Tresone Withinn,'" 21, implicitly share Trigg's understanding of allegory but consider that instead of overcoming their nature as personifications, Winner and Waster are unproductively constrained by it.

59. On exemplarity, see especially Larry Scanlon, *Narrative, Authority, and Power: The Medieval Exemplum and the Chaucerian Tradition* (Cambridge: Cambridge University Press, 1994); Elizabeth Allen, *False Fables and Exemplary Truth in Later Middle English Literature* (New York: Palgrave, 2005); and, with a phenomenological emphasis, J. Allan Mitchell, *Ethics and Exemplary Narrative in Chaucer and Gower* (Woodbridge, Suffolk: D. S. Brewer, 2004).

60. On the poem's treatment of waste as such, see Eleanor Johnson, "The Poetics of Waste: Medieval English Ecocriticism," *PMLA* 127 (2012): 460–76 (463–66).

61. Or so Winner seems to suggest by juxtaposing this description of indigestion caused by overeating with complaints about "your trompers, thay tounen so heghe / [That ic]he a gome in the gate goullyng may here" (358–59). Setting aside *MED* senses that refer to these lines only, *tunen* means to intone a psalm or recite Parnassan poetry; its negative redefinition here parallels the negative redefinition of *selcouth, wit,* etc. in the prologue.

62. Most careful readers of the poem note that Winner and Waster each accuse the other of misusing a common store of goods, but the issue becomes central for Roney, "'Wyse Wordes,'" and Bryant, "Talking with the Taxman."

63. On these images, see Claire Richter Sherman, *Imaging Aristotle: Verbal and Visual Representation in Fourteenth-Century France* (Berkeley: University of California Press, 1995), 83–92, and Breen, "Discipline and Doctrine: Inculcating Moral Habits in *Le Livre de éthiques d'Aristote,*" *New Medieval Literatures* 12 (2010): 209–50.

64. Trigg, "Rhetoric of Excess."

65. Aquinas, *Summa Theologiae,* 1a 2ae, q. 64, art. 1.

66. For these widely recognized parallels see, e.g., Trigg, *Winner and Waster,* 25n126, 37n317.

67. On this readership, see, e.g., Nolan, "'With Tresone Within'"; Bryant, "Talking with the Taxman"; and Thorlac Turville-Petre, "*Wynnere and Wastoure*: When and Where?," in *Loyal Letters: Studies on Mediaeval Alliterative Poetry and Prose,* ed. L. A. J. R. Houwen and Alasdair A. MacDonald (Groningen: Forsten, 1994), 155–66. Elizabeth Salter, "The Timeliness of *Wynnere and Wastoure,*" *Medium Aevum* 47 (1978): 40–65 (49–65), identifies the heraldic device of "thre wynges inwith wroghte in the kynde / Umbygon with a gold wyre" in lines 117–18 as the arms of the Wingfield family and proposes these prominent royal and aristocratic servants as possible sponsors for the poem.

68. On the traditional association between poetry and ethics, see Allen, *Ethical Poetic.*

69. Bestul, *Satire and Allegory,* 80.

70. I here subscribe to the majority opinion that relatively little of the original poem has been lost; for contrary views, based on assumptions about debate conventions, see Roney, "'Wyse Wordes,'" and John W. Conlee, *Middle English Debate Poetry: A Critical Anthology* (East Lansing, MI: Colleagues Press, 1991), 98n503.

71. Sherman, *Imaging Aristotle,* 86–87.

72. In the narrowest senses listed by the *MED,* a *baroun* is a lord summoned by writ to Parliament or a judge of the Court of the Exchequer; a *baroun upon þe benche* is specifically a member of the king's council. More generally, however, a *baroun* can be a feudal tenant, "any man of respect or honour," or the master of a household.

73. Hanna, "Alliterative Poetry," in *Cambridge History of Medieval English Literature,* ed. Wallace, 488–512 (510).

74. Steven Justice, "The Genres of *Piers Plowman,*" *Viator* 19 (1988): 291–306 (292).

CHAPTER SEVEN

1. Alan of Lille, *The Plaint of Nature (De Planctu Naturae),* in *Literary Works,* ed. and trans. Winthrop Wetherbee (Cambridge, MA: Harvard University Press, 2013), 21–217, 16.21. Citations of the *Complaint of Nature* refer to this edition.

2. Alan of Lille, *Complaint of Nature*, 12.3, 12.10.

3. Albert the Great, *Summa Theologia*, 1a, tr. 3, q. 15, c. 3, a. 3, in *Opera Omnia*, ed. Bernard Geyer (Münster: Aschendorff, 1951–), 34:1:81.

4. On Aquinas's treatment of these universals, which transcend the Aristotelian categories because they apply to each of them, see Gyula Klima, "Aquinas on One and Many," *Documenti e Studi sulla Tradizione Filosofica Medievale* 11 (2000): 195–215.

5. On this Bonaventuran synthesis of Augustinian and Aristotelian cognition, see Karnes, *Imagination, Meditation, and Cognition*, 63–110.

6. Newman, *God and the Goddesses*, 34.

7. Helen Cooper, "Gender and Personification in *Piers Plowman*," *Yearbook of Langland Studies* 5 (1991): 31–48 (38).

8. Noting that the *Psychomachia* fell out of favor as a school text in the later Middle Ages, Ad Putter argues that while "Latin allegorists up to and including Alan of Lille were still consciously recollecting Prudentius . . . later vernacular writers like Langland were not"; see "Prudentius and the Late Classical Biblical Epics," 370. He does not take into account the Latin and francophone *Psychomachia* tradition discussed in chapter 6.

9. On the history of the idealized plowman before Langland, see Lawrence Warner, "Chaucer's Non-Debt to Langland," *Yearbook of Langland Studies* 32 (2018): 353–74 (363–66).

10. In all of these scenes, one hears an echo of the Middle English proverb, "When Adam delved and Eve span, / Who was then a gentil man?" attested as early as the first half of the fourteenth century. See Galloway, *Penn Commentary*, 1:57–58, and *The Oxford Dictionary of Proverbs*, 6th ed., ed. Jennifer Speake (Oxford: Oxford University Press, 2015).

11. *MED*, s.v. "putten," sense 12c. Galloway, *Penn Commentary*, 1:57–58, links "potte hem to plogh" with the Middle English phrase "putten in ploughes," meaning "to begin to plow." Although both phrases are associated with beginnings, "putten honde to the plough" tracks the plowman's engagement with the plow rather than the plow's engagement with the field.

12. On the poem's "small anthology of poetic inception formulas," see Anne Middleton, "The Audience and Public of *Piers Plowman*," in *Middle English Alliterative Poetry and Its Literary Background: Seven Essays*, ed. David Lawton (Cambridge: D. S. Brewer, 1996), 101–23, 147–54 (152n34).

13. *Biblia Latina cum Glossa ordinaria*, ed. A. Rusch (Strasbourg, 1489), https://gloss-e.irht.cnrs.fr/index.php.

14. Traugott Lawler, *The Penn Commentary on "Piers Plowman,"* vol. 4 (Philadelphia: University of Pennsylvania Press, 2018), 58.

15. Raoul does offer his readers a clue to his biblical intertext. Lines 14–15 of the *Songe d'Enfer* ("Those who go to seek hell / find a pleasant path and a beautiful way" [Plesant chemin et bele voie / Truevent cil qui Enfer vont querre]) echo Matthew 7:13 ("For wide is the gate, and broad is the way that leadeth to destruction, and many there are who go in thereat" [Quia lata porta et spatiosa via quae ducit ad perditionem / et multi sunt qui intrant per eam]).

16. *MED*, s.v. "contenaunce," sense 3c, and "disgisen."

17. See Kantorowicz, *King's Two Bodies*, 314–450.

18. Cooper, "Gender and Personification," 39; see also Michael Calabrese, "Posthuman *Piers*? Rediscovering Langland's Subjectivities," *Yearbook of Langland Studies* 32 (2018): 3–36 (12).

19. On *roberdesmen*, see Pearsall, "*Piers Plowman*," Pro.45n, and Ralph Hanna, *The Penn Commentary on "Piers Plowman,"* vol. 2 (Philadelphia: University of Pennsylvania Press, 2017), 269.

20. Mary Clemente Davlin, "*Petrus, Id Est, Christus*: Piers the Plowman as 'the Whole Christ'," *Chaucer Review* 6 (1972): 280–92 (281).

21. On the association between the watchtower of Isaiah 21:8 and divine providence, see Galloway, *Penn Commentary*, 1:43–47.

22. Newman, *God and the Goddesses*, 14–19.

23. Middleton, "Narration and the Invention of Experience," 98.

24. Justice, "Genres," 296.

25. Heise, "Menippean Boethius," 126.

26. For a comparison of the initial appearances of Holy Church and Philosophy, see Justice, "Genres," 295. On the formal similarities between passus 1 and the *Consolation*, see Steiner, *Reading "Piers Plowman,"* 22–38. As their respective narratives continue, each personification takes on the roles of foster mother, teacher, physician, and psychopomp.

27. On the suggestive but not conclusive evidence that Langland knew Boethius, see most recently Grady, "Chaucer's Langland's Boethius."

28. See, e.g., Relihan, *The Prisoner's Philosophy*, and Marenbon, *Boethius*, 146–63.

29. Middleton, "Narration and the Invention of Experience," 102.

30. Johnson, "*Reddere* and Refrain," 9. For similar invocations of the *Consolation*'s "vertical dialogue" as a foil to *Piers*, see Grady, "Chaucer's Langland's Boethius," 278–79, and Nolan, "Fortunes of *Piers Plowman*," 13–14.

31. See Nolan, "Fortunes of *Piers Plowman*," 13–14, and Grady, "Chaucer's Langland's Boethius," 279–83.

32. The *MED*, s.v. "dor," sense 4b, lists the A text of *Piers* among the earliest uses of the collocation "dead as a doornail," none of which can be dated with precision. Galloway identifies a macaronic pun on *feet* and *faits* (Fr. "works"), which he associates with a "distinctive kind of 'harped preaching'"; see his *Penn Commentary*, 1:212–13.

33. See Alan J. Fletcher, "Line 30 of the *Man of Law's Tale* and the Medieval Malkyn," *English Language Notes* 24 (1986): 15–20, and Frederic G. Cassidy, "The Merit of Malkyn," *Modern Language Notes* 63 (1948): 52–53.

34. On Langland's restaging of the *Consolation* "*nel mezzo* rather than *in finem*," see Grady, "Chaucer's Langland's Boethius," 279.

35. Michael Calabrese, *An Introduction to "Piers Plowman"* (Gainesville: University Press of Florida, 2016), 293.

36. See, inter alia, David Aers, *Community, Gender, and Individual Identity: English Writing 1360–1430* (London: Routledge, 1988), 20–72; Derek Pearsall, "Poverty and Poor People in *Piers Plowman*," in *Medieval English Studies Presented to George Kane*, ed. Edward Donald Kennedy, Ronald Waldron, and Joseph S. Wittig (Woodbridge, Suffolk: D. S. Brewer, 1988), 167–85; Robert Worth Frank Jr., "The 'Hungry Gap,' Crop

Failure, and Famine: The Fourteenth-Century Agricultural Crisis and *Piers Plowman*," *Yearbook of Langland Studies* 4 (1990): 87–104; Anne Middleton, "Acts of Vagrancy: The C Version 'Autobiography' and the Statute of 1388," in *Written Work: Langland, Labor, and Authorship*, ed. Steven Justice and Kathryn Kerby-Fulton (Philadelphia: University of Pennsylvania Press, 1997), 208–317; Margaret Kim, "Hunger, Need, and the Politics of Poverty in *Piers Plowman*," *Yearbook of Langland Studies* 16 (2002): 131–68; Anne M. Scott, *"Piers Plowman" and the Poor* (Dublin: Four Courts, 2004), esp. 68–114; Kellie Robertson, *The Laborer's Two Bodies: Literary and Legal Productions in Britain, 1350–1500* (New York: Palgrave MacMillan, 2006), 45–50; Kate Crassons, *The Claims of Poverty: Literature, Culture, and Ideology in Late Medieval England* (Notre Dame, IN: University of Notre Dame Press, 2010), 30–40; and Rebecca Davis, *"Piers Plowman" and the Books of Nature* (Oxford: Oxford University Press, 2016), 186–92.

37. See D. W. Robertson Jr. and Bernard Huppé, *"Piers Plowman" and the Spiritual Tradition* (Princeton, NJ: Princeton University Press, 1951), 84; Katherine B. Trower, "The Figure of Hunger in *Piers Plowman*," *American Benedictine Review* 24 (1973): 238–60 (242); and R. E. Kaske, "The Character Hunger in *Piers Plowman*," in *Medieval English Studies*, ed. Kennedy, Waldron, and Wittig, 187–97 (190n2).

38. Hewett-Smith, "Allegory on the Half-Acre," 9.

39. William Rhodes, "Personification, Power, and the Body in Late Medieval and Early Modern English Poetry," in *Personification: Embodying Meaning and Emotion*, ed. Walter S. Melion and Bart Ramakers (Leiden: Brill, 2016), 95–120 (106).

40. For these echoes and allusions, see Hanna, *Penn Commentary*, vol. 2, notes on lines C.8.1–4 (Luke 10:2), C.8.35–55 (Luke 10:4), C.8.44L (Luke 14:10), C.8.98–99 (Luke 16:2), C.8.128 (Luke 14:21), B.6.181 (Luke 15:14–17), C.8.209 (Luke 6:30), C.8.246 (Luke 19:22–27), C.8.277–88 (Luke 16:19–31). Although I here list only the first version Hanna cites, most allusions occur in all three versions of the poem.

41. Pearsall, *"Piers Plowman,"* C.8.168n.

42. The B text offers a condensed version of this appeal: "'Now, by þe peril of my soule!' quod Piers, 'I shal apeire yow alle'—/ And houped after Hunger, þat herde hym at þe firste. / 'Awreke me of þise wastours,' quod he, 'þat þis world shendeþ!" (6.171–73).

43. Rhodes, "Personification, Power, and the Body," 104.

44. On Grosseteste as the vernacularizer of this motif and as Langland's source for an important stretch of B.18; see Nicholas Watson, "William Langland Reads Robert Grosseteste," in *The French of Medieval England: Essays in Honour of Jocelyn Wogan-Browne*, ed. Thelma Fenster and Carolyn P. Collette (Woodbridge, Suffolk: D. S. Brewer, 2017), 140–65. On the *Chateau d'Amour* as Langland's source for the episode of the four daughters of God, see Ronald Waldron, "Langland's Originality: The Christ-Knight and the Harrowing of Hell," in *Medieval English Religious and Ethical Literature*, ed. Gregory Kratzmann and James Simpson (Cambridge: Boydell and Brewer, 1986), 66–81, and Jim Rhodes, *Poetry Does Theology: Chaucer, Grosseteste, and the "Pearl"-Poet* (Notre Dame, IN: University of Notre Dame Press, 2001), 43–71. To my knowledge, nobody has proposed the *Chateau* as the source for B.9.

45. See *The Middle English Translation of Robert Grosseteste's "Chateau d'amour,"* ed. Kari Sajavaara (Helsinki: Société Néophilologique, 1967). The title *Chateau d'Amour* is modern.

46. For this history, see Evelyn Ann Mackie, "Robert Grosseteste's *Chasteu d'Amur*: A Text in Context" (PhD diss., University of Toronto, 2002), 75–80. Parenthetical citations refer to this edition.

47. Davis discusses Grosseteste's understanding of the Virgin as "the highest perfection of human nature," rendered yet more perfect by the incarnation; see *"Piers Plowman" and the Book of Nature*, 116–17.

48. Watson, "Langland Reads Grosseteste," 150.

49. Newman, *God and the Goddesses*, 36–37.

50. On the poem's difficulty as central to its pastoral goals, see Nicolette Zeeman, *"Piers Plowman" and the Medieval Discourse of Desire* (Cambridge: Cambridge University Press, 2006).

51. See A. V. C. Schmidt, "Langland and Scholastic Philosophy," *Medium Ævum* 38 (1969): 134–56 (152).

52. Anima is not the only personification whose represented gender clashes with the grammatical gender of the underlying noun (see, e.g., "*Latro*, Luciferis Aunte," B.5.477, and the pairing of the grammatically feminine Fides and Spes with the masculine Abraham and Moses). Anima is, however, the only figure to virtually force the reader into a solecism, since they are prominent enough to warrant discussion and lack any other nomenclature.

53. For these paraph marks and annotations, see C. David Benson and Lynne S. Blanchfield, *The Manuscripts of "Piers Plowman": The B-Version* (Woodbridge, Suffolk: Boydell and Brewer, 1987).

54. At least one English equivalent, "Þouȝte," may be a scribal intervention, appearing in some manuscripts (and some modern editions) but not others. It is thus yet another indication of the heavy scribal involvement in this passage. Anima's glossarial nature is also reflected in Schmidt's critical response, which he presents as a schema rather than continuous text; see "Langland and Scholastic Philosophy," 151–52.

55. Carruthers notes in "Allegory without the Teeth," 34n, that Amor and Conscience have been added to the seven qualities outlined in *Etymologies* 11.1.13.

56. *MED*, s.v. "conscience," sense 2a.

57. Paxson, "Gender Personified," 85, suggests that Anima's mouth without tongue or teeth is "a euphemism for the human vagina," while for Elizabeth Robertson "the 'thyng' seems to have been castrated—that is, it lacks the representation of the phallus, the tongue; its lack of teeth suggests at the same time that it denies the 'vagina dentata'"; see "Souls That Matter: The Gendering of the Soul in *Piers Plowman*," in *Mindful Spirit in Late Medieval Literature: Essays in Honor of Elizabeth D. Kirk*, ed. Bonnie Wheeler (New York: Palgrave, 2006), 165–86 (174).

58. Many critics note in passing that Anima changes gender between B.9 and B.15, including Joan Baker and Susan Signe Morrison, who consider the later Anima a strong masculine foil to the earlier lady in the tower; see "The Luxury of Gender: *Piers Plowman* B.9 and the *Merchant's Tale*," in *William Langland's "Piers Plowman": A Book of Essays*, ed. Kathleen Hewett-Smith (New York: Routledge, 2001), 41–67 (44). Paxson and Raskolnikov look at this transformation more closely, noting the indeterminacy of the second Anima's gender but ultimately concluding that they are masculine. See Paxson, "Gender Personified," 83–86, and Raskolnikov, *Body against Soul*, 190–94.

59. Robertson, "Souls That Matter," 174–75.

60. Carruthers, "Allegories without the Teeth," 34.

61. Griffiths, *Personification in "Piers Plowman,"* 15–16.

62. Helen Cooper, "Romance Patterns of Naming in *Piers Plowman*," in *"Truthe Is the Beste": A Festschrift in Honour of A. V. C. Schmidt*, ed. Nicolas Jacobs and Gerald Morgan (Oxford: Peter Lang, 2014), 37–63 (43).

63. Mary Carruthers, "Moving Images in the Mind's Eye," in *The Mind's Eye: Art and Theological Argument in the Middle Ages*, ed. Jeffrey E. Hamburger and Anne-Marie Bouché (Princeton, NJ: Princeton University Press, 2006), 287–305.

64. Stephanie L. Batkie, "'Thanne Artow Inparfit': Learning to Read in *Piers Plowman*," *Chaucer Review* 45 (2010): 169–93 (178).

65. On the dreamer as "a person with a soul," see Elizabeth Robertson, "Soul-Making in *Piers Plowman*," *Yearbook of Langland Studies* 34 (2020): 11–56.

66. In associating enigma with nominalism, I depart from Gruenler's *"Piers Plowman" and the Poetics of Enigma*, which treats enigma as inherently Neoplatonic and participatory. I do not claim, however, that enigma is necessarily nominalist—only that it plays an important role in Langland's characterization of Anima as a nominalist personification.

INDEX